VOTI

UNION OF THE IMAGINARY

A Forum for Curators

Edited by Susan Hapgood, Vasıf Kortun and November Paynter

Published online by SALT, Istanbul, 2013

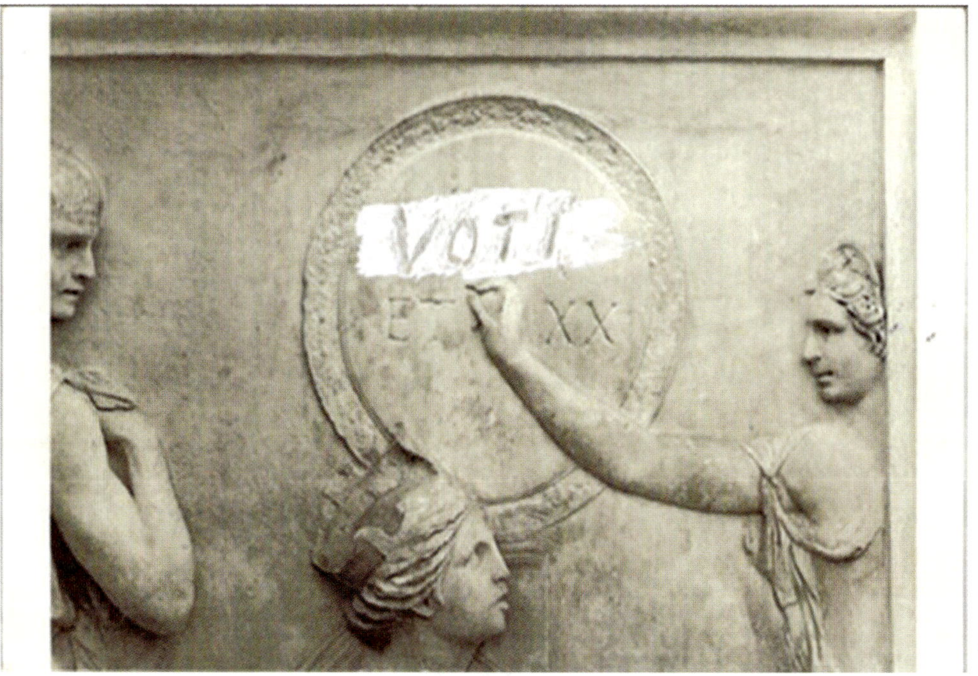

Postcard sent from Hans Ulrich Obrist to Susan Hapgood, 1998

Contents

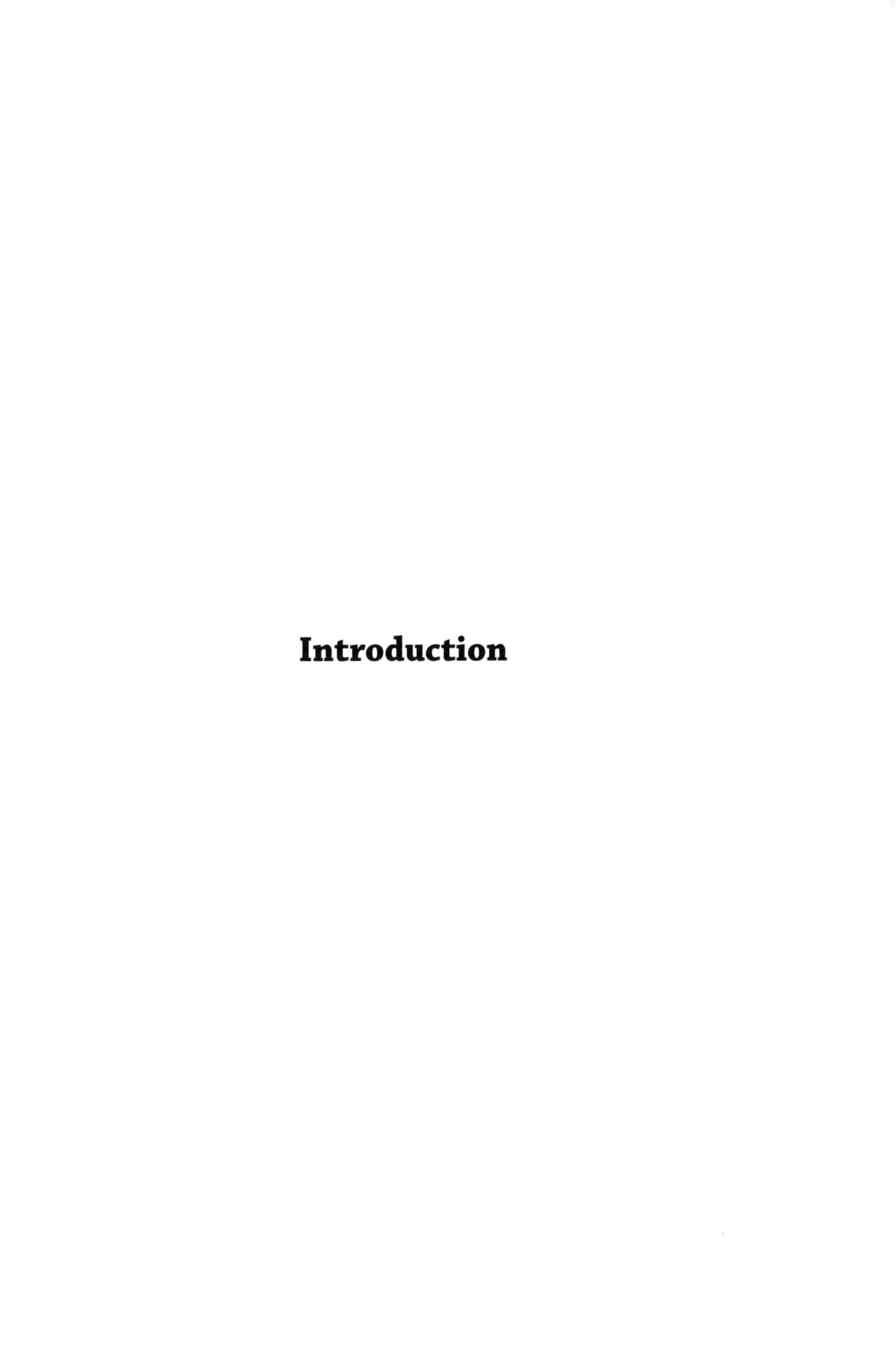

Introduction

Introduction

Susan Hapgood and Vasıf Kortun

For only a few years, just before the turn of the millennium, VOTI (Union of the Imaginary) flourished. It was an international forum that existed online, a digital place for discussion among contemporary art curators, many of whom are among today's most prominent museum professionals. Because members were writing from all over the world, geographic and cultural distances were oftentimes palpable, while at other moments invisible, when we met at this common digital forum. There were days and nights when discussions careened uncontrollably away from the original topic on the table, but for most members it was liberating to read what kindred spirits (or adversaries) were thinking and doing elsewhere, to hear their voices without any institutional or editorial framing and without any mediated filter. E-mail etiquette did not yet exist, so VOTI postings were unstructured, freewheeling, antagonistic, fleeting, exhilarating, ultimately amorphous and at times incoherent. Despite attempts to structure the forum with set conversations, the bigger picture was organic. It was above all a union where discussions were tough and uncensored.

The internationalism of the group was unusual, the instantaneity was novel. It gave us all a taste of the digital future. By this point, the "brand" status of curators had already been consolidated earlier in the 1990s by our predecessors. The chief curator of painting and sculpture of the Museum of Modern Art, Kirk Varnedoe, by 1998 had already posed for a full-page ad for New York department store Barneys. Kasper König, Rudi Fuchs and Jean-Christophe Ammann were invited to the Whitney Museum of American Art for the museum's *Views from Abroad* series in the late 1990s. Following Jan Hoet's celebrated 1988 *Chambres d'amis* (M KHA, Antwerp) project of artists' installations set in Ghent's private residences, Mary Jane Jacob's 1991 exhibition, *Places with a Past*, introduced a series of site-specific public projects rooted in the sociopolitical histories of Charleston, South Carolina, working entirely outside the museum and gallery system. In terms of mega-exhibitions, Harald Szeemann returned to the Venice Biennale in 1999, this time to extend the presentation to the Corderie and Artiglierie in the Arsenale, radically expanding the scope of the biennale. In short, by the time of VOTI's formation in 1998, the curatorial subject was already quite recognizable, the early curatorial-studies education programs were more than half a decade old, and yet the profession was not yet quite as fetishized as it has become today. Most importantly, the affairs between exhibiting institutions and guest curators were extremely problematic. Institutional mistreatment was not the only reason for the founding of VOTI but it was a thread running through many of the discussions.

E-mail

E-mail was still fairly new. It was commercially introduced in 1988, and by the 1990s many younger people were active on the Internet. These kinds of online discussion groups were novel structures. Not conducive to senior professionals, who were neither mentally nor technologically prepared to engage in generous, laterally-motivated discussions, these networked groups produced their own constellations, their own new communities. Older generations who were not familiar or comfortable with the e-mail format were excluded. Concurrently, e-mail was rapidly becoming essential to many curators living and working outside of major urban cultural centers. It was the sole means of keeping up with contemporaneity, short of travel, which was affordable to some but not all VOTI members.

Structure

There was an attempted structure, with Carlos Basualdo, Jordan Crandall, Susan Hapgood and Hans Ulrich Obrist trying to run the group as light-handedly as possible, all as volunteers. New members were suggested and invited to join the forum, and VOTI grew from a handful of interested colleagues to a much larger community of people who did not necessarily know one another at all. Selected discussion sessions were open (to anyone who was interested) or closed (readable only by VOTI members), depending upon the topic. As VOTI developed, moderators for particular discussions attempted to sustain, guide, and inspire the discussions, sometimes with great success, and other times with little response. The whole forum was run for free on the server of The Thing, artist Wolfgang Staehle's online social network, which was launched in 1991 and geographically located at offices in the Chelsea neighborhood of New York at the time. In these years, the Internet was not yet overwhelmed by private interest and a spirit of openness prevailed.

Organization of Contents

Whereas readers of this publication are being spoon-fed discussions composed around clear topics, VOTI members had to try to keep up with various simultaneous threads of conversation. When they were first written, these posts appeared in real time as they were sent; nobody was mediating the message order or screening them for content. At times it was extremely chaotic to read all of what was streaming onto our screens, to decide when to jump into the fray or remain silent.

Publication

A little more than a decade later, a number of VOTI contributors remarked on their interest to revisit what many of them remembered as a formative series of discussions. With this impetus we began to work from files disinterred from old servers, and e-mails searched out from aged computer memories, but ironically the bulk of the material in this publication was sourced from a stack of e-mail print-outs retrieved from a summer home.

Rather than try to replicate the original forum experience, or the salvaged archives, our co-editor November Paynter suggested that the material should be slightly sifted and organized, to order the discussions around particularly evident topics of discussion—some that were officially predetermined, and some of which emerged on their own. The brief introductions she has written to open each chapter provide a precise condensation of what will be found within. The dates of the different chapters' posts sometimes overlap, and in fact this new organization makes the discussions far more coherent than they initially were. Less than five percent of the material available to us was edited out of this publication and for those that were, the reasoning was simple: either a post's topic was random and could not be placed in a thread, the e-mail was personal, or layers of formatting from an e-mail having passed through various servers had left the text incomprehensible. The only exception to this rule is for the chapter on *Cultural Practice and War*. This discussion included numerous posts sharing copy-pasted news items and media coverage of the Kosovo War (1998–99), which were mostly edited out to maintain a rhythm of VOTI member postings. Regardless, all of this material is still available in the VOTI archives held at SALT Research.

Other editorial decisions have been made to facilitate easier reading in publication format. To avoid endless repetition while risking the loss of authenticity, the longer headings and footings that appeared on each original posting have been deleted. Part of the original VOTI footnote stipulated that all e-mail content was considered the property of individual authors and so SALT sought each contributor's permission to include their copy in this publication. In only a handful of cases permission was not forthcoming. Throughout the posts, new links have been embedded, citations added for people and events, and editorial notes inserted when e-mails could not be found or seem to be missing. Texts and other material that was posted in the forum, but which are too long to include in the chain of e-mails, are included in the appendix. A timeline for VOTI has also been drawn up.

Achievements

VOTI established solidarity among a core group of curators because it offered an opportunity to strategize professional agency in the face of institutional demands, and to communicate in a closed forum about very real long-term and immediate challenges. Some of these postings are brief and concise, some are long-winded exegeses. The professional exchange of information, about what it was to be a contemporary art curator at that time, about the inextricable relationship to the world economy, the problems of cultural translation, the communal outrage over museum directors and regional governments blithely trampling over curatorial rights—these were just some of the topics covered in VOTI's voluminous outpourings. Many of the curators were working freelance rather than on the staff of institutions at this point. There was an urgency to these situations and a very open sharing of concerns. Discussions were far-reaching in exploring new museum and curatorial models, in looking at the museum as a laboratory, and in powerfully articulating what it meant to be on the periphery in a newly-globalized field. These networked communications allowed for new kinds of professional connection, which eventually grew into solid and long-lasting bonds. While VOTI's technology seems humorously anachronistic now, the vital community spirit evident from the posts is quite evident, and many of the issues that arose still feel relevant today. This publication gives the Union of the Imaginary a second life, one that was never anticipated when the forum began.

VOTI Timeline

November 1997, Bonn: A gathering of 33 curators and leaders of the art world from many countries is organized by the Bonn-based Foundation for Art and Culture. The group, referred to as the Conclave, is asked to advise for a major exhibition titled *Zeitwenden*, due to open in December 1999. The Conclave selects five co-curators to work on the exhibition: Carlos Basualdo (South America), Dan Cameron (North America), Okwui Enwezor (Africa), Yuko Hasegawa (Asia) and Udo Kittelmann (Europe), who then select artists. Several participants express concern with the selection procedure that overvalues names and particular art practices. They encourage a more dynamic and fluid curatorial approach, yet because of continuing disagreement the project is discontinued.

January 1998, New York: Carlos Basualdo, Francesco Bonami, Dan Cameron, Okwui Enwezor, Hou Hanru, Matthew Higgs, Susan Kandel, Rosa Martínez, Åsa Nacking and Hans Ulrich Obrist are invited to present ten artists each for the first *CREAM* book to be published by Phaidon. In response to what they perceive to be a growing homogenizing tendency imposed on curatorial activity, Bonami, Obrist and Basualdo decide to organize a forum for contestation and resistance.

February 1998, Madrid: During ARCO art fair lectures, several meetings take place between Carlos Basualdo, Francesco Bonami, Dan Cameron, Okwui Enwezor, Hou Hanru and Hans Ulrich Obrist. They discuss the possibility of forming an organization to fight the homogenization of curatorial practice and to develop an understanding of the role of the curator in contemporary society.

March 31, 1998, New York: Carlos Basualdo and Hans Ulrich Obrist found the Union of the Imaginary (VOTI) in a meeting with Jordan Crandall, Director of the X-Art Foundation, which agrees to host a permanent digital forum for the Union. At this meeting, Basualdo and Obrist are named Secretarios, and Crandall is named Delegado of VOTI. VOTI is dedicated to the memory of Alexander Dorner (1893-1957). Individual curators are invited to join the VOTI forum.

May – June 1998, online: With an initial group of approximately 20 members, VOTI begins private discussion on "The Museum of the XXI Century." Throughout its existence, VOTI technically functions as an online discussion forum on the server of The Thing, a New York-based, artist-run, nonprofit organization, founded by artist Wolfgang Staehle.

October 11 and 14, 1998, New York: Planning meetings attended by Carlos Basualdo, Jordan Crandall, Hou Hanru, Susan Hapgood, Bettina Funcke, Hans Ulrich Obrist, Octavio Zaya. Susan Hapgood is named Archivista of VOTI, and the Oficina de Asuntos Publicos is announced, with Francesco Bonami and Octavio Zaya named as Oficinistas.

November 2, 1998 – February 28, 1999, online: Private discussion on "The Economies of the Art World" begins, hosted by Zdenka Badovinac, Vasıf Kortun, Jose Ignacio Roca, and Salon 3 (Hans Ulrich Obrist, Rebecca Gordon-Nesbitt and Maria Lind). Guest discussants are Brian Holmes and Liam Gillick, and Ben Kinmont is invited in January 1999 to join in. Discussion continues into early 1999, spurring several side conversations and actions.

December 1, 1998, fax: Collective VOTI action. All day long, the same letter signed by most VOTI members is repeatedly transmitted by fax from members' diverse locations to the Whitney Museum of American Art, New York. It accuses the director, Maxwell Anderson, of disrespecting curatorial practice and initiating a form of intellectual gentrification that borders on censorship after he fired two respected curators Elisabeth Sussman and Thelma Golden.

February 6 and 15, 1999, New York and Madrid: Two meetings; the first attended by Carlos Basualdo, Dan Cameron, Jordan Crandall, Bettina Funcke, Susan Hapgood, and Jens Hoffmann; the second attended by Carlos Basualdo, Ute Meta Bauer, Dan Cameron, Jordan Crandall, Rosa Martínez, Pedro Reyes, Octavio Zaya. Topics of forum discussions planned; preliminary discussions for VOTI to organize panels for ARCO art fair in February 2000.

May 1999, Venice Biennale: VOTI members Vasıf Kortun, Carolyn Christov-Bakargiev, Maria Lind and Rebecca Gordon-Nesbitt meet.

May 26 – July 26, 1999, online: The public forum on *Cultural Practice and War*, is presented jointly by the X-Art Foundation and VOTI. Catalyzed by the Kosovo War and NATO bombings of January to June of the same year, an extensive discussion of military strategy vis-à-vis culture ensues, with many postings by new voices to the forum.

February 11 to 13, 2000, Madrid: As part of the ARCO art fair, over 30 VOTI members speak at eight panel discussions on topics including curatorial practice, new exhibition models, curators' responsibility to society, independent curators, globalism and transdisciplinary practice. Panels conceived and organized by VOTI members Bettina Funcke, Susan Hapgood and Octavio Zaya.

April 4, 2000, online: VOTI assigns individual members specific days to post messages, timed roughly two weeks apart. Discussion continues into June 2000 with posts found dating up until September 1, when all goes quiet.

Members of VOTI, 1998 – 2000

Bruce Altshuler
Pedro Reyes Alvarez
Zdenka Badovinac
Wayne Baerwaldt
Carlos Basualdo
Ute Meta Bauer
Daniel Birnbaum
Waling Boers
Francesco Bonami
Dan Cameron
Christophe Cherix
Carolyn Christov-Bakargiev
Lisa Corrin
Jordan Crandall
Amada Cruz
Bart De Baere
Okwui Enwezor
Charles Esche
Robert Fleck
Douglas Fogle
Jesús Fuenmayor
Bettina Funcke
Rebecca Gordon-Nesbitt
Lars Grambye
Hou Hanru
Susan Hapgood
Maria Hlavajova
Jens Hoffmann
Udo Kittelmann
Vasıf Kortun
Aleksandra Kostic
Carin Kuoni
Marta Kuzma
Cornelia Lauf
Maria Lind
Rosa Martínez
Laurence Miller

Viktor Misiano
Akiko Miyake
Åsa Nacking
Michelle Nicol
Hans Ulrich Obrist
Adriano Pedrosa
Kathrin Rhomberg
José Ignacio Roca
Annette Schindler
Yukiko Shikata
Valerie Smith
Nancy Spector
Jon-Ove Steihaug
Stéphanie Moisdon-Trembley
Barbara Vanderlinden
Hortensia Voelckers
Octavio Zaya

Guest discussants:
Liam Gillick
Brian Holmes
Ben Kinmont

Vita VOTI

Jordan Crandall, 2013

In the late 1990s, when VOTI was formed, participation on the Internet was optional rather than obligatory. The World Wide Web, still in its infancy, had little commercial allure. You clicked through pages that were often slow to load due to the limited bandwidth of your dial-up modem, with minimal opportunities to input your own content. Blogging tools were beginning to become available, yet social media, at least as we know it today, was barely conceivable.

For discursive engagement, the action happened elsewhere. It happened in text-based environments like Usenet newsgroups, telnet-enabled role-playing environments, IRCs and listservs. The latter, also called mailing lists, were especially conducive to sustained conversation. They were popular largely because of their convenience. You did not need a special application. You could subscribe to them by e-mail. Once subscribed to a particular mailing list, you could send one message to the addresses of all the subscribers on that list. People's subsequent replies were then sent to all subscribers, and in this way an ongoing conversation would play out simultaneously in the e-mail boxes of all of the members of the forum. You responded at your own pace, in the context of attending to your mail.

Through this very simple technological means, complex and dynamic communities of interest were formed. They brought people together through shared interests and affinities. They were engaging to the extent that they were relevant to users, and so they ebbed and flowed in rhythmic undulations that were unpredictable, invigorating, and sometimes unsettling. The best listservs tried to stay relevant by maintaining a level of quality and focus sufficient to hold the interest of members. This often required organizational effort to ensure that topics were well-selected, that an adequate number of competent participants were invested and that conversational frameworks were conveyed with clarity. The organizational structure had to be firm yet agile enough to accommodate spontaneity: the unanticipated lines of action that could vitalize the discussions. The thrill of the unavailable had to be courted, yet this was not without risk.

Mailing list forums were like living things, strange conglomerations of urban actors, and they had rhythms, intimacies, and moods. Their instantaneity could be intoxicating, their silences haunting. Since participants were only visible through their writings, dialogue required careful attunement to quality of voice: not only what was said but *how* it was said. As an urban space, the openness of communication had to be respected, yet as in all social situations, forms of modulation and subtle regulation were crucial. An argument that got out of hand could gather momentum and completely subsume a forum; left unchecked, it could destroy it. Forum moderators were often required: an arduous job that was something like an air traffic controller, book editor, psychologist, and dinner host combined.

I was involved in organizing many of these forums in the latter half of the 1990s. They were interesting to me for the kinds of conversations they could enable and the kinds of communities they could help develop. They were also interesting to me as artistic forms in and of themselves: assemblages of people, technologies, places, rhythms, thoughts and sensations. I was interested in the formal and affective qualities of the global, networked spaces that they helped enable, cut through with unresolved localities, intimacies and divisions: volatile spaces that were never as unified or seamless as the lulling glow of the monitors suggested. I was interested in the strange new politics that they anticipated, centered around actors who were no longer bound by the same kinds of allegiances. Small, often situational networks of affiliation among dispersed constituencies, whether cultural, erotic or economic in nature, seemed to allow vibrant identifications that did not fully align with conventional boundaries.

It is important to remember that, during this time, the digital was defined by a condition of impermanence: it was the opposite of materiality. Concepts of virtual space, cyberspace, and virtual embodiment abounded, registering a dislocating dynamic that seemed to offer the abandonment of the complications of bodily identity and physical place. Yet at the same time, in the face of this seeming dissolution, the network was simultaneously working to enable new corporealities and localisms: frameworks of physical, cultural, and regional specificity that were not so divorced from history and territorial alignment. They were subject to the imperatives of new technologically-mediated economies, not free of them.

These were the conditions under which the planning for the VOTI discussions began. As Carlos Basualdo, Hans Ulrich Obrist, Susan Hapgood and I developed the architecture for the forum, we aimed to create conditions that seemed most appropriate for the discursive community we hoped to enable. We conceived a structure that would involve a fluctuation between private and public modes. In private mode, the permanent members of VOTI would have a space for discussing issues pertaining to their own curatorial practices, plan upcoming events and conferences, and develop topics for the public discussions. While this private mode was ongoing and free-flowing, the public mode was of a specific duration and organized around a particular theme. These open discussions, which aimed to introduce culturally diverse voices and perspectives, often focused on topics that concerned the relations between cultural institutions and the corporate world and the changing climate for cultural work as corporate management models were implemented. They focused on the economy of the art world in the context of globalization and the role of cultural practice in a time of crisis. The texts of many of these discussions are gathered and edited in this volume.

Creating an edited compilation of an online forum like this is an enormous challenge, since these conversations are multi-threaded and interwoven with events and communications that are not always at hand. They play out across different intervals and registers, poised as they are between writing and speaking, performance and elucidation. Voices coincide and diverge, presences come and go, thoughts migrate. The editorial team of Susan Hapgood, Vasıf Kortun, and November Paynter has aimed to produce a volume that does justice to the form. When I read these documents, I think of them situated in their time. VOTI aimed to facilitate exploration of the role of curatorial practice during a time of profound change. It sought to develop aesthetic, intellectual, organizational and political strategies that were informed by the urgencies of a particular historical moment. The discussions grapple with the transformations that were being wrought by critical technological and economic change, in order to explore their implications for cultural work. They concern the material situatedness of everyday practice across radically reconfiguring geographies and connective intervals: people writing from their studios, institutions, places of transit, in expressive forms that range from the poetic to the polemical, with varying senses of political and experiential urgency. They are comprised of spaces through which participants are assembled and coordinated, yet compelled out into the world as new cultural situations, conversations and identifications: urban spaces of the everyday, familiar yet foreign.

Forums like VOTI show that these kinds of connective experiences can materialize in ways that endure, however ephemeral they may seem. Their effects are subterranean, flowing into other networks, communities, discourses. Ideas, relational forms and affective bonds morph and transform, reconstitute and reproduce, often at long intervals, and in the most unexpected places. In these ways the VOTI discussions contain lines of flight that can, from the standpoint of this historical moment, be traced. They are clusters in nets that have become vast. Such network space, once thought the most transitory of landscapes, is etched with generative chords.

In Conversation

Carlos Basualdo and Hans Ulrich Obrist, 2013

Carlos Basualdo: We could try to remember how VOTI started, but we should also try to remember why we felt it was important, and what did we want to do with VOTI, what were the things that we were really keen on doing. Because it's important to remember that when we were thinking about VOTI, first of all, we were thinking about May 1968, that's why we had the Imaginary in the title. '68 was resonating strongly for us. But there was also a question of organization, the organization of a certain practice that had to do with exhibitions at a time when there were not really so many courses on exhibition history or curatorial practice and the like. I will always remember that when I had my first conversations with you, I was at the time invested in working with histories that were not so present, working with artists coming from different parts of the world, from South America and so forth, which at the time were not sufficiently recognized, but for you what was very clear was your interest in what an exhibition can do, and at that time there weren't many people thinking in that direction.

Hans Ulrich Obrist: Yes, our conversations were full of ideas about the exhibition as a medium—I found this fascinating. I have some very specific memories of the beginnings of VOTI, and New York was really the city where it was born. We must have started the conversations in '97?

CB: I think it was the question of the medium of the exhibition, I mean, the question of the acknowledgement that there is something that gathers us, and what gathers us is that we all work with exhibitions. And exhibitions are cultural artifacts that have a history. To me it was a revelation that had to do with meeting you, and my own interests in exhibitions and the history of exhibitions came from that meeting, when you were talking about certain key historical figures, like Alexander Dorner, of course.[1]

HUO: And Willem Sandberg, Félix Fénéon.[2]

CB: Yes and all the people from the '60s. From Harald Szeemann to Pontus Hultén... and at that time there was not a structured way by which one could access that kind of information.[3]

HUO: And in the early days of the Internet, there were not so many databases—a lot of this information had not yet been digitized. It was a form of amnesia and protest against forgetting that coincided with me doing the series of interviews commissioned by Jack Bankowsky for *Artforum* with pioneering curatorial figures such as Walter Hopps, Pontus Hultén and Harald Szeemann.[4] I remember that this was the same period, '96, '97, '98—it seemed an important time for better understanding and promoting the work of our professional forebears, for speaking to the people at the forefront of these generations in person while we still had the opportunity. Almost like grandparents, they had become a generation of mentors: Szeemann, Hultén, and Hopps. Later the *Artforum* interviews became a book and I also added interviews with Jo Cladders, Lucy Lippard, Jean Leering, Walter Zanini, Seth Siegelaub etc.[5] These individuals were mostly in their seventies or eighties at that time, and of course now some of them are no longer with us. We had a desire to explore this increased interest in curating, something that had exploded in the '90s. There were more and more curating courses in art schools, yet there was no history available. It's very interesting that the first chapter in the book represents a protest against forgetting, and, in a non-nostalgic way, to think that the past could actually be a toolbox—as Erwin Panofsky so beautifully pointed out—for the future.[6]

CB: What I want to emphasize is that our interest in these key figures was absolutely revelatory for our generation. I mean now it seems a bit redundant to point back to them, but at the time it was not; because we were all coming from different backgrounds and meeting around contemporary art, and some of us felt an urgency to work, as I said, to address histories that were at the time not part of the main conversation, but the fact was that we were all using the same tools and talking in a similar language. What that language could be, I think it was not clear.

HUO: Do you remember some of the roles? We were something like the "Secretary Generals," Susan Hapgood was "Master of Archives..." [7]

CB: We were called Secretarios and she was Archivista. I think we used names in Italian and Spanish. I was reading Guy Debord, and VOTI was conceived as a Situationist union of sorts.

HUO: That's right Spanish! The titles were inspired by your Argentinian background. It was a sort of Borgesian fiction, it wasn't a Brechtian institution, it was more a Borgesian institutional fiction. Fiction connected to play, as Robert Louis Stevenson said: it's through fiction we change the atmosphere and tenor of life.

CB: Let's also not forget that there was *humor* in VOTI, I mean, VOTI was about being free to play.

HUO: And Jordan Crandall's role was essential as he really brought the forum to reality.

CB: Indeed!

HUO: Yes, and the incubation was during '97. We were keen on the idea that there should be participants from every continent. It is fascinating to read José Roca's conversations about the incredible dynamics of the Colombian art world at that time. The voice of the Colombian art world was new. Many people in the art world didn't know about its remarkable energy. Today everybody knows about Slovenia and the amazing success of Ljubljana, but at that time, Zdenka Badovinac had just started to tell us about the Slovenian miracle.[8] This proliferation of voices and the polyphony of centers was really so exciting. It is worth mentioning that VOTI did not only involve curators; there were also museum directors and scholars, theoreticians, art historians and so on. Bettina Funcke was writing an art historical thesis at that time, and subsequently went into publishing and editing.[9] Brian Holmes has always been an activist as well as a translator.[10] From the beginning it was very much about pooling skills and knowledge. As an artist Jordan obviously had lots of connections to new technology…

CB: It's important to stress the fact that VOTI involved an artist [Jordan Crandall] from the very beginning and that we were interested, in a sense, in creating an open community, an intergenerational, international platform including people from different fields. I think that was very unique.

HUO: There was always something both poetic and political from the very beginning, I would say. In those very first conversations in your loft, and with Okwui [Enwezor],[11] I remember us discussing the idea of a union being a very concrete and organized action—a *self-reliant* action. And that seemed important. It became apparent that there was a very clear difference from the previous generations of curators. Our practice is defined by these extraordinary people from the '60s and '70s—people who really fought for contemporary art and were such an inspiration to us. It was this approach that allowed people to found new kinds of institutions. Douglas Gordon referred to our practice as a "promiscuity of collaboration" and I think that we as curators felt very strongly that yes, we were promiscuous in our collaborations, but at the same time were very loyal to each other.[12] It is fascinating to think that many of our dialogues date back to the beginning of the '90s—we've known each other for more than twenty years— and somehow it is still like the first day we met. We continue to see each other; we continue to be in dialogue; we continue to collaborate.

CB: Absolutely, and we keep learning from each other, looking at what we do very closely, which is a beautiful opportunity, because one knows how to look at the work of someone who is older, but how do you look at the people of your own generation? I think that the museum directors of the sixties did not have that same level of self-consciousness about the tools that they were working with, and I think that's what we brought to the table, and also, one thing that we quickly found out was that there was a certain brotherhood or sisterhood, if you wish, among independent curators, right? I mean, I think that what VOTI stood for, was an experiment in trying to understand, for those of us who were not working in institutions or were only working with institutions in a sort of tangential way, about the different set of interests between curators who were working in institutions and independent curators. The membership of the Union was open; you and I, Jordan and Susan had many conversations about how to define the membership and I believe at some point we arrived at the formula that anybody who was interested in curatorial practice should become a member, regardless of what they were doing.

HUO: And also regardless of age. The other day I was speaking with Jens Hoffmann and he told me that he had pretty much just entered the art world at the time of VOTI—it was among his first experiences.[13] There was also the idea that a memorable exhibition could no longer be centered around one person, and this actually had a lot to do with Francesco Bonami's 50th Venice Biennale in 2003, in which you curated a section, I teamed up with Molly Nesbit and Rirkrit Tiravanija, and Hou Hanru curated a section.[14] That was very much a continuation of VOTI's activities, because almost all the curators, including Francesco, were members.

CB: It is important to look at VOTI from the perspective of its potency. What was the potency that VOTI expressed? It expressed a generation, and it was the medium through which the conversations that were defining to us took shape. And then it expressed a generation that was invested in collective work, which one could say is still apparent, as was also manifested very clearly in the 50th Venice Biennale which to a certain extent was part of the same narrative.

But I do remember that there were fractures along the lines of the divide: independent/institutional curators. I mean, it was difficult to create a common ground there because the curators who were more closely associated with institutions would not feel they had the same things at stake. That impossibility is even more acute today, so, in a way, VOTI very much continues in our conversations. But also a certain difference between the way institutions think about exhibitions and the way in which some of us think about exhibitions also continues, wouldn't you agree?

HUO: Of course, I think many of the VOTI conversations are still relevant now.

CB: *Zeitwenden* was important.[15]

HUO: A trigger.

CB: Yes. Because *Zeitwenden* was in '97.

HUO: And where was it?

CB: The curatorial meeting organized for *Zeitwenden* took place in Bonn, in the fall of 1997, I believe.

HUO: Oh, it was *that* gathering!

CB: The Conclave!

HUO: It was the Conclave where we also felt uncomfortable, right?

CB: Well, the Conclave, what had happened was that this organization—

HUO: Because Nancy [Spector] mentioned it [in her e-mail],[16] she says: "Is this comparable to what happened recently in Bonn? Was anything done about that?"

CB: So there was the so-called "Conclave" organized by the Stiftung für Kunst und Kultur in Bonn and there were 33 curators invited from all over the world and we were the youngest people in the room.[17] I remember Yuko Hasegawa and Dan Cameron and Nancy and Barbara Vanderlinden and Okwui and Udo Kittelmann, yourself and myself.[18] We were supposed to, once again, come up with a list of artists and the organization was going to do a show about the end of the century. And then I believe it was Nick Serota who said "We are curators, we don't do shows by lists.[19] We are going to select seven people who are going to do the show." And then we started working on the show, and the team selected was you and Udo, Yuko, Zdenka, Okwui, Dan and myself, I believe.[20] And I think our proposal was, and this was 1997, that we were going to work with an interdisciplinary approach and mostly with artists' collectives. Those were the guiding principles for our project. Of course we involved a wide variety of people from Jeff Wall to Maurizio Cattelan, but the organization wanted something more traditional.[21] They were thinking more in terms of painting and sculpture, and so, soon after we presented our proposal, they fired us.

HUO: That's it! We got fired!

CB: We were actually fired.

HUO: This is so fascinating that you remember that because thinking back, it was actually a really important moment. ...but it was considered to be un-phrased, unformulated... But yes, that was a very strange thing.

CB: I don't remember exactly what they said about firing us, but it was pretty clear that it happened because we were not going to work with some of the artists that they wanted us to work with. And there was, I believe, quite a buzz in the media at the time in Germany, and we were defended by Harald Szeemann and Nick Serota, publically. And that created for us the sense of a new generation coming into being.

HUO: So again, there is an underlying sense that we came together through such moments—moments defined by some kind of friction or resistance. I think the Conclave was important. There's a group photo of the Conclave. And who was it that fired us?

CB: Walter Smerling. Do you remember Walter Smerling?[22]

HUO: It was also the beginning of online publishing because all of these debates about Bonn, about VOTI, and also about the letter to the Whitney Museum, they were recorded by *Nettime* and *Artnet*.[23] It was the start of a different form of press. The emergence of VOTI coincided with the early days of online press.

CB: I recall that our conversations started to take shape at the time when we were all invited to work on *CREAM*.[24]

HUO: The *CREAM* book started to take shape in '97 and it was a new experiment by Phaidon. What they basically wanted to publish was an exhibition in book form. And that's obviously a very sensitive matter because as curators, we were very aware of the book being used as a medium by curators like Seth Siegelaub and Lucy Lippard. Siegelaub would do exhibitions, for example, *The January Show*, the famous '69 exhibition with Lawrence Weiner, who coincidentally reminded me just last week how revelatory this exhibition had been.[25] At the same time there was Siegelaub's *The Xerox Book*, and then Lippard's exhibition with the cards, the Seattle show, and the exhibitions where the number of inhabitants in the host cities gave the exhibitions their titles.[26] The instruction cards and manuals for the exhibition were very inspiring for *DO IT*.[27] So basically this idea that an exhibition can be a catalogue was very much at the front of our minds.

We therefore resisted Phaidon's proclaiming this publication to be an exhibition as *CREAM* was a book about artists but not by artists. The reason we felt this way was because all we would actually be allowed to do was nominate the artist, write a little text, and then Phaidon would do the layout with the graphic designer. We couldn't control the pages. We kept saying that making an exhibition in the medium of a book should mean that *we curate* the pages. We all became quite concerned about it not really being an exhibition in book form. We were also concerned about the fact that Phaidon as a publisher would not tell us how many copies of the book were going to print and we were questioning the idea of a curated book in relation to curators' rights.

I remember Okwui was one of the first curators involved in these VOTI conversations and one night at an opening on the street, we had a very febrile, feverish conversation about being curators, basically asking, "what does it mean?" Here we were, supposedly curating a group show for a book, but in our view the book pages were not a valid exhibition space, and in this sense it betrayed our key conviction. Would it mean that we would have to find our own structure? There was the strategy of infiltration, as we had seen in the late '80s when Félix González-Torres brought up the idea that we should infiltrate institutions like a virus and then replicate.[28] The analogy of the virus was an interesting one. So we were having a big discussion as to whether the strategy of infiltration had run its course, and that maybe it was time to set up our own structure. I remember at that moment we both had the feeling that we should self-organize. We talked about Magnum, in which the photographers had organized themselves as a kind of artist-run production structure, and we thought about a similar kind of curator-run production structure. These were some thoughts at the beginning.

CB: Yes, absolutely, there were these two points: on the one hand, a common interest in a certain praxis and the idea that this praxis was related to a form of knowledge, and the radicality of this form of knowledge at that time for us. There was a kind of self-consciousness of curatorial practice itself, something that our generation projected onto the past. Sometimes I feel that we somehow produce our own antecedents instead of the reality of what's there. I think it's *always* like that; we produced our antecedents around this specific notion of practice, around this notion of exhibition making that was being developed. At the same time, the other component was the "Union," the idea that we have to defend ourselves, that we should be paid properly, that we should be treated properly, that we could represent a sort of new intellectual class. I think there were lots of conversations about that new intellectual class, a new form of creative agency, and so on. I think that the Union was supposed to work on these two levels: to produce knowledge related to a certain praxis [exhibition making], which somehow gathered us, and to give us a voice and a certain leverage in terms of determining the basic conditions under which a curator is able to do his or her work.

HUO: Exactly, and something referred to later, which also revealed itself as a battle line, was globalization and the forces behind it. We are not talking about the first wave of globalization (there have been moments of globalization ever since the Roman/Greek empires), but I mean an extreme form of globalization that was affecting the art world and the field of curating, with all its new possibilities and dangers. I suppose this was why we felt that it was important to gather, to reflect upon how we can engage in a global dialogue and actually produce difference and not annihilate it, how can we produce what Edouard Glissant called *mondialité* as a sort of collective force.[29] I remember you talking about the urgency of developing an institutional model that could be adjusted to the conditions of countries both in the center and the periphery. There was a proliferation of centers and within this Rem Koolhaas' thinking also played a big role.[30] We talked a lot about Koolhaas and we were very interested in this idea of an analogy between curating and urbanism. Had this whole thing happened ten years earlier, the debate would have been limited to very few centers. It's really fascinating how even by '97 the debate was everywhere.

CB: Yeah, it was kind of fantastic. I didn't remember it was so global from the very beginning.

HUO: And that's what happened in the '90s. It was this very specific moment in the art world when one center grew to become a number of centers, then suddenly exploded into a proliferation of centers.

CB: And the reason was clearly the use of the Internet. I think we were interested in what certain people were doing with electronic media and the ways in which they were experimenting with the Internet. I remember that it was clear that we needed to establish an online platform. Jordan Crandall immediately became a partner. The Internet allowed us to operate in a delocalized manner, it allowed us to include in our conversations people who were living in different parts of the world. I think you can say that we were primarily motivated by an interest in a certain practice, in constructing a pioneering cartography of that practice, which for us consisted of a specific form of knowledge production. Secondly, there was a strong desire to imbue those ideas with a politics of agency, the agency of curatorial practice and to have those politics play out at a global level through the Internet. I would say those were the key components of VOTI: to recognize the specificity of a certain practice conceived as a model for the production of knowledge, to invest it with a politics of agency and to activate that agency online.

HUO: Those were the ingredients, definitely, and we had conversations with Jordan about how such a platform could work. Obviously, this was pre-social networks, it was pre-blogs, but there was this desire to have regular exchange.

CB: There were lists at the time, do you remember? There were e-mail lists.

HUO: Like *Nettime*?[31]

CB: Yes.

HUO: I always followed *Nettime* at that time.

CB: I think that the e-mail lists allowed us to engage in these discussions online, and there were many interesting discussions.

HUO: Let's consider the chapter *The Economy of the Art World* because that leads us to a very concrete aspect of VOTI.[32] We wanted to call it *Union of the Imaginary*. We wanted it to be a union, yet at the same time, we wanted it to be poetic and "dystopic." "UOTI" didn't really work phonetically, and so we had to call it "VOTI." I don't remember how this idea came about, do you remember?

CB: We came up with the name of the Union and then you sent me a postcard. It had a picture of an ancient relief where you could see a Latin inscription. The "V" was like the Latin version of a "U."

HUO: Ah, great, so that was the beginning, the postcard. I had forgotten about that. That's also kind of interesting—it was the age of the Internet and we were still sending postcards.

CB: Absolutely, yes.

HUO: *The Economy of the Art World* resulted from a discussion I had in New York about the necessity of the curatorial contract. We looked into different contracts in history. Guy Debord, for example, published a book about his contracts with publishers and film producers...[33]

CB: And of course Seth Siegelaub's model for an artist's contract...

HUO: Yes, and don't forget we interviewed Siegelaub about his *Bob Projansky Artists' Reserve Rights Transfer*.[34] So the content of what is now the second chapter became concrete.

CB: Yes, because it was about concrete things, and that was a very important concept. It was also the period when we were discussing Roberto Mangabeira Unger's book *Democracy Realized* and it was essential for us that the utopian angle would be articulated through a number of concrete proposals.[35]

HUO: I feel I should say that these chapters did literally come out of these conversations—they were not artificially devised.

CB: I think that one important action for the Union was the protest that we did when two curators at the Whitney were fired, Elisabeth Sussman and Thelma Golden.[36] To this day, Thelma is still very thankful to us for doing that. We organized a protest by which we were sending faxes, basically to the Director of the Museum.

HUO: Yes, let's talk about the Whitney response, because this came after talking very concretely about the question of the contract and economy. Obviously it's also important to say that almost none of us were making a living at the time. That was another subtext of it. Do you remember how it started? It was after the Whitney Biennial, was it not?

CB: Curators are unfairly fired all the time, unfortunately, but this was particularly hard to make sense of because these were two very bright, very brave curators and there was a new director and they were simply dismissed. We saw them as curators who were really pushing the boundaries to a certain degree. And look at what happened! Thelma went on to do an amazing, incredible job at the Studio Museum and Elisabeth is back at the Whitney. So obviously it was a decision that didn't go very well. But there have been many instances, recently, of situations similar to this or even much worse than this…and nothing has received a collective response. You know Charles Ray's sculpture of *Boy With Frog* was removed from Punta della Dogana, and there has not been an international collective response.[37] The field has not been able to come together and oppose this action.

HUO: It's very interesting because Nancy kicked off the forum conversation on the 10th November 1998 by alerting everybody to what had happened at the Whitney. She already had a more institutional role herself at that time, but while some of the group worked for museums, most of us did not. I didn't have a fixed job at a museum at that time—I was working for the Musée d'Art Moderne de la Ville de Paris as a *Migrateurs* curator. It was more like a freelance position, but I did have my own office. And you weren't at an institution at that time either. That's why it's interesting that Nancy raised this issue. We had thought that maybe VOTI was more oriented toward the needs of independent curators, yet the forum started to raise this issue of the Whitney and said that we should also see what's happening to curators within the institution—what are their rights, what are their contracts? What about sabbaticals? Nancy raised the issue of research sabbaticals. I think that very few museums in the world have research sabbaticals and the Museum of Modern Art (MoMA) has them because it was something that was introduced very early on. A couple of years ago Barbara London told me she was on a one year travel research sabbatical after twenty years at MoMA.[38] I think you can count on one hand the number of museums that offer this… So Nancy raised a key issue here.

I remember we wrote to Maxwell Anderson…[39]

HUO: He also remembers it?

CB: Yes. We spoke about it a few years ago. And it's interesting because it really had an impact. You know, certainly from the perspective of today, when any form of community action in regards to curatorial practice seems almost inconceivable. It's kind of romantic that we felt we could do things like that, but, we tried, we did it, in a way, and it produced effects.

HUO: It is really intriguing that Chapter III is all about the making of a letter. It was the collective production of a letter.[40]

CB: We were adopting a collective mode of production via the Internet that then became more evident as a possibility but at the time it was not. And at the same time, by working together online, we created the form of a community.

HUO: Then there is the chapter *The Trial of Pol Pot* that grew out of a polemical debate, though I was less involved in that conversation, relating to an exhibition that Philippe Parreno and Liam Gillick did in Grenoble in 1998—and it became a conversation mostly between Brian Holmes and Liam Gillick. You and I were absent from this conversation.[41]

CB: Ah that is why I don't remember it very well.

HUO: Yes we were absent. It is also interesting that in some kind of way, after having triggered VOTI, it started to self-organize, self-regulate...

CB: I mean, absolutely, that is exactly what we wanted. And then there was VOTI at ARCO, do you remember? ARCO was very important for VOTI.[42]

HUO: ARCO was important for our generation. It was the first art fair that by the mid '90s had already begun to invite many curators.

CB: And it was a kind of dysfunctional art fair, which was the beauty of it, because let's also remember that this was long before art fairs became what they are now. To start with, there weren't so many. There was Gramercy Park, and, of course, there was the Chicago Art Fair and Basel and one would never go to them. And possibly because ARCO was not so commercially powerful, and it was also publicly sponsored, they decided to organize all these scholarly conferences around the Fair. We would have the best of times in Madrid and Rosina Gomez who was wonderful and very, very progressive, allowed herself to be convinced that we needed to devote one entire session of ARCO to VOTI.[43] That was the year 2000, I think.

HUO: Yes there were these meetings at ARCO, they were sort of a critical mass. They brought dozens of us together. And in many ways it was actually not so much about the conferences happening there, it was what was happening at breakfast, what was happening at dinner or late night in the bars of Madrid what was happening in these interstices. This was how our generation got to know each other better. Many of us had met online through VOTI and obviously we knew of most of the people and had encountered their work, but many people had not yet met each other in person, so I think that many were meeting for the first time in real space.

CB: And that was also something we very much wanted, we were keen to have the online experience but also we wanted VOTI to be an opportunity for people to meet offline and be able to work together.

HUO: In '99 there was the forum *Cultural Practice and War,* an online art forum presented by the X-Art Foundation and VOTI.[44]

CB: The X-Art Foundation was basically Jordan.

HUO: Yes, and it became a more public forum––more and more people joined, people we didn't know so well, and in this way VOTI really became more like a community over time.

CB: What was the last VOTI activity?

HUO: That's something I was wondering about. Perhaps it's a useful question with which to conclude this conversation: how did it end? I don't remember…

CB: I think it ended, to a certain degree, with ARCO. Because I think that the conference was our last organized activity. It was a culmination of sorts because there were around 70 people invited, I remember it being quite massive, and then the question was where would we go from there, and at that point, it wasn't clear what could have been the next step. I think the next step should have been to create some kind of institution, but at that point, I don't think we had the resources that we could have now if we would like to do that.

HUO: Also, I think there was a certain feeling that it had a limited lifespan, and that maybe it had organically come to an end. Cedric Price talked about the limited life span of buildings.[45] We felt the same was true for VOTI.

CB: One of my posts reads, "The VOTI list has been quite inactive lately, that may be because activity has been displaced to the live meetings, the one in New York and the one in Madrid. Both have been very productive and Susan is working on a long posting about them."

I think that when we organized the VOTI meetings at ARCO we thought it was going to be a point of arrival at least.

Based on a conversation between Carlos Basualdo and Hans Ulrich Obrist, May 2013, London.

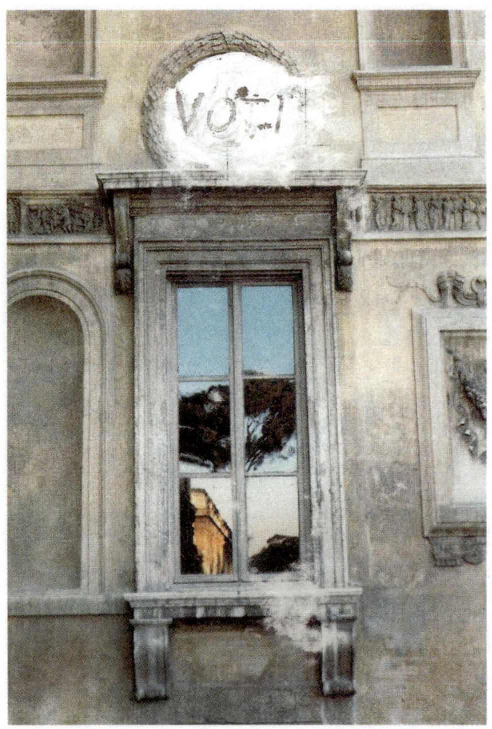

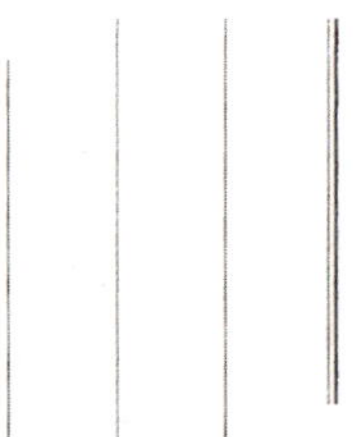

ACCADEMIA DI FRANCIA A ROMA
Villa Medici, facciata sul giardino

© Carte Segrete - Roma - Foto: Marc Le Mené

Postcard sent from Hans Ulrich Obrist to Carlos Basualdo, 1998

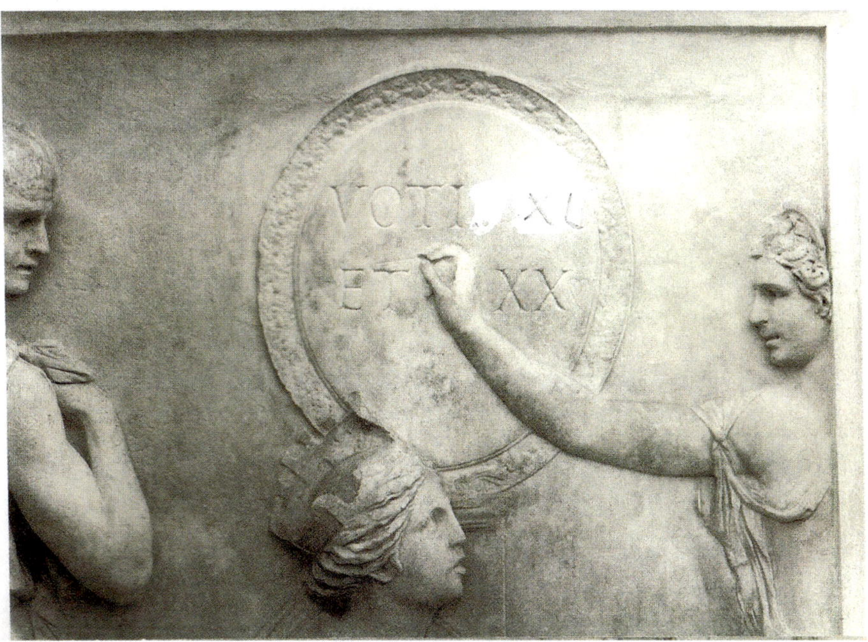

Rilievo della facciata di Villa Medici, con iscrizione per
i voti dell' Imperatore (dettaglio).
*Relief de la façade de la Villa Médicis avec inscription
pour les voeux de l' Empereur (détail).*

Postcard sent from Hans Ulrich Obrist to Carlos Basualdo, 1998

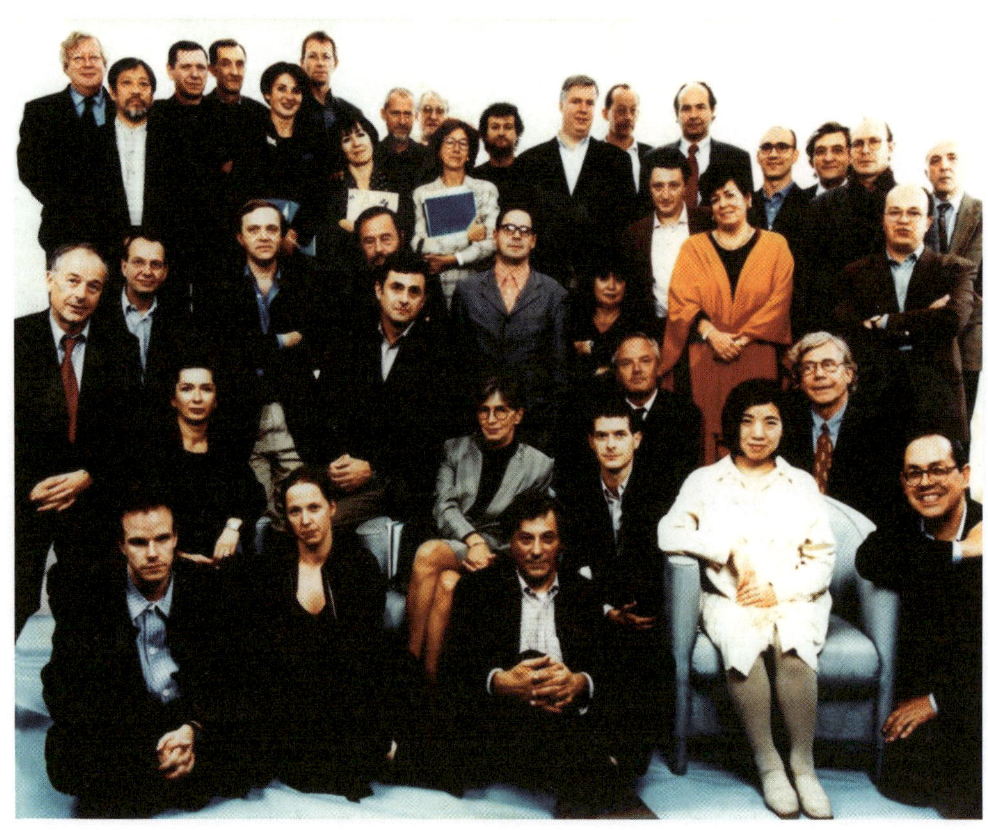

Group photograph of the "Conclave" of curators invited in 1997 to advise on the *Zeitwenden* exhibition in Bonn.

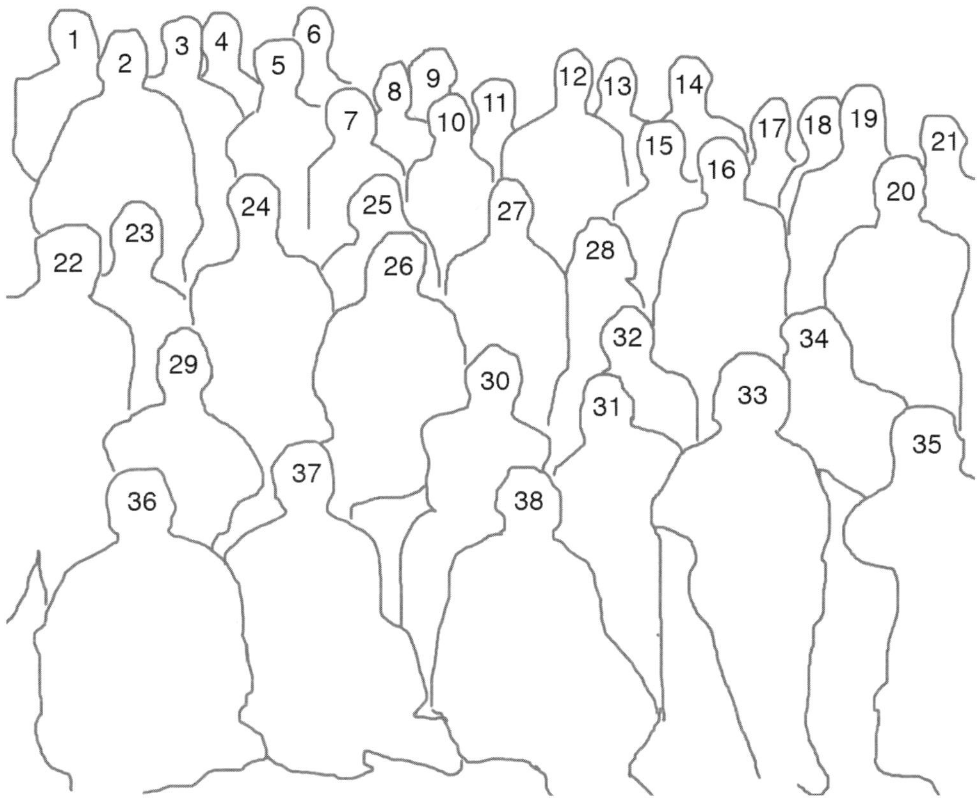

1 Rudi Fuchs
2 Li Xianting
3 David Elliott
4 Leon Paroissien
5 Suzanne Pagé
6 Nicholas Serota
7 Rosa Martínez
8 Lorand Hegyi
9 Jürgen Harten
10 María de Corral
11 Danilo Eccher
12 Lars Nittve
13 Kasper König
15 Viktor Misiano
16 Carolina Ponce de León
17 Carlos Basualdo
18 Walter Smerling
19 Alfons Hug
20 Necmi Sönmez
21 [unknown]
22 Uwe M. Schneede
23 Jean-Hubert Martin
24 Robert Storr
25 Harald Szeemann
26 Neal Benezra
27 Udo Kittelmann
28 Katalin Néray
29 Zdenka Badovinac
30 Anda Rottenberg
31 Dan Cameron
33 Yuko Hasegawa
34 Bazon Brock
35 Paulo Herkenhoff
36 Hans Ulrich Obrist
37 Barbara Vanderlinden
38 Jan Hoet

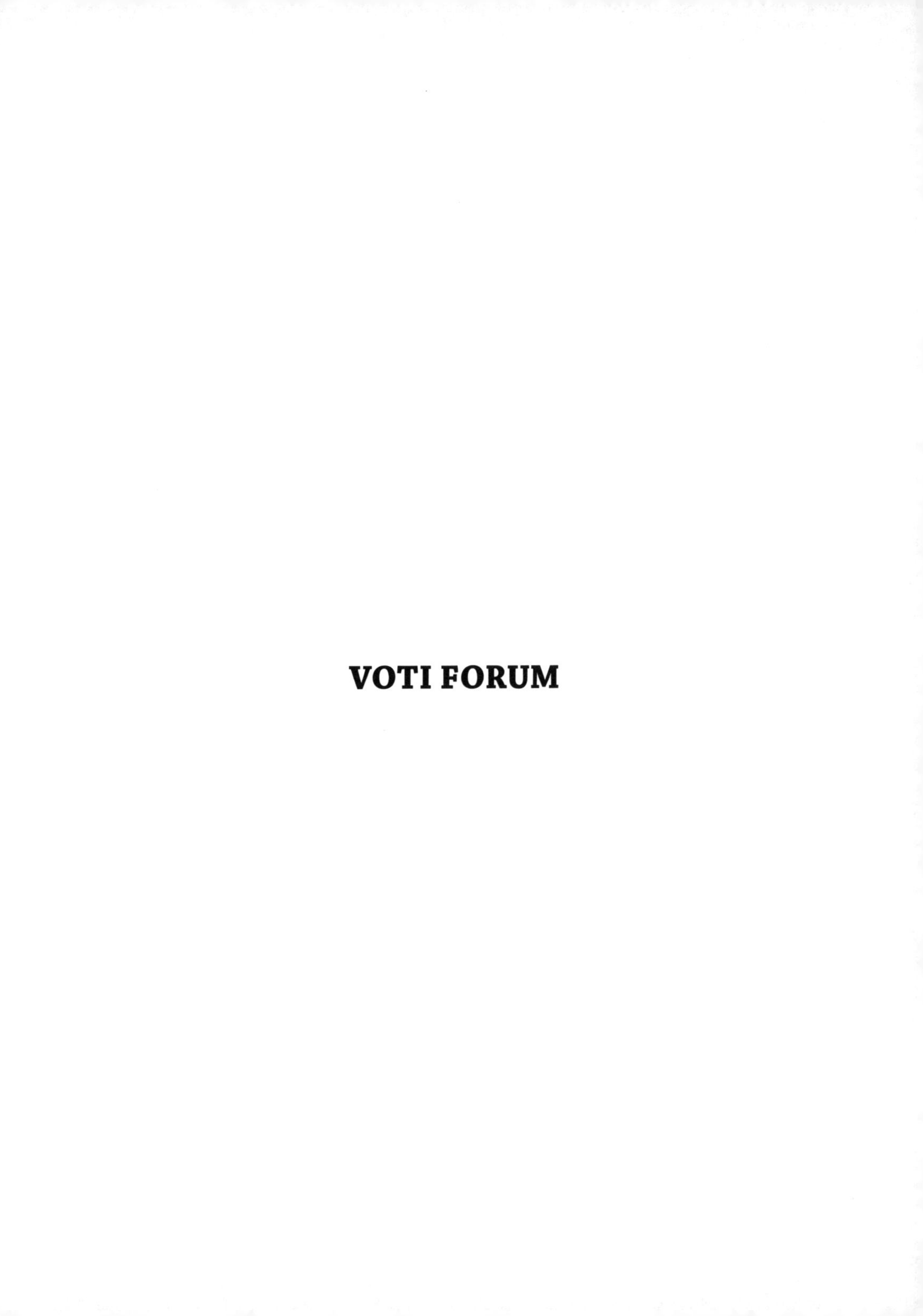

VOTI FORUM

The first two e-mails of this introductory section of VOTI share personal messages sent between Carlos Basualdo and Hans Ulrich Obrist in January 1998, in which they pinpoint a name for the forum – Union of the Imaginary. The two pages are included as scans to show the original form of the e-mails of the day and how they appear in the sourced archives that are now held by SALT. The following e-mails are the official welcome announcements for VOTI as sent by Jordan Crandall to those invited to contribute to the first session of the forum.

Date: Sunday, January 25, 1998 7:59:29 PM
From: Cbasualdo
Subj: A suggestion
To: HUO@compuserve.com

"An international association of Situationists can be seen as a union of workers in an advanced sector of culture, or more precisely as a union who claim the right to a task now impeded by social conditions; hence as an attempt at an organization of professional revolutionaries in culture." Guy Debord. "Theses on the Cultural Revolution," 1958.

Dear Hans,

Francesco told me about your idea of producing some kind of anti-homogeinizing manifesto in Madrid. I love the idea. May I suggest that we consitute the basis of a new kind of union, a Union of the Imaginary?

I look forward to hearing from you.

Best,

Carlos

Date: Sunday, January 25, 1998 9:25:05 PM
From: HUO@compuserve.com
Subj: A suggestion
To: Cbasualdo@AOL.COM

UNION OF THE IMAGINARY
VERY BEAUTIFUL
LETS DO IT
best
Hans Ulrich

---------------------- Headers -------------------------------
Return-Path: <HUO@compuserve.com>
Received: from relay13.mail.aol.com (relay13.mail.aol.com
[172.31.109.13]) by air07.mail.aol.com (v37.8) with SMTP; Sun, 25 Jan
1998 21:25:04 1900
Received: from arl-img-5.compuserve.com (arl-img-5.compuserve.com
[149.174.217.135])
     by relay13.mail.aol.com (8.8.5/8.8.5/AOL-4.0.0)
     with ESMTP id VAA16121 for <Cbasualdo@aol.com>;
     Sun, 25 Jan 1998 21:21:35 -0500 (EST)
Received: (from mailgate@localhost)
     by arl-img-5.compuserve.com (8.8.6/8.8.6/2.10) id VAA06627
     for Cbasualdo@aol.com; Sun, 25 Jan 1998 21:21:29 -0500 (EST)
Date: Sun, 25 Jan 1998 21:21:04 -0500
From: Hans Ulrich Obrist <HUO@compuserve.com>
Subject: A suggestion
Sender: Hans Ulrich Obrist <HUO@compuserve.com>
To: Cbasualdo <Cbasualdo@AOL.COM>
Message-ID: <199801252121_MC2-309E-3386@compuserve.com>
MIME-Version: 1.0
Content-Transfer-Encoding: quoted-printable
Content-Type: text/plain; charset=ISO-8859-1
Content-Disposition: inline

From: Jordan Crandall
Subject: invitation to VOTI
Date: Tuesday 02 June 1998

Dear ____________,

Carlos Basualdo, Jordan Crandall, and Hans Ulrich Obrist would like to invite you to join the Union of the Imaginary (VOTI).

VOTI is a permanent forum for the discussion of issues pertaining to curatorial practice in the context of contemporary society. Its goals are to promote discussion and collaboration among curators; to develop a progressive understanding of the role of curatorial practice; and to fight homogenization and instrumentalization at every level of culture. VOTI encourages an open discussion of issues that concern the present and future of curatorial activity, particularly in its relation to intellectual production and the politics of everyday life.

VOTI is a laboratory, a think tank for the testing of ideas both concrete and utopical. It is primarily structured as a private Internet forum, with discussions among members occurring via e-mail. An archive of the discussions, accessible only to Union members, will be housed on the Web. The forum will be hosted by the X Art Foundation as part of its Blast 7 program.

The Union will occasionally organize special sessions for the discussion of specific topics. On these occasions, guests will be invited from various disciplines, and the forum will be opened to a wider audience. Public Web archives will be created for these sessions, and offline events and publications may accompany them.

As a VOTI member, your only requirement is to participate actively in the discussions and collaborate in the organization of the special sessions.

Please reply to this message with a confirmation of your participation. If you would like to discuss any of these matters beforehand, please e-mail us.

Below you will find a preliminary list of invitees, and a brief history of the Union. VOTI has emerged in the intersection between the need for a stronger communication among curators and the expertise and deep commitment of X Art Foundation and Blast to the field of cultural practice in the network. (For recent Blast discussions, see http://www.blast. org/eyeblast.html and http://www.thing.net/~xaf/documenta.) VOTI was conceived as a network organization that is structured according to the dynamics of the medium.

We are very much looking forward to your participation in VOTI.

Carlos Basualdo
Hans Ulrich Obrist
Secretaries

Jordan Crandall
Delegado

"With the courage of the unacademic and the radical, according to the necessities of contemporary art."

Willem Sandberg

From: Jordan Crandall
Subject: WELCOME
Date: Friday 19 June 1998

Dear Members of VOTI,

On behalf of X Art Foundation and Blast, it is my pleasure to welcome you to the <voti>
forum. We are pleased to host this project in conjunction with the newly-formed Union
of the Imaginary (VOTI). I am personally delighted to be operating as Delegado of the
Union and to be working alongside Secretarios Carlos and Hans Ulrich. We are eager to
help realize the vast potential of the Union and are very much looking forward to the VOTI
conversations, meetings, and projects in the months to come.

As you know, the <voti> forum is private, accessible only to Acting Members. We hope to
create a comfortable atmosphere for you to participate in the discussions. The forum is
structured as a private laboratory or think-tank, where everyone is free to propose even the
most impractical ideas. With this in mind, none of the material generated here should be
made public without the specific consent of its author. We ask that you respect the private
nature of the proceedings.

Periodically, we will open the <voti> forum to the public for scheduled symposia. The
topic for the first symposium is "the museum of the 21st century." We will be discussing
this project in the weeks to come, and we look forward to your participation in these
discussions. Each public symposium may involve offline components such as panel
discussions and printed compilations. Each event may be developed in association with one
or more sponsoring organizations.

A private archive of the <voti> forum is accessible to you on the Web at http://www.thing.
net, in the "Threads" section. This archive will always remain private. We will create new,
publicly accessible archives for each of our scheduled symposia.

If you have colleagues that you would like to suggest as candidates for VOTI membership,
please let us know by sending private e-mail to Carlos, Hans Ulrich, or me. We have
developed the following procedure for recruiting new members. Potential candidates will
be invited to participate in the scheduled public symposia. At the close of each symposium,
those candidates who have contributed substantially to the proceedings may be invited to
stay on as Acting Members.

Lastly, and perhaps the most important thing: how to post a message. Please address
your e-mail to voti@llistproc.thing.net, or simply hit the Reply button on any of the VOTI

messages that you receive.

A warm welcome to everyone, and onward with the VOTI!

Respectfully,

Jordan
VOTI Delgado

From: Hans Ulrich Obrist and Carlos Basualdo
Subject: (unavailable)
Date: Wednesday 24 June 1998

Dear acting members of VOTI,

It is a great pleasure for us to welcome you to the Union of the Imaginary. First of all we would like to thank you all for participating in the Union. VOTI would not exist without the input of many of you.

We want to thank especially Jordan Crandall for being our fantastic Delegado and host at Blast, Francesco Bonami for his early encouragement of this project and all our colleagues who gave us all their support since the idea of the Union was first mentioned: Hou Hanru, Viktor Misiano, Dan Cameron, Octavio Zaya, Jens Hoffmann, Nancy Spector and Rosa Martinez are some of them.

As Jordan has mentioned, one of the goals of the Union will be to maintain this permanent forum where we can openly discuss issues pertaining curatorial practice. We would like to start our special sessions with a discussion on the Museum of the XXI Century. We would be glad to receive your suggestions regarding possible guests for the session. We will invite the guests to express their opinions on the subject of the session and to discuss it online with us. The Union belongs to the acting members, so please feel free to come with whatever suggestions you may have for the better functioning of the forum.

The Union is also an open space for us to talk about the things that shape our practice as curators. This means that VOTI has not fixed rules, the rules are set by the members and the forum can be used for whatever activity the members decide it should be use. This is your home in the Internet and we hope you enjoy it and care for it.

So please come in, and let's let the talk begin.

Hans Ulrich Obrist and Carlos Basualdo, Secretarios

From: Jordan Crandall
Subject: VOTI
Date: Monday 17 August 1998

Dear ___________, Welcome to the VOTI forum!

You will start receiving the forum posts as of today. To post to the list, send a message to: voti@listproc.thing,net Or simply hit "Reply" to any of the messages.

An archive of the discussions is available to you, at http://www.thing.net, in the "Threads" section. Since the archive is private, available only to VOTI members, there are a few steps that you have to take in order to access it. It is complicated at first, but after you initiate the account, it will be very easy thereafter.

Here is how to do it.

1. Go to http://www.thing.net. Click on "new member"

2. Fill out the form. You will then get a password by email.

3. After you get your password by email, go to
http://www.thing.net again, and fill out your name and password in the boxes. Hit "login."

4. Send an email to Max at kossatzdthing.at, requesting access clearance to the VOTI archive.

5. Thereafter, you will find the VOTI archive in the "Threads" section.

Please let me know if you have any questions.

We are looking forward to your participation in VOTI.

Best regards

Jordan

Chapter I

The Museum of the XXI Century

The first special session of the VOTI forum was launched in June 1998 under the discussion
heading "The Museum of the XXI Century." On the first day of the forum Jens Hoffmann
shared a series of questions he had received for an upcoming publication on contemporary
"young" art in the '90s. These questions and a follow up e-mail from Jordan Crandall, which
re-introduces a previous Blast forum thread "The museological and the urban," kick off
the discussion. Initially the conversation revolves around what the site of a XXI Century
museum can or should be.

Questions raised included: Can a museum function within a shopping mall and what is the
mechanism of culture today in relation to commerce? Several e-mails shift the conversation
back to focus on individual curatorial practice, questioning the role, purpose and future of
the Curator. These concerns are also considered in relation to context and local conditions.
Several contributors talk about their personal work, in particular citing the difference
between how a museum can function on the periphery as opposed to a museum located in
an urban cultural center.

In order of appearance:
Jens Hoffmann, Jordan Crandall, Carlos Basualdo, Hou Hanru, Rebecca Gordon-Nesbitt,
Francesco Bonami, Okwui Enwezor, Nancy Spector, Hans Ulrich Obrist, Rosa Martínez,
Jose Roca and Zdenka Badovinac.

From: Jens Hoffmann
Subject: [unavailable]
Date: Friday 19 June 1998

dear all,

i got the following questions today for an upcoming publication on contemporary "young" art in the 90s:

1) there has been a noticeable increase in attempts recently to draw a clearer dividing line between entertainment, commercial art and so-called serious art. for what reason would such a differentiation be acceptable to you, absolutely necessary, irrelevant or simply impossible?

2) how do you evaluate the significance of exhibitions as a form of presentation for contemporary art? has their significance changed in the last 10 to 20 years? and if so, why?

3) a preoccupation with history and past utopias is evident in the current art world. does this historicist practice influence the context in which "young" art is placed for you? do you find that "young" art conforms to this practice or do you see signs of contradictory tendencies?

4) what do you find young about the "young" art of the late nineties?

5) what demands do you make of an exhibition that sets out to present "young art '98"?

let me know your thoughts,

all the best,

jens hoffmann

From: Jordan Crandall
Subject: the museological and the urban
Date: Thursday 25 June 1998

Many thanks to Jens for kicking off the discussions.

Hans Ulrich and Carlos suggested that we might include one of the discussion threads from the previous Blast forum—a thread called "the museological and the urban." This thread has many provocative ideas to consider in the context of developing our first public VOTI forum, on the museum of the 21st century.

Rather than posting the whole thread, which is quite long, I thought I would post a short summary of the discussions.

So here goes:
Hans Ulrich Obrist gave two examples of curators whose work he felt was pioneering—Félix Fénéon and Alexander Dorner.[46] Each "contributed to the mutation of existing museums and exhibition structures but also pushed the boundaries towards the invention of new interdisciplinary structures." The importance of Dorner, Hans Ulrich writes, lies in the fact that he anticipated very early the urgency of issues such as: "the museum in permanent transformation within dynamic parameters, the museum as an oscillation between object and process, the multi-identarian museum, the museum on the move, the museum as a risk-taking pioneer: to act and not to wait (!), the museum as a locus of crossings of art and life, the museum as a laboratory, the museum as a relative and not an absolute truth, the elastic museum: both elastic display and elastic building."

Alan Sondheim writes that a great deal depends on the demographics and asks how can one intervene on this level. "In the United States, the museums are more popular than ever, in part due to the production of spectacles and accompanying connoisseurship that began in the 1980s. As a result, viewers might know, say, about King Tut, but nothing else about Egypt."

Carlos Basualdo responded to Hans Ulrich's post, writing that "this leads us to the urgency of developing an institutional model that could be adjusted to the conditions of both the countries of the center and the peripheries. I would like to suggest here that the exhibition as a model of understanding of art production should probably be emancipated from the museum and be considered an institution of its own." Carlos suggests that in order to realize Dorner's vision "the museum as an institution would have to become the exhibition as a temporary (urban) museum."

Hans Ulrich reported that, during a panel discussion on Museums of Modern Art in the Twenty-First Century, which took place in 1996, Rem Koolhaas pointed out that he sees the museum less as an issue of architecture and more as an issue of urbanity. "I think rather than architecture, which always induces enormous anxiety in its either/or logic—since architecture is, just like MoMA...about exclusion—the urban is the ideal medium, combining the unpredictable with a degree of organization. Because a city of course never preempts what is going to happen, rather, it offers the latent potential for things to happen...in a kind of related way."[47]

Carlos Basualdo writes that such a museum might be based and constructed upon the instability of the archive. He reports on a recent article on the structural instability of digital archives. Carlos remarks that we may be losing a lot, but he does not think we are losing much. "Eternity is the ultimate dream of authority, perfect wholeness forever. The traditional museum relies on this dream—or nightmare." The challenge, Carlos suggests, is to conceive a museum that is structured on transience and not to attempt to reform the Museum of the Eternal. The issue of memory then becomes fundamental. Carlos likes Koolhaas's suggestion that the museological and the urban can become the same. Carlos writes that when he mentioned the possibility of replacing the institution of the museum with the exhibition as an institution, he realizes that it would "rely entirely on the city as the privileged reservoir of memory. Not only memory as information, but memory as lived memory, a know-how of everyday life, memory as inscribed in the body." Lygia Clark's therapy provides us with a model of this kind of memory, Carlos suggests, "a model that could potentially be related to an archeology of the urban."[48]

Paul Miller pointed out the extreme unwillingness of the Western art hierarchy to look at examples that have already been at work in the European and American contexts for the last several centuries. Paul writes that outsider artists like Sam Doyle and Bill Traylor, operating from the late 19th century up until the mid 20th, provided a visual archive referencing blues and jazz as vessels for cultural transmission.[49] Even the Gypsies in Europe, he writes, as one of the few groups to retain pre-Roman pagan traditions, of course never make it to the official discourse ("globalization, etc."). "The art world is in a crisis precisely because of these issues: how an institution based on Feudal European structures can survive the dissolution of the social hierarchies that formed it should be the context that these issues are explored from."

Franklin Sirmans wrote that not only is the Western Art Hierarchy unwilling or slow to look at such examples that already have been at work, "they're pretty slow just to realize that it isn't all still white and male." There is a place for recontextualized museum space, Franklin writes. Somewhere, and not only on the Internet.

Simon Biggs brought up encoded mnemonics in the context of Frances Yates's book "The Art of Memory."[50] According to Simon, her thesis is that in many cultures memory was seen as important and as artful as logic or poetics. Carlos pointed out that the notion of memory engraved in the city comes from mnemonics, of course, but is also evident everywhere. "The old section of Rome is one of the best examples for me of a city where the urban equals memory equals art." Carlos proposes Lygia Clark's work as a model of embodied memory, and mentions that a parallel with de Certeau could be established.[51]

Brian Holmes elaborated on the technique in Frances Yates's book: the association in one's mind of the images of specific places—palaces, rooms, streets, theaters—with important bits of knowledge and narrative sequences. He explains that "the idea was to select an architectural environment, often one with niches, and to use it literally as a 'topos,' a palpable place in which to organize a more far-ranging cultural memory. It was a self-fashioning technique, or what Foucault calls a process of subjectivation, intimately connected to the collective dimension of experience because of the use of architecture as a mnemonic support, but at the same time, seemingly a much more fluid and personal way to build one's self than by subjection to the tightly delimited structure of the authorized book (which ultimately replaced the *ars memoria* as the primary technique of self-fashioning in bourgeois Western cultures)."

Brian writes that the relation between determinate urban space and a fluid individual-collective use of memory is something that surges up with every social revolution, when artistic practice really gets out into the streets. He wonders how computer memory could be used to further such individual-collective self-fashioning processes—"in experiments which at once recognize the binding weight of historical reality and yet aim toward material and symbolic transformation of it."[52]

From: Carlos Basualdo
Subject: The Museum of the XXI Century
Date: Tuesday 30 June 1998

Dear members of VOTI,

I am very curious to hear your reactions about Jordan's posting on the "Museological and the Urban." Do you think that reflecting on those issues could be a good way to start our session on the "Museum of the XXI Century"?

Are you specifically interested in developing any of the arguments that were addressed in that discussion? And, finally, whom do you think we should have as guests for the special session?

I look forward to hearing your opinions soon.

Carlos Basualdo

From: Hou Hanru
Subject: Re: The Museum of the XXI Century
Date: Thursday 9 July 1998

What about a "museum" in a shopping mall?

Hanru

From: Rebecca Gordon-Nesbitt
Subject: Re: The Museum of the XXI Century
Date: Thursday 9 July 1998

We now have an office in a shopping mall—Salon3.[53]

From: Carlos Basualdo
Subject: Re: The Museum of the XXI Century
Date: Thursday 9 July 1998

Well, guys, at this point it would be very interesting to say why no and why yes. Francesco, what is the reason why you would abjure of the idea of a museum in a shopping mall? And Hou, do you have any specific examples in mind?

We know that there are more and more shopping malls—or rather their smaller versions—inside many museums. Shows are becoming like movies in the sense that there is a lot of franchising produced after them. Rodchenko umbrellas and so on. In Buenos Aires there is a new space for contemporary art, the Borges Foundation, which is actually inside a shopping mall... This issue touches on many others; I think, for example, of the traditional relationship between a building as monument and archive as house for a collection. What happens when the environment where the exhibitions take place is no longer connected to issues of memory but of pure spectacle and consumption? Is it possible to compete with the display of commodities?

Carlos

From: Francesco Bonami
Subject: Re: The Museum of the XXI Century
Date: Friday 10 July 1998

Yes it is true people go to a Museum and shop but most of the time they first go into the museum. Now in a shopping mall I doubt that people would first shop and then go in the museum. I doubt that because the product they buy is not related to the one in the museum. The idea of the museum shop is to fool people and let them believe that they are buying some kind of memory of what they have seen. They feel less guilt because they are buying some kind of "Culture" transformation or derivation.

How can this be applied to people that buy popcorn or underwear in a shopping mall? There is not the sublimation of culture and guilt. So the museum will rest empty while the people will keep shopping. I feel it is at this moment a waste of energy. After all what museums are trying to do is taking the presence of shopping mall, see Bilbao. People go there because it occupies a physical space in such a way that cannot be denied. Yet, if someone wants to try to open a museum in a shopping mall. Good luck. The problem is not to hide in people's weaknesses but to try and create a strong necessity outside the shopping mall. People get depressed in shopping malls even if they don't know it.

From: Hou Hanru
Subject: Re: The Museum of the XXI Century
Date: Sunday 12 July 1998

Dear Carlos, I'll let you know my examples shortly. I just got back from Hong Kong where shopping is the "mainstream" culture and shopping malls are the places for everything, replacing culturally and symbolically all traditional venues in a city such as churches, museums, political institutions, and so on... I am developing some ideas about it...

Best,

Hanru

From: Carlos Basualdo
Subject: Re: The Museum of the XXI Century
Date: Sunday 12 July 1998

Dear Hanru,

Here's some more information on the Centro Cultural Borges.[54] The space is located at the top floor of the Galerias Pacifico, right in the heart of downtown Buenos Aires (Avenida Cordoba y Calle Florida). The building is late nineteen century building that functioned as a sort of local version of the Parisian "galeries" until the seventies when it was closed down. Now it's been remodeled and revamped as a shopping mall. The old building had a rotunda with frescos by the most important Argentine artists of the forties and fifties, like Antonio Berni. Those pieces were restored, and, to keep up with the original intentions, the company that remodeled the Galerias decided to build a cultural center on the top floor—as a contemporary counterpart of the frescos I guess. That is where it is now. The space is quite amazing but the exhibition program is uneven. They have shows of young artists along with surveys of well-known local artists.

How do these spaces work in Asia? Do the audiences mix? I do not think they do so much at the Borges...

Carlos

From: Francesco Bonami
Subject: Re: The Museum of the XXI Century
Date: Sunday 12 July 1998

But you see it's on top of a building, at the end of a building, then outside the building. People do not pass by; they have to get up there. Shopping malls are architecturally flat, even if they are on more than one floor.

FB

From: Hou Hanru
Subject: Re: The Museum of the XXI Century
Date: Monday 13 July 1998

A shopping mall can be of tens of levels! There are many of them in Hong Kong and Asia, which are very complicated architecturally, just like a whole city!

From: Hou Hanru
Subject: Re: The Museum of the XXI Century
Date: Sunday 12 July 1998

Where's the ideal location for you?

l' artiste.

Hou Hanru

From: Francesco Bonami
Subject: Re: The Museum of the XXI Century
Date: Sunday 12 July 1998

The ideal location would be in this huge semi truck travelling around Europe or US or Asia with a real travelling exhibition. The truck would be the event, like when they bring the biggest whale of the world. I still think that is the unexpected that people are waiting for; in a shopping mall people are expecting everything included a museum.

From: Hou Hanru
Subject: Re The Museum of the XXI Century
Date: Monday 13 July 1998

But, don't you think people would expect to see a kind of circle truck when they see the truck coming in town? Then what's the difference from what one expects to see in a shopping mall?

From: Okwui Enwezor
Subject: museums and inequality
Date: Sunday 12 July 1998

Distinguished Members of VOTI,

I do not know whom this is reaching, but so far, I have had the displeasure of reading what
has been posted so far, and quite frankly, find it both irritating and dismaying. I am afraid
that the entire Notion of what this membership is supposed to be about, that is, to kick start
some serious discussions amongst curators who are presently working in very precarious
situations with very little leverage and financial support is entering the space of banality.

One question I have for Hanru, Carlos and Francesco, is: why are you guys so obsessed with
museums? Why is the museum such an important structure for curators like you who see their
practice as not at all dependent on the way museums have been and are presently constituted?
I find that without a thoroughgoing analysis of the political and economic models of culture in
general, we may never be able to do much with museums other than apply for jobs there. I am
afraid that this obsession with museums is akin to that utopian, fake critique of the institution
that many so-called conceptual artists, after a fashion, embarked on, and when it was no longer
interesting, went back to their studios to make some paintings to sell to collectors and museums.
We all know where all those yellowing pieces of paper of conceptual critique went: directly
into the vault of the museum and presided over not by curators, but by conservators. Let's
face it, it's such an old and by now uninteresting argument to carry on about museums, history
and memory when within our own practice we are not proposing new models and structures
through which our ventures could be made legible in a meaningful and rewarding manner. I
feel that part of what our discussion needs to focus on is what kinds of challenges face curators
today who will be working well into the first quarter of next century, when museums are going to
become increasingly irrelevant as they compete with other, more powerful and efficient sources
of distribution, communication and information. I feel also that part of our so-called critique is
an engagement of doubts we may be experiencing at any given time. We equally need to discuss
the notion of courage as one of the aspects of what curatorial practice could be. By courage, I
do not mean some heroic, self-immolating gesture; or an attempt to foretell the future and win
a place in the grand halls of curatorial hall of fame, à la Szeemann, but courage in the sense of
trusting our own impulses, the peculiarities of our own ignorance, confronting the limits of our
knowledge, sharing information, being less competitive and more trusting in our colleagues,
instinct and ideas and finding ways to present them in the public sphere. As part of this, we
need to ask ourselves what represents the public sphere for us and in what ways can they be
imaginatively and productively reinvented and made useful.

Another issue for all of us to ponder is how willing are we to have our faith in all we believe in
shaken to the point where we become apostate and begin to reconsider the ways in which we
look at art from outside the comfort zones we presently all occupy? I think that there needs to

be not just a crisis of confidence in the museum or other such institutions, but also a crisis of confidence in our own beliefs, in our references. I believe as curators we need also to discuss such unthinkable notions as passion, responsibility and other such active verbs as a way of describing and proposing what we do to the public. We need to go beyond the grand ideas, and begin to work from the basis of a micro-politics of culture. I mean how many of us who live in New York City ever venture to areas like Queens, Bronx, Harlem, Yonkers and the like to look for art and artists. Frankly, I believe none. The list of artists in our shows betrays that quite easily.

So let's leave off museums, and begin from the gaps in our own practice. We need to interrogate them thoroughly before we arrive at what it is we need to do about museums in shopping malls, which is nothing new even in a literal way. It's been happening in Japan for some time now with department stores opening their own museums and galleries. I have absolutely no quarrels with the kind of real estate where museums choose to put up their signs. After all Andreas Huyssen smartly wrote about the museumification of just about everything in the common culture. In this museumification, he talked about the persistent hunger to own a fragment of the past, as if it were history and memory itself.[55] He gave a really great example with the proliferation of flea markets and antique shops. Now for me those are the museum sites we have not considered. We all know what the thrill is, and how triumphant we all feel when we find that "rare" vintage, tweed boucle suit by Chanel or Mainbocher, circa 1947, in a flea market or antique shop. We know what they mean. They are not just historic references for fashion designers or aesthetes, in the rarity and surplus memory and nostalgia they possess, they are as much presiding personages of our collective belief about elegance, taste, connoisseurship, etc. as they are museum pieces worthy of the costume department at the Met or Art Institute of Chicago. Now that's shopping and culture coalescing in an odd and fantastic manner.

So who will be the first to forget museums and shopping malls and stage a show in a flea market? There are several famous ones on 26th street in Manhattan, Portobello and Camden Market in London; you all can add the rest. But please let's not all carp anymore about museums and such.

Okwui

P.S.

My suggestion on maximizing this forum is that there should not be any wankers. If you do not have anything to say please restrain yourself until you have something to say. One word postings are irritants and not helpful at all. Another suggestion is, in proposing other models of exchange and encounters, that we should use our own projects as concrete examples. Using our own projects as examples could be a good way of making visible the transformations we see out there in the nebulous world of the MUSEUM.

THANKS ALL

From: Carlos Basualdo
Subject: Re: museums and inequality
Date: Sunday 12 July 1998

I basically agree with Okwui and I think this is a great point of departure to start a fruitful discussion at VOTI. This is actually the main reason for VOTI to exist, and I will be glad to hear what the rest of the members have to say about Okwui's intervention. In any case, I would like to rephrase his proposition this way: how can we, as curators, take into account in our practice the existence of tremendous inequalities in the contexts where we develop our work? What is the relation between the curator's work and the local conditions of production? Is there a possibility of developing a curatorial framework that will work both in the countries of the North and the South (or the East)? I will be pleased to see some debate on these issues. But I also think that the discussion that Hou started on museums and shopping malls points to some of these issues in an indirect way. In my interventions at the Eyebeam symposium (the ones summarized by Jordan under the thread "the museological and the urban") I tried to propose this idea of the exhibition as an institution, thinking specifically about the South American experience. I would like to ask Okwui about his experience working with institutions in the North and with exhibitions as institutions (like the Johannesburg Biennial) in the South. How do you translate your own work in these circumstances? And Hou, once again, could you please clarify your position regarding the museum and the shopping mall? Are you just describing a situation of trying to propose a curatorial strategy that would allow the curator to deal with these phenomena?

Carlos

From: Hou Hanru
Subject: Re: museums and inequality
Date: Monday 13 July 1998

Well, I don't think I am obsessed with MUSEUM but just use the term to indicate the venue of exhibiting and animating art... However, I think either way, we have to deal with and work within a certain institutional framework whatever we may call it. The real challenge for us is to bring art beyond the established confinement of museums and bring it back to real life in order to catch up with art's evolution ... shopping malls as one of the most "popular" forms of living, entertaining and perhaps embodiment of our culture, in both 'North' and 'South' provides us a relevant place to reconsider a series of questions regarding art's social status and meaning. The issue of curatorship seems to be under rather than above this larger question. Of course, the shopping mall is only one of the possibilities of reinventing the 'institutional framework' ... Activities in such a place have to be flexible, evolutionary, unpredictable and therefore deconstructive. It is in such a place that the deconstruction of the established notions of institutions, including museum, become possible and can evolve continuously along with real life.

As independent curators, we have to negotiate with the establishment of institutions for more freedom and better conditions. Proposing to bring art out of conventional museums and position it in the opposite form of what it is supposed to be, is essential... It is in such a negotiation that we can reformulate and consolidate our positions.

From: Nancy Spector
Subject: Re: museums and inequality
Date: Monday 13 July 1998

Dear Voti members,

I finally feel compelled to respond to the postings so far, but mostly with questions, some intentionally provocative.

As a curator very much employed by a cultural institution—one, by the way, that is redefining the notion of the museum, for better or worse—I find the discourse of institutional critique as it appears here somewhat nostalgic.

We all know that the strategies of breaking down institutional boundaries and challenging the commodification of art (and artists) have been well rehearsed since the 1970s (as Okwui has so eloquently pointed out). We also know that the museum itself has continually transformed itself in order to accommodate, promote, and even collect such critical practices. My favorite example of this is a comparison between Gordon Matta-Clark's community-based restaurant Food, which was intended to subvert the market system by making an affordable, collectively-run place for artists to eat, meet, etc. and Rirkrit's work.[56] This is nothing against Rirkrit, but he cooks within the museum and the museum collects the artifacts of his actions. Granted, he introduces cross-cultural narratives and issues of global economy with his temporal gestures, but these become incorporated into the institutional framework.

My question is, what is it that we hope to achieve beyond the museum/gallery/biennale exhibition/Internet (which is increasingly Invaded by museum web projects) context? The curator him or herself carries the legitimizing element of the "museum" within. Whether the "exhibition" happens in a shopping mall, a truck, a magazine, a flea market, a hotel room or is dispersed throughout an entire city, the curator invests the project with a certain credibility. The act of choice conveys value. Whatever "site" is selected, no matter how nomadic this site may be, it takes on an "institutional" function even if for a limited time.

Let's discuss the role of the curator—what is its purpose, what is its future?

Yours,

Nancy

From: Jordan Crandall
Subject: voti dialogue
Date: Monday 13 July 1998

Okwui: I appreciate your concerns, and just wanted to quickly respond to your initial comments about the VOTI dialogue. Based on my experience, online forums are interesting to the extent that they balance substantive content with a social dynamic, which often can be quite playful. They exist somewhere between writing and speaking. Sometimes a quick sentence can be just the thing that is needed. With VOTI we hope to create a comfortable space of experimentation in which we feel we can take chances, and where we're not afraid to sound impractical at times. We decided to keep the forum private at this stage, for these reasons and others.

It takes a while for a space like this to find its "voice." We are all new here. We jump in with some thoughts, and soon the protocols start to be established. We have to be patient with each other as we each find our own route in here, and our own mode of interfacing.

Jordan

From: Jordan Crandall
Subject: malls, markets, museums
Date: Tuesday 14 July 1998

I like Francesco's image of the huge truck coming into town. A powerful vector through the forum.

Maybe the agenda is first to understand the structures of commerce—the 'shopping systems'—and the kinds of built realities that they produce/register. For example the shopping mall is already being replaced in many senses—through superstores and warehouse shopping corridors (there is a huge corridor in New Jersey leading into Manhattan), through urban entertainment centers (42nd Street and other Disney-esque, Photoshopped constructions) and through new urbanist recreations of city streets and public spaces built entirely for shopping (CityWalk, etc.). Witness the impulses behind the new Venice recreation in Vegas (FULL-scale replicas of the Doges Palace, the Campanile, etc.—not even reduced like the mini-Manhattan!) that is rising on the ashes of the old Sands Hotel. Even if you think about the difference between the shopping mall and the warehouse shopping corridor you can see how the structures are part of completely different systems of commerce, the latter enabled by info & communications technologies through which things and people 'move' in a different fashion, and through which the tiniest impulses and behaviors are trackable. Already now there is a lot of talk about the Internet and its potential for "disintermediation," cutting out the middleman, along with just-in-time delivery, built-to-order products, zero inventory, etc. The online bookstore Amazon.com—a huge success—is the perfect example. We will see many more in the coming year as online commerce comes into its own. A lot of this talk is now accompanied by a focus on 'reintermediation' that is, rather than eliminating the middle man (e.g. Barnes and Noble becoming obsolete), its role and function changes. The fact that Barnes and Noble becomes a library-like public space where one socializes and can loll about all day is certainly part of this repositioning. So it's not about the shopping mall per se or the net per se but how they are embedded within and informed by commerce systems as linked to built realities. How they endow a subject with capacities and desires.

What is registered in this shift from developing enclosed mall environments to developing simulated urban spaces that are more 'real' (not to mention safer, cleaner) than their predecessors?

And then a basic question: what is art in this landscape, what is the reintermediation of the curator, what is the institutional complex that informs and gives value. And then there is historical memory (which we really no longer have in America anyway), as partially transferred to the machine (database).

Carlos asks: is it possible to compete with the display of commodities? No. But we have to understand the mechanisms, as part of our 'institution' (and here a revived institutional critique would focus on the culture industry—its effects, its mechanisms of legitimization, its harnessing of the museological, etc). And then to insert the curatorial function there. What is the 'reintermediation' of the curator? Nancy suggests to look at how the curator carries the elements of legitimization, how it carries the weight of the institutional complex and endows artistic value.

Jordan

From: Okwui Enwezor
Subject: Re: voti dialogue
Date: Wednesday 15 July 1998

I would like to respond simultaneously to the questions posed by Carlos, Nancy, Hanru, and Jordan. Firstly, Jordan your point is quite well taken on the notion of giving this network and its various meanderings an organic kind of substantiality, so that we can allow our thoughts and ideas to germinate in a transparent kind of way. However, what I was pointing to should not be viewed as a case for minimizing experimentation, but its use value, hence my caution against becoming self-serving. I was also reacting to the notion that is often floated out there that the net is some kind of free-for-all, stream-of-consciousness bubble where anything goes. That is, if you have a thought, you just get it out there; perhaps it will stick; without ever allowing ourselves the opportunity to sift, process, and organise those thoughts in a way that is cogent, productive and useful for people who receive them. I am not saying that everything put out here should be of earth-shattering intensity. I accept there can be some profound transformations that can occur in the kind of mundane, everyday chatter we engage in that can lead us to genuine questions, and I encourage that.

Nancy, I agree with your question very much, it really sits at the heart of this discussion and will remain so for a long time. To use your word "provocation" and following on that most essential of questions, what do curators do, I want to propose to all the curators in this discussion to summarise what they consider their work as curators to be. I have often come up short when asked by people about what I do and I tell them that I am a curator and they ask what that is. I suppose the idea behind the question is how does one define a curator within the kind of division of labor that compartmentalises professions. In this sense, the question lies at the root of what the identity of a curator is. How would each of you define your identity as a curator? What is it that you do and how do you explain it to someone without sounding like you are some functionary? Secondly, Nancy, I have a more specific question for you. You stated that for better or worse, the Guggenheim is reinventing the notion of the museum. In what way is the Guggenheim doing this? How do you see this happening? And where is the better and where is the worse in this scenario?

Carlos wrote in responding to my post: "I would like to rephrase his proposition this way: how can we, as curators, take into account in our practice the existence of tremendous inequalities in the contexts where we develop our work? What is the relation between the curator's work and the local conditions of production? Is there a possibility of developing a curatorial framework that will work both in the countries of the North and the South (or the East)? I will be pleased to see some debate on these issues. But I also think that the discussion that Hou started on museums and shopping malls points to some of these issues in an indirect way. In my interventions at the Eyebeam symposium (the ones summarized by Jordan under the thread "the museological and the urban") I tried to propose this idea of the exhibition as an institution, thinking specifically about the South American experience.

I would like to ask Okwui about his experience working with institutions in the North and with exhibitions as institutions (like the Johannesburg Biennial) in the South. How do you translate your own work in these circumstances? And Hou, once again, could you please clarify your position regarding the museum and the shopping mall? Are you just describing a situation of trying to propose a curatorial strategy that would allow the curator to deal with these phenomena?"

I do not believe that Carlos's position rephrases the core issues of my initial questions as to what curators do today and could become tomorrow and our relationship with institutions (museums, exhibitions, shopping malls, etc.), the location of our practice, the subject of our work and so on. What Carlos and Nancy have added are other layers to a very complex issue. On the issue of working with institutions in both the North and South, my insistence is that not all subjects reverberate the same way in the institutions of the north and south. It all depends. For example what are the emergencies, desires, hungers, complexes? What is the meaning and reception of modernity in each location? What is tradition for the inhabitants of each place? How do we account for how various constituencies sift and graft various experiences, encounters and socialisations to their acts of looking? In fact, what constitutes a history of looking, as Barthes would put it, in such places and how do we insert our work into those arenas? In each case the question is: what options and support is available to the curator on both a practical and political level? And what is the curator's subject, and what are the intentions behind its proposition? It all depends. Hence, for every institution and place, new strategies and an understanding of the standard etiquettes and politics of each are required.

Curators who work in this way, in my view, are involved in very profound questions that go beyond issues of cultural practice, but also their translation and interpretation within highly contingent political and social circumstances. Obviously all curatorial work is developed in two different spheres: in the lifeworld of the mind, deep within the structure and meaning of the subject of each exhibition including all its references, and the other in the lifeworld of the everyday, in the common culture of each location. This push and pull situation, because of poorly developed "alternative structures," needs the institution in one way or the other, so I am not about to give up the institution so soon. For me I work in the reality of each circumstance. I translate each space into a constitutive map of the kind of dialogue and engagement I am willing and able to have with each. That is I learn from the beginning what is possible, what is an ideal and what won't be possible.

Increasingly, I find that it is independent curators that have the perverse luxury of being in this kind of situation in which one's critical position could simultaneously signal a political position and cultural one. So in the end, is the shopping mall an answer? It could be one of multiple answers. Having grown up in Nigeria, famous for its sprawling urban markets (Ochanja, Jankara, Balogun, Ariaria, etc.) I for one do not have any fascination for the kind of agglomerations and shopping corridors Jordan wrote about, culturally speaking, that is. Again, these are options in a vast network of other options. Also I am a bit surprised at the fixation on the very western concept of shopping malls, and how limited the references being proposed are. Nobody has considered for example the open markets of many West African cities and their reinvention elsewhere in places like London (Brixton Market, to start with). Another example is the way Senegalese street traders have replicated the markets and medinas of Dakar right on the streets of Harlem, (have any of you New Yorkers travelled up there) in many ways turning it into a deeply inflected ideological, political and cultural economy, and more importantly, a nationalistic space of the new diaspora. In fact, Michael Taussig is coming out with a book on this very subject sometime this year. Similarly you find the same phenomenon of Senegalese traders in Rome, Madrid, Barcelona and, of course, in Paris. This is a really important body check on the notion of shopping malls. Equally, we have ignored the souks and medinas of the Arab world, throughout North Africa and the Middle East, the bazaars of India and Pakistan. There are so many examples. Each of these spaces constitutes a different notion of time and space, and attracts different issues of culture. For me it's not the vastness of shopping malls that are interesting, but the behavioral and class issues associated with them. Moreover, what about the little neighborhood shops that for me mark the stress points of global commerce and culture. In my neighborhood, I could go to the Mexican shop for chilies and cactus and pulque or to the Nigerian shop for Egusi and dried fish or to Atlantic Avenue (blocks mind you) for North African and Middle Eastern provisions. What about such places, are they spaces worthy of consideration?

Okwui

From: Hans Ulrich Obrist
Subject: Re: voti dialogue
Date: Sunday 19 July 1998

Dear Members of Voti

In his first mailing, Okwui suggested that we use Voti-mailings as concrete examples of our projects.

I think that this is a good idea in order to make the discussion more concrete, to talk about the daily practice of curating. With regard to the ongoing museum discussion and the question of the role of the curator I would like to mention again Alexander Dorner (see the Eyebeam discussion).

Dorner has, at the beginning of our century, invented a type of mutating museum, which even on the brink to the 21st century remains a mostly unrealised project. Joan Ockman called it "the road not taken." Some of Dorner's key ideas were aiming at self-transforming and self-organizing museums (very interesting and highly contemporaneous issue in the context of complexity theory of the 90s): non-linear Museums, flexible Museums (according to Dorner, the institution would have to transform to accommodate the artist's project rather than the other way round. That's why it is interesting to look at artists unrealised projects, which within the existing often static parameters of museums and other institutions cannot happen but which within flexible circumstances could easily happen and which very often are the most interesting projects of artists), active, participatory museums as loci of crossings, the museum as a network etc...

Dorner succeeded in "challenging the institution from within" (Ockman); he spoke about the idea of being an " infiltrator," an issue about which Felix Gonzalez-Torres said, "I want to be the one who looks like something else, in order to infiltrate, in order to function as a virus. The virus is our worst enemy but should also be our model in terms of not being the opposition anymore, not being very easily defined, so that we can attach ourselves to institutions which are always going to be there and as Althusser said, these institutions or these ideological institutions are always replicating themselves, and if we are attached to them as a virus, we will replicate with these institutions...." (Felix Gonzalez-Torres in a museum in progress interview for Der Standard, Vienna, re-published in the catalogue of Manifesta II).

Felix Gonzalez-Torres leads us to museum in progress, the Vienna organisation that was founded by Josef Ortner and Kathrin Messner for whom I frequently curate projects. museum in progress is a structure providing access to different media where artists are invited to make interventions: clips on TV, pages in daily newspapers and weekly magazines, billboard projects all over Vienna. The aim is to make these media spaces, which are usually difficult to access and very expensive, available for interventions of artists. (museum in progress: http://www.mip.at)

One of the biggest projects in which the museum space became totally global was in '93-'94 with Alighiero Boetti who made an all-year exhibition on board the whole fleet of Austrian Airlines.[57] The project consisted of thousands of jigsaw puzzles that were distributed on board upon request. The show was carried to all the destinations of Austrian Airlines and therefore totally scattered.... I recently found one of the jigsaw puzzles on a flea market in Paris. As far as the question of the role of the curator is concerned: I see the curator as a catalyst, as Marcel Duchamp told Walter Hopps: A facilitator who should not "Barrer la route", who should not stand in the way. [58]

Another modest definition of the curator which I like very much comes from Suzanne Pagé who refuses the pretentious and disciplinary word Commissaire (French word for curator) and talks about the curator as the "Commis de l'artiste".

Hans Ulrich Obrist

P.S. some more websites
http://www.artnode.se/artorbit
The second issue of this Swedish online-magazine came out a few weeks ago. http://www. medicis.org/jardin

From: Carlos Basualdo
Subject: Re: voti dialogue
Date: Tuesday 21 July 1998

Just a couple of things. Besides discussing what our practice already is I think it would be quite useful in this context to imagine what it could or should be. Personal experience should not bar the imagination. I feel that curatorial work needs to be more fictionalized, and this forum could be a great opportunity to do that. This of course taking into account that today's fictions will be tomorrow's realities, as Borges put it so often. I would like to see curators collaborating with artists, scientists, and urban planners, acting and reacting to specific social conditions. In Bogota I met with Jaime Iregui, an artist who runs a non-profit space called "Espacio Vacio" (The Empty Space). One of the "exhibitions" that Iregui and his team organized recently was a group show where a number of Colombian artists interacted with the people who live in the houses located on the same street where the "Espacio Vacio" is—in a low middle class neighborhood of Bogota. The artists did not just installed their pieces in the houses of the neighbors, but developed artistic strategies in collaboration with them, according to their needs and demands. After the process was finished, an exhibition of the work done in cooperation was exhibited both in the houses and the "Espacio." As a result of the process and the show, the neighbors started to cooperate actively with each other in the preservation of their neighborhood, with one of them even entering the macropolitical arena.

In a city like Bogota—where the social and urban tissue is constantly on the border of disappearance, and extreme violence is an everyday reality—the relevance of such processes is tremendous. The "Espacio Vacio" is, for Iregui, a reservoir of energies that are aesthetic as well as social and political. In New York, Kyong Park, the Director of the Storefront for Art and Architecture is currently coordinating a project that involves the production of an economically viable process to recycle an old Pachard factory in Detroit and turn it into a factory for refabricated houses. In his project, Park is working with a team of artists, social activists, economists and urban planners.

Experiences like these ones are, in my view, one of the most appealing possibilities of curatorial practice today. In that sense I do not think that curators have to be neutral facilitators. I think it is quite funny that Duchamp told Walter Hopps that curators should not "stand in the way." Especially because that's exactly what he was doing all the time: standing in the way of conventions, traditions and prejudices. I think all of us will agree with the fact that an exhibition is not a transparent medium. I think that curators, as producers of culture, should be able to stand strongly in the way of their subject—the cultural construction that we call "art history"—ready to change it and to force it to interact closely with the social. I would like to see curatorial practice departing critically from the impulse of the most radical artistic practices of the century in order to expand them, translate them and actualize their premises.

Carlos

From: Jordan Crandall
Subject: museums/localities
Date: Wednesday 29 July 1998

Okwui has made some important body checks on the notions of both shopping malls and museums. In the case of museums he asks "what kinds of challenges face curators today who will be working well into the first quarter of the next century, when museums are going to become increasingly irrelevant as they compete with other, more powerful, and efficient modes of distribution and communication?" On the other hand, Hans Ulrich reifies the museum as a construct to be re-invigorated from within—becoming agile, adaptable, flexible, networked, in line with the demands of the global economy. Okwui feels that "without a thorough going analysis of the political and economic models of culture in general, we may never be able to do much with museums" and on the other hand Hans Ulrich implies that the museum could be some kind of workable context for pursuing these analyses. Where Okwui laments the obsession with museums, Hans Ulrich works from the premise that, in the end, the museum is all we have.

Nancy suggests that the museum functions as a legitimizing agent, which invests the curator and the project with a certain credibility. I am wondering what would take its place, in confronting some of the observations that Okwui offers. What does the curator invoke, that banks his/her position?

Okwui proposes that everyone in this discussion summarize what they consider their work as curators to be. "How would each of you define your identity as a curator?" What is it that you do? I think this is a good base to depart from. It would be helpful also, in the sense of introducing everyone in the forum, and giving a sense of the local realities that this forum connects. Where are we? In Istanbul, in Maribor, in Tokyo? Right now there are 27 of us. What is our local working situation, what do we do in our daily practice? It is crucial, if we want this forum to be a productive "virtual" space embedded into specific cultural realities. If we don't invest it with this specificity, it is detached, just floating "out here."

From: Jens Hoffmann
Subject: [unavailable]
Date: Sunday 2 August 1998

dear members of voti,

thanks for all the mails i was lucky to receive over the last weeks.

when okwui asks "what challenges face curators...when museums are going to become increasingly irrelevant..." he does not only describe the difficulties of curatorial work within a museum due to "more efficient modes of distribution and communication." he also points right to the current situation of museums as real life institutions to present art. these "more efficient modes of distribution and communication" of the last years such as, tv, the www, shopping malls, clubs etc. might lead to a disappearance of the museum, to a liquidation of his role within a social structure. the reasons for this disintegration, which actually also defines the reason why the museum will survive all this, however, comes from within the foundation itself.

the museums start to flood with their collections since they cannot escape from collected and overproduced art. all aspects of life seem to have found their place within the museum. the museum as institution and authority within a cultural hierarchy is not able to define clear borders for what should be included in the ARCHIVE and what should not; it seems that only with the inclusion into a museum collection or an exhibition, art actually becomes art. today an artist does not have to be dead to get a retrospective, and more and more art becomes unspecified in terms of its medium. the different medias do not need to reach a point of entirety anymore; the radicalisation of a medium like malevich's black square, which brought painting to point zero, is not the issue anymore. the level of reflection about how something is consumed defines the notion of art today. that means: strategy became the "handwork." the question is, how can we establish a situation inside a museum where art can be recognised as what it is without necessarily becoming part of the collection or an exhibition? all the attempts of avoiding the cultural hierarchy and to present art outside of the museum context—fluxus for example—always worked with very traditional methods. it always happens within a certain context, a FRAME, which you do not need within the museum. the presence of the artist always functions as his SIGNATURE. this construction of frame and signature, or better, of FRAME and NAME, functions as a sort of art id-card. a minus of museum always creates a plus of other signs.

the paradox lies within the whole cultural hierarchy. every attempt at deviation to withdraw from the hierarchy formulates a new demand a new quality within the discussion itself therefore immediately becomes part of the ARCHIVE since it tries to disintegrate it. see the ready-made as one of the best examples. the museum can actually be seen as an archive that collects all the deviations, since the museum's structure gives us absolute freedom.

the freedom of absolute deviation. i can show almost everything; i am not dependent on a certain form or structure within the museum, the museum is the authority that defines what is art and what is not. outside of the museum, i have to find other signs for the FRAME and the NAME. i do not believe that it is unimportant to work outside of a museum. but i think it is uninteresting in the sense of what arises NEW. the NEW originates in the museum. outside of the museum, i am interested in the identity of art. how has art to be, to look like, to be recognised as art; where are the borders between fiction and reality, see for instance christoph schlingensief, a film and theater director who is running for chancellor in germany. in a museum, art shows us its non-identity; outside, we see the identity. it has a lot to do with what the audience expects from art. how has art to look like according to the norm? nobody knows that and if someone knows it, it is very difficult to deviate from it. art it is. always about for filling the norm and deviating from it at the same time.

already kant told us that an educated mind cannot trust art anymore. kant left his house and walked around in the park. here, surrounded by nature, he saw what he thought art might be.

jens hoffmann

From: Rosa Martinez
Subject: Various
Date: Wednesday 5 August 1998

Dear VOTI members,

I am so glad to receive all your e-mails and to follow the discussions even if I do not have the time to participate very actively in them for now. Being a freelance curator is so hard sometimes. I am overloaded with work but I have not been yet paid for the projects I have done in the last months so I am in a spiral trying to do more things to survive economically. I think ideological and conceptual discussions are extremely important for our work but it is also important to be able to pay the rent, the telephone, etc ..

Should we also open a part of our forum to discuss what institutions are not paying, how we should educate them, how important it is to sign a contract, etc .. What do you think about this perspective of approaching our reality to keep on being imaginative, critical and flexible but also strong curators?

Love.
Rosa

From: Okwui Enwezor
Subject: Re: museums/localities
Date: Monday 10 August 1998

Jordan has provided good ground rules for what I hope will open up to more discussion and elaboration of his summary of Voti. I am presently in Johannesburg and will travel to other parts of South Africa and to Mozambique where I will be conducting research. This means that there will be specific contexts in these places that may provide further questions on the notion of the "Location of Culture," but also its dislocation as far as the globalist perspective many of us in this forum share. I am in Johannesburg where the value of its currency following the Asian financial crisis fell by 40% in one week and where the "Truth and Reconciliation Commission" has just finished its work.

It's quite clear from my discussions with many people: artists, professors, writers, ordinary people, that these are anxious times. Not as tense as during the immediate period after democracy. Clearly there is a loss of confidence in some way; people are not as optimistic as they were, say, in January or even in March. The reality fundamental to globalisation, where countries like South Africa negotiate their positions and the value of their economic viability from positions of extreme weakness, without any leverage whatsoever, is beginning to sink in. The Johannesburg Biennale is bankrupt, and some of its former acolytes are dejected and frustrated. Young artists are making their way "West," where presumably the opportunities are. So much for South-South discussion, which was what I attempted to negotiate in the 2nd Johannesburg Biennale. My interest then was a rejection of anything that could remotely be considered "Third World" as some kind of strategic negotiating position. For South Africa, now that apartheid is gone, many artists, intellectuals, and writers have lost a potent subject. If there is a crisis of the imagination, it's partly because of this loss. But the loss isn't a terminal one. Very slowly, good productions are coming out again from the theatre world, novels are being written, and artists are slowly recovering from the stupor of political contestation, music (especially from the Townships) is more vibrant, experimental and hardcore as ever. This makes South Africa a good place to look at art. I am now searching for what culture means for those people engaged in it at this particular time in this place.

As for my own situation, I live simultaneously, literally and psychically across many territories as both rooted and exiled subject. I consider the second part as one of terminal condition, which I suspect many in this forum share whether they live at "home" or "abroad." So what does it mean to live as an exile in all the complexities of its meaning? What then constitutes home for the curator? I have written somewhere in the past, that beyond the specific conditions of exile such as dislocation, homesickness, the exile of the mind from the life world and sustaining *nostos* of one's language and culture, one could also be an exile even within the rooms of home. This has to do with not the kinds of loss we associate with exile in the political sense, but a loss related to the inability to find within one's work a meaningful community. Are independent curators then exiles from the museum as a structure? What constitutes home for those of us out there who do not have any kind of affiliation in the museum? "Exile is strangely compelling to think about, but devastating to experience," wrote Edward Saïd. Is the hunger for the institutional legitimate, a hunger based on homesickness, that is, if we are to believe that the true home of the curator is the museum? So does *nostos* (meaning home) joined with *algia* (longing) produce the nostalgic curator? Does anyone here think of their work in relation to the notion of exile in its most complicated terms i.e. linguistically, intellectually, culturally, politically, socially, institutionally, etc.?

I will write more during my travel.

Okwui

From: Carlos Basualdo
Subject: Re: museums/localities
Date: Wednesday 12 August 1998

So here we are, almost there at the Union, and I am glad to be reading the very disparate recent postings after a few days offline, installing a show in Caracas. Then, coming back home, to my home in NY and our place on the Internet I found:

1. Some information about the upcoming members projects. That was very welcomed, but a little too little for my expectations. Maria, Rebecca and Hans, could you tell us more about your motivations for doing a project at the Elephant & Castle Shopping Centre? Why there, and how do you see the exhibition interacting with the environment? And what is Salon3? Vasif, could you elaborate more on the implications of opening a space like yours in Istanbul?

2. Rosa made a great point bringing VOTI back to one of its *raisons d'etre*: I also think that the Union should be a place where curators discuss issues related to their economic survival and also help ensure the survival of the figure of the independent curator. Hans suggested in a meeting that we had in New York that we should elaborate a model for a contract and I think that is a great idea. It would also be very good to discuss which are the institutions that do not pay in time. As you all know very well, we seem to be at the very bottom of the scale when it comes to our payment. I think that there is a lot to gain also in this aspect if we can constitute a strong community gathered around common interests.

3. In response to Okwui's posting I would like to imagine VOTI as a possible community. Not the re-creation of a traditional community, but a new form of it. Only strong communities can produce strong fictions. And if the museum is, and was, some kind of fiction, it would be a matter of imagining a new one, a possible home for the independent curator. Even if this imaginary museum would differ radically from the traditional institution, to become a political gesture, a temporary statement of a fragmentary wish. Okwui's posting has summarized brilliantly many of the questions at stake in the discussion about our relation to the institution, and I hope we will be able to hear more from him as well as some responses from other members.

Carlos

From: Jose Roca
Subject: localities
Date: Saturday 15 August 1998

Dear VOTI members:

In response to Okwui's proposition, I shall make a brief description of my work, which is embedded right to the core of an institution, more so if we consider that the Luis Angel Arango Library (in fact a vast cultural complex that occupies two complete blocks in the heart of the historic district of Bogota) is financed by the central bank of Colombia. As chief of the Visual Arts department, I try to exercise a creative opposition from my position that undermines institutional assumptions (as Hans Ulrich put it, "the museum as a construct to be re-invigorated from within"), since the main interests of the institution are geared towards becoming a venue in Latin America for important traveling exhibitions involving well-known artists and patrimonial concerns. This attitude is not, from my point of view, to be scoffed at or neglected, but rather put into the right context, since for a city of nearly seven million people like Bogota, without a solid and well-funded system of Museums, Galeries and Collections, the task of responding to the young people's varied interests (the Library receives a daily average of eleven thousand people from 8am to 8pm) is a clear and unavoidable social role. In one exhibition on selected works from the MASP at Sao Paulo that we held in 1995, which showed works of nineteenth and turn-of-the-century masters including—for the first time ever in our country—a work from Van Gogh, we received, along with an unheard-of response in terms of attendance, several letters and statements of which I remember one: "I have taught art history for twenty years at a school; thank you for allowing me to see what I had talked about for the first time ever." When even a national historiography of art is yet to be developed, the role of Museums in bringing access to the history of western art permits, at the same time, development of a real perspective on matters such as our relation with our cultural references and paradigms. So, within the Museum, I try to propose a space for the discussion about contemporary art, in the form of exhibitions (such as Concrete Dreams, curated by Carlos Basualdo), seminars (such as parallel strategies for the diffusion of contemporary art, detonated by the presentation of the DO IT project), cycles of conferences (Catherine David's presentation of the making of the Documenta), or a series of travelling exhibitions I call La Mirada Transversal (The Transversal Gaze) in which artists are invited to curate a thematic exhibition on the basis of taking our Collection as a "material" to be looked at from a fresh perspective. I also "publish" a fortnightly column on art criticism called Columna de Arena that disseminates via Internet. Colombia is a country of profound contradictions, one that provides an unrivaled entry to the Museum of the Macabre, more than 30,000 violent deaths each year (yes, thirty thousand, which means that every fifteen minutes a young man under thirty is assassinated), but one that at the same time has an enormous desire to make things, a country of optimism, humor and what I call "selective amnesia"—we still call the fifties *la epoca de la violencia*, the time of violence, as if it had stopped since—that makes living and

working here especially stimulating and that provides the feeling (is it a mirage?) that our work is really crucial to the country's development.
I will develop later on.

Jose ROCA.

From: Zdenka Badovinac
Subject: museums at the periphery
Date: Friday 14 August 1998

The postmodern museum has often been described as a place of intense experience similar to the euphoria of Disneyland or a rock concert. This description undoubtedly fits the museums of rich countries, but such an experience would be difficult to find in those of the Third World or Eastern Europe. Museum standards have developed mostly in Western Europe and the United States, while museums in peripheral countries outside western cultural centres have mostly remained pale shadows of their idols. Are museums on the margins of the developed cultural world doomed to offer poorer programmes and weaker incentives to their visitors because of less funding and a poorer infrastructure? Is it at all possible to avoid the logic of capital and form a museum whose creativity and imagination would rival the spectacle offered by the more wealthy museums?

Apart from the universal standards which are increasingly being adopted by museums from the margins, the significance of one's own particular experience has gained in importance; only recently, in postmodern times, have museums started to transform themselves into spaces of imagination and creativity.

Within the context of discussions about the issues of the centre and the periphery, I must describe the place where I work as peripheral, regardless of the fact that Ljubljana is located in the centre of Europe and that, even internationally, it has become one of the more interesting cultural environments.

Based on my own experiences, or the experiences of Moderna galerija (Museum of Modern Art), an institution that I have been managing for the last six years, I can say that we have been trying to turn the drawbacks of the periphery in our favour. The drawbacks of our environment are very similar to the drawbacks faced by art institutions all over Eastern Europe. These drawbacks are the heritage of a socialist regime, problems of transition to a new system, insufficient state funding and sponsorship, and a relatively underdeveloped infrastructure. Regardless of these facts, the remaining issues concerning the role of the museum and the role of the curator are highly academic.

The more art turns towards life, the greater the responsibility of the curator, who now no longer simply has to explain an isolated art object but also relate the context of its creation. Several years ago, the full weight of the issue of the relationship between art and life and the responsibility of the curator fell on my shoulders. The time of the Balkans war proved to be a great challenge for the functioning of our museum. How to react to the war was, at that time, the question of the role of the museum and the curator in society. With the help of certain projects (the "Living with Genocide" symposium and the Museum of Sarajevo, among others), we came to the conclusion that the international network of artists, curators and intellectuals in general did not react to the war in Bosnia-Herzegovina at all. It became evident that contemporary artists and intellectuals were apolitical and incapable of carrying out broad international campaigns, such as those at the time of the Spanish Civil War or the Vietnam War. It is true that art and with it, museums, increasingly turn to the social environment, but it must not be forgotten that this usually represents a narrow and particular environment and not a broad, international social and political community. During the time of the Balkans war, I participated in several international conferences of curators and artists where we discussed AIDS, women's issues, multiculturalism and so on. The war in Bosnia-Herzegovina, which was taking place at the same time and which claimed more than 200,000 lives, was never a topic of these meetings; it was hardly even mentioned. Unfortunately, it wasn't raging in an area that was part of the international art system.

One of the paradoxes of the contemporary global society which has developed universal standards and tools for the art system is that it has failed to develop a method of focusing beyond the limited social and political problems of its own country, or its own neighbourhood. The turning of art towards life is sometimes understood as a particular, isolated experience. It is similar to our understanding of the art of the periphery in terms of its peripheral characteristics.

In its relationship with the centre, the periphery must strive to solve the paradox of the global village or else it will remain caught in the "multiculturalism or cultural logic of multinational capital." This is one of the creative potentials of museums at the periphery: to define themselves before they are defined by the Other.

Zdenka Badovinac

From: Carlos Basualdo
Subject: Greetings from New York
Date: [unavailable]

Dear members,

My good friend Viktor Misiano wrote this text about Museums on my request for the Argentine magazine *Tres Puntos*, a weekly on culture and politics. I asked his permission, and gladly got it, to post it in our forum. Things have been a bit too quiet this summer; I hope that Viktor's piece will stir some reactions. Many members have told me about how impressed they were with Jose Ignacio and Zdenka's postings, but I would actually prefer to see their comments in writing. I hope you all have a nice vacation and I look forward to an active forum.

Carlos

A Museum "here and now"

Museum (in a sense of a museion) is losing its sense along with the end of the World history. A Museum of contemporary art (in a sense of MOMA or MOCA) is losing its sense along with the end of Modernity. The dimension "here and now," determining modern civilization, is incompatible with the usual concept of the museum.

As far as art is realized in the sphere "here and now," it loses stable objective forms and comes to an event. Thus, the museum is becoming a center of social animation, a center for projection of events that can occur mostly besides its borders.

As contemporary art is not anymore unique and universal visual language but existing within a row of others, thus, its only peculiarity is to be the unique language reflecting the nature of visuality itself. Consequently, the museum is a laboratory, an investigation space where different visual languages are compared with each other and with visual objects of the past.

Therefore, as the civilization has plunged into the flatness of "here and now," the museum is the last place where one can experience temporal deepness. It is possible to reach one only by mobilizing all suggestive and shock resources. Consequently, the museum in a consumerist society is a unique place where a work of art can be publicly destroyed. Consequently, in "the risk society" the museum is a unique place where one can experience reposing boredom.

Therefore, the existing global order is not at all global; a lot of things are left besides its borders and inside this order is not homogeneous. Consequently the museum is still a propagandistic device of power, a proof of the existence of modernity and linear historicism.

Despite the fact that art has done everything not to be an element of a power show, museum-monuments are still being built and will be built; their self-valuable expressiveness is more than everything inside them.

Obviously, all versions of the above-mentioned museum institution are not compatible to each other. Here is the main conclusion: the Museum cannot and should not exist, only museums have a right and should exist. Including those, which are not foreseen by the above-mentioned typology.

Viktor Misiano

From: Jordan Crandall
Subject: Re: museums at the periphery
Date: Friday 30 October 1998

I appreciate how Jose and Zdenka's posts help lo locate them in a specific cultural situation while at the same time setting forth a general problematic. Zdenka: what I think about in terms of your text is how the net helps to "turn the drawbacks of the periphery in [your] favour." It is interesting how some of the strongest artistic work online has come out of Ljubljana and other areas of East Europe, transforming it into a center. But interestingly enough, this work is rarely political, at least overtly; it rarely deals with the situation in the Balkans, for example. There might be more politically-oriented work circulated on the email lists, but not in English anyway (there is an email list coming out of Novi Sad called CyberNS for example but the language barrier limits its ability to engage in broader international dialogues—this is not a criticism—I mean it only to indicate the language problematics that continually limit our ability, often productively, to figure translocalisms).

You wrote that, among the broader artist-curator-intellectual community, discussion over the war in Bosnia-Herzegovina and the Balkan crisis in general was curiously absent.

It seems that most of the work of the young artists in the former East (at least those who have "entered international net space" anyway) are interested in the net as an autonomous space of invention—a transnational, regionless space that is often self-reflexive (about its communications protocols, its interface conditions, etc.). I spent some time in Slovenia recently, and this is really true for many of the artists that I met with. Lev Manovich, a Russian-American critic at UC San Diego, often writes about the conceptions of the net in the former Eastern Bloc—how artists from the East conceive of net space and how they situate representational structures within it. He suggests that for many young artists, the net is a way to transcend locality and enter the global space of modernity, and that therefore we should look to the ways in which artists do this, rather than for regionalistic approaches or "national schools." But such an approach is contested by many artists who are attempting to use the space of the net to emphasize regional situations and to develop new forms of local political intervention. The example of the Zapatistas is a perfect one. Through the use of networks they have focused enormous attention on the situation in Chiapas and developed new ways in which one can politically intervene in a remote place. The Mexican government finally understands this threat to national hegemony.

In very similar ways to what you are saying, networks can bring the periphery into the center. They can make one a borderless citizen, at least partially, or provide very potent means of local articulation. Often it is a strange mix of both. And the situation is the same for the institution, which has the opportunity to redefine itself. What are the more adequate ways in which we can conceive of center/periphery relation in the network, and how can we ground the museum in the space of transmission? In so many ways we are all trying to understand this space (this hybrid space, combo of transmission and transport) and the kinds of presences, formations and allegiances that it facilitates.

Jose: what a fascinating description of the museum at the intersection between public and private space. I am trying to think about the relays, the switching-points between.

Jordan Crandall

Chapter II

The Economy of the Art World

"The Economy of the Art World" was again a forum session pre-defined by VOTI. This time the conversation was open to members and two specifically invited guests: Brian Holmes and Ben Kinmont. The forum aimed to "address the roles of curators, contractual agreements and related issues of money and commitment."

The chapter opens with Hans Ulrich Obrist's e-mail, which appears to be a precursor for the official forum topic launched several months later. Brian Holmes enters the conversation with a text he has been asked to share, titled *TNCS, Networks – Civil Society – Transnational Corporations – Democratic Governance* " (p.385), a piece of political critique with a broad analysis of the new world economic system and a viewpoint on some of its consequences." Two evidently key posts from Okwui Enwezor and Bart De Baere, referred to by several writers, could not be found. Yet, in his post on November 17, 1998, Jordan Crandall, as he often does throughout the forum, sums up some of the content of Enwezor's text and Holmes adds further information in his following e-mail. These e-mails and others' responses organically shift the conversation away from a focus on economy and it gathers momentum around notions of the local and the global under the e-mail subject lines: "Gare de l'Est" and then "Gare du Nord."

The chain of e-mails ends with Susan Hapgood's posting of Siegelaub's and Projansky's *The Artist's Reserved Rights Transfer and Sale Agreement* (p.393) and a final comment from Ben Kinmont.

In order of appearance:
Hans Ulrich Obrist, Susan Hapgood, Bettina Funcke, Carlos Basualdo, Jose Roca, Zdenka Badovinac, Brian Holmes, Jordan Crandall, Bart De Baere, Vasıf Kortun and Ben Kinmont

From: Hans Ulrich Obrist
Subject: CURATORS CONTRACT
Date: Thursday 13 August 1998

Carlos evokes the discussion Okwui, he and I had in New York about the necessity of a curator's contract. Lets start to ping pong ideas.

1. Guy Debord published in 1995 a small booklet called *"DES CONTRATS"* published by *"le temps qu'il fait."*[59] The book gathers the unusual contracts between Debord and his publishers and producers, contracts for the present, contracts for life and not financial speculation. Some extracts:

"Rien n'est egal dans de tels contrats; et c'est justement cette forme speciale qui les rend si honorables."

"L'artiste n'avait, en aucun cas, à expliquer comment il choisirait de s'y prendre pour venir à bout d'une sorte d'exploit apparemment insoluble, et qui ne pourrait donc qu'etonner."

"Tous ces contrats, en outre, n'auront pas manque d'etre assez bien calculees…en restant incontrolables a tous les points de vue; ni sans jamais avoir revele rien de trop, fut-ce simplement. Solo vivimos dos dias (nous n'avons que deux jours a vivre). C'est un principe naturellement peu favorable a la speculation financiere."[60]

2. Seth Siegelaub's and Bob Projansky's "Artists' Reserved Rights Transfer and Sale Agreement."[61]

It is interesting as an example for the elaboration of a contract from scratch, which, through the involvement of many people, tried to get to a point where it could be used as a model contract by artists. Here is an extract from an interview with Seth Siegelaub in 1997:[62] HUO [Hans Ulrich Obrist]: In 1971 you worked with Bob Projansky on the "The Artists' Reserved Rights Transfer and Sale Agreement," which I recently saw in New York in an exhibition about artists' economies and contracts organized by Ben Kinmont. How did you conceive the "Artist's Contracts"?

SS [Seth Siegelaub]: Its intention was just to, first articulate the kind of interests existing in a work of art, and then, to shift the relative power relationships concerning these interests more in favor of the artist. In no way was it intended to be a radical act; it was intended to be a practical real-life, hands-on, easy-to-use, no-bullshit solution to a series of problems concerning artists' control over their work; it wasn't proposing to do away with the art object, it was just proposing a simple way that the artist could have more control over his or her artwork once it left their studio. Period. But the broader social-economic questions of the changing role and function of art in society, the possibility of alternative ways of art making or the support of the existence of the artist; all these important questions are not addressed here. As a practical solution, the contract did not question the limits of capitalism and its private property; it just shifted the balance of power in favor of the artist over some aspects of a work of art once it was sold.

HUO: Did you work with a lawyer on this?

SS: Yes. But many of the provisions drafted in the contract for the United States, already have a certain legal existence in Europe in various droit de suite and other well-recognized artist-related laws. Whether or not they are enforced is a different question on another level of power relations between artists and collectors, but there are certain laws that give an artist a tremendous amount of moral control over his work, even after he is no longer the "legal" owner of his work. This is not the case in the United States, and this contract was just an attempt to obtain some of these rights for the artist.

The problem of art as private (capitalist) property, of the uniqueness of objects, this was certainly a problem in the air during the 1960s and behind certain art-making projects. But it wasn't just a theoretical-political problem, in the context of art making at the time it was also a practical problem, in that the selling of ideas or projects was something that the art world had never come up against before on any generalized scale. This has to do more with questions of how to transfer property ownership of an artwork, and these questions were "more-or-less" resolved by treating them in a way similar to the rights and interests given to authors or composers.

Hans Ulrich Obrist

From: Susan Hapgood
Subject: VOTI Plans
Date: Saturday 17 October 1998

The Union of the Imaginary–VOTI Summary of Recent New York City Meetings

October 11th
The Meeting, attended by: Carlos Basualdo, Jordan Crandall, Hou Hanru, Susan Hapgood, Bettina Funcke, Octavio Zaya

October 14th
The Necessary Additional Meeting, attended by: Carlos Basualdo, Jordan Crandall, Susan Hapgood, Hans Ulrich Obrist, Octavio Zaya

In order to succeed, The Union of the Imaginary encourages your continuing participation! During the October 11th and 14th meetings, there was impassioned discussion on this subject. To be a dynamic forum on issues of curatorial practice, VOTI must have contributions and dialogue from everyone involved. A short text, a long essay, it does not matter. What matters to VOTI is that the dialogue goes on and the members contribute to it. But if, on the contrary, you are finding your inbox crammed with VOTI e-mail postings that bring on a migraine, it is advisable that you ask to be removed from the VOTI list.

The forum operates in two modes—private and public. The private session, limited to acting members of VOTI, is the one that we are in now.

The public session, on the other hand, is open to everyone. We are planning our first public session, "The Museum and Beyond," for March, April, and May 1999. During that time, the doors of VOTI will be open. At the end of May, the public session will close and we will then return to the private session. At that point, we may invite new members—those individuals from the public session who have participated significantly in the discussion and will have much to contribute to VOTI on an ongoing basis. In this way, the acting member base of VOTI will continue to grow.

VOTI will continue to develop through a series of private and public sessions alternating with one another. In this way it expands and contracts.

Upcoming Pre-session: The Economies of the Art World
During the next few months, until March 1999, VOTI will host a discussion (limited to members and a few invited guests) about the economy of the art world, addressing the roles of curators, contractual agreements and related issues of money and commitment. Several artists whose work has dealt with these subjects will be invited to join this pre-session, the topic of which was partly inspired by Seth Siegelaub's creation of an artist's

contract in 1971. Since that era, many museums and auction houses seem to have turned toward models of multinational corporate conglomerates. In the current climate, curators may find themselves engulfed in corporate culture, marketed as stars, compensated for their expenses but not their ideas or otherwise involved in deals they never made.

This discussion is intended to generate and define a set of key issues for curators to bear in mind as they work. If you feel inclined to play host at this pre-session, to stimulate the flow of ideas and to keep things cogent, please relay your interest to Susan Hapgood.

Public Session, March 1999: The Museum and Beyond
VOTI will invite discussion about curatorial practice as it relates to both museums and to extra-institutional projects in the spring. We will consider the proliferation of international biennials over the last five years, and the issues they raise about curatorship. Online exchange about the nature of recent projects occurring outside museum walls may produce new ideas about presenting contemporary art, assessing the purposes and audiences of such presentations as well. Artists' participation in this forum will be crucial to assessing the viability of different formulations.

More Future and Not-So-Future Activities

1. Oficina de Asuntos Publicos (OAP): In the near future, a statement of purpose will be available from the OAP of VOTI, currently in formation. Octavio Zaya and Francesco Bonami have become our first two Oficinistas. All inquiries regarding publicity will be directed to the OAP. Archivista Susan Hapgood has recently joined VOTI. She will be the first Archivista, and as such will help stage activities, format and foment.

All dialogue is being archived, with the intention of publishing it at a future date. Bettina Funcke is currently putting together a small VOTI archive, with some basic information about each member.

3. VOTI encounters in real time: Symposia are under discussion as well.

From: Susan Hapgood
Subject: The Economy of the Art World
Date: Monday 2 November 1998

Dear VOTI members,
Our online discussion, "The Economy of the Art World," begins today. The conversation is being hosted simultaneously by the following VOTI members spread almost halfway around the globe:

Zdenka Badovinac in Ljubljana
Vasif Kortun in Budapest
Jose Ignacio Roca in Bogota (visiting New York this week)
Salon 3—Hans Ulrich Obrist, Rebecca Gordon-Nesbitt and Maria Lind—in London

In the coming public and private sessions, we hope all VOTI members will volunteer to play host. Thus far, we have two guests planning to join this discussion: Brian Holmes, a cultural critic based in Paris (please correct me if this is not what you call yourself, Brian), will partake for the coming two or three weeks. In January, Ben Kinmont, an artist in New York, will join in the discussion. We would like to invite additional guests whose work or thought is relevant to the subject, so please let me know of potential guests.

As VOTI continues to evolve, we hope to strike the right balance to keep the conversation flowing and stimulating, and thus we envision the hosts' roles as crucial in this regard, during this pre-session and during the public session that will follow. To reiterate, this particular session is private—that is, only members and announced guests have access to the discussion.

One more announcement: Salon 3 is in the process of planning a live event at their London space in December to coincide with this VOTI discussion.

Here are a few questions to get us started:
VOTI asks about the roles of curators within the art world economy. How might contractual agreements define and defend what it is that curators do? Working within institutions, or on an independent basis, what do we think about the increasingly corporate atmospheres of museums, and the way they affect our practice? Changes in art have undoubtedly precipitated shifts in curatorship as well; should we try to identify these shifts and figure out how they might be stated in contractual terms? How do we own our ideas; how is our intellectual property also a form of cultural currency?

In 1971, Seth Siegelaub and Bob Projansky drew up an "Agreement of Original Transfer of Work of Art" for artists and collectors, also known as the "Projansky Agreement." The need for that contract reflected significant changes in art of that time, changes that seem relevant to VOTI and to this discussion (one clause of that 1971 agreement, for instance, addressed the need to maintain the integrity and clarity of the artist's ideas). As Siegelaub told Hans Ulrich Obrist in a recent interview, the contract was "intended to be a practical real-life, hands-on, easy-to-use, no-bullshit solution to a series of problems concerning artists' control over their work."

Perhaps VOTI will devise a curator's contract or identify the issues that might comprise such a contract as this discussion evolves.

All best,

Susan Hapgood

From: Bettina Funcke
Subject: [unavailable]
Date: Tuesday 3 November 1998

Dear VOTIs,

I think an important aspect to this discussion to begin with is to step back and to look on the situation as a wider historical development and to be aware of the conditions of dependence of artistic practice and its (re)presentation that always have been existing. The actual shift that has taken place is the process of the abolition of the political by economics. Art used to be involved in political representation, but the development of the last 150 years that has led to imperialism over colonization to the current so-called globalization, which also produced the depolitization we have to deal with today. There is a book by Slavoj Žižek, "A Plea for Intolerance," that criticizes this process.[63] Multiculturalism for him is only the effect and epiphenomenon of an economically based globalization. This is the very problematic background that I think we have to deal with when talking about the "independent" curator.

From: Susan Hapgood
Subject: [unavailable]
Date: [unavailable]

Dear Bettina and VOTI members.

I'm of two minds on this subject. My reference to owning ideas and to ideas as cultural currency has to do with what curators do, what it is that we offer in exchange for pay. Wasn't the formation of VOTI partly in response to curators' ideas, identities and choices being marketed by companies (and institutions?) for capital gain?

I agree that curators are conduits for ideas, and that ideas are in the air. But copyright and protection of intellectual property are concepts designed to protect creators in a capitalist system, and as strange as they may seem (especially the oxymoron, "intellectual property"), they exist because people got sick of seeing their concepts distributed in mangled forms, and they want a way to have some control over them. A more cynical view would be that they are just devices to make sure the creator doesn't get cut out of profits. The "Projansky Agreement" was certainly related to these concerns.

There is a policy on some websites called "copyleft"—an idea first introduced by Richard Stallman that has evolved to mean that whatever you can download online can be freely distributed, but not for profit.[64] The idealism of the copyleft idea is refreshing, and perhaps the Internet, by its very nature, will persist in this direction.

Susan Hapgood

From: Carlos Basualdo
Subject: globalization and independence
Date: Wednesday 4 November 1998

Bettina and Susan's interventions made me think about the curator's position regarding intellectual (transmissible) knowledge as somehow situated between Lacan's "the Symbolic belongs to everyone" and the laws of copyright. I say "intellectual" knowledge to define it in opposition to "practical" knowledge, that it is a lot harder to communicate but quite essential (I believe) for the curator's practice.

The formation of the Union was definitely, as Susan points out, in large part "a response to curators' ideas, identities and choices being marketed by companies (and institutions) for capital gain," that's for sure. On the other hand, any attempt to respond to this situation through a paranoid system of copyright would be totally misleading. I think that for curators it is necessary that information about our practice circulate as freely as possible so we can all benefit from it and enhance our activity. On the other hand, we should be able to develop mechanisms to protect that information from being appropriated by the institutions and marketed without our participation (or by diminishing our participation as much as possible).

I believe that VOTI could be instrumental in allowing us to experiment with a freer process of information exchange while ensuring that the information will still belong to us somehow, "us" defined as a whole group rather than as single individuals. But of course, a true cooperative attitude on the side of the curators is a basic requisite for this to happen. My question is: is there any possibility for us to develop a contractual form that would not block the exchange of information among curators but that would, on the other hand, protect their ideas from being capitalized without their participation in the process?

Carlos Basualdo

From: Jose Roca
Subject: Re: globalization and independence
Date: Friday 6 November 1998

Dear VOTI:

The problem of the separation between property rights and intellectual (moral) rights is certainly not new, and it surfaced not so long ago on the occasion of the removal of Serra's Tilted Arc.[65] In the hearing prior to the removal of the work, several arguments were deployed, but the final outcome proved one thing: as Serra himself put it (in America) property rights are rather clearly defined (and protected), whereas moral rights are not. That is, commodity prevails over ideas. The United States, in particular, has not been willing to sign the 1886 Berne Convention regarding copyright, and only very recently has begun to put in place a protocol to acknowledge part of it due (according to Serra), to extensive pirating of the American film and book industry abroad.

How does this precedent apply when faced with Carlos's proposition for a Contract that would protect the work of independent Curators? Serra insisted, in a much-cited statement that "to remove the work is to destroy the work." Applied to curatorial practice, to—purposefully or not—ignore the nature of a curatorial project, to interfere with its internal logic or to appropriate it for other (commercial, ideological) purposes other than the original agenda the project intended to address, is to destroy the work of thought the curator has construed, and these possibilities for the misreading, misinterpretation or outright violation of a curatorial project should be put within a framework—at least in formal, if not yet possible in legal, terms.

How can we define what is exactly expected from a curator when she or he signs an agreement with an institution?
First of all, one ought to define the exact nature of curatorship, as far as an institution is concerned. In mine, for example, (which is maybe not the best example, because Curatorship as a profession is not widely known nor acknowledged in Colombia) external curators are expected to fulfill three practical tasks so the administration gives its agreements before the payments: a. a precise list of works; b. an n-page text for the catalogue and texts for information within the exhibition and c. to make an initial contact with the artists and to do a follow-up of the mounting process of the exhibition. The conceptual framework that permits a curatorial project to be carried out is either taken for granted when the Curator is invited, or expected to be implicit in the list of artists and their works. If Curatorship can be understood as the definition of a series of parameters that permit that the ideas that have taken form in the works of an artist or a group of artists sum up to construct a new set of meanings by association, juxtaposition and accumulation—the much-resisted Szeemann's "total work of art"—then we are not being explicit enough when

hiring a Curator, because the very core of the nature of our work is precisely left out of the agreement, probably because its complex nature is impossible to enunciate in a formal manner, resulting in an inevitable act of faith.[66]

From: Zdenka Badovinac
Subject: Re: The Economy of the Art World
Date: Wednesday 11 November 1998

Dear VOTI members,

Before starting our discussion, "The Economy of the Art World," we all agreed—or should I rather say, nobody expressed his/her disagreement—that all our texts launched in the VOTI discussion are to be "the property of individual authors / no circulation elsewhere without permission."

We live in a time in which we, on the one hand, no longer believe in the absolute originality of ideas, and on the other, it seems that our products are increasingly being alienated. The end result of our debate on the roles of curators within the art world economy could probably have an entirely practical form—it could be a proposal of how to protect the curatorial product, how to prevent its alienation. I do not believe that there is total freedom in the circulation of ideas—there are always centres of power channelling these ideas in this or that way. One of the issues we are interested in here is where and in what way the curator's ideas are going to be realised, and what is going to happen to them. If we do not provide concrete examples, the "Economy of the Art World" discussion will bring no practical results. This is a "guild" discussion on how to facilitate efficient work conditions for ourselves. I therefore think it is time that we go ahead to concrete examples of the area in which we mostly feel our curatorial work is being alienated. Before coming to general conclusions, we will probably have to find out in what way our work is most commonly misused. Therefore I am inviting all VOTI members to submit their concrete examples, for maybe by doing so it will be easier to resolve the dilemma clearly opened up by Carlos.

Best regards,

Zdenka Badovinac

From: Brian Holmes
Subject: TNCS[67]
Date: Tuesday 10 November 1998

Hello VOTI members—

My name is Brian Holmes, and I thank you for inviting me to join the forum. I find this opening discussion on contractual law and freely exchanged ideas really interesting; we should push it farther. Clearly there will be increasing amounts of contracts to craft and obey as the marketplace extends its reach, transforming what used to be considered spiritual, philosophical, friendly and intimate expressions into transmissible and saleable information—art, ideas, gestures and styles, games and patterns of play, self-images, sexual energies, even genomes. But the question for me is, how to refuse the reduction of intersubjective experience to merely contractual relations? I tend to agree with Jose Roca when he says that the complex nature of a cultural production—an art show, in this case— "is impossible to enunciate in a format manner, resulting in an inevitable act of faith." The thing is always, where do you place your faith? Why? How far can you go with the relations, contractual or otherwise, that it makes possible?

The text I've been invited to present to you—a rather long one by email standards—is a piece of political critique with a broad analysis of the new world economic system and a viewpoint on some of its consequences. People aren't likely to agree with every detail of this, but I guess the idea of bringing in such a reflection from outside the professional field of curatorship is to provide a general framework for the discussion of how economics affects the practice and presentation of art. What's key here is the effort to locate oneself within the worldwide relations of production and exchange—the effort to become conscious of where you're placing your faith. That's why I've tried to identify the ambiguous position of the "networker": a person making his or her livelihood by a use of the transnational networks of transportation and communication but also trying to sound out the possibilities of those nets and to appropriate them for non-systemic ends. It seems to me that curators today are particularly likely to be in that ambiguous position.

I'd be curious to hear some descriptions of actual situations, to find how it works for you, what the parameters of your networking existence are. I'd be equally curious to find out how people face their inevitable systemic involvement with the transnational corporations and how they deal symbolically with the split between the networked and the non-networked worlds, in terms of the art they stage, write about and promote. I'll have some comments to offer on my own location. But for now, here's the text:

TNCS

Networkers - Civil Society - Transnational Corporations - Democratic Governance

Brian Holmes

PS—In October '98, the MAI talks were killed in the OECD by the withdrawal of the French government that quietly proposed to move the discussions to the World Trade Office.[68] Democracy ever wrestles with the undead...

From: Jordan Crandall
Subject: Re: globalization and independence
Date: Tuesday 17 November 1998

I very much appreciate the posts of Brian and Okwui and would like to briefly make a few responses.[69]

Brian: why do you refer to networkers as a class? What criteria are involved in grouping them as such? I ask because you seem to imply that in order to achieve agency as a networker, one must have access to communications media and be "conscious of the welter of connections that make up the global economy." Especially when you refer to networkers as "the people whose labor actually maintains the global economic webs," I wonder what type of agency is possible for disadvantaged economic actors. Will participation in transnational civil society require a modem?

Just as you are very right to emphasize non-corporate aspects of economic globalization in the face of overarching emphasis on the multinationals, it seems important to emphasize the role of MICRO-NETWORKS and LOCALISMS in the face of the overarching emphasis on globalizing, locality-evacuating networks. These kinds of micro-networks might connect those immigrant communities who do not necessarily aspire to any political agency in one state but whose interests are located in cross-border social, cultural, and economic nets. These networks have nothing to do really with having access to the Internet but are nets maintained primarily through other channels. (When we speak of networks today should we incorporate this multiplicity? Networks do not equal the Web but are most often cross-format information and communications channels that bind distant places and peoples in shared interests, ties and formats of exchange, subject to the imperatives of new technologically-mediated economics.) Networks are rough, patchy, uneven, home to so many subcultures and regions, so many situated, embodied dynamics. At all turns they disrupt conceptions of over-arching globality and give rise to new politics of the local.

Brian I know you are talking about these issues already when you emphasize the role of the nation against the "Oneworld" (though you may be emphasizing the nation too much), when you call for spending time away from computers and out of airports and when you call for the need to expand the "magic circle of empowerment to people and priorities which have been marginalized and excluded." What I am wondering is if you are positioning this as somehow outside the network or outside the class of networkers or whether you are calling to extend our conceptions of the network itself.

In this context I can't help but think that in Okwui's text there is something of the conflict between corporate capital and the new immigrant workforce, which Saskia Sassen locates as part of a new transnational politics, a politics of those who lack power but now have "presence."[70] How could anti-multiculturalist currents be seen as kinds of reactionary impulses within this landscape? I mean this more in terms of the general hostility to political correctness that Okwui locates, rather than in terms of the specific Whitney ouster.[71]

On that note: personally, I feel that Okwui has introduced urgent issues that call for a response from every single member of this forum. Several members have spoken for the first time in response to the Salon3 press release and mailing list request. Surely, then, you have time to respond to these issues, which cut to the very core or curatorial practice today. At the very least, to show where your priorities are.

From: Brian Holmes
Subject: TNCS, curating, public space
Date: Wednesday 18 November 1998

Dear VOTI members,

I'd like to answer Jordan Crandall's questions concerning my essay on transnational civil society, and go from there to reflections on curating. It may seem odd, but the two poles have links.

The essay does posit a transnational "class," composed of people working with and profiting from worldwide transportation and communication networks (and not just the Web!). I distinguish this rising class from the vast majority of people in the world whose livelihood does not involve any direct use of those networks. Marxists talk about a "hyper-bourgeoisie," but it's more complicated than that, 'cause lots of people are just plain working with those networks, like independent curators, for instance—they're usually a little better off in the new economy than most others, but they have no managerial control or capital stake. I also point to the very real possibility of using the information-gathering and communication capacities of transnational networks for nonsystemic, i.e. non-capitalist or non-corporate ends. Democratic ends, for instance.

It's also true that there now exists a large transnational labor force, physical, factory-type labor I mean, as well as a very large number of people whose daily working patterns are conditioned by transnational product and info flows. Manuel Castells even distinguishes between the networkers and the "networked." That's too brutal for me. I think there are new social relations of production in which all players have agency—we just don't understand those relations very well yet. I'm extremely interested in what Jordan calls micro-networks, as well as the "politics of presence," which is a new and promising form of media politics for the disenfranchised. In fact my major point is that, while transnational corporations exist in and for the(ir) networks, the world is much bigger than that, and I don't want to play just the TNC game, or blindly participate in a "civil society" that fine-tunes the status quo.[72] So I try to look outside the center-cities and the dominant circuits of exchange, to see how people are getting along in the face of what are often very difficult times, and I try to look at what you might call the transitional networks, the places where people are struggling to make their localism, i.e. their lives, get taken seriously by those with power. If I stress the national locus, it's because that's where most "public" institutions still reside. And those public institutions are an important means for translating local or existential values and aspirations to larger scales, the scales where most power lies. Of course, money is also a great translator—but every translation conditions the message, so my experience says you need more than one way to go about it. Only people like Luciano Benetton want art, the international market and politics to perfectly coincide, to become one. Oneworld.
So you better have damn good contracts when you cut deals with Benetton, Tom Pachett,

Hugo Boss, Philip Morris, Deutsche Telekom, that's right! But anyway, they'll pull out when there's no advantage. There's a clear limit where they'll fire you or not call you back. And public institutions that define civil or "civilized" society by the standards of these corporations and their stockholders will not tolerate the challenging practices of those for whom multiculturalism, for instance, isn't synonymous with niche-market consumerism. Unfortunately, Okwui Enwezor has had to demonstrate the pertinence of my discussion of Clinton/Blair-style centrist politics and their effects on the tacit social consensus. I'm referring to just this one sentence of Okwui's very careful and probing comments:

"It seems to me rather ironic, that the news of the Whitney putsch, occurred within twenty-four hours of last week's election in which the American public deemed it necessary to repudiate the right wing's encroachments into individual rights, and to humanize the political debate around questions of representation on both a social and cultural level."[73]

It is ironic. People in the representative democracies want more humanistic societies, but how are they even going to see what's going on in crucial institutions of representation such as museums, if we the people working directly with those museums do not speak up and challenge the consensus? If we don't challenge the "civilized" agreement not to talk about anything, that's supposedly bad for business?

Okwui is right, American public art institutions have been losing the extraordinary gains made since the sixties. Not coincidental, the loss has occurred in parallel to the reassertion of American economic power in the world since the mid-eighties. Corporate penetration of the museum has been a big factor. But let's not just talk about America in this forum. Each one can talk about his or her own experience. The situation in France, where I live, is very different. Almost no corporate penetration, a huge public art sector. But what is mostly done with it? On the one hand you have the old-fashioned French institutional conservatism that academically replays what's been accepted as good. And on the other hand you get an embarrassing mimicry of everything that's trendy and international: computers, interactivity, nomadism for the rich, variations on commercial cinema and haute or not-so-haute couture, and the casual, deskilled photography of sophisticated consumerism. In other words, everything that can somehow correspond, on the symbolic level, to the immaterial exchanges of speculative or "fictional" capital. And in the face of this, I can't help but think of the old colonial phrase: "the natives are getting restless." It's not just the neofascist groups who protest against the French commitment to public art in order to push their own nauseating agenda. In the last 3-4 years there has also been a significant number of politicians and intellectuals from the socialist party, often in the "provinces," who lash out at what they see as pointless, disconnected posturing. These people, operating at ground level, don't know what to do with the split between the ins and the outs, the networked and the unemployed. And so they panic. Can't we help them a little? Can't we find art that addresses the deep complexity of social relations and not just technological complexity or fast-changing media styles? Can't we treat museums as public places for debate over the representations of what life is about, what time is for, what communication can bring to people? Wouldn't that be a way of easing the transitions to a global economy, and widening the circuits of immaterial exchange, opening them to other contents, taking the blinders off? Personally, that's what I try to do in my relations with museums. And that's why in recent years I've gone back to using that nasty word "class," though I use it as a question, and not with the dogmatism of former generations. I don't see how I can do that anywhere but in the public space, with public institutions as central pillars of that space. I'm not simplistically against the very existence of transnational corporations and markets; they even have some liberating possibilities, like the art that goes with them. But I think the questions that Okwui Enwezor and Nancy Spector have raised are the right ones. How to consolidate the public space of art?

Brian Holmes

From: Carlos Basualdo
Subject: Gare de l'Est
Date: Sunday 6 December 1998

Brian and Bart's interventions left me wondering about what are we supposed to do with the notion of the local. As Brian states in his essay, the function of the TNCS as described by Gramsci it is to legitimize the status quo, in this case an incredibly unjust world where globalization basically acts as a re-mapping of the globe that completely excludes certain areas while it intensifies the connections among a few others.[74] In that landscape, the work of the revisionist art historian or curator may end up being dangerously close to the traditional functioning of the TNCS. Revisionism attempts to reconstitute the canon by invoking the histories that were initially set aside. By the same token, it might run the risk of sacrificing sometimes the local specificities of the contexts where those practices took place in order to translate them to a more international discourse. My question to Brian would be: how can we, as curators involved in a revisionist approach to the canon, inscribe in the art historical narrative these non-canonical practices without losing the radical potential that they enacted in their original contexts? Brian gives us a hint of an answer when he suggests that we, as networkers, should be paying a lot of attention to the local contexts. But, practically, how would you do that in an exhibition that takes place in Europe or the States? On the other hand I feel that the traditional concept of the local is too oppositional and grounded in the genealogies of romanticism.

Bart suggests that the French Right could be more in tune with the local needs than other political parties and that this might be one of the reasons of its apparent success in certain areas in the South of France. Sincerely, I doubt that this concept of the local really fits into an accurate description of the inner dynamics of those places. After all, their economies are completely intertwined and dependent with the State and the European Community as a whole. This dependence is a paradoxical but inescapable condition of the globalized areas. We might be able to still use the traditional concept of the local when speaking about a small village in an area that is structurally irrelevant for the global economy, but I do not think it is valid when discussing Buenos Aires, Johannesburg, Montreal, Marseille or Nantes. If this is the case, then our job is a double one: we have to rethink the notion of the local and we have to redefine the way in which we can stop dissociating the local and the international in our practice as curators.

Carlos

From: Bart De Baere
Subject: Re: Gare du Nord
Date: Thursday 10 December 1998

One of the phrases of Jimmie Durham worth remembering, is when he once talked about the time he was an activist and organisor of the American Indian Movement.

The people with whom it was most hard to have a meaningful discussion concerning the AIM, he said, were the left-wing New York intellectuals. Each of us can identify with that side. Aren't we all a bit—but not completely—left-wingish, New Yorkish and intellectuals?

Dear Carlos,

Thanks for your generous and well-considered e-mails. It would be good to have a list of the individual e-mails so that specifics can go partially outside of the general platform, even if that might reduce this platform still more into a place for information & congratulations.

The situation in France is very different from the Whitney case, Octavio. In France, some of the most ardent curators are under attack and populism, and fascistoid methods can be seen on the 'progressive' side as well. I'm sick of this kind of collective action.

The position of Robert was grand at that moment—he went all the way then and wrote clear letters—and his change now is grand too.[75] With all my profound estimation for you, Octavio, the question is not, as you state (it is really too simplistic), "an apology for collaborating with fascism (whatever the merits of particular cases)?" A meaningful question may be: under which conditions can the mediation between art and audience be senseful and ethically acceptable? That's one I tried to answer.

As I wrote before, each of us is compromised from the very start because we essentially negotiate between the conditions that are and the engagements we take. To deny that would be naive hubris.

The equation of fascism and rightwingism and managerialism with evil may very well cover up the really problematic, even unacceptable, aspects of our position. To take the French debate jusqu'au bout would mean that we can't allow collegues to act with public money at all anymore in most of Africa and in large parts of Latin America and Asia. And as far as I'm concerned in the United States, where a lot of private money is, for me, more problematic and much more unacceptable than the public money in France. This money, by the way, doesn't come from the Front National but from the tax payers, and is distributed by a democratic system, not by the Front National.

I think you are right, Carlos, when you reenter that damned term of the "local." And when you indicate, it's irresolvable. Don't get me wrong about the extreme right wing. It's more a question of questioning ourselves, continuously, profoundly. Shouting "collective action" is easy and hip. I don't see many people who take real consequences, a real constructive hour, a real thousand dollars. In the end, it's not economy that rules the world, as Yugoslavia shows in a sad way. It's culture, for the better or the worse. The extreme right uses themes that are there, on the street. They magnify them. As a culture we fail to unmask this magnification, as a society we fail to counter those problems, as arts people we fail to effectively develop and implement more profound and open themes.

The local I believe does still exist, and it's really local. It's not an abstraction like we tend to take it for. It's different around every corner. It's part of streets and neighbourhoods and identification patterns of a majority of the populations in Europe, at least. Perhaps we'd like it to be different. Perhaps we'd like everybody to be mental nomads like we are.

The local is several militants I spoke with during the last weeks, who said things they wouldn't have said five years ago. If you think it ain't a problem for people to cease being able to greet their neighbours, you'll have an easy ride.

Yesterday I went to a think tank for a city festival. There was a presentation by a team of urbanists that has been analysing the nineteenth century extension around Ghent. This banlieue is the zone with most poverty, the zone which traditionally votes socialist and which is now the main zone of recruitment for the extreme right. The urbanists gave a survey of their study. No social functions or few of them, no supralocal functions, dense inhabitation in dilapidated housing, the links with the central city often even physically severed...These severed links—the suburbs being isolated by railroads and highways—are a symbol for what happened. The core city, the city of which the culture crowd and the politicians are part, has lost touch with its wider population.

A European Utopia of spreading culture has been given up (it was a failure anyhow, to a large extent) and the top professionals have continued to do their thing, improving themselves. The urbanists had asked permission to come. They came with a question. An open question. Whether the arts could be part of a solution. Whether we could develop that. The city of Ghent may after the next local elections be the only large Flemish city without major problems with the Vlaams Blok, an extreme right party that has become so cunning it can't even be chopped down as racist anymore. They have the best publicity, sharp, focussed analysis, they know what's happening, they are developing neighbourhood organisations like the socialists once did but fail to do these days. Antwerp, Mechelen, Brussels may become hard to govern. If Ghent stays out of that mess, it's not because our policy was better. It was a tiny bit less horrendous, but if you're serious, we failed dramatically as well. The cultural sector at large. We're less serious than the Vlaams Blok. The misdemeanor is not caused by the extreme right but by the powers that are. Those we accept. The fact we feel it's acceptable that people are working in the Whitney at all. Reconsideration of the 'local' seems indeed to be important. Perhaps it might be addressed as "the specific" and the ways in which the specifics that always inform art can be highlighted, channelled and, especially, validated through our processes as organisors. No exhibition takes place in Europe or in the States at all, any exhibition takes place somewhere, really somewhere. This somewhere is a context which may be taken as one of the valid references or not.

This is incompatible with the 80s type of internationalism. It can be as international, though, but may have more aims, more layers of effectiveness. It means its sense is here and now, or there and then, which is to a larger extent how artists act than how curators act. Perception & validation. The last Sao Paulo biennial was for me a magnificent example of this possibility.[76] It was very much timely for Sao Paulo, its present and its future, it was very aware of the impossible hardships of that reality. The result was very much for an international audience too. It even developed proper curatorial practices ("contamination" being an important one) and a discourse.

Most of us, I guess, are in, or related to, positions of authority and different sons of power. How effective are we?

Vasif refused a position as director in a major American institution to start up a small center in Istanbul because he wants the potential he sees there strengthened by an interesting debate. I guess he does this in a slow, low-key, grass-roots-like way. Years of invisible work.

Zdenka has substantially added to the continuation of contemporary art as a motoric point of reference in Slovenian society. As such, she acts in the prolonging of the civil society movement and the intimate links between the culture, people and the opposition in the period before independence. In one way or another parties (fun, not political) seem at present to be very effective there as part of the mix.

The problem is that cultivations of the specific cannot be generalised. They can be developed through experience, and at best be transformed when being reapplied to another place. They are slow. It's hard to inscribe non canonical practices into an art historical discourse - or any generalistic discourse, for that sake. Perhaps they're "fitting," rather than "radical." Perhaps this quality of "fittingness" is more important as a possibility for their continuation than the possibility to interpret them as "radical."

Sitting in the car with a left-wing Brussels intellectual. Important Arts Person.
"The ideologies should get more attention again," he says.
"Well if any, anarchism."
"That's not an ideology," he says.
A rapid end of a conversation. How did we get from a call for collective action against the National Front to consider the "truthfulness" of the fascist drive?' Too easy. Too fast.

Bart

From: Vasif Kortun
Subject: Re: Gare du Nord
Date: Friday 11 December 1998

Dear Carlos,

Let's take as an example the most recent Sao Paulo Biennial that turned the linear Euro-North American art historical model and substituted with a topical Brazil-centric one, for Brazilian communities first, and Latin American later, and finally for the global art audiences. Do you consider this project to be a revisionist one, firstly for Brazilian audiences, and secondly for the entire canon? I ask this question to draw attention to other, and not-so-incompatible positions of contamination in historical East Europe and Japan for example. Each inclusion is also a marker of limits.

I remember you had said a while ago that only strong cultures create strong fictions. Will it be possible (ever) to disassociate the concentration of Capital from the concentrations of cultural nodes? The possibilities of little histories are visible, but how do those become impactful on the main story, and there is still a main story, albeit a new one in action that keeps on being written.

Consider, for example today, the plethora of exhibitions that arrive on the scene under the general rubric of Asia, when we all know too well that "Asia" means only certain concentrations in South Asia. When we say "Africa" we only seem to imply the Sub-Sahara. And when we say "East Europe" we only imply the traditionally SCCA supported areas.[77] So on and so forth. Geography is only part of the problem, and it obfuscates specific economic class differences, proximities to state apparatus, the precisely different cultural situations.

Additionally, it is nearly impossible today to speak of a place to be completely structurally irrelevant from the global economy. We are all penetrated by invisible wires. However, the transmissions received by different receptors, produce completely different readings and results. In a way, it is always local. Tender readings of different humidities, intensities are essential.

Finally, how does one articulate the space between the site of borrowing, and the site of delivery? Cultural translation remains a problem. From the culture of the "local" to the culture of the powerful?

Just some wandering thoughts

Vasif Kortun

From: Carlos Basualdo
Subject: Re: Gare du Nord
Date: [unavailable]

I would like to begin by responding to Vasif's question about the SP Biennial.

I think that using "antropofagia" and a blueprint to re-map the history of international contemporary art is not a revisionist gesture, but an oppositional one. It consists of replacing one local narrative (Euro-North American) for another (Brazilian). Now, what does this gesture entail, both for Brazil and for that other fiction "Latynoamerika," as Glauber Rocha used to write? Well, it is obviously a fantastic thing to do if considered in the Brazilian context because it has the potential of centering the discussion around the cultural history of the country, acting as a catalyst for arguments around the current cultural conditions of production. "Antropofagia" has a very specific history in Brazil, starting with Oswald de Andrade's *Manifesto* in 1928, and continuing with the critical rediscovery of its problematics in the late sixties, with "Tropicalism."[78] "Antropofagia" has always being part of the construction of "brasilidade" (Brazilianness), that strong fiction that vertebrates that continental-country. Lately, in the last five years or so, "antropofagia" has re-emerged in the critical discourse hand-in-hand with the work of contemporary musicians such as the late Chico Science and events like the funky parties in the favelas. Now, some Brazilians friends of mine told me that they thought that the Biennial staged antropofagia in a spectacularizing manner. What they implied is that the show did not help to problematize the question of the construction of a national culture in Brazil, but rather made a logo out of the issue.

This is an interesting question, because it can be generalized; I agree with Bart when he says that a show happens in a specific place—not in Europe, but here, in this particular town, in Cordoba or Rotterdam—but does that mean that we have to reify what we think it is the main problem (or problems) that affect that locality? Going for the local in such a way may easily end up turning the questions into ready-made answers. Maybe this means that a show never happens only in one place, that it is always somehow displaced. The locality would be made of a set of conditions that involve the aspirations of the institution as much as the socioeconomical and cultural histories of the audience, as much as the inner dynamics of the practices that are exhibited. And in that sense, the Biennial had several coexisting readings; in the rest of "Latynoamerika," for example, the show could have easily been perceived as a reaffirmation of Brazil's isolationism and aspirations to south-continental hegemony.

At some point I wrote that strong fictions produce strong cultures—not the other way round—and I believe that strong cultural contexts can emerge anywhere: in Rio de Janeiro, New York or Cape Town. Borges found the "Aleph" in a lost basement in the middle of a marginal neighborhood in Buenos Aires. I strongly believe that the centers of power and the centers of culture do not necessarily coexist.

Irit Rogoff, writing about audience participation in the Black Male show at the Whitney, mapped the capacity that a show has of inventing its own public.[79] The audience of an exhibition, she seemed to imply, may become an instant community that has the potential to last longer. That community is not in a place, it is a place. Our concept of the local might be redefined as that future community that we have to produce through our curatorial efforts -not only us, of course, but us among other cultural producers. The local will have to be produced through interaction and audience participation; it would never be the result of the imposition of cultural or political logos. I believe it is a process of collective action, and it relies on individualism only to supersede it.

Carlos

From: Bart De Baere
Subject: Re: Gare du Nord
Date: Tuesday 15 December 1998

Carlos,

Antropophagia was indeed staged in a spectacularizing way. Many other agendas were there at the same time, though, often implied by the choices and placement, situating the female as constitutive for Brazilian culture, not only participative, the myth of racial equality in Brazil, or the difference of colours in different climates. Beside this, it seems to me that "antropophagia" was dealt with in a multi-levelled way and the aim was not so much to state an answer to it as to activate its mutation into contemporary possibilities, as well by the openness of the total textual construction as by the curatorial practices. The generalisation was indeed there, as an instrument with as both local and international targets. The ready-made answer was given, not as an end, but as a beginning; it was not the only layer. The theme, by the way, was epaisseur, not antropophagia. The institution and its transformation was a main drive (in which the clear goal was to focus the biennial back onto contemporary art, even if there was an astonishing historical part, starting from the 16th century). Perhaps this multiplicity of layers can be the start of a methodology that includes the local; the coexisting readings are indeed a goal to be cherished.

The idea of the future community is an arousing one. Perhaps this one too can be put into a qualitative plural.

Bart.

From: Susan Hapgood
Subject: Part 1: Contracts
Date: Friday 15 January 1999

Dear VOTIs.

I've been offline for a long while, but following the discussions with great interest. Since there's a little lull, it seems to be a good time to reintroduce the contractual materials pertaining to the stated topic of this VOTI session, "The Economies of the Art World," which will extend through March.

We agreed, in the fall, that we would look at ways to characterize what it is that curators currently do and see how this activity can be defined, qualified and quantified, perhaps translated into workable contractual terms. For inspiration, we cited a contract from 1971 as our model, a contract intended to help artists control the use of their work and take part in whatever economic gains it might generate once they no longer own it. Drawn up by Seth Siegelaub, esteemed dealer of Conceptual art, and Bob Projansky, a New York attorney, it is officially titled "The Artist's Reserved Rights Transfer and Sale Agreement," but also is known as the "Projansky Agreement." You'll find the full texts of Siegelaub's introduction and the agreement itself in my next two postings, and if you want to see what it actually looked like (sans-serif, no-nonsense style), you can view largely illegible images of it at http://www.blast. org/contracts.html.

I have thanked Jerald Ordover, attorney, on behalf of our forum, for graciously supplying us with the agreement. The Guy Debord contracts, which might also inspire us, are in my hands, but we need them translated. Is anyone willing to translate them as a service to VOTI?

The Projansky agreement is intriguing as a glimpse into another, perhaps more idealistic (but also more sexist and naive) time than ours, and I'm impressed by the respect it demands for artists and their work, a kind of respect that they still are not necessarily accorded in many private and public situations.

Some of the basic points from the contract that may be applied to curatorial practice are the aim "to establish recognition that the artist maintains a moral relationship to the work, even as the collector owns and controls it," and the agreement that "the parties wish the integrity and clarity of the artist's ideas and statements in the work to be maintained and subject in part to the will or advice of the creator of the work." How and why do such understandings go awry? Perhaps we could start here…

Since one of our current guests, the artist Ben Kinmont, has dealt extensively with contractual agreements, I expect he'll be posting on this subject soon. He has written of:

"contracts as formalized relations between two, as promises made and remembered ideals once had. Although artists have begun to use contracts with increasing frequency since the late 1960s, there are many who remain uninterested in using legal language to formalize a promise or relationship...as money becomes a greater factor for artists, artwork production, dealers, and institutions alike, it becomes increasingly difficult for many to operate on verbal contracts alone and, in consequence, the legal profession grows to accommodate our insecurities, need for control, and curiosity."

(Excerpts from Ben Kinmont's "Promised Relations: or, thoughts concerning a few artists" contracts, 1996)[80]

What issues are crucial in defining our relations with institutions, publishers, sponsors, artists? What rights and responsibilities do we expect?

Susan Hapgood

From: Ben Kinmont
Subject: contracts
Date: Monday 18 January 1999

Dear everyone,

Thanks for the invitation to participate. Although I know some of you out there, many I do not, so by way of introduction, I am an artist who makes public projects. Most occur initially out on the street, some end up in strangers' homes and museums, and all involve the distribution of texts ("catalytic texts") and direct interaction with people not usually considered to be within the art world. Typically archives are made of these projects, and it was after consideration of the life of these archives that I began to write contracts for their ownership and, later, for their exhibition.

The "Promised Relations" show was simply put together from bits of my own research into various artists' uses of contracts, ranging from artworks in and of themselves, to functioning contracts used to define a legal position.

Although I too am concerned about the entrance of corporate culture into the art world (Susan H. 17 Oct.), it should be remembered that the contract is not an exact document. A few lawyers interpreting a contract are no more likely to come up with an agreement that a few art historians considering a Cezanne.

The contract is interesting in that it attempts to define a space between two points, between the two signees, each with different motives and values. Jose Roca mentioned in his 5 Nov. posting that curatorship creates "a new set of meanings by association;" in this way, I would argue that the contract is the perfect exhibition space. Its history and purpose is to discuss not only the two points, but the association between the points (what I have in other places referred to as "the third sculpture"). Approached as a friendly medium, it may even allow us to "push the limits of our own practice" (Okwui, 11 Nov.), or to empower ourselves (Carlos 16 Nov.) if we use this tool, the contract, for our own purposes.

Ben Kinmont
From: Susan Hapgood
Subject: Re: contracts
Date: Tuesday 19 January 1999

Dear Ben and VOTIs,

Just a quick clarification in response to Ben's recent posting: the idea of devising a contract to help curators was not intended to be interpreted as a sign of the encroachment of corporate culture into our field; it is a way VOTIs can define the association, you might say, between the corporate culture of some institutions, and curators who work with them. Depending on how a contract is formulated, in other instances, the same contract might encourage new models for practice.

Susan Hapgood [81]

Chapter III

The Whitney Letter and FRACS

The first spontaneously formed VOTI debate, and one that results in the first collective action by VOTI, is inspired by an e-mail from Nancy Spector who raises concern over the sacking of two curators from the Whitney Museum of American Art, New York, in 1998. There appear to be some conversational e-mails missing that prompt Susan Hapgood to draft a letter to be sent from the forum to the then-director of the Whitney Museum, Maxwell Anderson, "stating deep concern for the treatment of curators Thelma Golden and Elisabeth Sussman." Following this post, a fast-paced succession of e-mails ensues, involving many VOTI members. The discussion revolves around how best to agree on the contents of a jointly composed letter, how the letter should be sent and what it means to voice individual concerns versus composing a union-style statement. There are also questions raised at this moment about how VOTI is perceived by non-members, given the lack of any manifesto on the project, or a public announcement about the forum. During the Whitney debate, Robert Fleck introduces the contemporary situation in France and the funding problems being encountered by the Regional Endowments for Contemporary Art (FRACs). In support of Fleck's e-mails other members add that similar cases exist internationally and VOTI should aim to be more globally oriented.

The chapter closes with the sending of a final letter (p.400), signed by a long list of VOTI members, to Maxwell Anderson by fax from all over the world creating a fax jam in the offices of the Whitney.

In order of appearance:
Nancy Spector, Susan Hapgood, Francesco Bonami, Rosa Martínez, Michelle Nicol, Brian Holmes, Dan Cameron, Bettina Funcke, Hou Hanru, Jens Hoffmann, Octavio Zaya, Carlos Basualdo, Douglas Fogle, Robert Fleck, Zdenka Badovinac, Jose Roca, Christophe Cherix, Carolyn Christov-Barkagiev, Bart De Baere, Vasıf Kortun, Rebecca Gordon-Nesbitt, Aleksandra Kostic and Udo Kittelmann.

From: Nancy Spector
Subject: Re: globalization and
Date: Tuesday 10 November 1998

Dear Voti Members,

I am wondering with our current discussion regarding curatorial contracts and intellectual property, whether we want to comment on the current events at the Whitney. While many of the concerns addressed in this forum are, perhaps, more related to the needs of the independent curator, I find the way the situation was handled at the museum deeply problematic. Its implications for our profession are troubling. Are curators really so expendable? Museums pride themselves on their proximity to an academic environment, positing scholarship as one their highest goals. I am not arguing with this in principle, but if those standards are to be met, why are curators not protected by the same vehicles offered in the university system, such as tenure? Not to mention paid research sabbaticals.

In the area of contemporary art, I do believe that a certain amount of fluidity and change must be encouraged. Whether we like or not, I think this is a generational issue. Nevertheless, I find the Whitney's actions bordering on a kind of intellectual gentrification, if not censorship. They no longer have a curator versed in the history of cinema. And they no longer have a curator of color.

Should we, as a fundamental part of the art community, comment on this in some public fashion? Is this comparable to what happened recently in Bonn? Was anything done about that?

Yours,

Nancy

From: Susan Hapgood
Subject: Whitney letter
Date: Thursday 19 November 1998

Dear VOTI members,

Here is a draft of a letter, adapted from many of our recent messages that I hope we can finalize in the coming week if it is to remain timely. Do you think it reflects the situation, and our position, accurately? Now is the time to establish how it will be distributed, as this will also affect its content. Please post your response.

Susan Hapgood

Dr. Maxwell Anderson
Director
Whitney Museum of American Art
945 Madison Avenue
New York, NY 10021

Dear Dr. Anderson:

We wish to express our deep concern about your treatment of curators Thelma Golden and Elisabeth Sussman. Your recent restructuring of the curatorial departments at the Whitney Museum of American Art are indicative of prevalent attitudes that have been slowly developing over the past several years in many major art museums. Beyond our wish to show support for fellow curators Golden and Sussman, we see your recent actions as signals of a subtle yet pervasive disrespect for curatorial practice and as signs of aversion to controversy.

Curators at many institutions today are caught in a kind of double bind. Art museums pride themselves on their proximity to an academic environment, positing scholarship as one of their highest goals. Yet due to shifts in the infrastructure of funding, museums have also adopted corporate management models—this has had a corollary effect of treating curators as expendable workers. Contrary to both of these models, curators do not have the job security and intellectual support enjoyed by professors in the university system, nor do they enjoy salaries comparable to corporate employees. As a result, they are forced to stand on increasingly shaky ground, while serving as the primary source of ideas for their institutions' exhibition programming.

We find your actions in regard to these particular individuals to be a form of intellectual gentrification, if not censorship, as well. You no longer have a curator versed in the history of cinema, nor do you have a curator of color, and you have not announced any plans to make up for these gaps, perhaps because you do not believe that such issues reflect your agenda for the Whitney. This troubling direction reflects a conservative trend, a mistaken attempt to return to an outdated approach to cultural history.

We feel it is imperative to bring attention to your actions both publicly and privately, lest they be misperceived as the innocuous restructuring of an organization.

Sincerely yours,

[to be signed by VOTI as a union, with members' names listed
or
with a long list of individuals and no mention of VOTI
or
to be distributed as each member decides]

From: Francesco Bonami
Subject: Re: Whitney letter
Date: Thursday 19 November 1998

I think that the equation "no curator of cinema, no curator of color" doesn't make much sense, like saying "You have no business card and no hot water." I wouldn't mix gender and curatorial field. The issue is in the method of action, the attitude of a structure toward professional individuals no matter their specificity. What if the curator of color was also the curator of the Olography department and the other one of the Embroideries? Would the institution behaviour be more justified or more wrong?

F. Bonami

From: Rosa Martinez
Subject: Re: Whitney letter
Date: Friday 20 November 1998

Dear members of VOTI,

I will be very happy to sign the letter addressed to the director of the Whitney. I want to thank the people who have given their time to write it. I think we should send it individually by fax, all of us using the same text but without mentioning VOTI. Please inform me what is the final collective decision.

Bestest,

Rosa

From: Michelle Nicol
Subject: Re: Whitney letter
Date: Friday 20 November 1998

Members of VOTI

I agree with Rosa and would be happy to send an individual fax to the Whitney and in doing so—as HUO suggested—collectively "jam the fax machine of the Whitney."[82]

I think it's a good idea not to mention VOTI. Otherwise, as again HUO has pointed out, Voti will be perceived as some kind of lobby.

Best,

Michelle Nicol

From: Brian Holmes
Subject: Re: Whitney letter
Date: Friday 20 November 1998

Dear VOTI members—

I think the letter to the Whitney is intelligently drafted and reflects the concerns of those who have expressed themselves here. Good work Susan!

It would have been useful if the letter could have been sent individually, signed by the sender with the name of the VOTI network. There is more power in the combination of individuality and numbers. But since some people hesitate before this course, their reasoning should be respected.

One sentence is in dispute:

"You no longer have a curator versed in the history of cinema, nor do you have a curator of color, and you have not announced any plans to make up for these gaps, perhaps because you do not believe that such issues reflect your agenda for the Whitney."

My suggestion is:

You no longer have a curator versed in the history of cinema, which amounts to a denial of the complex interdisciplinary exchanges that have led to the use of the term "visual arts." The fact that you also no longer have a curator of color, though it is of a quite different order, suggests that even more complex social and cultural relations may be similarly denied. You have not announced any plans to make up for these gaps, perhaps because you do not believe that such issues reflect your agenda for the Whitney. Etc.

I hope that is helpful, best to all.

Brian Holmes

From: Susan Hapgood
Subject: Re: Whitney letter
Date: Friday 20 November 1998

Thanks, Brian! It is much clearer now. Any responses regarding the newspaper question? For those of you not in the United States, next week this country will be frenzied as everyone prepares for Thanksgiving, which is on Thursday. Perhaps we could do the faxjam on Monday afternoon or Tuesday? Or should we wait until after the holiday?

Susan

From: Dan Cameron
Subject: Re: Whitney letter
Date: Friday 20 November 1998

Dear Members of VOTI,

I'm proud to be able to join with the rest of the group in faxing this letter to Maxwell Anderson. Thanks for producing such a moving and determined response to the Whitney's high-handed behavior.

Dan Cameron

From: Bettina Funcke
Subject: Re: Whitney letter
Date: Saturday 21 November 1998

Dear members of VOTI,

I will be very happy to send a fax to Maxwell Anderson. I agree with the suggestions of Francesco Bonami and Michelle Nicol.

Being in the Whitney Independent Studies Program right now, I can experience half-close how the curators in this program are forced to ridiculously simplify their proposals for their exhibitions. Besides the treatment of curators—that urgently needs such a comment—it becomes obvious in a frightening dimension how complex and precise ideas with some kind of a critical or experimental dimension are cut down to culture that fits the consumption of the masses—which was, if one wants to give it a radical perspective, the strategy of dictators to flatter their peoples. This is the challenge we are facing now, of the economical that is abolishing the political these years.

And Hans Ulrich, I like your idea about more real-life-events and interdisciplinary discussions to keep this discussion simultaneously as imaginary and real-life as it is going right now.

Bettina Funcke

From: Hou Hanru
Subject: Re: Whitney letter
Date: Saturday 21 November 1998

Dear Friends of VOTI,

I have been too much on the run for the last weeks and am sorry to be somehow detached from the forum...but reading the letter to the Whitney, I feel it's urgent and imperative to respond to such a new danger to curatorship, and to contemporary art in general, in our own manner. Of course, the intellectual and cultural landscape in the U.S., which is being increasingly influenced, even dominated, by the corporate "culture" and rule. It's also true that this "model" is now being brought to many other places, including Europe and Asia, along with globalisation. What's happening in the Whitney could happen somewhere else tomorrow. And it is probably happening. On the other hand, there is more and more political and moral censorship in many places. In France, the increasing influence the far right wing has in the political arena is now threatening the art world...in the region of Lyon, a part of the public funding for a contemporary dance festival has been retreated due to the pressure of the Front National in the regional administration while the conservative parties are accepting such blackmails. We are curious about what's going to happen to the Lyon Biennale in 2000...

It's now clear that the letter to the Whitney is a first collective action of VOTI to negotiate with the neo-conservative reality... It gives a real significance to the foundation of VOTI itself. I'm very proud to be a part of it.

In the long run, we must develop our discussion on alternatives to the existing museum establishments. The issue of "the museum and beyond" that we tried to carry out during our meeting in New York last month should be brought to our agenda of discussion soon.. It's only by proposing and practicing new forms of experiments that we can respond to the threatening reality efficiently and effectively.

Hou Hanru

From: Jens Hoffmann
Subject: Re: Whitney letter
Date: Monday 23 November 1998

dear members of voti,

i am very happy about the last emails and specially about hans ulrich's and hou's carefully critical but also enthusiastic postings which both seem like an extreme "call for action."

i do not share the opinion that we should only sign the letter individually, we definitely should also sign the letter to the whitney collectively with Union of the Imaginary, since the letter is a collective form of protest i do not see the point to sign it only individually; if you like to sign it only individually, write your own letter! in a situation like this we cannot afford to be afraid of rumours and gossip about what voti is or not. what we need is a collective statement even if it means to take the risk to be seen as a lobby, etc.

i definitely think the letter should be made public as well!!!!

only my very best,

jens hoffmann

From: Hou Hanru
Subject: Re: Whitney letter
Date: Monday 23 November 1998

Dear Jens and others,

I totally agree that we should sign the letter collectively, and this should be done immediately.

Best

Hanru

From: Octavio Zaya
Subject: Re: Whitney letter
Date: Monday 23 November 1998

Dear members of VOTI

I sincerely appreciate Susan's work and dedication regarding the Whitney letter that we are discussing, and I also share the members' desire to go on record about this most disturbing affair, but I honestly find the tone of the letter somewhat "soft," considering the magnitude of the situation.

As many of you have repeatedly stated, this situation is a symptom of the corporate management models, which US cultural institutions have been adopting. But it is also the result of the relentless campaign of defamation and intimidation that the conservative species viciously directed during the last few years against the controversial programs presided by David Ross at the Whitney.[83]

Remember the culture wars? This particular campaign—you may remember—was assisted by the vitriolic insinuations of Hilton Kramer from the pages of The New York Observer. The right wing just got another battle won under its belt. And as Okwui said, "it is because of our silence that today the Whitney has forever banished any art or exhibition with a political dimension."

That's precisely why I don't feel that we should express just "our deep concern" but our crystal-clear repulsion towards this well-orchestrated political assault.

At the least I would like us to unequivocally express not only our support for Thelma Golden and Elisabeth Sussman but also our appreciation and defense of their work—Mentioning in the letter Black Male, as well as the 1993 Whitney Biennial, as examples of the brave, audacious and challenging dispositions that have characterized both their curatorial practices, will clarify our intentions.[84]

Regarding the way the letter should be signed, perhaps Jens is right in suggesting that it should be the Union, but considering that VOTI has not been properly introduced to the public I still can't grasp the point. I guess the whole list of members could also distract from the issue at hand. Whatever the case, I agree with Jens about making the letter public and Hans's suggestion (jamming the Whitney fax machine) sounds very appealing.

Octavio Zaya

From: Dan Cameron
Subject: Re: Whitney letter
Date: Monday 23 November 1998

Dear members of VOTI,

I just read Octavio's e-mail about the Whitney letter, and I think that signing a collective letter is much less effective than "jamming" the Whitney's fax lines with individual letters of protest. A single letter with lots of (virtual) signatures can be dismissed quite easily, but a stream of faxes from around the world makes a powerful impression. Also, AICA's annual awards ceremony will take place this week at the Whitney, with Max Anderson as the presenter.[85] Since I assume many VOTI members are also AICA members, perhaps we should be enlisting Alexandra Anderson's (no relation) support in this.[86] For an international organization of AICA's status to acquiesce to receive Anderson's blessing seems to read as the opposite: us giving our blessing to him. Perhaps someone who is attending the award ceremony can be called upon to interrupt the proceedings by pointing out how grotesque the image of Max A. handing out awards to curators (among others) is, considering the circumstances...

Sincerely,

Dan Cameron

From: Susan Hapgood
Subject: Re: URGENT
Date: Monday 23 November 1998

Dear VOTIs,
To try to get a quick sense of consensus, can everybody please post his or her position on these 3 issues right away?

1.
"Need stronger letter, as Octavio suggests"
or
"Letter fine as is"
or
"Letter too strong and accusatory" (I've heard this, privately, from at least one VOTI member.)

2.
"One letter, signed by VOTI and with a list of members"
or
"Fax-jam by individuals"

3.
"Alert the press"
or
"Keep this between us and the Whitney"

I think Dan's suggestion sounds great—is there someone who can do it? What do others think? If that can't be done, a week from today for our action would probably work fine.

All best wishes,

Susan Hapgood

From: Octavio Zaya
Subject: Re: URGENT
Date: Monday 23 November 1998

Dear Susan,

Thank you so much for the fantastic work you are doing.

My position is as follows:

1. As I mentioned in my previous posting, the letter needs some corrections. The Whitney's new direction shouldn't get away so easily with what it did. It sets a bad precedent to imitate, and it could be any of us next time.

2. Fax-jam by individuals

3. Alert the press

All the best

Octavio

From: Jens Hoffmann
Subject: Re: Whitney
Date: Tuesday 24 November 1998

dear susan, dear all,

thanks for the email messages.

1. i agree with octavio's suggestion to make the letter stronger, to be honest i have the feeling that most of us are so much involved in the structures of the art world and actually totally dependent on the system that they do not want to take any risk and try to be careful, i understand that to a certain degree but at the same time i do not see the chance to create anything that matters out of this situation.

2. fax-jam by individuals signed individually and by voti!!!

3. if possible make it public

my very best,

jens

From: Michelle Nicol
Subject: Re: URGENT
Date: Tuesday 24 November 1998

hello susan

1. stronger letter

2. fax jams by individuals signed also by VOTI

3. alert the press

best,

michelle nicol

From: Carlos Basualdo
Subject: Re: URGENT
Date: Monday 23 November 1998

1. Letter is fine.

2. Fax-jam by individuals.

3. Alert the press—in this case we should sign the letter collectively and also add some extra-VOTI signatures.

Carlos

From: Bettina Funcke
Subject: Re: URGENT
Date: Tuesday 24 November 1998

Dear VOTIs,

Thank you for all the e-mails.

1. The letter should be stronger.

2. The letter should be faxed individually and signed by VOTI.

3. It should be published including signatures by non-VOTIs, too.

4. It should happen VERY soon.

All my best

Bettina Funcke

From: Douglas Fogle
Subject: Re: Whitney letter
Date: Tuesday 24 November 1998

I might be wrong, but didn't Chrissie Isles replace John Hanhardt as the curator of film and video?[87] Then wouldn't it be inappropriate to say, "You no longer have a curator versed in the history of cinema"? But perhaps I'm missing something.

Douglas Fogle

From: Robert Fleck
Subject: Re: URGENT
Date: Tuesday 24 November 1998

Dear friends of VOTI,

I was just following the discussion during the last weeks, did not really find the point where to connect into the discussion. I am not informed about all the details of the Whitney events, but I would also agree to sign Dan's letter collectively. For many reasons, first it is a very intelligent argument, and last it seems also politically a good moment to appear with such a point.

But also in general, of course I would say that I agree with everything you sign collectively, until I am not expressing my disagreement. If we proceed like that, we are able to react in shorter terms.

Here in France, the next two weeks will show if the regions where the front national is participating to the regional governments, such regional institutions as FRAC Languedoc-Roussillon (Ami Barak), FRAC Rhone-Alpes (Yannick Miloux), FRAC Bourgogne (Emmanuel Lattreille), FRAC Picardie and FRAC Centre will still be able to do independent work. The budgets for 1998 will be discussed and decided within two weeks. In the regional elections in March 1998, the Left was the winner in these five regions. The former, conservative regional governments maintained their ruling position by associating the Front National to the regional government. The FRAC-institutions in France are regional institutions—run by the regions, they are under the law of the regions and the president of the region is appearing on every invitation card. I therefore suggested to these five colleagues in March/April 98, to retire from their position, because it would be impossible, at least for me, to work for fascists. Nobody of the five colleagues retired, or expressed public disapproval for the semi-fascist government in their region. I understand their position—they are struggling hard, every day, to maintain the activity of their FRAC-institution. And they do not have any other job proposal in exchange. But I think that we should issue a collective declaration if the FRAC-institutions in these five regions in France where the Front National party is associated to the regional government, should be impeached to work as before. This can occur within two weeks, with the budget decisions. Ami Barak, two weeks ago, seemed very much in fear for his future. I think that we should support them, if the fascists in the regional governments in France interfere in their work.

Best Wishes,

Robert Fleck

From: Zdenka Badovinac
Subject: Re: Whitney
Date: Tuesday 24 November 1998

1. Susan's letter is very well composed. This is VOTI's first collective act, and therefore we should maybe consider the possibility of introducing a stronger stance. Why not simply condemn the Whitney scandal, instead of expressing "our deep concern"?

2. That letter should be faxed individually and signed by VOTI.

3. Alert the press.

Best,

Zdenka Badovinac

From: Brian Holmes
Subject: Re: URGENT
Date: Tuesday 24 November 1998

1. Stronger letter—"deep concern about" could be changed into "total opposition to" or something equally clear.

2. Fax-jam by individuals indicating membership in VOTI (non-members can also send their letters)

3. The press will certainly report "a global revolt against the Whitney" or some such blather. Best to ensure that the letter is published in full.

Proofreading: In the second sentence of the letter—the verb should be "is," no?

And far more importantly—can someone in New York verify what Douglas Fogle says:

...didn't Chrissie Isles replace John Hanhardt as the curator of film and video? Then wouldn't it be inappropriate to say, "You no longer have a curator versed in the history of cinema"?

It's best to get things accurate before going ahead with an action...

Brian Holmes

From: Jose Roca
Subject: Re: URGENT
Date: Tuesday 24 November 1998

Dear VOTIs,

1. Stronger letter; what should this mean? What is exactly our leverage? Is it merely symbolic?

2. Fax-jam by individuals; as Dan put it, a stream of fax paper is visually appalling indeed.

3. It will, in all cases, leak to the press; why not go public right away?

Abrazo,

Jose Roca

From: Christophe Cherix
Subject: Re: Whitney letter
Date: Tuesday 24 November 1998

Dear Voti Members,

Sorry not to have replied earlier about the Whitney letter. I don't have enough information about the Whitney affair, but fully share Voti concerns on this matter.

1. Would be glad to sign the letter collectively.

2. I think a single letter has more chance to get an answer.

3. Alerting the press is necessary.

I agree with Robert Fleck's proposal about the FRAC's situation in France. A collective declaration seems urgent to me.

Best,

Christophe Cherix

From: Susan Hapgood
Subject: Soon
Date: Tuesday 24 November 1998

Thanks for all the response. We're working on all these issues as fast as we can and will be posting again soon.

Susan Hapgood

Archivista

From: Carolyn Christov-Bakargiev
Subject: Re: Whitney letter
Date: Tuesday 24 November 1998

Dear friends, colleagues and members of VOTI,

I have remained silent until now for a number of reasons. I would like to first of all say how fascinating and enriching it is for me to take part in this association of people and exchange of ideas and I would like to thank Hans Ulrich Obrist and Carlos Basualdo for inviting me to take part.

Although I still do not feel able to add much to the discussions going on, I do feel the urgency that many of you are expressing about the events at the Whitney in New York. I also remember that VOTI was born also as a way of providing mutual support to practitioners round the world. So I would like to now tell you all that I agree with sending the letter of protest to the Whitney. I am not sure whether it is better to sign collectively, individually, with VOTI mentioned or not, however. I do agree with Hans Ulrich Obrist's remarks about the risks involved in making such an embryonic grouping public so early on.[88] However, trade unions do act as a group more effectively than as individuals only. I guess I shall go with the majority decision therefore.

I appreciate the energy put into VOTI by those who take part frequently and those who are now promoting the Whitney action. However, I do want to say that I felt slightly ill at ease when I read Carlos Basualdo's remarks about the fact that all of us should take actively part in the discussions or be removed from the association ("people who are not interested in participating in the discussion should ask to be removed from the list so that the rest can speak freely and productively").[89] I'm sure he did not mean exactly that. I, for one, feel that silence is very important and that it does not at all mean that one is too busy or not willing to share and participate in communication. It may mean that there are different notions of time in relation to productivity and different times of elaboration: it will take Roman Opalka a whole life to paint one single white painting![90] I mainly have not participated as I still am getting acquainted with the modes of relation, which are occurring and being set up here.

In any case, at this stage, I would like to send only a few comments and impressions, in the chaotic order in which they appear in my mind:

I was very interested in Bettina Funcke's initial remarks of 12 October about how it might be possible to envisage a form of asceticism, modesty and unpretentiousness in both curatorial and artistic practice today as a way of escaping the fact that "everything seems to be liberated and possible now" without this meaning a conservative turn.[91] This seems close to some thoughts I have been having about the way the notion of "experience'"—a progressive, advanced notion in the sixties when Ronald Laing was writing The Politics of Experience—has become an element of a by now commoditized model for life, a new dominant paradigm which may alienate more than liberate.[92] We are almost "obliged'" to have as many experiences as possible, navigate the net all over, update software, etc. I would like to recall Emily Dickinson's poem: "to make a prairie/ you need a clover and a bee/ one clover and a bee/ and fantasy. / Fantasy will do/ if bees are few."[93]

I am very interested in the different levels of messages being sent: essays, long remarks, short informal messages, etc. I would like to understand more about the boundaries and blurring of boundaries between private and public today and of course Luce Irigaray's notions of democracy starting with "two" subjectivities refounding their relations, comes to my mind.[94] How does one create "intimate" art exhibitions, for instance? How does one avoid considering the audience as an abstract "multiplicity"?

Also, we speak of contracts and defending curatorial practice and intellectual property from being misused and redirected towards finalities we did not have when producing it: this is fundamental, and at least where I live and mostly practice, independent curators are unfortunately totally expendable currency (by the way, there is tenure in museums here in Italy, Nancy, and it does not work here: it has only produced a cast of funzionari who are totally out of touch with real art being produced—no longer curators but bureaucrats). So there should be a way of increasing the recognition of the meaning of curatorial work and empower the curators. Yet, at the same time, I would like to keep our practice fluid and open, as free as possible as HUO often suggests (and contracts do sometimes limit what we could do through improvisation, even though they defend our rights), also because of the ethical issues that are raised by what we do when professional curatorial practice dispossess artists themselves from self-organisation and presentation (many artists are also curators, and most of the most interesting movements and art practice throughout our century has happened not in the curatorial, critical field, but among artists themselves, as we all know).

I was totally surprised to learn that in New York, "multiculturalism," or whatever we want to call it, and "political correctness" are out of fashion. This to me is new. Where I practice, some of us are still trying to create an awareness that there are different histories and different geographies, different notions of what gives "value" to works of art and how "coded" our parameters are in this field. So maybe, we are so late and out of sync with the "center" that we could again be avant-garde! Certainly, even the notion that art and art exhibitions are forms of research, inquiry and debate is not even accepted here at an institutional level. Something that has bothered me for many years and may be of interest to you is the question of why the progressive left in Italy has been reactionary and conservative in the realm of advanced art (for instance supporting Renato Guttuso's realist/ expressionist painting in the post war period, even pushing artists such as Carla Accardi and Giulio Turcato to leave the communist party). In many ways, this is still occurring.

The babysitter is now leaving so I must end this first message and go back to little Rosa! All the best to all of you, those I have met and those who are just names and words for now!

Carolyn Christov-Bakargiev

From: Bart De Baere
Subject: Re: URGENT
Date: Wednesday 25 November 1998

Dear VOTIs,

Just came back, found the mailbox blocked by emails, got them as a zipfile, read them through, can't assess yet, so will go with whatever happens. The letter is fine and has triggered a lot of attention.

At the same time.

If we're honest, what do we think it'll initiate? Shrugging one shoulder at the Whitney? Hardly even that, it'll be thrown straight into the paper bin, also if it comes in twentyfold. Having it published in the press? An open letter? Goes without consequence.

If this is a point to focus on, and I believe it is—Bernice Murphy resigned last week as director of the Sydney Museum of Contemporary Art, which I heard during a radio discussion in which she hammered on the danger of management strategies taking over from cultural questions—why not be thinking instead of signing people? Why not each of us write their own substantial reflections, about the wider situation and the weakness of the W. within it, offering the W. the challenge to think, letting Mr. Anderson receive one fax after another of reflection and reflecting ourselves too, sending them around in this forum at the same time?

And why not send at the same time copy of those to a limited number of well situated writers who may publish interesting reflective articles from this momentum onwards, which may have more effect than an open letter?

Sorry for entering so rude, reading all of the emails one after the other gave me the feeling that it's hard to reach a true consensus concerning the approach of a question like this. No consensus but intense ideas may be a simple way to address the issue without having to find a polished middle ground.

At the same time: happy to sign, if that's the outcome.

Bart De Baere.

From: Francesco Bonami
Subject: Re: URGENT
Date: Wednesday 25 November 1998

1.Letter is fine.

2.Fax-jam by individuals.

3.Alert the press

F. Bonami

From: Hou Hanru
Subject: Re: URGENT
Date: Wednesday 25 November 1998

My position is the same as Francesco, Octavio...and all others:

1.Letter is fine.

2.Fax-jam by individuals.

3.Alert the press

Hou Hanru

From: Rosa Martinez
Subject: Re: VOTI ACTION
Date: Wednesday 25 November 1998

Dear VOTIs,

1. Letter is fine

2. Faxjam by individuals mentioning VOTI and all other individual memberships (AICA, etc.)

3. Alert the press.

Rosa Martinez

From: Susan Hapgood
Subject: Re: VOTI ACTION
Date: Wednesday 25 November 1998

VOTI ACTION
Monday, November 30
10-11 am—fax the letter on your own
12 noon—letter faxed from VOTI, with names of members

By our general agreement over the past several weeks, VOTI is responding to recent events
at the Whitney Museum of American Art. Members are encouraged to sign and fax the
following letter on their own, from 10 am to 11 am, New York time, on Monday, November
30. In addition, non-VOTI colleagues who agree with this letter are welcome to fax it on
their own letterheads.

At 12 noon on Monday, a final letter sent by VOTI, listing the names of every VOTI member,
and additional individuals who express their wish to be included, (please e-mail or phone
VOTI to let us know), will be faxed to the Whitney and to the New York Times. Further
discussion of press issues should be addressed to the Oficina de Asuntos Publicos of VOTI
and sent by e-mail (hit "reply")

Monday November 30, 1998

Dr. Maxwell L. Anderson, Director Whitney Museum of American Art 945 Madison Avenue
New York, NY 10021
Fax 212-570-18XX

Dear Dr. Anderson:

We wish to express our opposition to your treatment of curators Thelma Golden and
Elisabeth Sussman. The recent restructuring of the curatorial departments at the Whitney
Museum of American Art is indicative of a managerial approach that has been slowly
developing in a number of major art museums. Beyond our wish to show support for
fellow curators Golden and Sussman, we see your recent actions as signals of a pervasive
disrespect for curatorial practice, and as signs of aversion to some of the most aesthetically
and intellectually challenging experiments in contemporary art.

Curators at many institutions today are caught in a kind of double bind. Art museums pride
themselves on their proximity to an academic environment, positing scholarship as one of
their highest goals. Yet due to shifts in the infrastructure of funding, museums have also
adopted corporate management models with the corollary effect that curators are treated

as expendable workers. Contrary to both of these models, curators do not have the job security and intellectual support enjoyed by professors in the university system, nor do they enjoy salaries comparable to corporate employees. As a result, they are forced to stand on increasingly shaky ground, while serving as the primary source of ideas for their institutions' exhibition programming. The door is then open to all kinds of abuses.

We find your actions in regard to these particular individuals to be a form of intellectual gentrification, if not censorship. The fact that Thelma Golden and Elisabeth Sussman presided over the controversial 1993 Biennial Exhibition, one of the most stimulating and contentious contemporary art exhibitions presented after the gutting of the National Endowment for the Arts, or that Golden then went on to curate "Black Male: Representations of Masculinity in Contemporary American Art," are coincidences that hardly escape us. Since when did exhibitions that set attendance records and raise genuine intellectual questions become a failure? Of course no one is required to subscribe to the aesthetic options of these two curators, but to admit that they are part of an important debate, itself linked to a vibrant focus of artistic experimentation, is surely necessary for a public institution that seeks to represent artistic practice today. To sidestep this debate over politics and identity in a multicultural, globally integrating society is to set a timid, unproductive, yet perhaps more easily manageable agenda for the Whitney. This troubling direction reflects a broader conservative trend, the mistaken return to an outdated conception of cultural history.

We feel it is imperative to mark our opposition to your actions, lest they be misperceived as the innocuous restructuring of an organization like any other in the private sphere. Curating is an eminently public activity and must remain so, if the visual arts are to continue to generate the curiosity, the enthusiasm and the commitment that sustain our efforts as professionals in this field.

Sincerely yours,

Member

From: Vasif Kortun
Subject: picketline?
Date: Thursday 26 November 1998

I grew up in the 70s as an organized socialist. Hence, the hoopla over the exit of curators of symbolic impact of yet another dull and historically irrelevant NY institution, forces me to recall a few instances of being bored to tears at the nitpicking over the arrangement of words in protest notes, declarations and manifestos. I cannot sign a letter that I've not authored, and collective action is a remnant of industrial massification that I suggest "we" better not mingle with... Alternative? Wage individual campaigns, be sincere with your reasons, assume complete responsibility. Secondly, the inter-geographical obsession with a NY situation locates this town as the center for the VOTI community. Maybe it was naive to believe that the dispositions of our community would not be symmetrical to the condensations of Capital. Shall we please get over this obsession and stop acting like a labor union gang? Was the Whitney on a better course a few months ago? How did they deal with "third-party" curators? How did they deal with other institutions? We all have some ghastly stories to tell.

I would like to exercise the possibility of carrying on a discussion as if Whitney did not ever exist.

Sorry for the interruption.

From: Brian Holmes
Subject: Ideas and questions...
Date: Thursday 26 November 1998

Dear VOTI members—

I can't just make believe that the Whitney and even New York don't exist, as in the e-mail I just read—but still I got a good laugh out of the idea!

It isn't all happening in New York, and for instance, Carolyn Christov-Bakargiev's more ex-centric viewpoints were very engaging for me, particularly the notion that "experience" and subjective involvement have been normalized and made profitable. There's a recent book in French by Andre Gorz, "Misères du présent, richesses du possible," that goes into some dimensions of that idea; it's worth reading.[95] And Carolyn, I'd be curious to hear more of your views on that, in this forum or directly to me. (Posso leggere anche l'italiano, il mio e-mail e 106271.223@compuserve.com).

Bart de Baere's point is well taken. There's a need and also a chance now to do some serious thinking and to address it to specific cultural actors, to build up momentum, as Bart says. That's a real network approach. Collective letter-writing and position-taking is still important, despite the disappointments of the 70s—I'd say it's essential, but nowhere near enough. Take the nasty situation that Robert Fleck has brought up, the neofascists in the French regions and their possible effect on the funding of the Regional Endowments for Contemporary Art (FRACs). I'm for almost any protest against the National Front, and certainly not just ones that I have personally authored. The symbolic level is always somehow collective. But on the other hand: What is this new fascism? Where does it come from? What are the real relations with globalization? How is it connected to certain rejections of contemporary art? How can art practice keep all its intimacy, all its experimental richness, all its intellectual complexity, and at the same time be an "art against fascism"—an art that offers not just the necessary opposition to racist fear and hate, but also a real emotional and symbolic alternative? Is it possible to be "against Le Pen" without plunging back into questions of social and economic relations, on the local as well as the international levels? I'd like to hear more from people working on such questions...Gerard Paris-Clave and I are going to Belgrade tomorrow for a Ne Pas Plier presentation, and to look in the faces of the latest in fascism. We're working and looking for partners. But we don't have the all the answers, far from it.

Best to all,

Brian Holmes

From: Carlos Basualdo
Subject: Re: Ideas and questions...
Date: Thursday 26 November 1998

Dear VOTI members

What course of action shall we take in regards to the FRAC situation? I would be happy to hear more about the way in which VOTI can react to that. I would also like to hear more about what alternative actions Bart thinks could be developed in conjunction with the letter to the Whitney. This situation has pushed VOTI to the public sphere and it would be interesting and urgent to debate how the Union shall shape its participation in this arena, beyond the Internet discussions.

Carolyn, I do mean what I wrote, and I am very glad that it might help to prompt some very substantial reactions—among them your fantastic posting. I believe that active participation by all members makes this forum feel more as a lounge and less as a conference room, and I guess that's a more comfortable feeling for all of us. On the other hand I do agree with your remarks about the need to allow a coexistence of many different subjective times at the forum. So I guess it is a question of how to navigate between the time needed by each of us to process and elaborate the information and the timing required by VOTI's internal dynamics. After all, it is also a subject(ification process) that we are tentatively improvising here.

Best.

Carlos

From: Carlos Basualdo
Subject: Re: picketline?
Date: Thursday 26 November 1998

Dear members of VOTI, dear Vasif,

I get your point, but we have to start somewhere, right? And I think it is because of the Whitney situation that we came to hear about the FRACS in France. VOTI is seriously intended to function in a horizontal, non-hierarchical manner, but we have to understand that there are strong dynamics inscribed in the way in which information flows and we have to slowly learn how to deal with them, so as to alter them in the process of our communication. I agree with you on the fact that a collective letter is not a very original way of reacting to a situation like the Whitney's, but besides that, what complementary collective courses of action would you suggest we should take? (I have to confess that I do not get your point about "individual campaigns" less I understand why that should be considered more effective than a collective letter. Wouldn't those individual campaigns become finally collective if they are to produce some effect?)

It seems to me that Bart's and your postings express a certain mistrust of the more traditional ways in which a group reacts to a specific political situation. That's great, after all VOTI is some sort of think tank, so it would be very interesting to come out with new ways of thinking about situations like this. I took forward lo hearing more from you.

Best,

Carlos

From: Vasif Kortun
Subject: soft belly
Date: Friday 27 November 1998

Needless to say, I did not claim that NY did not exist; nevertheless I remain apprehensive about the incessant centering of that situation. My reaction is to the grave drama that lasted quite a few days about the wording of the protest letter. The multiplicity of individual responses is far more significant than the soft heroics of group actions.

On that front, Bart's suggestions present individual coherency, and Robert's posting has an urgency of no less significance than the Whitney, it is not only happening at the almighty Whitney, and there are certain linkages between these seemingly unrelated incidents. The reasons run deeper than political inclination. I operate in Turkey often under radically barbaric conditions, and should I begin to relay some of the precise situations I face, I would be cluttering valuable reading time. In other places, things are more disguised, subtle, gentle and civilized, but not altogether different.

Perhaps, a more fundamental question is not only to produce responses against new kinds of corporate fascisms, but also review at the same time the histories (and presentation histories) of contemporary art? Yes, we have to defend, but also undo the institutional setups, exhibition-audience relations we have inherited. A blanket support is not sufficient. For example, do you not think that FRAC's need to be reimagined? What are the reasons for the near absence of independent curators in a place like France?

Vasif Kortun

From: Carlos Basualdo
Subject: Re: Ideas and questions...
Date: Saturday 28 November 1998

One of the things that seems to be at stake here is the possibility of collective action. I believe it is still fundamental to maintain and develop a cooperative, collective way of reacting to these clearly political situations—like the Whitney and the FRACs. In my previous email I suggested the need to develop alternative, original ways of collective action in order to combine them with more traditional methods, such as our collective letter to the Whitney. But to abandon the idea of collective action sounds to me like a terrible mistake, and we only need to look around to see how bad things get when there is no coordinated response to these kind of situations. I totally agree with Robert in his appreciation of the political dynamics of the art world as opposed to the more progressive and dynamic approach that other artistic disciplines maintain regarding situations like the FRACs. That does not only happen in the France but in the US as well, and I guess it is the main reason why the art environment is so conservative here. Basically, I do not think it is a question of opposing persuasion to enforcement or individual reactions to collective action. I think that, here in VOTI, we should develop original ways to operate within those terms. Because, as Bart says in his posting, it is in the name of an audience, of a people, that these issues should always be addressed.

Carlos

From: Bart De Baere
Subject: Re: Ideas and questions...
Date: Saturday 28 November 1998

Dear VOTI,

Carlos, if anything may change it's because ideas are heard. Collective letters of protest are worn out as a medium. They cause a psychological refusal (the us & the others effect, the others becoming "some protesters"). They can be grasped.

What may be more effective, I feel, is seriously and openly making your point as an individual. I'm willing to address Mr. Wellmax Anderson if he's the best addressee, to plant some doubt in his heart.[96] The raison d'etre of management in art institutions/the grandness of long term cultural visions/using curators as disposables.

Some of it would be:...I heard that (...heard through VOTI that if this would let him start to fear this unknown word through the succession of letters)...have the impression that...I might speak of this one Whitney Biennial as a focal point of an important development (not all beauty, though) and about a lecture by the now London based philosopher Irit Rogoff, one of the nicest lines of thinking I ever heard about audience participation, a lecture which focused on the Black Male exhibition.[97] I can make an effort because I trust your positions, but it'd better be my effort.

Letters seem more apt than fax in this for me. Technically. They hit better. They're opened and read with more respect. They're classified. These little things make the difference between being read and being forgotten. There might be better addressees for us, one bright or powerful—or both—member(s) of the board of trustees might do more. Or even an outsider with authority in that scene. Would have more effect. Would be more serious. Scaring people with their own shallowness, developing a ground in which the debate may become substantial again.

Yes, we shouldn't be silent, we should be talking every moment we can, and direct that as brightly as we can.

Same for the FRACs. I don't agree at all with Robert Fleck that the directors of those FRACs should have resigned. I spoke with Ami Barak today. He pointed out quite rightfully that by resigning he would be as well professionally as personally a winner. Applause. But that not everybody went to London in the Second World War, that there was resistance too. He said he is there first and foremost for the artists. I add—Ami would agree—and for the audience.

What's this, working for fascists? No, for a coalition including a fascistoid party. No, for a population of taxpayers. Leave the area bare? Let culture further collapse? People in Ami's position should start considering to resign as soon as they would be censored. He's not, as yet. If a fascistoid fraction of government—because of fear, ignorance or brightness—allow the other to be present, that's fine for me.

Since the Second World War, democracy has developed another set of tools besides elections only. It is established and accepted, the acceptance of specialists to whom politicians hand out part of their decision making power. This democratic instrument is still intact in the case of these FRACs. Contemporary art: I'm not wild about it but go ahead, that's what most of us experience, in the best cases.

Besides, aren't we all experiencing limits all of the time? Is there anything like a free zone? Is there a London today to go to? If you can develop things you want to engage with, but not all of them and not all of the ways you can engage through, is that enough to resign? Let's all resign then, from any activity beyond our kitchen.

Be honest, everybody's censored in this free world. Everybody gets money for certain things and no money for others. Every one of our actions is negotiated. Nothing is no strings attached. There are always expectations, traditions, formulations that will block communication, certain hardships we avoid like we choose for other hardships to endure them. I don't think that even in case of censorship you can draw a clear line of resignation. That's naive. Most of the censorship is implicit. And even, where to draw the line between cultural codes and censorship?

People in Ami's position should resign as soon as they're ordered to do things they can't engage with. Until then we should help them with whatever they ask us to help them with, for their artists, for their audience.

One step beyond that, what should we do? Perhaps we should take these extreme right wing parties seriously. Perhaps we should think there's some truthfulness in their drive. Perhaps we should try to figure out why they got this success, why people vote for them. Perhaps it's not only that their conclusions are wrong, but also that our cultural construct is vastly defective. Perhaps we have left them huge areas of culture. Perhaps we're the ones who are not serious enough. Perhaps the society of which we feel to be part is shallow and leaves a lot of people out in the cold. One example, the paysment de la culture from the extreme right. Isn't it normal people want to feel at home, and want their culture to be at home too? It's a much more complex game, much more time and energy consuming, much less buoyant and hip and easily transportable and reproducible also, to ground something in a local situation (and let it go beyond also). It means you never find the answer, it means you engage with messy, irresolvable questions.

Our local extreme right wing here is called "the Flemish Block." 25% In the city of Antwerp now, going on 40. Our artists and all of us dealing with contemporary culture used to state that art is art, not Flemish. Isn't it more interesting to continuously problematise this, to reclaim it, to develop visions of multiregionalism (we're this and that and that, each of them in an endless series of contradictory approaches, we're here and open nevertheless, we're us and of mixed origin nevertheless).

When Sarit Shapira made her Wandering Show in the Israel Museum, that was very precise.[98] Since then Nomadism became an easy variant to universalism, a way to avoid, rather than include. Perhaps we need slower, less immediately visible ways of dealing with art, more complicated ones rather than more complex ones.

Well, feel guilty for the length. Won't write for a week.

Is there a London today?

Bart De Baere.

From: Robert Fleck
Subject: Re: soft belly
Date: Saturday 28 November 1998

Dear Vasif Kortun,

1. Yes, it seems clear that the French FRAC institutions need to be reconsidered. The good ones, directed by Ami Barak (Languedoc-Roussillon), Nathalie Ergino (Champagne-Ardenne), Yannick Miloux (Rhone-Alpes) and Francois Taddei (Pays de la Loire), are very much discussing about it and they are trying to change very much their ways of working. But there is so much political intervention (on the local and the national level) that it is not easy for them.

2. Reasons for the absence of independent curators in France: the answer is easy, because everybody in France is working for the Ministry or the FRAC. No, not everybody, because there are two independent curators in France, Hans Ulrich and Hou Hanru...

Best Wishes,

Robert Fleck

From: Robert Fleck
Subject: Re: Ideas and questions...
Date: Saturday 28 November 1998

Dear Bart,

Thank you very much for the VOTI message. As some paragraphs concern my message
of Tuesday, just a short reply: I agree with you that the directors of these FRACs should
not resign now. After two days of talks in the "2eme Congres interprofessionnel de l'art
contemporain," in Tours, I am afraid about the violence of some attacks concerning
Ami.[99] I was not at all informed about some unacceptable things against Ami—we should
defend him. The whole thing became public this week: *Le Monde* made a big article about
attacks against Ami, and others, and there is a young artist who is doing anti-Semite and
xenophobic attacks especially against Ami. Perhaps we should express our solidarity with
Ami within some days.

About the question if the five FRAC directors should have resigned in March 98 when
de Front National was associated in five regions to the regional government: it is now a
kind of academic discussion, because these five FRAC directors decided not to resign (it
is their choice and we have to respect it), and it is clear that TODAY they cannot resign.
I still think that everything would be much clearer today if they would have shown any
reaction (to resign, or just to publish a clear statement) in March, when the Front National
entered five regional governments. The problem is, that the art scene in these regions did
not say anything and now they are forced to run after this early opportunity. By making
a collective and clear decision in March, they would have put an obligation to the French
Ministry of Culture to clarify its position towards the local authorities, and it would have
been possible—I am sure—to transform the five FRAC in these regions into independent
organisations, controlled by the state and no longer by the region. Then, everything would
have been clear. Instead of resigning, they also could have transformed their FRAC into
resistance laboratories, or whatever. But they just continued to work and to do exhibitions
as if their employers would not have changed from democratic to totalitarian parties.

Because any clear strategy is missing until today, the actual situation is getting worse and
worse every week. Everybody in the French art scene is accusing everybody of being unclear
towards the Front National, and the visual art scene is considered, by the public opinion,
to be very unclear with the Front National (the dance scene, the theater people, the music
scene are very active in the cultural resistance against the Front National, only the visual art
scene is appearing to be more and more compromised with the Front National—if this is true
or not, this is now the image in the public).

What is very special in the attacks against Ami is, that some people, especially one young
artist, are expressly accusing Ami to work for the Front National—and the same accusations

are clearly anti-Semite and directed against the only foreigner (besides Werner Spiess, director of Musee national d'art moderne) who is directing a French collection.

I also have to say, in my defense, that I never made any public declaration about this. In March, I wrote some private letters, to Ami, to two members of his board whom I know well, and to Yannick Miloux (FRAC Rhone-Alpes), saying to them that I will not work, in no way, for the FRAC of the five regions now co-directed by the Front National, adding that I personally think that they should resign and that we could help them to make a national event out of such a decision. My letters were known by everybody in the French art world within a week (I don't know how).

For me personally it is clear that I would immediately resign if the Front National were associated in the City Government of Nantes, where I am directing the post-graduate. I would even not wait one minute. My parents were big Nazis and it is physically impossible for me to work for Nazis. That's all.

Best Wishes,

Robert Fleck

From: Rebecca Gordon-Nesbitt
Subject: Re: Ideas and questions...
Date: Saturday 28 November 1998

Dear Robert,

I must congratulate you on your engaging and empowering VOTI posting. I absolutely agree that fascism/anti-Semitism cannot be tolerated under any circumstances. I find it hard to believe that Ami Barak could be associated with the Front National & agree that a message of support to him should be forthcoming from VOTI. He is widely known amongst the best British artists as an artists' hero.

Best regards,

Rebecca

From: Octavio Zaya
Subject: Re: Ideas and questions.
Date: Monday 30 November 1998

Dear members of VOTI,

1. By signing VOTI's "Whitney Letter," I'm just exercising my right to be disgusted at the new censoring policies of the Whitney Museum. I'm just expressing my solidarity with two courageous colleagues who have been wronged by this museum. I don't want to convince Mr. Anderson or his trustees. I don't have such illusions. I just want him to know that there are a lot of us who don't like what he is doing, who will confront him at every turn.

2. How did we get from denouncing the treatment of two colleagues to an apology for collaborating with fascism (whatever the merits of particular cases)?

How did we get from a call for collective action against the National Front to consider the "truthfulness" of the fascist drive?

Perhaps equating/confusing resistance to collaboration (as Bart seems to be doing) can help explain the ellipsis.

Who's talking of a free zone? Who's looking for a "London"?

3. Regarding the reasons for the extreme right parties success in France and other European countries, conveniently ignoring how they relentlessly play out the unemployment and racial cards at election time against immigrants and non-whites (residents and citizens alike) could definitely keep us wondering about their "truthfulness."

4. I appreciate your posting, Carlos. And I thank you Robert for yours. Please let us know what you think we should do to help your colleagues.

Yours truly,

Octavio

From: Aleksandra Kostic
Subject: sparks from Maribor
Date: [unavailable]

Dear VOTI people (reminds me of Village People),

This is my first approach to you. As many other people I read over in one extended evening all messages from you and here I am. I'm with you.

I agree with Robert Fleck about silent agreement until we are not expressing our disagreement (Carlos would say this is for lazy ones, ha ha). This is about Whitney letter and all collective activities in the future. But I think we should understand if Vasif Kortun or someone else is not emotionally loaded about certain problem, which sometimes seems to be far away. For me it exists as examples. Positive ideas, yes! But what is this?

If we are talking about political orientations, what you should be or not as a curator, I would like hear how is this connected to certain art problems. I'm a bio-communist and art for me is life itself. Left or right, all forms are implemented in life. I can't remember, do I know any right oriented curator? How does it look, a right curator or artist. The right one—the real one, the left one—the virtual one?

As far as I get, you are pretty anxious about curatorialship. In this case I must tell you something optimistic. There is a Slovenian weekly magazine for women, called Jana— Jane (Tarzan doesn't exist unfortunately)—that is one of the most popular magazines in general in Slovenia. Jana has every year a vote action for Slovenian woman of the year. Around ten women of different activities and age are nominated and this year is for the first time nominated a woman curator, a manager of the biggest Slovenian institution for contemporary art, Zdenka Badovinac, a VOTI member. The winner is promoted like a president in Slovenian mass media. Concurrence is heavy, but we in Kibla will vote for Zdenka, because we think that she is the right person. Hermeticism is a grave. At the same time I'm asking for permission to publish interesting issues of VOTI. "Who is afraid of a black man?"

Aleksandra Kostic[100]

From: Robert Fleck
Subject: [unavailable]
Date: [unavailable]

Dear Rebecca, dear VOTI,

Some more normal information from France:

Last week, November 26 and 27, the SECOND NATIONAL CONGRESS FOR CONTEMPORARY ART was held in Tours, France. The meeting was attended by nearly all directors and curators of FRAC, museums, Centre d'art etc., by the main art critics and all important people of the French Ministry of Culture. The general subject was *"art—une education a faire"* ("art—an education to do"). Therefore the main subject was the idea that the French art scene has to find a new relationship towards the public. There were two events occurring (besides artists talks of Raymond Hains, Luciano Fabro and Francois Morellet, which were the best things in the whole event):

The minister, Catherine Trautmann, declared in a very convincing speech that 1) she personally will not tolerate any main influence of the extreme right wing people in national cultural politics, 2) that after five years of continuously reduced budgets, 1999 will bring about 14 million dollars more budget for the contemporary art department of her ministry (which is a big sum), 3) that she will stay in function until the next presidential elections in three years (against many rumors that are saying she would leave to a cultural job in the European Community), 4) that these three years will be mainly orientated to have more exchange between French artists, institutions abroad and programmes for foreign curators in France.

Speaking for the association of the French curators, Nathalie Ergino (FRAC Champagne-Ardenne) read a manifesto saying that the association will back any colleague who will be censured by the right/extreme right-wing governments in some parts of France. This declaration was very clear and determined.

The ten artists of the post-graduate-programme in Nantes, which I am directing, interfered in the congress with a two-minute-video, which was projected at the beginning of every speech in the congress (like the advertising films in a cinema before the main film), declaring that all these people were expressly invited for a free studio visit to the artists. The ten artists of the Nantes post-graduate 1998/99 are:

International Post-Graduate Programme, Ecole Regionale des Beaux-Arts de Nantes.
1998/99: Peio Aguirre (ESP), Simona Denicolai (IT), Dettie Flynn (IRL), Thierry Froger (F), Uta Kollmann (A), Renata Poljak (HR), Tanja Ostojic (YU), Diego Schindler (D), Nina Sidow (D),

Liena Vayzman (USA) Information: Robert Fleck February 10-27, 1999: Post-Graduate Nantes at ARCO-International Art Fair Madrid + Exhibition Sala de Juventud, Comunidad de Madrid.

(In fact, besides Fabro, Ami Barak and myself, the post-graduate artists were the only foreigners participating in this congress.)

Best Wishes,

Robert Fleck

From: Susan Hapgood and Carlos Basualdo
Subject: Re: Whitney Action
Date: Monday 30 November 1998

Before we send the collective letter to the Whitney (which we will do tomorrow at noon),
it is important to make clear that it will list all the names of the members of the Union who
have not asked to be excluded from it—so far, only one. We understand that unless clearly
stated, everybody else is in conformity with the decision of the majority. So please, if you do
not want to participate, let us know before tomorrow at 12 AM. We also wanted to remind
you that the Whitney action started today with people faxing the letter on their own.

Thanks a lot.

Susan and Carlos

From: Udo Kittelmann
Subject: Re: Whitney letter
Date: Monday 30 November 1998

Dear Susan,

I apologize sincerely not being in touch with you before regarding the letter that should be sent today to the Whitney, but I had not received any e-mails since 23 November. The reason might be that all e-mails addressed to me are going first to my girlfriend and afterwards to my office at the Kunstverein. I just spoke to Carlos and he informed me about the recent development and he asked me to contact you right away. Of course, I am proud to join with the rest of the group in signing the letter and also I will fax it individually to the Whitney. But may I ask you to make it possible to fax it or to e-mail me once again the recent version of the text.

As I got from some older e-mails, you worked mainly on the draft joining all ideas together—thank you so much for doing that work.

All my best,

Udo

From: Susan Hapgood
Subject: what models do we have?
Date: Monday 30 November 1998

There is a somewhat obvious but important point no one has made in the recent heated discussion about how to make a difference, or just to express one's position regarding situations one is averse to. In distinct contrast to the seventies, and to "worn-out" letters of protest, the Internet encourages new forms of collective action. I understand Vasif's dismay over the New York-centric situation and the labor-union collective approach, but that doesn't negate the potential we have in our hands. Because of its medium, VOTI can be relatively loose, efficient and potentially powerful. It seems evident that VOTI is very adaptable and amorphous, ready to focus on whatever its members choose to focus on.

I don't believe that anyone, on their own, would have done anything about the Whitney situation without the collective online dialogue and the particular group dynamic that spontaneously combusted here into a heartfelt call for action. Vasif and Bart, what kinds of collective actions do you think would be effectual for VOTI to consider (keeping the Internet as a factor in the equation)? Or do you think it's better as a think tank, and that individuals should take action rather than the Union as a whole?

All best wishes,

Susan Hapgood

From: Susan Hapgood
Subject: Report
Date: Tuesday 1 December 1998

The following letter was faxed today to the Whitney and the New York Times.

Dr. Maxwell L. Anderson,
Director Whitney Museum of American Art
945 Madison Avenue
New York, NY 10021
Fax: 212-570-18XX

Dear Dr. Anderson:

We wish to express our opposition to your treatment of curators Thelma Golden and
Elisabeth Sussman. The recent restructuring of the curatorial departments at the Whitney
Museum of American Art is indicative of a managerial approach that has been slowly
developing in a number of major art museums. Beyond our wish to show support for
fellow curators Golden and Sussman, we see your recent actions as signals of a pervasive
disrespect for curatorial practice, and as signs of aversion to some of the most aesthetically
and intellectually challenging experiments in contemporary art.

Curators at many institutions today are caught in a kind of double bind. Art museums pride
themselves on their proximity to an academic environment, positing scholarship as one of
their highest goals. Yet due to shifts in the infrastructure of funding, museums have also
adopted corporate management models with the corollary effect that curators are treated
as expendable workers. Contrary to both of these models, curators do not have the job
security and intellectual support enjoyed by professors in the university system, nor do they
enjoy salaries comparable to corporate employees. As a result, they are forced to stand on
increasingly shaky ground, while serving as the primary source of ideas for their institutions'
exhibition programming. The door is then open to all kinds of abuses.

We find your actions in regard to these particular individuals to be a form of intellectual
gentrification, if not censorship. The fact that Thelma Golden and Elisabeth Sussman
presided over the controversial 1993 Biennial Exhibition, one of the most stimulating
and contentious contemporary art exhibitions presented after the gutting of the
National Endowment for the Arts, or that Golden then went on to curate "Black Male:
Representations of Masculinity in Contemporary American Art," are coincidences that
hardly escape us. Since when did exhibitions that set attendance records and raise genuine
intellectual questions become a failure? Of course no one is required to subscribe to the
aesthetic options of these two curators, but to admit that they are part of an important
debate, itself linked to a vibrant focus of artistic experimentation, is surely necessary for

a public institution that seeks to represent artistic practice today. To sidestep this debate over politics and identity in a multicultural, globally integrating society is to set a timid, unproductive, yet perhaps more easily manageable agenda for the Whitney. This troubling direction reflects a broader conservative trend, the mistaken return to an outdated conception of cultural history.

We feel it is imperative to mark our opposition to your actions, lest they be misperceived as the innocuous restructuring of an organization like any other in the private sphere. Curating is an eminently public activity and must remain so, if the visual arts are to continue to generate the curiosity, the enthusiasm and the commitment that sustain our efforts as professionals in this field.

Sincerely yours,

Monica Amor
Zdenka Badovinac
Bart de Baere
Wayne Baerwaldt
Carlos Basualdo
Daniel Birnbaum
Francesco Bonami
Dan Cameron
Christophe Cherix
Carolyn Christov-Bakargiev
Lisa Corrin
Jordan Crandall
Amada Cruz
Okwui Enwezor
Robert Fleck
Douglas Fogle
Jesus Fuenmayor
Bettina Funcke
Rebecca Gordon-Nesbitt
Hou Hanru
Susan Hapgood

Jens Hoffmann
Brian Holmes
Udo Kittelmann
Aleksandra Kostic
Maria Lind
Rosa Martinez
Laurence Miller
Viktor Misiano
Akiko Miyake
Louise Neri
Michelle Nicol
Hans Ulrich Obrist
Kathrin Rhomberg
Liisa Roberts
Jose Ignacio Roca
Yukiko Shikata
Nancy Spector
Barbara Vanderlinden
Peter Weibel
Octavio Zaya

From: Susan Hapgood
Subject: a few announcements
Date: Thursday 24 December 1998

Dear VOTI members,

Our letter to the Whitney has been posted online by *Nettime* and by *Artnet* Magazine, and it has been sent to several magazines.[101] Incidentally, Lisa Phillips, who was the museum's chief curator, recently announced that she will be leaving the Whitney to become Director of the New Museum of Contemporary Art.

Closer to VOTI, Francesco Bonami has recently been named Senior Curator of the Museum of Contemporary Art in Chicago, where he will begin January 1, 1999.

We'll be resuming our conversation about the art world economy, the roles of curators, contractual agreements, and related issues of money and commitment, after January 1 with artist Ben Kinmont as our guest.

But send messages whenever you wish—many of us will presumably be online throughout the holidays.

Merry Christmas and Happy New Year!

Susan Hapgood

Chapter IV

The Trial of Pol Pot

The opening e-mail from Brian Holmes is a response to a conversation about the "local" being held within a series of posts that can be read in the second half of Chapter II *The Economy of the Art World*. Yet, by citing a specific exhibition, *Trial of Pol Pot*, which Holmes had recently seen at Magazin, Centre National d'Art Contemporain, Grenoble, as an example for his argument, he launches a whole new chain of e-mail correspondence. The *Trial of Pol Pot* was initiated as a research project and later formed as an exhibition by artists Liam Gillick and Philippe Parreno. Although invited as a guest commentator to the VOTI forum "The Economy of the Art World," Gillick sends his first e-mail to the forum in response to Holmes' comments about *Trial of Pol Pot*. A heated and fast-paced debate between Holmes and Gillick, with Rebecca Gordon-Nesbitt, one of the coordinators of the exhibition and a VOTI member also commenting, lasts for several weeks early in 1999. It gradually moves away from specific references to close on ideas around networks and channels.

During the making of this publication a research document for the project *Trial of Pol Pot* was shared by Gillick (p.403).

In order of appearance:
Brian Holmes, Liam Gillick, Carlos Basualdo, Rebecca Gordon-Nesbitt, Jordan Crandall and Cornelia Lauf.

From: Brian Holmes
Subject: territories, cultural actions
Date: Tuesday 15 December 1998

Hello Votis

I'd like to answer Carlos and contribute to the general thread of the past few days. For me, the question of fascism comes down to another question: the local. By that I don't mean romantic rootedness in a place, a language, a tradition. Nor an exoticizing ideal of "authenticity." The local is the people in front of you, their ideas, attitudes, emotions—which might include notions of rootedness, authenticity, white or black identity...The local is what you have to live with.

Since the eighties, the global has been a way to construct a locality in a nomadic, abstract space of flows. But that locality is only open to a small fraction of the people living on any given territory. Fascism, wherever it arises, asks the question: can you still live with the majority of the people on your local territory? Violence from the suburbs and the ghettos asks the same question, but so far the answer has been a cop or a wall. Fascism is political, seeks to be hegemonic, and in many places now stands a chance of giving orders to the cop, of deciding to put "us" up against the wall. Which at least forces people like us to recognize their own complicity and to take the question seriously.

Bart said it all with one image: a banlieue severed from the core city, thrown back on its own frustrations while the professionals perfect their skills and their global deals behind a wall of freeways. That's why I was not so keen on the curator's contract debate. Focusing on the perfect security of individual rights can be an effective set of blinders. Every good professional becomes a nomad monad: travel light, travel alone. Meanwhile the local keeps pressing its questions, first with a rock in your face, then with organized thugs backed up by a political program and maybe a set of loyalty oaths—like the university professors just got in Belgrade.

The best economic and social analysis of globalization doesn't help anybody if you do nothing but analyze. That's what the politicians do in France, talking on the left and the right about the *fracture sociale*. Then when the unemployed start demonstrating, they say "we're waiting for economic growth." As if the others could just keep on waiting!

You get the same thing in so-called communicative, "relational" art: like the "Trial of Pol Pot" that I just saw at the Magasin in Grenoble.[102] Who are these artists relating to, why, what for? That installation isn't just a refusal of history and a denial of any public capacity for judgment in the "postmodern" age. As an art piece it's also hermetically closed to the understanding and the use of most everybody living on the territory of Grenoble. Sorry folks, I hate to say it, but a lot of the art being shown in France now is the prestige game of an elite protecting its delocalized privileges. Carlos, the idea of producing the local through interaction and audience participation is right on, and I agree that it depends on a strong fiction. One so strong that it can touch the ideas, attitudes and emotions of the people in front of you, so real that it can cross the freeway dividers, put the city back in touch with the country, or the North back in touch with the South. Not to make them think the same "collective" thoughts—just so they can start talking again.

At some point I got bored with most of what I see in the museums. It's interesting to work with people outside your immediate horizons. I do a lot with the group Ne Pas Plier—activist stuff, graphic art in the streets for political demonstrations, with unemployed groups, Algerian exiles, neighborhood committees. Turning the street back into a public space and working in the art scene that's considered outdated, which means not formatted for New York and LA, or more precisely, for a curator's fantasy of cultural rivalry with the metropoles. But there are lots of ways to revise art history, and you can start outside the museums.

Marc Pataut and I are doing a project that is not just an exhibition but a way to publicly raise the question of the territory, by looking into the notion of the *pays*—which would be a typical neofascist theme. In French, *pays*, is ambiguous; it means "the country," at once a rural area and the nation. We're working with a popular-education group, Peuple et Culture, in a little town called Tulle with a small industrial core on a rural territory. The kind of town left washed up by globalization. The idea is to make images of the area by listening to the people, hanging out with them, enjoying life and finding out what this place means to those who live there. Then, as the work is produced, we're going to show it in the context of public discussions about the economic and social future of the *pays*. We always aim to strike a debate, with concrete issues, politics and economics, made more emotionally real and hopefully more open by the artistic activity. As that debate unfolds, an artist named Francois Deck is going to gather questions—not aesthetically scrambled information, but comprehensible questions, carefully framed by the people with a stake in finding the answers. When the whole thing is over, we'll go elsewhere with the pictures and the questions—from one local reality to another, just like we already brought images from a Paris banlieue to Tulle. We'll bring Tulle back to Paris too. Everybody in the country matters.

Revisionism in one *pays*? Bart's right, the European utopia of spreading culture from the top down has been a failure. But today in France we can look back to a left-wing cultural organization like Peuple et Culture and try to remember what made it such a popular and intellectual success in the fifties and sixties. We can try to revise our views of what audience participation might be, what links can really be made between art and everyday life. That kind of activity might help win a local audience back for wider themes of international solidarity. It might also help get rid of the whole idea of a "canon"—which isn't much use in democracies anyway. But to make any social change, you've probably got to step outside your strictly professional milieu. Give up the monad thing, go into the backwaters, the forgotten places—like the street, the neighborhoods—not just the countryside.
And what about displacement? I'm an American, but I live on the outskirts of Paris, that's

my territory. I try to make what I know of the US-centered world system available to people who have to deal with its effects on their lives. Everywhere is connected to everywhere else—there's also an European Commission program on the idea of *pays*, for instance. But I think the EC planners' idea of "territorial governance" will just be the self-administration of frustration, unless the people out in the countryside force the country as a whole to wring some other changes from the EC. People are starting to realize how to pull the strings of power in the displaced localities. Activism has become very interesting.

Communications and information are an issue in even the smallest corners of the world. You can curate a show with help from sociology—check out Alain Touraine, "Critique of Modernity":

"How much longer will it take to rediscover human beings and social relations behind the technologies and to understand that everywhere there is a confrontation between socially opposite ways of using information and organizing communication: either abstractly, to reinforce information flows which are also flows of money and power, or concretely, to strengthen the dialogue between speakers situated in unequal relations of power and authority?"[103]

That's the question that the fascists are asking too—but they've got the worst answers.

Can artists and curators come up with better ones?

Brian

From: Liam Gillick
Subject: Re: territories, cultural actions
Date: Wednesday 6 January 1999

Brian Holmes shows off his lack of agency and incomplete relation to the culture around him; if he had made an effort to even glance at the invitation card, he would have noticed that one of the coordinators of the show is also on this voti list.[104]

I am amazed by his lack of faith and patronising approach to the "people of the territory of Grenoble," whatever that might mean, a typical example of his strangulated language.

I am sure if we passed on his generalised received ideas to the people of the territory of Grenoble, they would have a good laugh. If Brian Holmes was keeping in parallel with the cultural activity around him, he would have noticed that to focus on territory is not to focus upon anything at all, but to avoid dealing with any specific issues from the recent past or the near future.

The biggest refusal of history would be to ignore the specific events, and keep yourself within the abstract territories of neo-academic abstraction, just where the fascist powers you mention are happy for you to remain.

Best wishes

Liam

From: Brian Holmes
Subject: Re: Trial of Pol Pot
Date: Thursday 7 January 1999

Hello VOTIs and Happy New Year—

Liam Gillick is irked by my remarks (in a December 15 post) on his and Philippe Parreno's exhibition, "The Trial of Pol Pot"; he thinks such remarks had no place in a forum that includes one of the coordinators of the show. But I understood this forum as a public space, just as the show is presented publicly, for all eyes and all opinions. So rather than retracting my comments I'd just like to clarify them. Which requires describing the show a little.

The project is about "the faculty of judgment, about judging and the multiplicity of viewpoints with regard to an event of which it has been impossible to find a representation or produce an image." It's said in the introductory brochure that Liam Gillick and Philippe Parreno decided not to try to document the mysterious trial of Pol Pot by his comrades in Cambodia. "Instead, they chose to conduct a research project involving a dozen artists and curators, or 'supervisors,' to whom they submitted for approval or correction the successive stages of the project, along with a set of questions, in order to obtain a multiplicity of viewpoints."

What one saw in the multiple exhibition spaces were phrases in French and English, printed in large black characters at varying heights on the wall. A few examples: "judgments multiple et divises" (multiple and divided judgments)— "broadcasting from one location while receiving from another location and then suppressing the results of the entire process" —"what do I care about the stupid things I did yesterday?"—*"jusqu'a quel point sera-t-il necessaire de juger de l'efficacite des solutions proposes?"* (to what extent will it be necessary to judge the effectiveness of the solutions proposed?).

Apparently the communication process that generated these sentences took place by "Internet and e-mails," but the artists wanted "an element in the project that couldn't be sent over the Internet," hence the "fading light in different colors" that completed the scenography. But there was also a "present" for the visitor; a beige poster with garbled black texts. These, it is said, were the last comments sent by the "supervisors," all superimposed "to make a picture in words of what it might look like if you really did apply one idea and then another and then another." That's the image you're supposed to take home.

Why am I critical of this exhibition? Simply because of what it represents, or more precisely, because of the reasonable interpretation I make of the relation between its content and social reality. Democracy stands or falls on processes of collective deliberation, involving judgment on possible actions. New communication technologies have opened up a lot of interesting possibilities in that area, at a time when the expansion of democratic debate across national borders has been made even more necessary by the globalization of economic power. But this show denies the possibility of making sense through deliberative procedures.

There has been a lot of 90s art which purports to be about debate, and only presents garbled information or empty stage scenes. This show is exemplary because it asserts the impossibility of judgment. It is as though the show tried to capitalize on the renewed interest (here in France anyway) in procedures of political debate and deliberation—but with no chance to even imagine an expansion of the debate beyond the inner circle of those directly involved. That's why I said the show is hermetic, closed to local input as well as possible understanding. As Serge Daney wrote: "In a period where contradiction is no longer the motor of anything, the compromise formation that Freudians know so well risks becoming the major trope of social communication."[105] Here the compromise seems to be: we'll present a debate about an international issue, conducted with the latest technology, but we'll keep the proceedings for ourselves and show only gibberish. I think that's a cynical picture of a new and important possibility for communication. And I'm tired of that kind of cynicism being exalted artistically, so I prefer to clearly say what I think about it.

If the impossibility of participating in the publicly funded international communications game were to be doubled by the impossibility of even commenting on it, then the compromise-formation (or representation) would effectively become a social symptom, with all the passivity and repression that implies. But the conformism that keeps people silent in the face of mystification—or that keeps them "in parallel with the cultural activity around them," as Liam Gillick would have it—is hopefully a thing of the past.

Best to all,

Brian Holmes

From: Liam Gillick
Subject: Re: Trial of Pol Pot
Date: Thursday 7 January 1999

Carlos wrote:

Sorry Liam, but I feel a little bit lost after reading your posting. Could you please clarify to which of Brian's interventions are you responding? Some more background information on the subject of your posting will also be appreciated so we can make this discussion wider.

Thanks,

Carlos Basualdo[106]

Liam replies:

Dear Carlos,

I was responding to a few remarks in Brian's contribution the other day where he mentioned the research project Philippe Parreno and I proposed for the Magasin in Grenoble earlier this year so that he could talk about his own project and define it by default.

Liam continues:

Here is my comment upon his comment. I think that the points he raises about compromise and his perception of a singular and ignorant audience are interesting and need some more general discussion. I think it might be better to open this up and address some issues that arise from the matter rather than keep to the details of Liam and Brian. But here is some more ping-pong just to make things clear.

Brian Holmes comments in relation to my response are interesting but fundamentally flawed. First he has not read my short response properly. I was not suggesting that discussion of the project is to be suppressed in a forum such as this. I was merely pointing out that from the tone of his initial remarks it was clear that he was not aware that one of the coordinators of the project might be close at hand and therefore available for direct communication.

I wrote:

Brian Holmes shows off his lack of agency and incomplete relation to the culture around him; if he had made an effort to even glance at the invitation card, he would have noticed that one of the coordinators of the show is also on this voti list.

By this I meant to imply that had he noticed that my name is on the Voti list, he wouldn't have made his comments so indirectly as a way to puff his own project by default. Anyway.

His arguments remain occasionally pedestrian, strange and weirdly defeatist.

Why be so proud of such distance from contemporary discourse in the field of visual culture? Why be so sure that the "people of Grenoble" are so incapable of deconstructing the show? Goodness, what would they do without people like Holmes to tell them they can't possibly understand something. This was not our experience in Grenoble, and I repeat that the arrogance of his assertion is as much an insult to the developed critical culture there as it is a perverse distancing device employed by him in order to justify his role as some latter-day torch-bearer who obviously sees himself as leading the culturally impoverished through the maze of cultural signifiers without ever turning back to notice that they are not following him. That he only finds gibberish in quite clear statements in English and French combined with the contextualising structure of a contemporary art space and a recent event is beyond comprehension. He has an implicated role in the definition of our culture and is not a passive receiver of presented art works any more than anyone else. Art can function well to provide a way to negotiate events in a form that is not already used up within anthropology, context art, television, film and other communication media. Maybe he would prefer the neo-Duchampianism of a reading/information room or better still that we ignore ethical complexity and stick with abstracted misreadings of Deleuze in the form of claiming to deal with "territory." Such a lapse back into the comfort of the seventies would be irresponsible and dull.

As for this passage:

There has been a lot of 90s art which purports to be about debate and only presents garbled information or empty stage scenes. This show is exemplary because it asserts the impossibility of judgment.

It is here that we get to the heart of Holmes's problem. Debate was at the centre of our project; it was the result of debate. It couldn't have occupied the gallery without the process of debate that he himself describes in his lengthy response. So it does not purport to be about debate; it is the result of debate. If that debate appears garbled to him, then maybe he should question his own perception rather than resorting to the classic conservative line of suggesting anything that he doesn't understand must therefore be about the "impossibility of judgment." His fear of negotiating the constant reformulation of compromise in the hands of corporate and governmental agencies is his problem, not one that Philippe or I have shied away from.

Having said all this, there are many details that Holmes brings up in his writing and his direct comments on this matter that have either been influential upon Philippe and myself, or were starting points for our project. So maybe it is time to broaden the debate and as Brian

Holmes himself suggests, look at some issues beyond our small group. I trust my comments are received in the spirit of this forum, which is the way they are intended and we can use the complications thrown up by this issue to develop some new strategies.

Best wishes,

Liam Gillick

From: Carlos Basualdo
Subject: Re: Trial of Pol Pot
Date: Friday 8 January 1999

I think that at this point it is important to clarify that besides the VOTI members, Brian Holmes, Liam Gillick and Ben Kinmont have been invited to be part of the VOTI list as guests for the current forum on "The Economy of the Art World." Brian was the first guest to join us, as did sometime later Ben and Liam, in that order—hi Ben, are you there? The constituency of VOTI has been changing since the Union was founded and it changes all the time—Jordan, could you please post an updated list of the members?—so it is no surprise that at some point we do not know who is in the list. Having said that, we will do our best to keep you updated on the most recent changes. And besides, I believe that the discussion that Brian and Liam are sustaining is a good example of what VOTI should become: a really open and free forum where we can express our intellectual concerns, in the understanding that we will be always ready to open our arguments to a wider discussion.

Carlos

From: Brian Holmes
Subject: Re: Trial of Pol Pot
Date: Friday 8 January 1999

Dear Liam Gillick:

In comparison to the first, I find your second response to be a good deal closer the spirit of polemical debate, which I like. You have not yet in the least convinced me though—I think your show is very characteristic of a kind of ironic presentation which, rather than providing anything which a viewer can use and build on, seeks instead to evoke sheer admiration for an elaborate bluff. For me, in that show, you are working in prestige market, which I would find simply uninteresting were it not so widespread that I feel like actively opposing it.

That said, why don't we see what happens if you, I and potentially others on the list take the time to actually talk about the specific content of a show, its style and what its intervention in various cultural contexts can mean or evoke? That kind of debate is what the game is about, no? We might learn something. Unless you or others think it's boring, in which case I have plenty of other things to do.

Just one further point for now: I could hardly have been more direct in choosing your show to illustrate my remarks. I might have said something vague and general to illustrate my ideas. But I prefer to name things, so I gave the title of the show. Having had no contact with you before now, I didn't feel particularly compelled to say, "You know, Liam, your show was seriously flawed." Of course, that people should get pissed off when you criticize their show is kind of natural, and generally whether you address them directly by name or not, they'll take offense and find fault with the form of address. It can be interesting to go a lot further with specific questions of form.

Best,

Brian Holmes

From: Brian Holmes
Subject: Re: The Trial of Pol Pot
Date: Sunday 10 January 1999

Hello Votis!

It's possible to do really good TV. Yesterday while traveling I was thinking about an episode from Chris Marker's TV series, "L'Histoire de la Chouette," where Cornelius Castoriadis maliciously describes just how unruly the Athenian democracy was—all the rhetorical mud-slinging that could go into the process of arriving at a collective decision.[107] Apparently it got nasty sometimes. And yet Castoriadis had the highest ideal of that process.

I couldn't shake this Pol Pot thing off my mind, and since no one else has written in the interim, I'm really going to try to read the show in detail, to see what can be understood from the form and expression. I think the effort is justified, because I've seen many shows that derive from the same basic principles. What follows is a continuation of what I wrote earlier, so I won't re-quote the statements written on the walls of the show. What I will do is to respond to the serious critiques that Liam Gillick made of my argument—beyond all the mud-slinging, I mean. The best place to start is with this question from his January 7 post:

"Why be so sure that the 'people of Grenoble' are so incapable of deconstructing the show."

First off, I guess most people don't waste their time deconstructing it. But anyway: to propose something elaborately contrived for deconstruction is also called irony: you say something you don't believe in, as a challenge for the listener to figure out what you do believe, or as a wink to a third party who knows what you believe and enjoys watching the listener squirm. Assuming we're in the first case, what's the veiled message? The brochure says the whole thing's about Pol Pot, but that we know nothing about Pol Pot's trial, that "we have no images of the period when Cambodia was ruled by the Khmer Rouge," so that the "research" would have to be a matter of exchange among the artists and their so-called supervisors—and that "one of the essential questions of this project is whether we are still capable of judging without having recourse to images." Despite that metaphysical anguish, the brochure also states:

"Philippe and Liam...believe that if you are interested in the details of events like these there are plenty of direct sources of information, from newspapers and magazines to the Internet and e-mails...They think art becomes useful when it tries to find a way around all these forms of information exchange. Art can offer us a route through complicated ideas without making precise pictures or just presenting documentation. In a way what they have done is present a psychological portrait of an event."

So they have a psychological portrait—the fragmented phrases on the wall, referring not to Pol Pot's reality, but to their group psychology—plus what they describe as a "picture in words"—the garbled poster of the supervisors' final comments, superimposed one on the other. Images of another sort. To read all that ironically and to reach the conclusion that Liam Gillick suggested in his January 7 reply to me—that the show is about "the constant reformulation of compromise in the hands of corporate and governmental agencies"—the people of Grenoble and everywhere else have to assume that everything said not just on the walls but also in the brochure is a contrivance, a bluff. So in this ironic reading, even the "psychological portrait of an event" is just bullshit, and the supposed "debate" can only have been about how to contrive this very-hard-to-deconstruct object, which ultimately leads us to shadowy corporate and governmental agencies and their reformulation of an unidentified compromise. The "debate" is then itself a shadowy, veiled process—and the artists themselves have moved very close to the shadowy people they are supposedly talking about.

But wait, there is more: the words on the walls are said to be not only "a territory from which questions can arise," but also to be "the set of a film or TV studio waiting for shooting to begin." And the brochure (not the artists, because this is all ironic!) says at the end that the first idea was to invite Robert De Niro "to explain the concepts behind the show and to attempt to find a way to play a character that cannot be represented." Now that the show is done, the brochure says, they are going to invite him again to come and "explain everything" (the killing fields and their show?). They'll film the whole event, which will be private, and then they'll make a book out of it. They say.

Irony or not, what's the interest here? If you can stomach all this confused fiction or veiled debate being applied to the trial and therefore judgment of Pol Pot—which I find hard to do because we're talking about one of the major cases of genocide in human history—then the ironic reading or the so-called "deconstruction" apparently delivers this message: corporate and government agencies reformulate the international compromise about mass murder through the creation of phony Hollywood images, which can still be judged, unlike individual viewpoints which are multiple, fragmented, scrambled. Again, so what? Is this a more convincing critique of the spectacle than Guy Debord's? Have we really learned anything about the supposed role of the Internet in this, much less the economy? Just how long are government agencies—in this case, an art center—going to go on dishing out recycled, conventionalized critique of the "spectacle society" to the public? And then snickering when you point out that they too have mounted a spectacle, and trying to make you squirm by saying "Yeah, that's just it, our nihilism is so total, didn't you get the irony"? I got it a long time ago. The question about whether one can only judge on the basis of images which are presented as always being phony is a way of hanging onto, maintaining, and in a certain way even promoting the situation that the artists claim to be critiquing. It's zero art, hot air and it fills up institutions which otherwise could contribute in all kinds of ways to making the world a better place to live in.

Liam Gillick accuses me of being attached to the dull seventies. That was the time when the hierarchical powers of the western societies had to deal with what Michel de Certeau called la prise de parole—the fact that people spoke up, refused to be sheep.[108] You stand up, say who you are, what your viewpoint is on a situation, and what your intention or question is. Since '68, it has been forbidden to forbid that freedom of speech, even in the mass media. That's a lasting victory. One of the major ways that has been found to stifle that victory is to fragment people's speech so that they're supposedly represented, but no intention or question gets through. Another way is to blur their presence, to jam their speech, to drown it out by overload or superimposition. Anybody who speaks up today knows that. When you question people like Liam Gillick or Philippe Parreno whose artwork reflects this dynamic, they're likely to borrow your argument and say they are critiquing exactly those two procedures for stifling individual speech. I think it's interesting to ask oneself: are they not just mimicking how the dominant processes work? Aren't they engaging in that mimicry because they've found that it works, that it keeps them in the international prestige market, comfortably far from any territory and anything specific to deal with? If they really wanted to critique or change things, wouldn't they do something else, something deeper, more precise, riskier, with more content, more communicative power?

Look at one of Liam Gillick's pieces as it's reproduced on the cover of a major catalogue documenting twenty years of exhibitions at the Consortium in Dijon: you see a "conversation" table, empty but for a water carafe and a few glasses, with designer chairs around it. In the background are four washing machines where Maurizio Cattelan has supposedly put the notes taken by the artists during the preparation of the group exhibition of which this table is the emblematic piece. In the text published in the catalogue, Gillick expresses evident admiration for a friend who, after a short stint in the advertising industry, got a job in the government: that way, whenever he wants to talk with somebody he goes straight to the top, he doesn't have to deal with any intermediaries. There's the fantasy, the object of mimicry. But once again, apparently the show is all about some TV program, "Moral Maze."

The reason I don't like this stuff is that it's so vapid, so cynical, so useless. As though Pop art marked the historical limit of people's ability to know and transform the world—Liam Gillick mentioned fear in his January 7 post, he said I was afraid of what's being negotiated in the world today. Fantastic things are going on in the world today, right alongside very scary things, brutal things, slow exterminations as well as fast ones. A large amount of real debate is taking place because people are at once afraid and amazed to discover that there are great possibilities to speak, to enter into relations, to do something different, or on the contrary, to give new breadth to what they've been doing all along. All these people try in various ways to convince "the people" that the world can be different—because the people, popular sovereignty in a democracy, are the only even partially effective ethical procedures we so far have for making collective decisions by other means than sheer power and covert influence. Even if the institutions for articulating that popular sovereignty—courts, schools, the press, museums, etc.—are flawed and are also sorely damaged by the worst aspects of the contemporary media, that's no reason to flush them all down into some cesspit of obscurity.

Finally, the question of territory. Many people now think, like me, that it's important to take stock of the differences between the levels of transnational circulation and the physical, territorial conditions that affect human beings where they live, drink the water, raise their kids and so on. These people don't get the idea of territory from misreading Deleuze, as Liam Gillick suggests, but from their experience and their contact with other inquiring minds. But anyway, there are thousands of reasons to speak up, thousands of effects or non-effects of it. There are artistic ways to speak up, indirect, emotional, subterranean, powerful ways. And there are thousands of ways to distort, neutralize, convert singular speech into consensus, domination or convention. No one can tell you what is what. You have to judge, you have to choose—or you can simply enjoy not judging, not choosing, or being afraid that such outdated gestures as talking about what can be done with the means of communication would be considered simplistic and "dull."

Best to everyone

Brian

From: Carlos Basualdo
Subject: Re: The Trial of Pol Pot
Date: Sunday 10 January 1999

In a recent essay about the work of the Argentine artist David Lamelas and describing one of his pieces from the early seventies, Benjamin Buchloh writes, "yet in Lamelas' rigorous reduction of the filmic image to its most elementary functions (pure duration, pure recording, and pure indexical presence), the dialectic of late modernist rationality suddenly appears: that the elimination of narrative and agency, of representation and the imaginary from the (filmic) image, driven by the desire to dismantle the ideological conditions of media representation, manifests the very order of technocratic and administrative rationality that the calculated and industrially produced forms of narrative and myth conceal... It was this dialectic that conceptualism radical critique of representation considered least. To the degree that it eliminated representation as a privileged convention of artistic knowledge and historical memory, it also prolonged—at the very center of a cultural practice of resistance—the elimination of experience that the principles of a technologically advanced culture of spectacle enforced."[109]

So, abstracting Brian's argument on Liam's show, I guess similar things can be said about tons of contemporary art and maybe a few exhibitions as well: irony is always too close to mimesis with the object that it ironizes, its distancing effect being too easily recuperable by a standardized logic of spectatorship. Now, as Brian points out, this strategy was also that of Pop, but I guess its limitations are already very clear for everybody. On the other hand, I am extremely suspicious of a recourse to "communication," and I wonder what does Brian exactly mean by that. Artistic practice, after all, is so much about "communication," but it is always redefining what that is, critiquing and complicating its assumptions.

Now, my question is, can we be skeptical about the possibilities of linear communication and still not fall prey of an excessive faith in the powers of irony and deconstruction? And how to articulate such a fragile position? I realize that this is a very old question, and a very difficult one as well, but I would like to pose it in regards to the way in which we think of exhibitions and curatorial practice. What notion of communications underlines our curatorial efforts? What notion of the audience was involved in Liam's exhibition and Brian's comments? And finally, does it make sense to think that our notion of what an audience is should change according to the place in which we do our shows—and according to the subject that we choose to tackle?

Carlos

From: Rebecca Gordon-Nesbitt
Subject: Re: The Trial of Pol Pot
Date: Monday 11 January 1999

As a supervisor of "The Trial of Pol Pot" and a member of VOTI, I feel somewhat implicated in the current debate and would like to respond. It is important to state at the outset that the exhibition was founded on debate—between ourselves and the coordinators—a process which was instituted to compensate for the lack of satisfactory discourse and resolution within Cambodia. The impact of genocide was in no way intended to be trivialised. Understanding the mechanisms of power is the first step in understanding how this could have happened and the perpetrators not brought to justice.

The form of the constantly evolving exhibition has been much criticised by Brian Holmes. I can only respond by saying that the statements on the wall were not deliberately obtuse, rather a concise and powerful rhetoric. Not ironic, a contrivance or a bluff (Liam, correct me if I'm wrong). My understanding is that the show was in no way deliberately contrived for later deconstruction by the viewer but was developed collectively as a resolution for certain complex ideas. Rather than a critique of spectacle becoming a spectacle itself, these collected statements and questions became a provocative call for judgment and reflection that I am sure the audience was more than capable of processing. Admittedly, the poster that contained all the supervisors' suggestions became a little difficult to read as it veered from the literal to the metaphorical. Initially all our suggestions were to be literally layered directly over the coordinators ideas, although this was probably decided against precisely because it would have been too banal. Brian, would you prefer exhibitions to patronise their audience by emulating some of the retinal one-liners that have characterised many recent artworks?

From: Brian Holmes
Subject: Re: Trial of Pol Pot
Date: Monday 11 January 1999

Rebecca, I'm not so crazy about one-liners or exhibitions that patronize their audiences in any way. As for the show being "contrived for deconstruction," I understood that from Liam Gillick's remarks here, but also from the form of the show and the surrounding material, particularly the Robert De Niro bit, which strongly suggests irony. I've read the show from an outside point of view, which is, after all, the public viewpoint. My interpretation may have failed to grasp the artists' best intentions. But it's hard to see how "the lack of satisfactory discourse and resolution within Cambodia" could be remedied by phrases such as the ones I've quoted. Who would remedy what, for whose satisfaction? On the other hand, it's true that the whole thing provoked me, and as it referred so very little to Cambodia, I found myself judging the show itself.

Carlos, I think your point is well taken. Under the conditions of globalization, communication is being defined as the encoding and exchange of the most diverse realities by means of universal equivalents. Thus, all production is encoded as money and is exchanged on the stock market. Visual art seems increasingly to be encoded in the vocabulary of Hollywood cinema, and to a lesser extent, of "fashion" as created by designers and magazines in LA-New York-London-Paris. But communication can also be defined as the constant effort to translate one singularity into the terms of another, to make one local reality comprehensible in another place, to exchange meanings in a way that does not reduce both parties to a common standard, linguistic, monetary or otherwise, but always adds new possible meeting points between people. Art is an ideal field within which to carry out this kind of work, which could become a cultural project for globalization—if more space can be made for it within our societies, and particularly, our institutions.

All the best,

Brian

PS: It turns out that the text from which I have extensively quoted is available at www.magasin-cnac.org, along with a few pictures and other materials. So anyone frustrated by this debate about an unknown object could get at least some idea of the exhibition from the Magasin website.[110]

From: Jordan Crandall
Subject: Re: The Trial of Pol Pot
Date: Monday 18 January 1999

Brian,

I really appreciate your posts and my own views tend to be close to yours. But in all fairness
we have to realize that aesthetic strategies are rarely political ones, and that there is a
difference between artistic and political intervention, even as that difference is always an
open question. Even as we question the validity of aestheticizing communication—why not
just establish a direct communications link, we ask—we have to understand the relevance of
visual work on the field of signification, which often must hinder that link.

Even if this is "in a certain way even promoting the situation that the artists claim to be
critiquing"—if it's "hot air," filling "up institutions which otherwise could contribute in all
kinds of ways to making the world a better place to live in"—we have to realize that is our
mistake to assume that artistic practice must have a clearly articulated goal or even any kind
of moral or ethical agenda at all.

I am really surprised that your remarks haven't roused anyone here—I mean, you offer vital
challenges to the very conditions of aesthetic practice. It also points out that in art, we have
no responsibility to defend ideas either, or to really be issue-driven at all.

"If they really wanted to critique or change things, wouldn't they do something else,
something deeper, more precise, riskier, with more content, more communicative
power?"—that's a subjective measure of the success of any work. With the networks,
we now have potent means of communication, and the means to structure real debates.
But Carlos is right to be suspicious of your recourse to "communication" in art. He
asks some important questions: how "can we be skeptical about the possibilities of
linear communication and still not fall prey of an excessive faith in the powers of irony
and deconstruction? And how to articulate such a fragile position?" "What notion of
communications underlines our curatorial efforts?" Further: even as we mourn the lack of
engagement of communications networks in the art world, we have to realize that the nets
pose a direct threat to the status quo, to the structures of power that keep the art world
together as an object. We also have to remember that often networks don't work, and art
can speak of the lack.

Statements like these of yours I find highly motivating: "A large amount of real debate is
taking place because people are at once afraid and amazed to discover that there are great
possibilities to speak, to enter into relations, to do something different, or on the contrary,
to give new breadth to what they've been doing all along." You are the real thing, Brian. We

need you in the art world. But in terms of visual art you've got to give some space for other kinds of intervention, which might be closer to the poetic or the anarchic. But on the other hand perhaps it is we who need to better articulate the terms of our engagement.

From: Brian Holmes
Subject: Re: Trial of Pol Pot
Date: Monday 18 January 1999

Jordan, your comments are welcome. I agree, the signifying conditions of the artistic frame are essential. I don't think art should be "communicative action" as Habermas would say. It's more about representation, display of experimentation, in all kinds of ways. You speak of giving space to poetic or anarchic qualities, no problem! But the artistic frame has various definitions—like everything cultural, we create it. To define art as public today, it might be important to recognize several things:

First, access to the "means of representation" means power in the information age: the power to broadcast, to touch people's senses and minds. Second, a lot of access is legitimated with the claim that the artwork is relevant, a model for experience, a reflection of social conditions. Third, even the most anarchic or poetic gestures have "symbolic power," which means they contribute to the viewer's general idea or grasp of the world and of human relationships, on an emotional level too.

All these things make publicly presented art something worth debating over, even intensely, as though it were political. It's one of the ways to make art really exist. You know, to argue about a show you have to spend some time on it! And it's worth spending time. One reason is that in the post-industrial societies, artists dealing with information, communication and technology are at a powerful juncture, of the kind we've seen throughout the twentieth century: dadaists, futurists, constructivists, pop artists, situationists, rational or not, agenda or not, they all have had real effects, through direct presentations and through the spin-offs of their work in other fields. It's all about shaping the ways we get along with each other, the use we make of tools, of Institutions. As a critic or just a viewer, there are times to praise, times to whisper encouragement, times just to dream off on your own, times to respond to artworks with other artworks. And somewhere in the midst of all that, there are times to be polemical, to hunt for some definitions, to point to how art fits into a broader context, political, economic, psychological, social. The relation to politics can make art much more vibrant, that's why public art has come to be defined in ways like the one I've offered. But like you say, the curious thing about art is the uncertainty of all those different moments—when to do what?

Best,

Brian

From: Jordan Crandall
Subject: network practice
Date: Sunday 31 January 1999

In many postindustrial economies, increased bandwidth is just around the corner, which will allow live video transmission over the net with the quality of television. Even the third generation of mobile phones, now being developed, will allow video to be recorded and transmitted in real time (the US and Europe are currently fighting over standards). This playing field is animated by so many competing interests: from the jockeying of media conglomerates over who will set the standards, control of access, etc., to the immersive commercial information society now in formation. We are talking about a system from which most of the world will be excluded. It is crucial to pay attention to who will speak, who will be represented. As cultural workers we are not acting fast enough, we are leaving the field of symbolic production open for total appropriation by the media industries. Right now our work at Blast is wholly about developing ways of bringing others into this system, of interjecting diverse presences, opening up heterogeneous cultural axes, pushing toward a politics of presence in the networks. The stakes are high.

For those who think 500 channels is a lot, well, soon we will have 500,000. Where do you want to go today?

We are not only talking about a medium, but a new kind of urban space—a space with new claims upon it.

Brian Holmes wrote:

...communication can also be defined as the constant effort to translate one singularity into the terms of another, to make one local reality comprehensible in another place, to exchange meanings in a way that does not reduce both parties to a common standard, linguistic, monetary or otherwise, but always adds new possible meeting points between people. Art is an ideal field within which to carry out this kind of work, which could become a cultural project for globalization...

In our work at ENSBA in Paris, we are developing a format for a netcast channel.[111] Here is how it works. Each "program" revolves around a particular news event—say, a recent American strike in Iraq. There is a central switching-station, which can route a series of live or recorded video feeds, which are sent from local stations or personal video recorders. These transmissions are very particular regional perspectives on the event—local articulations that see the same event differently. On the interface itself, the links allow you to access these perspectives. Therefore, you read the event by viewing it through several cultural conduits at the same time. The event provides a rallying point around which many people speak, and through which many presences become known. A public space is opened up around it.

The event can be interpreted via commercial broadcast or personally, by recording it as it occurs, by recording its aftermath, by recording the impact it is having on local culture, by recording a specific cultural reception of it, etc., or by simply turning the camera upon oneself and speaking about it, assuming the role of a newscaster.

There is a captioning bar below the image providing information and speech, which can be translated into several languages when translation software improves. One can flag the system and "pull up a chair" to intervene. The only requirement is that one deals with the same event. Rather than sampling many news events around the world from one viewpoint, like CNN does, and rather than providing a batch of links that disperse one's attention and encourage surfing, as is the rule on the Web, this channel stays focused on one event for a substantial period of time. It fractures open the singularity of the event, by probing deep within it and scattering the places from which you are seeing it. It forces you to move about, occupying several, often incommensurable, positions in a kind of movement that is very different from hyperlink clicking. It uses the event as a device to probe and foreground networks, to mobilize diverse presences, to introduce ranges of issues. These issues are further dealt with in net-based discussion venues, continuing what we have been staging with Blast.

In this channel, artistic image strategies will have a place alongside established news media. The critical will have a place alongside the commercial. There is no prioritizing one over the other. This is very important, as there are no venues on this scale where critical network practices can hold their own against commercial media, existing side-by-side. We have to invent them.

Brian writes that "access to the 'means of representation' means power in the information age: the power to broadcast, to touch people's senses and minds". Yes. And for those of us who do have the power of access there is the responsibility to project the outside into the field of view. Against the popular representations of the net as a clean, smooth, unified, transnational space that sweeps over regions as the very space of modernity, it must be positioned as a space of contestation—a heterogeneous tangle of intersecting micro-networks, indelibly bound up in urban processes and embroiled in various procedures of "becoming present."

The question is: when we do have the video cameras in our hands, when we do have the access to this enormous medium of distribution, exchange, and presentation, what will we say? How can critical media gain power, how can it have a space in the public eye? In building up this netcast format we are simultaneously developing a network of institutional relationships. We need bonds and alliances. The corporations are doing it, and so should we, and not entirely separate from them.

From: Cornelia Lauf
Subject: Re: network practice
Date: Sunday 31 January 1999

I've just spent the day with someone who sells sheep for 4800 lira each, less than what his father received for them twenty-five years ago (≈3 dollars). This man tills the earth and herds the sheep from 5 a.m. until 6 p.m. He is educated and as smart as you or me. It took me twelve years for him to tell me something about prices and about the economics of farming because he is Sardinian, and it is not his nature to complain, despite living in an unheated house with one fireplace, three children, and a TV, right in the middle of Tuscany. A TV that doesn't have 500,000 channels, but enough to see what he is missing, and that he has no way to get it.

I'm wondering how to reconcile the reality of this life, responsible after all, for the lamb chop we order at the Blue Ribbon or wherever, and the myriad possibilities offered up by staying tuned to a computer or TV the livelong day. I am working hard just to collect my e-mails, and keep a career simmering, with two kids, and I would like to know a really quick way to brush up on the entire world, in between dumping a load of wash into the washing machine, dragging a kid off to the bathroom, and trying to write three articles, and curate a cockamamie show. Which channel will it be?

From: Brian Holmes
Subject: Which channel?
Date: Monday 1 February 1999

Scales are the enigma of cultural projects today. Weighing the balance, feeling out the range. When so much right next to you is so full of beauty and suffering, and yet so far out of reach, and yet tied in so closely to vast networks of power and control. Where to begin? How to stay there? What limits not to set? Which openings are fatal?

Jordan writes about a handheld, multi-angled version of CNN. And Cornelia writes about sheep, lamb chops, lira and another load of wash. One tries to open viewpoints, raise voices. The other leaves us pondering over silences and scales of involvement. No one is right, there is no formula. The channels of communication are like the old canals, networks of flowing water barred and joined by locks, held at all different levels of potential, articulated by people who open the locks and then close them again, letting the boats pass smoothly where a waterfall would have been.

Me too, I'm playing with the corkscrews of some cockamamie show out in the countryside, and wondering by which currents it won't all overflow—too much, I mean, or too soon, or not enough, so that in the end we get somewhere, without entirely leaving where we are.

Chapter V

Frieze and *Artforum*

Outside of the official forum sessions Carlos Basualdo asks for comments about a text on VOTI written by Ralph Rugoff and published in *Frieze 44* (January - February, 1999) (p.414). Just a few weeks later a column on VOTI, written by Matthew Debord, is published in *Artforum* (March, 1999). On reading these articles, concern over the outside perception of VOTI is again raised by several members. In response, Susan Hapgood posts an official forum e-mail to all members requesting they each "post a message about where you think we should go with Voti."

The lack of international distribution of major art periodicals at that time is made apparent by the number of VOTI members requesting a faxed copy of the articles. The *Artforum* column appears in the appendix (p.406) and a link to the *Frieze* article is located in the Endnotes.[112]

In order of appearance:
Carlos Basualdo, Hou Hanru, Jose Roca, Marta Kuzma, Nancy Spector, Susan Hapgood, Vasıf Kortun, Jens Hoffmann, Rosa Martínez and Carolyn Christov-Barkagiev.

From: Carlos Basualdo
Subject: Re: contracts
Date: Thursday 21 January 1999

Has anybody read the article against independent curators of our generation—sounds very much like it's against us to me—that Ralph Rugoff published in *Frieze*?[112]

Shall we react somehow?

Carlos

From: Hou Hanru
Subject: Re: contracts
Date: Friday 22 January 1999

Dear Carlos and others,

I read the piece and it is more destructive than constructive...why should we bother about this kind of thing which proposes nothing but personal complaints, also, this matter makes us think how important it is to continue stimulating the change of the definition of art in contemporary culture and breaking the border between disciplines, including the "stability" of art and the art world itself...

Best to you all,

Hou Hanru

From: Jose Roca
Subject: Re: contracts
Date: Friday 22 January 1999

Hi, everybody, hi, Carlos.

Frieze doesn't circulate in Colombia; is it easy for you to scan it and post as an attachment?

Thanks,

Jose

From: Marta Kuzma
Subject: Re: contracts
Date: Friday 22 January 1999

Hello, Carlos.

I have the same request as Jose. No recent Frieze to be found in Kyiv. I'd also appreciate it if you might scan and post it.

Thank you,

Marta

From: Jose Roca
Subject: Re: contracts
Date: Friday 22 January 1999

Yes, dear Carlos: how common is our common ground of discussion?

Jose

From: Nancy Spector
Subject: Voti Content-Disposition
Date: [unavailable]

Dear Carlos, dear Hans Ulrich,

I am assuming that I am no longer on the Voti list since it has been weeks since I have seen a posting. Perhaps this is because I have not had the time to participate fully or because I voiced concern over publishing information on the group before it had been allowed to truly evolve into a productive and supportive entity, where people felt free to share ideas and concerns. I saw the *Artforum* article this morning and it proved two things to me:

No one in the art world believes in something unless they see it validated in print. The more mainstream the venue the better.

The art world is still dominated by men.

Yours,

Nancy

From: Carlos Basualdo
Subject: Re: VOTI
Date: Sunday 28 February 1999

Dear Nancy,

The VOTI list has been quite inactive lately, but that may have been because the activity has been displaced to the live meetings—the one in New York and the one in Madrid. Both have been very productive and Susan is working on a long posting about them. The article in *Artforum* is quite bad, and it confirms Hans Ulrich's worst fears about the ways in which the press misrepresents and manipulates information. He was very right, all along. In any case, I feel that it is our responsibility to work on the way in which we think VOTI should be perceived. If we do not do it, the press will keep on doing it for us. After I read the piece, and once I overcame the feeling of embarrassment, I sent an email to Hans, Jordan and Susan expressing my concerns and also the need for VOTI to come out with some sort of press release soon.

Maybe we should post this conversation on the list? I only hope that the article will help us focus on these issues...

Besos,

Carlos

From: Susan Hapgood
Subject: Re: Letter from Basualdo, Crandall, Hapgood and Obrist
Date: Wednesday 24 March 1999

Dear Voti members,

The recent short piece in *Artforum* about Voti skewed us in an alarming direction—a bit like a sexist, private coterie of curators. We need to better define ourselves and make our decisions clear during the coming public session.

We would like to ask everyone in the forum to post a message about where you think we should go with Voti. We are going through a hopefully productive crisis, a moment of doubt, of decisive (re)definition right now. As we open the doors for the first public debates, we need to assess where we have come from and where we need to go. We need to isolate core issues and strategies. What is our purpose? What are the pressing issues that we must now tackle? How do we organize ourselves and our debates to best meet these challenges and increase our efficiency? What do you really care about now, what needs immediate attention? What are the urgent burning issues? What do we want to change?

Besides the public forums, we think it is important that Voti can fulfill the simple function of having its members talk to each other, non-publicly, to inform each other more in depth about activities, to share experiences, to think about new forms of collaboration.

We are still working on plans for the upcoming public forum, revolving around issues of the museum. Can everyone also please send the names and e-mails of two people (not just curators) we should send announcements of the forum to?

Carlos Basualdo
Jordan Crandall
Susan Hapgood
Hans Ulrich Obrist

From: Vasif Kortun
Subject: Letter from Basualdo, Crandall, Hapgood and Obrist
Date: Sunday 28 March 1999

Are we having problems with the *Artforum* piece because it presents VOTI as a boy's club, or because of the spillage of the writer's sexism—his selections and highlighting processes—in his text? There is still obviously an institutionalized, operative practice that is exclusionary. Persons may not be exclusionist, racist and so on, but the institution in the abstract remains racist and exclusionist. This provides an individual cordon sanitaire for the person with the open mind and spirit although, in the long run, it may function within an affirmation of the status quo. Shall we hold in exception the Whitney example that was a blatant reversal to a pre-1989 paradigm? Such a reversal has shown us the presence of the abstracted racism and sexism of the institution taking form in the person of the Whitney director.

VOTI could function as a transcendent space that needs not only operate at a level of representation, while, at the same time, not forgetting that representations exist. I do not think we have to define ourselves, but we suffer from a lack of critical debate on exhibition practice. Rather than the discussion of the issue of Museum with a capital M, I am drawn to innovative exhibition practices, possibilities of liberated circulation of art works and ideas. Women curators have reinvented many aspects of the practice in recent years, why do we not hear more on this now? Women curators who have been extremely important to my formation such as Mary Jane Jacob, Lisa Corrin, Suzanne Pagé (History of the Museum exhibition in Paris almost 9 years ago), and Susan Vogel whose contributions would be critical to VOTI.[113] I also love certain postings of HUO on Dorner for example, or the interviews in the last few years with the curators. Also can we get permission from Rosa to circulate her Szeemann interview for VOTI? These tickle the mind and soul much more than generalized discussions.

Love,

Vasif Kortun

From: Jens Hoffmann
Subject: JensforVoti
Date: Tuesday 30 March 1999

dear all,

i very much share the opinion of vasif when he points out the urgent need of a critical
debate on exhibition practice; we witnessed an enormous increase of exhibitions, biennials,
etc. during the last years of which most unfortunately seemed very similar to each other.
what we see is not the real body of an artistic practice anymore, what we see is only a
shadow; we see the soulless shifting of information from one side of the globe to the other,
these forms of culture entertainment do not satisfy the cultural necessities of our times
any longer and just as some of us were pointing out, we feel very uncomfortable to discuss
issues of contemporary exhibition practice while a war is going on in yugoslavia. our time
needs a curatorial practice that tries to explain our present position in history, our time
needs cultural manifestations which have a deeper and more active approach to reality,
society and their questions, these manifestations can be of course exhibitions but hopefully
also other more radical forms of curating which will help us to understand the meaning
of current conflicts. i am personally very much interested to understand the individual
motivations and ideas of curating expressed in individual or collective manifestations in
relation to what we call the real world. my most urgent question is: why do most exhibitions
not reveal anything new in terms of the circumstances of our time and why do they not
formulate new curatorial and artistic practice ALTHOUGH curated by DIFFERENT individuals.
i strongly believe in curating as a highly CREATIVE process and do not believe in the curator
as the executor of the ideas of artists, therefore i believe in a personal, individual idea of
curating, and i am more eager than anything else to understand the motivations of other
curators for doing what they do. as someone who was trained and educated as a theatre
director, i have lots of faith in collaborations of all forms and all disciplines therefore i think
that a trans-disciplinary approach is the only way that art, if it still wants to play a key role
in the development of our society, can find an adequate form to tell us something about
our current existence. only a trans-disciplinary approach will be able reveal the complexity
of today's society and the diversity of aesthetic practices it has produced. the hierarchy of
the disciplines has to be deconstructed as the only adequate development to link artists'
practice with the complex structure of society, which can open a space that makes these
cultural manifestations productive fields of energy for everyone.

yours,

jens

From: Rosa Martinez
Subject: Re: Letter from Basualdo, Crandall, Hapgood and Obrist
Date: Tuesday 30 March 1999

Querido Carlos,

Could you please send me by fax (+34.93.205.57.XX) a copy of the article about VOTI that appeared in ARTFORUM? I have not had the opportunity to read it and I would love to answer it if it deals with male/female curatorship...

VOTI is for sure necessary. We are inventing it and constructing it.

Best

Rosa

From: Carolyn Christov-Bakargiev
Subject: [unavailable]
Date: Tuesday 06 April 1999

Dear Voti,

I too have not had a chance to see the Artforum article. Can anyone fax it to me as well, at:
0039.06.687XXXX

or email it to me?

Thank you,

Carolyn Christov-Bakargiev

Chapter VI

Cultural Practice and War

After several e-mails from VOTI members about the Kosovo War and the situation in the Balkans, which question what VOTI means at that moment and whether it can provide some form of support to the artists and others in the region, Jordan Crandall proposes a public online forum presented by the X-Art Foundation and VOTI, titled *Cultural Practice and War*. It launches on May 28, 1999, and is proposed to run for three months closing on September 1. A huge number of e-mails that included posted content are sent during this period mainly from VOTI members and contributors to previous Eyebeam Blast forums. To keep this chapter succinct and with clear narrative thread, only e-mails written personally, or posted content that was then responded to, have been incorporated here. Additionally, given the dense amount of content and information in this chapter the public period of the forum has not been end-noted. The e-mails not included here, often posted under a pseudonym, were agent-blast posts composed by interns in order to share news content and topical texts for general reading.

Two short conversations introduce other e-mail chains within the general discourse of this chapter. The first is a discussion about the Venice Biennale and the problems being experienced by the curator and artist of the Bulgarian pavilion. The second is an impassioned debate about the role and scope of the curator given the topic of this forum, grouped under the e-mail subject line: "megalomaniac curators."

As personal postings diminished in number over the summer of 1999, the forum was mainly kept active by news postings from the Blast agents. Jordan Crandall announced that the Blast office would be closed from July 2 to 6, and, based on concern from Robert Fleck and others that VOTI had turned "towards a kind of 'all-over' military discussion," he proposed that a new theme be considered for the following period.

In order of appearance:
Carolyn Christov-Bakargiev, Hou Hanru, Carlos Basualdo, Robert Fleck, Bart De Baere, Bettina Funcke, Zdenka Badovinac, Cornelia Lauf, Jordan Crandall, Charles Esche, Ute Meta Bauer, Iara Boubnova, Nedko Solakov, Trevor Batten, Angus Trumble, Joseph Nechvatal, Bronwyn Mahoney, Simon Biggs, Brian Carroll, Aras Ozgun, Sina Najafi, Marina Grzinic, Andrej Tisma, Saul Anton, Teo Spiller, Barbara Kuon, Bennett Simpson, Olu Oguibe, Vasıf Kortun, Michael Benson, Edi Muka, Jose Roca and Robert Atkins.

From: Carolyn Christov-Bakargiev
Subject: Letter from Basualdo, Crandall, Hapgood and Obrist
Date: Sunday 28 March 1999

Dear VOTI,

It's good to hear from you.

I think it would be interesting to send information on the public forum on the museum to Lorenzo Romito (a young Roman architect interested in this subject, part of the artist/architect group called Stalker).[114] Also, Lisa Parola in Turin from the *a-titolo* collective curatorial group.[115] He's now also preparing a meeting on this subject for 12-13 June in Rovereto (near Venice).

I have missed reading VOTI postings, so this must mean that VOTI is important in some ways. I believe it should continue to function as a way of informing each other of our projects, also of exchanging ideas with people we did not know before.

At present I am particularly shocked by the bombings and war in the Balkans and feel art and discussions of ours are a bit impotent before such tragedies.

I'm interested in pluri-disciplinary projects and encounters, on how we can develop meeting grounds with other disciplines and not only science, but also poetry, cooking and such.

I look forward to the reopening of VOTI, and send best regards.

Carolyn Christov-Bakargiev

From: Hou Hanru
Subject: Re: Letter from Basualdo, Crandall, Hapgood and Obrist
Date: Monday 29 March 1999

Dear VOTI:

I share Carolyn's concern with the current bombing in Yugoslavia...again, we are in the same situation as the Gulf war and Sarajevo some years ago, and art seems to be so indifferent facing this...even some people start questioning if the Venice Biennale, situated in a neighbouring city, should take place this year while no end of the war seems to appear.
It seems a bit selfish and lacking in self-confidence to be troubled by a piece of paper in Artforum, or even by the mechanical "critique" from the "art world." It's more essential to worry about where is the place for "art" and curating in the world of real life... In a way, I think Vasif's mentioning of the female curators contribution is interesting: the real question is not how many women have been curating, but can we think about "femalisation" of curating? Probably this implies types of projects beyond the "male" hard edge institutional frames...

Best,

Hou Hanru

From: Carlos Basualdo
Subject: Re: Letter from Basualdo, Crandall, Hapgood and Obrist
Date: Tuesday 6 April 1999

Dear Robert,

Do you think that VOTI should get in touch with Dejan, Branislava and Bronislav? What do you think we can do in order to help these people—and this in the understanding that we will probably be able to do only very little?

Carlos

From: Robert Fleck
Subject: Re: Letter from Basualdo, Crandall, Hapgood and Obrist
Date: Tuesday 6 April 1999

Dear Carlos,

Yes, I think it is a good idea to get in touch with our colleagues there, even if the only thing we can say is "we did not forget you."

Yesterday I was in touch with a composer in Belgrade—Radomir Stančić, he is the boyfriend of a young artist from Manifests 2, Tanja Ostojic, who is currently participating in our Post Graduate Program in Nantes. I had dinner with him on Jan. 2, never thinking that a war could become reality. To get a distance from these events, he is recording the noise of the NATO planes, the bombing and the alarm signals, for a much later use in his work. He was struck by the observation that everybody around him is with the government, since the war began.

This is the first war in the history of mankind, I think, where you can communicate, through email, in real time with the people on the other side...

Best Wishes,

Robert Fleck

From: Bart de Baere
Subject: Re: Letter from Basualdo, Crandall, Hapgood and Obrist
Date: Wednesday 7 April 1999

Milica Tomić, the Belgrade artist invited last year to Sao Paulo, had selected a sunny day to start the video-shoot of her new work. It was the same day NATO had selected for their first bombing. "Both worlds—Serbia and us—have become completely incompatible," she wrote today. They have been so, potentially in several aspects for several years. The observation of Radomir seems to be quite true.[116] For us too, there seems to be a lot we are not aware of.

Bart.

From: Bettina Funcke
Subject: curating and war
Date: Saturday 10 April 1999

Dear VOTIs,

I certainly share the feeling of Carolyn that the war in Yugoslavia is questioning our work. What we do is very little and looks decadent and helpless when confronted with this kind of situation. But at the same time I do not think it depreciates curatorial practice. I think the kind of work we do bears the responsibility to be political on some level but it can never be any form of political activism. I think it is rather the question of how to reflect on what is happening in Kosovo. Of course, this can always include more direct help or support on various levels but I think as curators, writers and artists we inherently are in a reflecting position that has to be articulated and also needs to find its manifestation and dissemination, which is already difficult enough.

I find it amazing that we are a group of more than 40 people who all supposedly work on reflecting today's state of culture and the changes society and the world are facing—but nobody is able or willing to take a clear position concerning the NATO interference in Kosovo. Of course, one can always argue not to know enough about the circumstances under which the war began. I think there is some kind of a vacuum—created by the radical opening of structures and the total instability in any direction—that makes it impossible for us to articulate a clear position and I think this could be an interesting point of departure for a discussion. This precariousness and instability is not the postmodern "anything goes" but rather one produced by the transition to the so called "New World Order" we are in right now.

I would argue that it is wrong to interfere within any civil war; on the other hand, it seems to be a responsibility to stop Milošević's "ethnical cleaning."[117] Since the breakdown of the conflict between East and West, the idea of two political poles, right and left, does not seem to exist anymore in the way we knew it. Everyone seems to be extremely right. At the same time Serbia is performing a crude and vulgar version of a fascist regime, the United States and their strategic interests lift up their action to a highly sophisticated version of Fascism. (The killing of tens of thousands in Rwanda happened without any international interference.)

I think this groundless instability for developing arguments towards a clear position within those conflicts is the actual challenge for cultural practice today: how to overcome this vacuum in order to create new forms of cultural manifestations which are able to find a position.

With my best wishes!

Bettina

From: Zdenka Badovinac
Subject: war
Date: Monday 12 April 1999

Dear VOTIs!

It was with great interest that I read some of the latest VOTI contributions relating to the war in Yugoslavia. During the war in Bosnia, we prepared a symposium at the Moderna Galerija, entitled "Living with Genocide" and addressing the issue of why the international art world did not react to the war in Bosnia.[118] The fundamental question was: What is it in the very structure of contemporary political theory and art that tolerates, or even dictates, the irrecognition and incomprehension of the clearly manifested evil that is taking possession of today's world, what is it that relieves us from the need to resist it, or even makes us abstain from offering opposition?

The papers presented at the symposium and the ensuing debates will be published in the upcoming special issue of our magazine *Wars*—I can send a copy to anyone interested in it as soon as it appears. I am sure that each and every one of us is prepared to help our colleagues and the artists in Belgrade (as well as in Kosovo and Macedonia). But what this is about is a humanitarian gesture—and I am sure that each of us who had the possibility of providing help during the time of the war in Bosnia and Croatia did so at that time, too. I absolutely agree with Bettina—I believe our debate should centre around a new articulation of the artist and intellectual's stance against war.

I find the letter written by Radomir Stančić very problematic, in particular the following sentence: "The protest in art here is no longer against the oppression of the regime, but the oppression exercised by the world powers against our small country." What the NATO strike brought about is a total victory for Milošević, since now, in the fight against the external enemy, he more than ever before enjoys the lull support of the Serbian people. Slavoj Žižek writes about this in the article from the newspaper Delo, submitted by HUO.[119] While protesting against the NATO bombardments with poetry and music, the people in Belgrade do not at the same time protest against the genocide taking place 300 km to the south of them—in Kosovo. I don't know whether anything concerning your questions is being prepared also in Venice. Perhaps VOTI could organise a debate on these issues. If the Venice Biennale will manifest no kind of reaction to the war in the neighbouring Balkans within its framework Biennale, then the nineties with its four editions of the Venice Biennale will prove that art is in fact incapable of articulating fundamental social concerns.

All the best,

Zdenka Badovinac

From: Cornelia Lauf
Subject: Yugoslavia/Kosovo
Date: Monday 12 April 1999

What about devising a letter listing all the artists in Yugoslavia—by first name and last initial, if their privacy must be protected—and publishing it in newspapers, magazines, and on-line, so that it is clear that there are individuals being bombed, and not just buildings being "degraded." And by the same token, could we do anything as a group to help the situation in Kosovo? We have so many strong voices in this forum…so many good writers.

Perhaps we could use VOTI to formulate public, humanitarian, social and political opinions, in a similar way that writers have at PEN.[120] Opinions that would transcend nationality and would hopefully function outside of our small and all too often mute art world.

C. Lauf

From: Bart de Baere
Subject: Slavoj Žižek: Against the Double Blackmail
Date: Monday 12 April 1999

Thank you for the Žižek article, Hans.[121]

I happened to be in Belgrade on the day the opposition won the communal elections, enjoying the spontaneous party on the main square in the night, gypsy bands playing between the audience, Vuk (of whom every informed person knew already then that he is of a nature very comparable to Milošević) raising the masses and putting on a second plan the leaders of the two other opposition parties.[122] The day after, in the offices of B92, I followed the information about the first moves to tamper with the results in the different cities.

Flying home, of course read the newspapers, hoping to find more information. Searching an *International Herald Tribune*, the paper in which you get the clues about what's going to be decided. Not a word. The day after, not a word.

The day after, I phoned to Belgrade, to find out what was happening, expressing my surprise about the absolute lack of information. Oh, they're all here, my friends said, even CNN is here, but they wait because today the American negotiator comes (for Bosnia, that is). He didn't have results.

From: Jordan Crandall
Subject: Re: war
Date: Monday 12 April 1999

I am really struck by the contributions of Bettina, Robert, and Zdenka and for the direction they have suggested for opening the doors of discussion.

Right now so many artists and cultural producers are struggling with what to do, clearly in a context when our work seems insignificant. How to navigate this relation between art and war. Between cultural practice and war machines. What are the terms of our involvement, do we fight at the frontlines or do we rather make strong, precise interventions in the realm of symbolic production—because clearly this is also a war of images, propaganda machines and networks. Writer Ivo Skoric's friend in Belgrade says, "If I watch television, I see that the Galenica Pharmaceutics factory is in flames, but if I look out my window, I see the same factory standing intact."

Where are we needed most, where can we do the most good? Have we developed better tools with which to decode images to greater value in a situation where television continually overwrites reality? Someone wrote on the net recently that they don't understand why NATO is bombing bridges, factories, etc., and leaving the broadcast networks unscathed, for clearly these transmission networks hold more power.

As critical artists and curators we can fight in this war.

Following the suggestions of Bettina, Zdenka, Robert and the concerns of Cornelia and others, why don't we open the doors of the VOTI forum right now, why don't we start our first public session immediately?

PS We can also set up a corresponding website—I have programmers right now with me, we can set up something immediately, please let us know right away if you think this would be beneficial and if so how this website can function in conjunction with the VOTI discussions.

From: Charles Esche
Subject: Re: war
Date: Tuesday 13 April 1999

Dear VOTIs

I take this sad opportunity to join the debate. I have valued enormously the breadth of access that VOTI has offered to opinions and responses about the war. It has become for me a prime source of information over the last days.

Žižek's text seems to me very pertinent to the discussion of how artists (and organisers) might respond to the events in Serbia. At this stage, taking sides is both pointless and demeaning. Clearly, neither army has a monopoly on right. Instead, we might follow Žižek in refusing the demands of the immediate crisis to create demons of either the Serbs or NATO. How we might (long after the war's end) "seriously constrain the unlimited rule of capital" seems instead to be the most pertinent question of all and one that we can (Yugoslavs, Allies, Kosovars and others) all share.

This is surely the point at which the significance of art and the production of artists might find a place—in the creation of imaginative spaces and projections that allow the language of doubt and difference to flourish. If art has a role in describing social and political events, it cannot lie in direct call and response methodologies. That way lies propaganda and a form of political activism that should be thoroughly discredited; instead, artists from any nation might provide the possibility, unavailable within the current terms of debate, to look beyond the immediate crisis and towards picturing what a "transnational" set of values might look like. If we are to provide some ground to anchor our positions amid this "groundless instability" (Bettina Funcke), we should try to discuss the work of some artists who we feel are touching on such areas as part of the debate.

It is interesting to me how much the current tribal/national wars in the world are being played out on the edges of former European empires—French, Austrian, Russian, British. It seems we are, at this global level, still mired in modernist models of internationalism, avant-gardism and the grand narratives of world history—leading nations coming together to change the world etc. Sitting in Scotland (for instance) and thinking about the actual differences between the aims of the KLA and the IRA from Serb or British perspectives has me wondering about perceptions of terrorism.[123] It may be, as Žižek suggests, that the old order is not the nationalism of Serbians but the internationalism of the US. Renegotiating that internationalism, self-critically and in the light of post-modern doubt, is perhaps our greatest task as a society.

As an international group, VOTI has something to offer to that—notwithstanding its impotence in the face of bombs and ethnic murder. In the period after the war stops, in the clearing up and making do, we all have a role to question and imagine the situation otherwise. As such, I would agree with Jordan Crandall that we open the VOTI network to all-comers.

Charles Esche

From: Cornelia Lauf
Subject: direct call and response methodologies
Date: Thursday 15 April 1999

Dear Mr. Esche,

I'm a fan of what you disparage as "direct call and response methodologies." And don't feel that they are propaganda or discredited political activism. While theory is undeniably valuable, here is yet another practical proposal.

A friend here in Rome, three hours by boat from Tirana, works at the UN agency that trucks, ships and airdrops food every day at the camps. This is a well-coordinated effort in place that VOTI could have access to. Us artsy types in turn have access to warehouses, lofts, alternative spaces, Kunsthalles, museum lobbies and visible, well-publicized spaces where food or clothes could be collected. Rather than yet another horse hair, bee pollen, gold leaf, or rubble art installation in the name of high culture, how about making a pan-European series of installations with big piles of FOOD donated by visitors to contemporary art exhibition spaces. Each space, one type of food, for "maximum media appeal." Pasta for peace. Bags and bags of Barilla. Or baby food. Or bagged bread. Or canned food. This winter, I met the Albanian minister of culture, Edi Rama. Other VOTI members probably know him as well. He is an eloquent spokesman for his country. And Mr. Rama is an artist whose dream, at least then, was to turn the many thousand Albanian military bunkers from the last war into an art project. They now are probably going to revert to their original use. At any rate, I am sure he would be sympathetic to something that would fuse art and humanitarian aims.

My own exhibition space, Camera Oscura, is 40 sq. meters, but I've proposed the food installation idea to an exhibition space in Milan. It could be easily replicated by anyone in a location accessible to the UN commission.

Cornelia Lauf

From: Bart de Baere
Subject: direct call and response methodologies
Date: Thursday 15 April 1999

Dear Cornelia,

Searched for an article in the *Times* archive but didn't find it, dealing with food and clothes deliveries, analysing aid efforts for the refugees. One of the lines I remember out of these analyses is that the well-meant donations lead to an organisational nightmare, another that the cost of the same food package acquired in England would be 40 £ as opposed to X £ when bought in Greece. The most helpful thing was money, one of the articles concluded.

Giving money, it's not a very sexy thing to do. Also, the question after this conclusion may be, where to give money to?

The problem in Kosovo was clearly ready to come for a long time, for anyone who wanted to listen to it. In this long time we (the West) have not spent much financial nor intellectual effort on it. We have not been spending an impressive additional amount of energy towards our Serbian friends that decided to stay in Serbia, nor even on trying to understand the complexities and ambiguities of the situation.

The problems in Yugoslavia were clearly outlined and analysed before any war broke out. At that moment we (the West) did not spend much financial nor intellectual effort on it.

At present there are vast catastrophes being prepared all over the former Soviet Union. The west is happy to have been able to let everything fall apart, to let different kinds of mafia takeover, to create, tolerate and assist extremely unhealthy regimes. We are not spending much financial nor intellectual effort on it. And so forth.

The question of where to respond directly—and spend, to put it in a practical way, money—is an urgent one. If we believe in visual arts to be a relevant part of a cultural setting—as has clearly been the case in Slovenia—we might spend our spaces not on food or clothes, neither on more horse hair, bee pollen, gold leaf, or rubble art installations, but at least partially on giving serious possibilities to artists from areas we don't consider at present, not as cheap shots but as serious people needing substantial financial and intellectual space. Needing the possibility to be part of something without having a system around them that enables them to be as exclusively available as artists from countries where the economy is powerful and everything seems obvious.

To do this optimally and seriously one needs more resources of all kinds than an exhibition from an artist down the road. To find a potential partner to engage with from such a situation requests more effort, to start with, because not much clarity has been prepared beforehand. It would be nice if these—technically more burdensome—engagements might be a natural part of our daily practices.

Besides the really urgent question of analysis—towards picturing what a transnational set of values might look like—and the question of practical proposals, there is a very problematic field of how to imbed theoretical notions structurally in practical frameworks, rather than how to implement them through exceptional practices. This middle ground of modalities is not given much attention to.

Bart De Baere.

From: Cornelia Lauf
Subject: Reactions
Date: Friday 16 April 1999

Honeybun Bart de Baere,

Ten thousand Kosovars are crossing the border into Macedonia right now. It is raining and cold here. Twelve thousand Italian troops were dispatched today. We are members of the countries that are bombing Belgrade and Kosovo. This is our war. And Martha Stewart has an excellent article on canapé knives and Easter egg decorating in the current issue!

You, lucky duck, have the potential Bob Geldof of the art world, Jan Hoet, at your side, with a lovely museum in the well-to-do, sophisticated town of Ghent.[124] Where's the Band Aid of this war, to mount some huge and useful action?

A deputy director of the World Food Program is intrigued by the resources of the art world. Unicef is aligned with actors and singers. Sherrie Dougherty, the WFP photo editor, said that the organization has burlap sacks for food collection and that a well-planned effort could actually get press, inspire donations, and feed people. There are many organizations accepting money, and I am sure we have all donated to them by now on an individual basis. But food fills a room, and can make an exhibition AND be useful—hell, ask an artist to install it. Piles of money would need armed guards and Wells Fargo.

The WFP is one of the few organizations running a plane to Albania. Most journalists I know are traveling by boat. Today, one of the WFP photographers had his wallet and camera stolen while passing out food in Kukes, Albania. According to Sherrie, there's limited room on the plane, in the event anyone from the "art press corps" wants to go. There are thousands of children there. As you perhaps read, they have only garbage to play with. Maybe one exhibition space could start collecting toys/art supplies for them. Anyway, I am going to pursue this idea as best I can.

As I said, my own venue is in a small village in the boot of the province of Siena, so I must use my laptop, wallet, words and VOTI as a forum. But you who have public spaces or big exhibitions to mount, couldn't you address the situation far better?

XOX Cornelia Lauf

P.S. The World Food Program is a division of the United Nations. It is an international humanitarian organization with headquarters in Rome. They deal directly with the United Nations High Commission on Refugees. I will get precise information on the planes and transport possibilities administered by the WFP, should anyone be interested.
P.P.S. I don't mean to be the VOTI hand-wringer. I suppose having written for and worked

with Hungarians, Serbs, Croats, Poles, Bosnians, Czechs and Russians over the last ten years has sensitized me particularly. And then there is the epic scope of the horror. And its proximity.

See below for plane information from the World Food Program.

Dear Cornelia,

WFP has started a regular passenger air bridge between Rome and Tirana and Skopje as of 9 April 1999 with a Beechcraft 1900 aircraft, which has a 19-seat capacity. Seats are open on a space available basis ONLY to staff of UN agencies, governments, NGOs and/or other entities involved in relief activities in the region.

Request from the media (journalists, photographers, video crews) will be considered on a case-by-case basis.

Passengers need to have all travel documents and visas required. Passengers will be asked to sign a waiver for insurance claims at the airport before departure.

Each passenger is allowed to check-in maximum of 20 kgs of luggage.
Dates of entry and exit are required, plus passport details. I can give you numbers of WFP Information Officers on the ground in Tirana, Kukes and Skopje. They can provide info on the current situation there, but they are not policy-makers, so it may be best to check the possibilities out first at a higher level here in headquarters vis-a-vis planning/development of project.

Requests for photographs can be directed to me. Please explain what type of images you are looking for, what format you prefer, your actual/real deadlines, how they will be used/ what context. Images are provided free of charge, but we do ask that WFP/photographer is credited each time an image is reproduced. We will have new material as of next week from a photographer just returning from Kukes. I can also direct approved requests to other UN agencies (or additional material.

More detailed info on bags and delivery points can be supplied early next week.

Hope to see you later tonight to talk further about this with the fellow I mentioned to you.

A presto,

Sherri

From: Bart de Baere
Subject: actions
Date: Friday 16 April 1999

Cornelia,

Didn't want to attack your programme—to do something is certainly better than to do nothing—nor your remarks as a whole. I'm surprised at how suddenly one catastrophe becomes topical, and then the next, and then the next, one topic at a time, two at most. And how in between these moments there seems to be not much structural change. As if these catastrophes were shaped to give neatly focused space to our good intentions, in order to divert us from pursuing long term remodelling. Obviously, and luckily, some people are nevertheless consciously doing that.

Warm greetings,

Bart.

From: Jordan Crandall
Subject: VOTI PUBLIC FORUM
Date: Tuesday 11 May 1999

Dear VOTI members,

Susan, Carlos and I are putting forth this idea for the topic of our first public VOTI session. It seems to us to summarize the recent direction of VOTI discussions. Please let us know what you think and give us any practical editing suggestions that you may have. We plan for the listing of forum hosts to include every member of VOTI—so if you object to this, please tell us now; otherwise we will assume it is ok.

We would also like to know if anyone would volunteer to moderate the discussions. We require 3 moderators, each working for a period of one month. As moderator, all of the email messages will come to you first, and you will have to approve the messages before they are posted. It is a difficult job because you have to regulate the amount of messages that flow through the forum. The challenge is: if people can only be reasonably expected to handle, say, 8 messages a day, what are you going to do with the other 8 that come in?

Best regards

Jordan

Cultural Practice and War

Artists, critics, curators and other cultural producers are today struggling with the terms of their own practice, In a global context of crisis when much of their work seems insignificant. How to navigate this relation between aesthetic and political intervention is a nagging question, made all the more acute during times of war. What are the terms of our involvement—do we fight at the frontlines, do we devote ourselves to humanitarian efforts or do we rather make strong interventions in the realm of symbolic production? Because clearly we are faced with a war of images, of communications networks and propaganda machines. Where are we needed most? Have we developed useful tools with which to decode images that can have practical consequences in a situation where television continually overwrites reality?

Recently an extraordinary thing has happened on the net. As Robert Fleck has pointed out, it is the first time we have been able to communicate nearly in real-time with people on the "other side" of a war front. The war in Yugoslavia has exposed the promise and limitations of the net and has revealed anew the tangled intersections of representation, politics and histories that must be navigated in order to engage in effective cultural practice. It has revealed many things about how such assemblages cross with daily-embodied realities, uprooting traditional formats of place, identity and geography especially during times of national and international crisis. As critical workers in areas of cultural production, we must learn to contend with the new forms of cultural identification that are arising, with the fault lines of ethnic tension that contest national borders, and with the underlying processes of militarization.

The first public forum of VOTI will address these issues in the form of an open Internet mailing list, running from May XX to August XX. In conjunction with this forum, a website will be maintained that will allow live and recorded video broadcasts to be integrated with the discussions.

From: Ute Meta Bauer[125]
Subject: themes
Date: Friday 14 May 1999

This message is for the VOTI board—

I am very glad to receive VOTI—even as I am not a frequent writer—but I am debating on what I receive and I write back individually, if possible. You do a great work in terms of giving access to particular debates as now on the war in Yugoslavia, Belgrade and Kosovo. And now on Indonesia. But violence, political violence is never far; it is as well in our closest neighbourhoods, just a bit more unseen. We had a terrible case in Austria—a Nigerian who has died on a transport out of the country by Austrian security people against his will. They glued a tape over his mouth during the flight and he could not breathe anymore. There are a lot of demonstrations and silent marches in Vienna at the moment, to debate this awful practice to getting people, who ask for political or religious asylum, out of the way. It is shocking that we are, at the end of the 20th century, so much unable to deal different with the tasks of our society we live in and I am sad we humans behave like we are unable to learn anything. Boundaries in terms of acting out heavy violence are even less high today. I consider this as a task for all of us working within the cultural field, everybody on their place and in their individual manner—as politicians seems to fail a lot. I hate even to speak like this, as it sounds kitschy and even moralistic.

I would appreciate if these emerging discussions could be as well considered as themes for the panels at Arco 2000. I still appreciate personal communication, reaction, feelings, and it was good to meet some VOTI members face to face, as I did not know all of you before. Therefore I am looking forward to Arco 2000, and I would put some effort to be able to attend. The busy Venice might not offer the possibilities to have the concentration to go into serious debates, as the Arco panels really could do, to my surprise. Nevertheless I would appreciate to meet up for a drink, or breakfast or whatever somewhere.

I appreciate all the work you do in NYC and I once wanted to thank you for that!

All the best

Ute

From: Bart de Baere
Subject: Re: themes
Date: Friday 14 May 1999

Ute,

In Belgium there was a very similar case last year, Semirah Adamu died when she was being brought to the airplane by the paramilitary police.[126] No tape glued, but use of a cushion that had been "officially approved." Was videotaped because earlier evictions had failed and the police expected trouble. Brought about a huge reaction too, and a far reaching debate.

By the way, even if the extreme right becomes a threatening power here, racism appears to be going down, recent polls suggested.

And a little story: a school friend waits for his future wife—she's from Niger—who has been caught and is now staying in the place in Bruges where they imprison illegals. She has to keep her mouth shut and sit there for several months. The period officialdom needs to be convinced she won't tell them where she comes from. After this period officialdom will let her go into free illegality again, because they can't evict her to somewhere. At the same time my friend is getting court permission to marry her, for which they need faked witnesses to make up for the non-existing birth certificate. This part goes well. Faked witnesses are accepting, the lack of a paper not. She, on the other hand, cannot tell she's going to be married soon, because then she would be identified and evicted.

All the best in Venice,

Bart

From: Carolyn Christov-Bakargiev
Subject: VOTI PUBLIC FORUM
Date: Friday 14 May 1999

Dear VOTIs,

I think this is really very important and I would like to know more. The letter speaks about an "attached letter" to Paolo Baratta.[127] Can you forward this to us, please, Robert?

Thank you,

Carolyn Christov-Bakargiev

From: Robert Fleck
Subject: [unavailable]
Date: Wednesday 12 May 1999

Dear VOTIs,

The Venice Biennial is refusing the participation of Bulgaria. See enclosed letter. Should we send a collective fax to the Biennale office?

The author of the letter is Iara Boubnova, (very good) curator in Sofia, ex-Bard College:

Dear Robert,

I learned from Kalin Serapionov that he is short listed for the program in Nantes. I'm very glad with that choice and our ICA community is very proud with it. I hope you'll find him as interesting and "obedient" student.

I address you now with an entreaty for support for Nedko Solakov's and my active efforts for the official representation of Bulgaria in the Venice Biennial. It's a long story, which Nedko and me started before 5 years with official letters to our Ministry of Culture, but without any result.

Later Nedko found a contact with the President of Bulgaria, who started the procedure of the country's application in Venice, where Bulgaria has no pavilion. In defiance of the local bureaucracy and collegial envy the competition for curatorial project was announced for May 4th, 1999 in a deep delay and after all the deadlines of the Biennial. Nedko and me are nominated for the participation with a really great, easy-to-be-done, cheap project, which is not engaged with the Biennial at all—very unusual one. Now the Biennial refuses the national participation, which is a big shock for us. Nedko who trusts in his project is going totally crazy.

I'm taking a risk to send you attached our direct letter to Paolo Baratta, the President of the Biennial, in which our project is explained as well as the whole story about Bulgarian and Italian bureaucracy. May be you can find a way to support our efforts. We are asking for such professional support not only you, but also a lot of our colleagues and friends who know what we are doing.

Sorry for abusing your time, but we know your interest towards such an unusual art ideas in trust in your professional influence.

Sincerely,

Iara Boubnova

From: Iara Boubnova
Subject: Bulgaria in Venice X
Date: [unavailable]

Dear Robert,

Please find the text, which you asked me for. As I know Nedko had sent it to Hans Ulrich Obrist and Ami Barak, as well as to Kim Levin, Zdenka Badovinac, Hou Hanru, Kathalyn Neray, Anda Rottenberg, Victor Misiano, "Parkett," Dan Cameron, Jeffrey Deitch, Rosa Martinez, etc. To a big group of people, whom we know personally. So, the big part of PR is done yet. Thank you very much for the addresses of French journalists.

Hope to be in touch anyway (I speak about any of Venice "ways," maybe we'll participate, with the help of Giancarlo Politi in an Albanian space, which he had arranged).

Yours,

Iara

To Mr. Paolo Baratta
President of The Venice Biennial
Sofia, May 8, 1999

Dear Mr. Baratta,

We are taking the risk to address you regarding the recently canceled by the Biennial authorities official participation of Bulgaria at the 48th Exhibition. This letter is our very last chance to try to convince you to look from another (maybe more artistic) perspective that unusual case.

We admit that your decision to reject Bulgaria has its right reasons—we know that it is ridiculous to include a country 30 days before the opening. You have shown a great deal of patience and a good will while waiting for the Bulgarian clerks to do what they had to do (to provide the necessary funds for the reserved space at Tese and to organize much, much earlier the nomination of the curator and the artist/s—in two words to do all the professional steps which a country, wishing to participate, must do). We are really ashamed for this lack of competence.

We wouldn't be discussing at all your decision to reject the project (the chosen one by the official jury from the Ministry of Culture of Bulgaria, May 4th, 1999) if it consisted of any other type of art work—an installation, paintings, high tech stuff, etc. In that case we would not have the right to argue—you have enough properly done works of this kind. But we would dare to say that our ANNOUNCEMENT project is an unique one, fits from all sides to this ridiculous situation and even reveals the acceptance by Bulgaria of your firm decision not to include the country in this year Biennial.

THE PROJECT: on 15,000 post cards (standard 10 x 15 cm size) with our national white/green/red colours as a background, is printed the following announcement in Bulgarian, Italian and English):

- Bulgarian text -
Awiso urgente
Dopo trentannt di assenza tra I paesi che partecipano ufficialmente alia Biennale di Venezia, la Repubblica di Bulgaria e' orgogliosa di annunciare di avere cominciato a prepararsi per partecipare adeguatamente alia prossimma editione delta Biennale di Venezia che si avra' luogo nel 2001.

Very Important Announcement
After nearly 30 years of absence from the officially participating countries at the Venice Biennial, The Republic of Bulgaria is proud to announce that it is prepared to properly participate in the next Venice Biennial in the year 2001.

On behalf of the missing (but almost ready to participate) country Nedko Solakov, artist and lara Boubnova, curator, generously sponsored by _______.

These cards can be distributed mainly by hand {by volunteers) during the press—and the official opening and also can be left on tiny (20 x 20 cm) little "key spots" in Giardini (with yours and the Chief Curator's permission). Also they can be sent to an enormously big mailing list world-wide, included in web sites, etc. The same message can be print over T-shirts, caps, umbrellas, etc. to be offered for sale at the Giardini bookshop.

And that's all—we don't need a space, no engagement at all for the Biennial's staff. Regarding the catalogue (which deadline for receiving the materials expired a long time ago) our eventual entry will consist only of a short text over white/green/red. No images, no scanning and you know well that such entry can be included into the catalogue even now—if you will take the decision.

You have to know a very important detail—the main condition for the curatorial contest (announced here in Sofia on April 19th, 1999) was the chosen curator to find the necessary funding required by the Biennial. The Kosovo crisis put Bulgaria in a total impossibility to fulfill the financial requirements. That was the reason for us to propose such project and that was one of the reasons for the jury to approve it. The sponsors who are waiting to produce the messages are Giancarlo Politi Editore and Eyecatcher International, Holland. Mr. Baratta, believe us—we do respect the Biennale's decisions. We are only begging you to take a minute from your busy schedule and to reconsider your previous decision. Take the risk to accept even on such a late stage this project from Bulgaria, as it reflects the complications not only in our country, but in the entire region.

Your decision will reinforce your reputation of one of the greatest ARTISTIC events, which deals with UNUSUAL ART WORKS. You know better than us that sometimes the artistic activities look crazy and don't fit to the rules (we were hesitating for a while shall we write "bureaucratic rules" or not, but finally we decided not to make you more angry, so we will not write down that word).

PLEASE, SHOW YOUR SENSE OF HUMOUR AND GIVE A GREEN LIGHT TO THIS PROJECT! WE STILL CAN MAKE IT. IF YOU SAY "YES," BE SURE WE CAN PROVE THAT IN ITALY THE WORD "BULGARIAN" HAS NOT A BAD CONNOTATION ONLY!

With a deep respect, sincerely yours

Iara Boubnova, curator
Nedko Solakov, artist

From: Cornelia Lauf
Subject: virtual pavilion
Date: Friday 14 May 1999

If Bulgaria does not need a pavilion, does it even need the acceptance of the director, or a physical presence at the Biennale? The hats, t-shirts, and postcards still sound expensive, as well as time and labor intensive. What about advertising your ideas and stated participation prominently? Piggy backing onto *Flash Art* or right into the main Italian newspapers, through purchased ads, during the opening of the Biennale.[128] You could call it an art project, or the truth, or whatever. Say what you want to say, and have someone else distribute it.

Just an idea.

Cornelia Lauf

From: Ute Meta Bauer
Subject: Biennale
Date: Friday 14 May 1999

Dear VOTI,

Considering Robert's [Fleck] letter—if it is fast done, as time is emerging short until the opening—maybe still Harald Szeemann can do something.

As there is as well a quite unclear situation about the national pavilion of Yugoslavia (who knows more about it? I would appreciate to have more details) Harald Szeemann shows some younger artists from Belgrade in his main exhibition, if there would be more precise information on the national pavilion of Yugoslavia—it would be good to react (I heard some bits of information, but not very clear, and I do not know the sources).

So Szeemann might be the better address to help Nedko Solakov and lara Boubnova, to participate, beside bureaucratic ways. Does Nedko want to participate in the Biennale or does he want to participate as a representative of Bulgaria?

Regards

Ute

From: Nedko Solakov
Subject: Venice X
Date: [unavailable]

Dear Robert,

Iara just forwarded me some of the VOTI responses—it is great that you are doing this!!!
Would you send me anyhow your original letter, posted to your VOTI list? It seems to
me especially from Ute's reaction that she doesn't understand right away what kind of
participation we were fighting for.

This is very important—the case is: we are officially selected from Bulgaria; the entry is too
late (because of the nonprofessional Bulgarian clerks), BUT our project ANNOUNCEMENT
deals exactly with that situation—so we have that Biennale bureaucracy which is enormous
and they firmly don't want this very specific project which can be included in any show even
the day before its opening. Briefly this is it.

Anyhow we are going to produce the cards with a short text on the backside explaining/
completing the artwork under the new circumstances. Did you post the original text of the
ANNOUNCEMENT itself (that "After nearly 30 years and so and so...") This is very important
for the people to know it—THAT THIS IS NOT JUST A CANCELLED NATIONAL PARTICIPATION
WHICH CAN BE A BIG INSTALLATION, A SMALL EXHIBITION (as an art work), BUT THIS IS A
VERY ADEQUATE ANNOUNCEMENT, EXTREMELY SITE, CONTEXT AND SITUATION SPECIFIC
PROJECT WHICH WORKS IN ITS BEST WAY ONLY WITH BULGARIA (35 years no presentation),
ONLY IN VENICE. ONLY THIS YEAR AND MAINLY—ONLY AS A NATIONAL PARTICIPATION. A
whole country shows its sense of self-irony (announcing this ANNOUNCEMENT) and few
Venice clerks apparently don't have any sense of humour.[129]

You have to know that I was very frustrated (and desperate)—now I am a bit more calm. I
was so shocked by the Biennale's President and Chief Curator's bureaucratic attitude that
I was speechless. Because one can't have any reasonable reasons against such an entry,
except only narrow minded ones.

If you want you can quote me.

Best

Nedko

From: Hou Hanru
Subject: Re: Venice
Date: Tuesday 18 May 1999

Dear Robert and other VOTI…

I replied to Nedko regarding the Bulgarian project. I think the question is not only specific to this Biennale but more general…It's worth debating…

Best Hanru

Dear Nedko,

Thank you very much for your email…sorry for the delay of response. I have been travelling all the time, and set up "Cities on the Move" at the Hayward Gallery in London lately. Then, I have to leave for Venice on Thursday to install the French Pavilion…I read your letter to Baratta again this morning. I appreciate very much the Bulgarian project for its perfect relevance as a clever reaction to the current situation. The emergency of the war, the delay of your application for financial reasons, etc. actually raise the question of how contemporary creation should exist and continue to function today…I think the point is not only a country should respect the application process on time, etc. On the contrary, the Biennale, as well as any institutional-bureaucratic machine, should follow the necessity of each creative project and provide facility to make it happen. On the other hand, I think it's also interesting to realize the project in Venice anyway, even if there is no official recognition. I believe the art community will recognize the importance of the project and evaluate it…

I'll try to talk to AFAA who organises the French participation (I'm a co-curator of the French Pavilion this year) to see if they can help at this point, via a certain "official" channel…[130] But anyway, I'm convinced that your project should be realized, even unofficially. Perhaps, it's "illegal" presence would provoke deeper thoughts about what is contemporary art's presentation and its relationship with institutions today… let's do it!

Best Hanru

From: Ute Meta Bauer
Subject: Re: themes
Date: Tuesday 18 May 1999

I have already some hope, if people go for any kind of march—even a silent one.

The 3 police persons got suspended from service on Monday (today) due to the strong public reactions. I knew about the Nigerian woman deported from Belgium (Bart de Baere mentioned it) and here I am glad the mass media talks about this cases, as they are nothing new, but they cannot happen that hidden anymore, if they get into wide public debate. There are artists and activist groups in Germany (Kein Mensch ist illegal, Kanak Attak ea.) and Austria (Vor der Information with their recent publication "Staatsarchitektur" focussing on various debates and initiatives concerning migration ea.) participating in taking action and circulating information.

I brought this up, as we wonder how situations could escalate into war, but war is everywhere and happens often just next door. Unrecognized.

As mentioned in earlier debates, French unemployed showed much different actions than the German movement and got quite organized in terms of offensive strategies and they got quite some sympathy from the public concerning their issue and demands. This encouraged parts of the German unemployment movement to be as well more offensive. And as always it was necessary to read and to hear about different actions, strategies etc., elsewhere to get encouraged.

How is it going with Nedko Solakov. I think that I understood his project quite clearly—and therefore I had suggested to get in touch with Harry Szeemann (to get the support needed, to have a platform for this contribution, as this seemed not to much). Was it not "Apertutto," Aperto everywhere, what Harry Szeemann announced as the overall theme for this year's Biennial in Venice? Why not declare any site or place as the unofficial Bulgarian Pavilion. But I agree with what Cornelia suggested: to use other channels for distribution for the addressed message. This was the reason why I asked if Nedko Solakov wants to participate in the Biennial as such—as a representative of Bulgaria or if he wants to reflect the situation of Bulgarian artists within bureaucratic systems like the state policy/bureaucracy of Bulgaria and the bureaucracy of the Biennial officials. (And he can be sure, he is not alone).

Best

Ute

From: Robert Fleck
Subject: Re: themes
Date: Wednesday 19 May 1999

Dear Ute,[131]

1) "No human being is illegal": of course these practices are incredible (as are the restrictions of visa for artists from Bulgaria and Romania, among other countries, to travel to Western Europe; can you imagine that French Embassies are refusing two-week-visas for artists that we selected to present their work to the jury for the next post graduate programs in Nantes? Western Europe has built a new wall, keeping the people of half of the continent away by visa politics…)

Could you tell more about these groups? It sounds very interesting.

2) Solakov/Venezia: it seems that things are moving, Nedko and lara are very happy about the reactions and the backing, if I understood well his last messages, they will do it anyway, of course.

Best Wishes,

Robert Fleck

From: Charles Esche
Subject: Re: themes
Date: Wednesday 19 May 1999

Dear All,

I have maintained some contact with the Serbian folk Robert Fleck first spoke of some weeks ago. It seems more than ever that the NATO action is a completely indefensible obscenity. From the English *Guardian* yesterday I attach a piece by John Pilger, which says much about our own lack of knowledge here in the UK.

As for Nedko, I have been in touch with him directly and it appears all is going ahead with their "unofficial" participation. Perhaps this is even preferable as it highlights the relationship between Bulgaria and the hosts more clearly.

Pilger follows:

Acts of murder
Up to 38 aircraft have been shot down or crashed. This is suppressed, of course.

By John Pilger
Tuesday May 18, 1999

Charles Esche

From: VOTI
Subject: VOTI PUBLIC FORUM
Date: Friday 28 May 1999

CULTURAL PRACTICE AND WAR
The summer of 1999
An online public forum presented by the XArt Foundation and VOTI

Artists, critics, curators and other cultural producers are today struggling with the terms of their own practice, in a global context of crisis when much of their work seems insignificant. How to navigate this relation between aesthetic and political intervention is a nagging question, made all the more acute during times of war. What are the terms of our involvement—do we fight at the frontlines, do we devote ourselves to humanitarian efforts or do we rather make strong interventions in the realm of symbolic production? Because clearly we are faced with wars of images, of communications networks and propaganda machines. Where are we needed most? Have we developed useful tools with which to decode images that can have practical consequences in a situation where television continually overwrites reality?

Recently an extraordinary thing has happened on the Internet. As Robert Fleck has pointed out, it is the first time we have been able to communicate nearly in real time with people on the "other side" of a war front. The war in Yugoslavia has exposed the promise and limitations of the net and has revealed anew the tangled intersections of representations, politics and histories that must be navigated in order to engage in effective cultural practice. It has revealed many things about how such assemblages cross with daily embodied realities, uprooting traditional formats of place, identity and geography especially during times of national and international crisis. Working in areas of cultural production, we must learn to contend with the new forms of cultural identification that are arising, with the fault lines of ethnic tension that contest national borders, and with the underlying processes of militarization.

The <voti><blast> forum will address these issues in the context of a 3-month online public forum, beginning today and ending September 1, 1999. We invite you to join us.[132]

FORUM HOSTS:

ZDENKA BADOVINAC, Director of the Moderna Galerja, Ljubljana, Slovenia
BART DE BAERE, organiser and writer, Stedelijk Museum voor Actuele Kunst, Ghent Belgium
WAYNE BAERWALDT, independent curator in Winnipeg and Santa Monica
CARLOS BASUALDO, poet and freelance curator, project director of Apex Art Curatorial Projects, New York
DANIEL BIRNBAUM, Director of IASPIS, Stockholm

WALING BOERS, curator and publicist, director of Biiro Friedrich, Berlin
FRANCESCO BONAMI, Senior Curator at the Museum of Contemporary Art, Chicago, Artistic Director Fondazione Sandretto Re Rebaudengo per L'Arte, Torino, and Artistic Director of Pitti Discovery, Florence
DAN CAMERON, Senior Curator at the New Museum of Contemporary Art, New York
CAROLYN CHRISTOV-BAKARGIEV, art critic and independent curator, Rome
UTE META BAUER, curator and head of the Institute for Contemporary Art at the Academy of Fine Arts Vienna
CHRISTOPHE CHERIX, curator Cabinet des Estampes, Geneva
LISA CORRIN, Senior Curator at Serpentine Gallery, London
JORDAN CRANDALL, artist and media theorist, New York
AMADA CRUZ, Director of Exhibitions at the Center for Curatorial Studies, Bard College, New York
OKWUI ENWEZOR, curator, Artistic Director of Documenta XI
CHARLES ESCHE, writer and exhibition organiser, Codirector of The Modern Institute, Glasgow
ROBERT FLECK, independent critic, curator, and director of the post-graduate program at the Ecole Regionale des Beaux-Arts in Nantes
DOUGLAS FOGLE, Curator of Contemporary Art, Walker Art Center, Minneapolis
JESUS FUENMAYOR, curator and writer, Caracas
BETTINA FUNCKE, associate publications editor, Dia Center for the Arts, New York, and doctoral candidate at ZKM Karlsruhe
REBECCA GORDON-NESBITT, curator, founding member of Salon3, London
HOU HANRU, independent critic and curator, Paris
SUSAN HAPGOOD, Curator of Exhibitions, American Federation of Arts, and Senior Fellow, Vera List Center for Art and Politics, The New School, New York
MARIA HLAVAJOVA, Director, Soros Center for Contemporary Arts, Bratislava, Slovakia
JENS HOFFMANN, independent curator, New York
UDO KITTELMANN, Director, Kolnischer Kunstverein, Cologne
VASIF KORTUN, writer, curator, educator and founder of the Istanbul Contemporary Art Project, Istanbul
MARTA KUZMA
CORNELIA LAUF, art historian and curator, founder and director of Camera Oscura, San Casciano dei Bagni, Tuscany
MARIA LIND, Curator of Contemporary Art, Moderna Museet, Stockholm
ROSA MARTINEZ, historian, art critic and independent curator, Barcelona, and curator of III International Site Santa Fe Biennial
LAURENCE MILLER, Founding Director of ArtPace, San Antonio, Texas
VIKTOR MISIANO, independent curator, Moscow
AKIKO MIYAKE, Program Director for CCA Kitakyushu, Japan
STEPHANIE MOISDON TREMBLAY, art critic and freelance curator, Professor at the Universite Paris I-St. Charles, la Sorbonne

ASA NACKING, associate curator at the Louisiana Museum, Denmark
MICHELLE NICOL, curator, art and film historian, Zurich
HANS ULRICH OBRIST, independent curator, Paris, Vienna and London, operator of the Migrateurs program at Musee d'Art Moderne de la Ville de Paris
PEDRO REYES, artist and critic, curator at the Museo de Arte Carillo Gil, Mexico City
KATHRIN RHOMBERG, curator of the Vienna Secession, co-curator of Manifests 111
JOSE ROCA, curator and critic, Visual Arts Department at the Biblioteca Luis Angel Arango, Bogota
NANCY SPECTOR, Curator of Contemporary Art at the Guggenheim Museum, New York
JON-OVE STEIHAUG, independent curator and critic, Oslo
BARBARA VANDERLINDEN, founder and director of Roomade, Brussels
HORTENSIA VOELCKERS, Director of the Wiener Festwochen, Vienna
OCTAVIO ZAYA, independent curator and writer, New York

TO SUBSCRIBE:

Send an email message with the following single line in the body of the message: subscribe voti firstname lastname
Presented by the XArt Foundation and VOTI as part of the Blast 7 program (http://www.blast.org/agencies)
The VOTI website is located at http://www.blast.org/voti
A forum on cultural practice and war presented by the XArt Foundation and VOTI (http.//www blast.org/voti)
Texts are the property of individual authors
No use without their permission

From: Robert Fleck
Subject: venice
Date: Monday 31 May 1999

Dear friends,

This "public forum" is a very good idea.

Is the email information to be spread out publicly? For any interested person?

Concerning the fact that "for the first time, we can communicate with people on the other side": all ground mail is stopped since 3 weeks between France and Yugoslavia, and it seems that the telephone system in Belgrade will be attacked (or has even be attacked), then even email would no longer work...

Best Wishes,

Robert Fleck

From: Trevor Batten
Subject: post-Global?
Date: Friday 4 June 1999

The Return of National Security

Well, I guess the good news is: You got it wrong the first time round—so maybe you've got it wrong the second time too!

It seems there is a mathematical law which states that for any series of points there is an infinite number of curves, which joins them. Translated into English this means: "Don't count your chickens until they hatch and even then you ain't sure the fox won't come 'fore you gets em to market!" Or, as Franklin D Roosevelt said: "It don't matter who fires the first shot—it's the last one that counts."

Maybe America is trying to consolidate the Pax Americana with military means to reinforce its economic dominance—but if it is so economically secure why the change of policy—and if it is not so economically secure then perhaps the military strategy will fail too?

Defeat is often snatched from the jaws of victory, and the counter-attack is often at its heaviest just before it collapses. So we may still be witnessing the fast death throes of the nation state. Perhaps America is simply trying to confuse and fragment Europe in order to defuse the dangers of a unified competitive block. Maybe it will work—maybe not!

Maybe peacekeeping will turn out to be more profitable than traditional warfare, so one needs a few flare-ups to keep the process going, but serious conflicts may be tolerated no longer by the international (economic) community.

Perhaps the international community will become nervous of the implications of the NATO attack (and the precedent it has presented to India—which may now also be followed by other countries or groups of countries) and will move to stop such things happening again. Some wars are profitable and some wars disrupt trade more than they encourage it. If destroying a country is profitable, then rebuilding it is presumably even more profitable, but to get this really going one needs to transcend local borders and have some kind of global trans-national support system. Life is full of paradoxes.

Who knows, even a consumer boycott against the unjustified military aggression of America, if it so continues. Historically, money and war may have been allies, but "money" has been consistently winning against "land." Feudal empires broke up into nation-states, and these units continued to be threatened by the demands of "regional autonomy." The bourgeois nation-state is an expression of western European individual liberalism against imperial absolutism. It may collapse inwardly or expand outwardly. History is full of the ebb and flow of consolidation and collapse.

Just like global warming—the pattern changes depending on the time-scale used.

It is not impossible that the end of the Nuclear stalemate was encouraged by ecological studies of the "Nuclear Winter"—or perhaps these ideas were simply propagated to mask the real reasons. Perhaps American colonial aggression is not sustainable on ecological grounds—look at the aftermath of the Kuwait expedition. Perhaps the "two systems, one country" policy of China and the diversity of economic system in Asia is not a return to Nationalism, but the end of American dictatorship and the beginnings of a new economic "ecology" of co-existent diversity, where the political structure to carry and mediate this diversity is not yet visible.

Maybe the global economy has not completely collapsed after pulling the plug on Asia because the money has to go someplace, so presumably somebody must win somewhere. On the other hand the BBC business reports clearly stated that the European aircraft industry was surviving better than the American because Europe relied less on Asia for the export market. Dropping a few bombs on somebody is a sure way of increasing industrial production in an otherwise failing economy. It is perhaps a bad thing for us all (including the Americans) that World War II got them hooked on the military industrial complex just at a time when the more social "New Deal" was starting to work.

Bombing the shit out of somebody from 15,000 ft. can also hardly be called "being prepared to die for one's country." In fact exactly because Americans were not prepared to go in and do the close ground work, the Nato/Serbian war was increasingly becoming a dangerous cock-up, which could not end without losing face (rather like Viet-Nam)!

A country that measures history in minutes should be a little careful of making a "historical" analysis.

Look how clever America was in forcing Japan out of her isolation and how surprised it was when she showed how well the lesson had been learned!

Those that ride the tiger should not be surprised if they are eaten by it, we should indeed not forget the world is naturally a dangerous place.

Trevor Batten

From: Cornelia Lauf
Subject: where to voti
Date: Friday 4 June 1999

What has been decided regarding the Venice summit? Susan, can you referee?

After breakfast but before lunch on Thursday? Late breakfast on Wednesday? No breakfast, no lunch on Friday?

As I have remarked in these pages before, I direct a community art center in a village of 400 somewhere north of Rome, south of Florence, and east of Siena. In August, Camera Oscura is sponsoring an international art competition on behalf of the wild boar, which is slaughtered grotesquely and methodically every fall, by hordes of Italian hunters. Every artist from Sunday painters to the headiest of the post-conceptual is invited to celebrate the noble savage, and as I hope this competition is world-wide, at least in theory, I would very much like to mail my fellow VOTI's a flyer.

Where are you? Is there a mailing list of members? Jordan?

And on that note, let us turn back to the killing fields of Yugoslavia. The VOTI exchanges are fascinating; I really look forward to the open forum, and have forwarded the post on to a number of colleagues, some outside art. Those downloaded news pieces passed on by R. Fleck, C. Esche, and others are the type of behind-the-scenes material that makes this forum so riveting.

Regards,

Cornelia Lauf

From: Angus Trumble
Subject: Making the absent present
Date: Saturday 5 June 1999

If Jordan and our other hosts do not mind, I would like to post the following essay about K.S. Inglis's book "Sacred Places" (Melbourne: The Miegunyah Press, 1998) (p.419). It may be of some interest to some subscribers who are currently experiencing the horrors of which there are only faint, if bleak, echoes where I live in Australia.

Angus Trumble

SACRED PLACES: WAR MEMORIALS IN THE AUSTRALIAN LANDSCAPE
by K. S. Inglis

MAKING THE ABSENT PRESENT

From: Joseph Nechvatal
Subject: insignificant/significant
Date: Friday 4 June 1999

Concerning the initial premises on which the on-line public forum called CULTURAL PRACTICE AND WAR operates, I'd like to make a few initial comments. I don't understand the assumption that artists, critics, curators, and other cultural producers more and more see their work as insignificant compared to political interventions (violent interventions in Yugoslavia's case) any more than one can say it is made insignificant by other non-art or minor-art forms—such as raves, stock fluctuations or wearable computers. Indeed, these three random examples are made more significant when folded into art practice (to me) and framed as works of art. No? So it is, in my opinion, with the consciousness of war.

Also, to me, cultural work appears even more significant by its comparison to bloody political intervention. It especially appears significant when the consciousness of the underlying process of militarization is encoded subtly in the manifestation of the cultural practice. In this sense, art today can follow an ancient African lead, which perseveres today. In Benin, Nigeria, chiefs still wear red cloth as part of their ceremonial court dress and red (by its association with anger, blood, war and fire) is regarded as pseudo-threatening. By the wearing of such an artistically ominous cloth a chief protects himself (his consciousness) from evil; that is to say, from witchcraft and from the magical forces employed by enemies. In like manner, our art, by displaying subtle encasements of certain aspects of our war cultural consciousness might protect us from the evil consciousness of (and for) war.

I convincingly encountered such reflection (and art practice) in my role as artist coordinator for "Consciousness Refrained 1997"—the first international conference to look at new developments in art, technology and consciousness (held at Roy Ascott's Centre for Advanced Inquiry in the Interactive Arts in Wales) where I observed (and participated in) a new sensibility emerging respecting the integration of certain aspects of art, politics, science, technology and consciousness. The following brief words are an attempt to outline what I took to be the core of this phenomenon in terms of politics/war by stating what I take to be the underlying causes which I observed advancing this developing sensibility.

In my interactions with them, I discovered that the art/science/politics/consciousness creators ensuing Ascott's lead are actively exploring the frontiers of science/technology research so as to become culturally aware of the biases of consciousness today in order to amend those biases. They begin with the realization that every [new] technology disrupts the previous rhythms of consciousness. Then, generally speaking, they pursue their work in an effort to contradict the dominant clichés of our time, as they tend to move in their regimented grooves of sensibility. In this sense their art research begins where the hard science/politics/technology ends.

This moderately negative sensitivity towards hard science, politics and technology can be understood best, however, as a trestle on which vine-like connections grow between technology and psychology. Digitization is a key metaphor for them only in the sense that it is the fundamental translating system today. Digital inventiveness, like consciousness, is made up of electronic signals, thus digitalia is no longer content with the regurgitation of a standardized analog repertoire of image-tropes—hence the fertile attraction towards the abstractions of advanced scientific discovery, now stripped of their fundamentally reductive logical methodology.

Most certainly the art/science/politics/consciousness creators whom I have met understand that in every era the attempt must be made anew to wrest tradition away from a conformism that is about to overpower it. Hence the role of the science/politics/technology/consciousness artist in the face of war is that of the explorer/researcher. The function of such an explorationally inclined artist however is not to find—but to participate in and foster a constant instability of consciousness, to mitigate against self-stabilizing formations so as to encourage internal mizomatic connections to sprout and expand. This clearly is opposed to the tabular thought nestled behind nationalistic, racial and gender biases which typifies the consciousness in back of the warring impulse.

For the art/science/politics/consciousness creators, electronically augmented consciousness is characteristically a form of encountering that precipitates internal shifts where the grammar of art can collide with and interfere with the adjacent discourses of science/politics and technology. This integration goes far towards exemplifying an aesthetic, which has a problematic relationship to material science/politics-based reality.

Though exemplified by the sensibility outlined above, these feelings and strategies of production have been at work for certain significant artists, in my opinion, throughout our bloody 20th century. For example, one might ask, as I did myself when researching a Ph.D. dissertation on the central characteristic of virtual reality (immersion), just why does traditionally framed pictorial art become progressively challenged and to a certain extent eclipsed by an ambient-immersive impetus following the Second World War (as we know, there has been a substantial eruption of this impetus following the war)? Evidently there was something endemic within the barbarous conditions of 20th century modern warfare, which facilitated this development at its onset, rather than any more laudable human aspirations towards the expanding of aesthetic perceptual consciousness. We can find examples of the construction of immersive cultural space previous to the war on occasion, but after it I began identifying a large increase in apparent immersive cultural intentions. Indeed I have deducted that something in the spatial consciousness of society was altered following the war and have further deduced that the bombing of civilian centers in the course of the war (i.e., Koln, London, Tokyo)—culminating with the American atomic bombings of the civilian Japanese cities Hiroshima on August 6th, 1945 (circa 140,000 victims) and Nagasaki on August 9th, 1945 (circa 70,000 victims)—changed the world's sense of cultural space radically.

However, Paul Virilio in his esteemed book "Bunker Archeology" indirectly suggested the initial date of this spatial consciousness transition as being 1943 with the Nazi preparation for the first operational launching of the V-2 ballistic missile. Although experiments were undertaken before World War I on crude prototypes of the cruise and ballistic missiles, modern weapons are generally considered to have their true origins in the V-1 and V-2 missiles launched by Germany in 1944 and 1945. Both of those Vergeltungswaffen (Vengeance Weapons) defined the problems of propulsion and guidance that have continued ever since to shape cruise and ballistic missile development. Indeed strategic missiles represent a logical step in the attempt to attack enemy forces at a distance. As such, they can be seen as extensions of either artillery (in the case of ballistic missiles) or manned aircraft (in the case of cruise missiles). In 1944 at the Peenemünde base on the island of Usedom in the Baltic, Wernher von Braun and his team created the V-2. The V-2 was 14.1 meters long 47 feet) and its payload was about 900 kg of high explosives. The horizontal range was about 350 kilometers (220 miles), and the peak altitude usually reached was about 100 kilometers (62 miles). It was first fired against Paris on Sept. 6, 1944. Two days later the first of more than 1,300 V-2s were fired against Great Britain (the last on March 27, 1945). Belgium was bombarded almost as heavily with them. Reaching a height of more than 160 kilometers (100 miles), the V-2 marked the beginning of the space age. After the war, both the United States and the Soviet Union captured large numbers of V-2s and used them in research that led to the development of their missile programs.

Nevertheless, Pablo Picasso's 1937 monumental 3.51 by 7.52 meter (11.5 by 24.6 foot) painting, "Guernica," presented into art consciousness an earlier (the first) civilian air-bombardment of innocent people at home in their city of Guernica Y Luno during the Spanish Civil War (1936-1939). Here 1,654 Basque people were killed, at the bequest of Francisco Franco Bahamonde (1892-1975), and 889 were wounded, including the elderly, women and children by Adolf Hitler's (1889-1945) Junker 52 and Heinkel 51 warplanes in the service of Spanish fascism.

Previously there existed a separation between military and habitational space, but with the bombing of Guernica Y Luno, the swathed immersive space of the tellurian domain was suddenly deemed defunct as previous earth/covering frontiers became increasingly porous to airborne invasions. This sense of airborne vulnerability soon extended itself further and further outwards with the launching of spy and then military-communications satellites (Sputnik in 1957), the first manned space flight of the Soviet military pilot Yuri Gagarine (1934-1968) on April 12th, 1961 (the first man in space), and then the first manned trip to the moon of the American Apollo Mission in 1969 which featured Buzz Armstrong's televised trek on the moon. Rocket technology enabled military forces to put nuclear weapons on intercontinental missiles, due largely to the former work of Russian rocket pioneer Konstantin Tsiolkovsky (1857-1935) (whose visionary ideals came from Nikolai Fedorovich Fedorov (1828-1903)), the American Robert H. Goddard (1882-1945) and the German Hermann Oberth (1894-1989). With rocket technology the space of military interaction clearly expanded and mirror-like entered the inner dimensions of the human psyche. Virilio verifies this shift in consciousness in his book "War and Cinema: The Logistics of Perception," where he traces the colonization of the unhurried gaze by military technologies and the introduction of military intelligence into the indoctrination of the non-combatant's perceptions. This "rational" scopic extension of vision is accomplished precisely at the loss of another sort of vision—the ambient/holonogic—as it involves a heightened ordering and sighting of linear perspectives and a consequent geometrization of both external space and the inner human.

This new sense of threatening external space perhaps is most strongly, and most fearfully, exemplified by what has become known as C3I (pronounced as see cubed eye) the electronic military intelligence spatial fusion of control, command, communication and intelligence which developed as the electronic/digital system of strategic command over the U.S. militaries' nuclear arsenal. A fine overview of this trend towards militarizing and sighting outer (and hence inner) space is provided by Herbert York in his essay "Nuclear Deterrence and the Military Uses of Space" where he outlines the Strategic Defense Initiative (SDI) program of the 1980s and its ensuing militarization of outer space. Indeed York makes the point that "from the beginning" the use of the space program has been "primarily of a military, not civilian or scientific nature". (York, H. 1985. "Nuclear Deterrence and the Military Uses of Space" In Daedalus: Weapons in Space Vol. I: Concepts and Technologies. Issue 114, No. 2, Spring 1985, p. 20) As part of the SDI program President Ronald Reagan put forth in a speech in 1983 his "vision" of what became pejoratively called Star Wars; perhaps the archetype of this oppressive spatial consciousness—now making a limited comeback under Clinton.

What I am proposing here, in agreement with Virilio, is that the sense of human enfolded space was radically transformed in 1943 when the German rocket-launched bombs began to fall without warning, shattering the common sense of civilized, non-combatant, protected space and that this remade human feelings towards external space thoroughly. As a consequence, I maintain, a consciousness of civilian aerial bombing, of atomic weapons, of military rocketry and of the eventual militarization of outer space has greatly engendered the abandonment of the horizontal line in art, which for thousands of years had been the basis of aesthetics and proportion. Of course accompanying this new sense of space was a general post-war urge to position one's artistic activities and ideas outside of previous contexts and, in Western art and philosophy's case, outside of Surrealism and Existentialism.

Western consciousness just following World War II's brutal demonstration of nuclear destructive power on Japan began to be reflected forcefully in vanguard art of the post-war period. Therefore it is no coincidence that places of worship figured prominently among post-war modernist architecture and became statements of yearning for a placid immersive cohesion with wholeness as we see with Le Corbusier's Notre-Dame-du-Haut Chapel at Ronchamp and the Claude Parent and Paul Virilio project for the church of Sainte-Bernadette du Banlay in Nevers, France, designed in 1964 and built in 1966. This project was based on the architecture of confinement and territorial closure, which the Nazis had built on the French Atlantic coast, as depicted and explained by Paul Virilio's classification of the bunkers in his book "Bunker Archeology." These imposingly beautiful concrete monoliths seem almost as if they are floating autonomously on the silt and sand and this sense of shifting edges was recreated in the church of Sainte-Bernadette du Banlay as the project took the form of a colossal cleaved bunker which is cracked in two-halves. This design was intended as a critical statement of contemporary society's association with the military.

Moreover, in 1963, Parent and Virilio set up the group Architecture Principe with the sculptor Morice Lipsi and the painter Michel Carrade so as to advance many *Gesamtkunstwerk* (total-art-work) ideals into the 1960s. In this respect I should also mention here the French-based international and multi-disciplinary Espace group, which was predicated on the idea of a *Gesamtkunstwerk* synthesis of the arts and on ideals of spatial unity and spatial continuity. Espace (which is the French word for space) was founded in 1935 by its chairman Andre Bloc (1396-1966), principally, an engineer working in rubber and a painter and sculptor, whose interests lay in the expression of an underlying quest for a new relationship to space. As such he founded the journal *L'Ait d'aujourd'hui*, which was the print medium for the Espace group. *L'Architecture d'aujourd'hui* in the 1930s was one of the first reviews concerned with modern architecture and was distributed widely. As such, it was the place where all the different schools of architecture exchanged theories, including those of the Dutch Neo-Plasticists, Auguste Perret (1874-1954) and Le Corbusier. One of Espace's vice-chairmen was the artist Fernand Ledger (1881-1955). The artist Sonia Delaunay (1885-1979), who took her version of the *Gesamtkunstwerk* synthesis of the aits into the creation of clothing and a matching automobile, was the general secretary. Sadly Espace's *gesamt* ideals of spatial continuity died out after the war since the hostilities overturned the conception of concordant space (in fact Andrid Bloc, who was Jewish, was forced to flee for his life) and it became more reactive towards the psychic effects of aerial-bombings on civilian populations and the persistent nuclear threat thereafter. Influential with the group were the ideas, work, and writings of Max Bill (1908-1994) and Paul Virilio, who was one of the first to explore space's social and political ramifications. Following the end of the war, Bloc still conceived of the exploration of this topological space in terms of unity, but it is certain that the war brought about a more dour perception of spatial consciousness based on non-holistic notions of fragmentation and discontinuity, thus putting a temporary end to approaches based on the unity of total design. Indeed, with a heightened consciousness of war synthesis seems impossible.

Verily, this warring fragmentational consciousness is only now beginning to be reunited in a more natural (borderless) post-Cold War Euro environmental continuity (despite the crises in Yugoslavia) and by inevitable benevolent connectivist features of the Internet.

As an American artist living often in Europe, I notice this process of synthesis (re-conceived of in micro self-segmented ways within modest programs) unfold nearly every day with the unification of Europe, even given the retained suspicions towards idealist illusions which counterbalance this humanist desire for diverse but harmonious co-existence. Hence it is pleasing to recall that the musician Edgard Varese (1883-1965) in conceiving his unfinished work "Espace," wanted there to be "voices in the sky, as though magic, filling all space, crisscrossing, overlapping, penetrating each other"—much as our words and thoughts will do here through electronic connectivity.

From: agent blast (Paul Virilio)
Subject: war space
Date: Sunday 6 June 1999

The military space is something people don't talk about too often. You find it in Clausewitz, but it hasn't really been taken up since. People speak of the history of war, of battlefields, of deaths in the family, but no one speaks of the military space as the constitution of a space hung its own characteristics. My work is located within this concept. I suddenly understood that war was a space in the geometrical sense, and even more than geometrical: crossing Europe from North to South, from the shelters of the German cities to the Siegfried Line, passing by the Maginot Line and the Atlantic Wall, makes you realize the breadth of total war. By the same token you touch on the mythic dimension of a war spreading not only throughout Europe, but all over the world. The objects, bunkers, blockhouses, anti-aircraft shelters, submarine bases, etc. are kinds of reference points or landmarks to the totalitarian nature of war in space and myth.[133]

From: Bronwyn Mahoney
Subject: Re: war space
Date: Monday 7 June 1999

Paul Virilio wrote:

The military space is something people don't talk about too often. You find it in Clausewitz, but it hasn't really been taken up since. People speak of the history of war, of battlefields, of deaths in the family, but no one speaks of the military space as the constitution of a space having its own characteristics.

"Theatre of war" perhaps evokes such a space. It speaks of a stage, where drama unfolds. It also adds a sense of unrealness to the euphemism, distancing and mythologising war and those involved.

Bronwyn Mahoney

From: Simon Biggs
Subject: Re: war space
Date: Monday 7 June 1999

Paul Virilio wrote:

The military space is something people don't talk about too often. You find it in Clausewitz, but it hasn't really been taken up since. People speak of the history of war, of battlefields, of deaths in the family, but no one speaks of the military space as the constitution of a space having its own characteristics.

My work is located within this concept. I suddenly understood that war was a space in the geometrical sense, and even more than geometrical: crossing Europe from North to South, from the shelters of the German cities to the Siegfried Line, passing by the Maginot Line and the Atlantic Wall, makes you realize the breadth of total war. By the same token you touch on the mythic dimension of a war spreading not only throughout Europe, but all over the world. The objects, bunkers, blockhouses, anti-aircraft shelters, submarine bases, etc. are kinds of reference points or landmarks to the totalitarian nature of war in space and myth.

You speak of the physical or geographical space of war, but what of the informational space? I do not particularly mean here the recent use of the Internet, nor the use of other media (such as print, radio or television) for propaganda (although that is part of what I refer to) but more the technologies of control and surveillance that underpin missile guidance systems, satellite tracking and battlefield reconnaissance. In *War and Cinema*, you wrote to some degree on this, in relation to cinema in particular and its relation to particular weapons technologies (the Gattling or machine gun).

Keeping in mind the sort of informational war space I suggest above, how do you think artists (who specialise in the representation of space) can intervene in or at least represent this space (I have in mind here the manner in which Picasso related war space to print, and newspapers in particular, in his painting Guernica, which I would regard as paradigmatic of an artist's representation of war). Do you agree with Paul Celan as to the role of the artist (or lack of it) after World War Two?

In a sense, is not war space another aspect of the culturalisation of geographic space, just like any form of architecture, transport system, ownership or representation of landscape?

Simon Biggs

From: Brian Carroll
Subject: Re: war space
Date: Monday 7 June 1999

An interesting book on the subject of war space is:

"The Cultivated Wilderness Or, What is Landscape?" by Paul Shepheard, MIT Press, 1997.

Landscape's too big a subject for ideas. It needs visions...

p. 191
It may be called a pyschogeography of war, a place of memories, memorials, bodies
decayed, the wilderness reasserted, the artifacts of the military exchange..."

Old soldiers have a vision of every battle as part of some great war that has been going on
since humans began. Some pieces of the landscape are so perfect for battle that they have
been chosen over and over again, they say, and one of these is the shoulder of northwest
France. The mud and the massacre that framed the battle of Agincourt is too like the battle
of the Somme deny the old soldiers' delusion. That is why one must write plays.

The Western Front... A blur of churned-up ground, only a few miles wide, whose few
remaining trees were decimated to stumps, pockmarked with craters, full of rusted metal
and debris and unexploded shells and the corpses of 4 million men, ran clear across France
for 450 miles, from the English Channel all the way to the Alps.

The ruination of the landscape...

... a little battlefield museum: theme-parking of the most basic kind.

(The~Western~Front-as~Theme~Park)

...the Western Front landscape has achieved something I would not have thought possible -
a secular sacred landscape."

excerpts pp.199-230[134]

From: Brian Carroll
Subject: Re: war space
Date: Monday 7 June 1999

By the same token you touch on the mythic dimension of a war spreading not only throughout Europe, but all over the world. The objects, bunkers, blockhouses, anti-aircraft shelters, submarine bases, etc. are kinds of reference points or landmarks to the totalitarian nature of war in space and myth.

I would add that war has spread to civilian objects, now, like barracks and bunkers. There are TV and radio stations and transmitters, power stations, phone exchanges...as part of the battlefield. The war space now sits on most every street (infrastructure), as both the Gulf War and Operation Allied Force demonstrate.

bc[135]

From: agent blast (Vicki Sowry)
Subject: stealth technologies
Date: Monday 7 June 1999

An examination of the contemporary concerns of military research and development shows that a major tendency is to create war machines which attempt to achieve increased speed through invisibility, an invisibility not just to the human eye, "but above all to the piercing unerring gaze of technology." These are the technologies of stealth, encapsulated by the F-117A fighter and the B-2 bomber.

In essence, stealth technologies are concerned with practices of invisibility, of what Virilio has called an "aesthetics of disappearance." This is currently achieved through a process of reducing what is termed the "signature" of a given machine (or weapon). A machine's signature is determined by its radar cross-section (RCS) and by the emissions of its communications and propulsion systems. By utilising an array of measures it becomes possible to reduce a machine's signature to the point that it becomes unrecognisable. An example of this is outlined in a House and Senate Armed Service Committee debate centred around the astounding reduction in the B-2's RCS: "When asked whether the B-2 RCS was most like that of aircraft, birds or insects, General Welch [Air Force Chief of Staff) replied that it is "in the insect category." He pleaded classification, however when asked which insect it resembled most."

Within such a frame, spatiality is only ever talked of in temporal terms. Reducing a machine's signature is a gaining of time: "if you can reduce the RCS of your aircraft by 10db, you gain a seven second advantage in launching your missile against a non-stealth adversary." Modern warfare relies entirely upon the deregulation and the convergence of time and space.

Another equally increasing convergence is that between the real/unreal—in this case, between what we perceive as "ocular reality" and the instantaneous mediated representation of that reality. The ocular reality of the B-2 bomber is an airplane standing 17-feet high, 69-feet long and with a wingspan of 172-feet. In its instantaneous representation on a radar screen this reality is totally displaced and the enormity of the B-2 has become no more perceptible than an insect—the B-2 can be apprehended as simultaneously real and unreal.

An interesting sideline to this are the simulation technologies that have developed for testing the capabilities of the B-2 and F-117A. Currently, test pilots spend more "flight-time" in the tactical simulator than they do in actual airspace. The repercussions of this situation, and its concomitant extension to notions of "real" versus "simulated" warfare, point to one area emerging as a site for analysis and possible intervention. Cf. the Kroker's assertion that the current situation is an opportunity for combat trainings

The development of technologies necessary for the building of the B-2 began in the early 1970s, leading to the construction of the first operational prototype in 1978. However, the B-2's existence only became known to the public during the 1980 presidential campaign, and even then no more was known than that—any other information about the programme was unobtainable and this remained the case until November 1988 when the official roll-out ceremony took place. Even at this public "unveiling" severe restrictions were placed upon what could be seen, and who could see it. (As a brief background, it had come to be seen as unfeasible to fly the B-2 only at night and only in remote areas. The Chiefs of Staff had decided to transfer the B-2 into an active flight test programme, that is, a programme where flights could be undertaken during daylight hours. It became a matter of political expediency, therefore, to provide the public with more information than had previously been forthcoming.)

This history is mirrored with the F-117A fighter. This aircraft first flew in prototype in 1977, entered production in 1981 and became operational in 1983. However its existence was not acknowledged by the Air Force until November 1988—a full eleven years after its first flight. (And this of course does not include the length of time spent in development on R&D design databases). In this fog of secrecy, one thing is clear—the ability of the military to classify security-sensitive technologies out of existence. Paradoxically, the "being-seen" of the B-2 and the F117A only highlighted the extent to which they remained unseen. (Haraway described something very similar, in referring to the cyborg: "They are as hard to see politically as materially.")

This is certainly the case for the B-2—although "officially unveiled" four years ago, details about its yearly budget and production schedule still remain "black" (the questionable moniker for absolutely classified projects). The obvious reason for such a classification is that it gives the B 2 an advantage in Congressional debates concerning Defense Budget allocation. However, through such evidence we can see that stealth technologies—and their underlying tenets of disappearance, deceit and decoy—are having an irrefutable impact upon concrete political process, an impact that is rapidly gaining momentum. For example, the funding for "deep black" projects has substantially increased in the last ten years, and now makes up thirty-five percent of the total Air Force procurement budget. Secrecy has also distracted observers outside of the Pentagon. Shielded from the radar of a potentially critical public, the B-2 and F-117A projects elude being focused upon to the degree of mare visible programmes such as the Strategic Defense Initiative, thereby ensuring that debate is restricted to the armed services and appropriations committees. Such secrecy, however, provides some disturbingly ironic drawbacks—even for the pro-military politician.

The same classification which guarantees the budget dollar also makes accountability for that dollar difficult, if not impossible, to achieve. This dynamic has been played out in the B-2 program with surprising force, in October 1989, a false claims lawsuit was filed against Northrop Corporation—the prime contractor involved in the project. The suit, brought by one current and five former Northrop employees, claimed that "the company wrongfully received more than $20 billion from the U.S. government...[and] that there was widespread and long-term mismanagement, fraud and abuse within the stealth bomber program that resulted in mischarging, false statements and misrepresentations to the Air Force concerning progress on the B-2."

The suit was defeated, but it did raise serious doubts about the desirability of continuing with the program. Congress, backed against a wall, agreed to continue supporting the project, albeit in a severely curtailed way. At the time of the rollout the Air Force was adamant that an operational fleet of one hundred and thirty-two bombers was necessary for the success of the programme. In January 1992, President Bush announced that the B-2 fleet would be held to twenty aircraft. This has required a redefining of, among other things, the proposed strategic role of the B-2.

By concentrating on the technologies of stealth favoured by the military it is possible to recognise some major operative trends, which form the component parts of a framework around which a technics of domination is emerging. Noted above are some brief examples of ways in which stealth has impacted upon governmental process. Of far greater importance is the need to identify the ways in which stealth technologies will broaden their reach into the broader political and cultural realm.[136]

Vicki Sowry

From: Jordan Crandall
Subject: Re: stealth technologies
Date: Tuesday 8 June 1999

Vicki Sowry wrote:

By concentrating on the technologies of stealth favoured by the military it is possible to recognise some major operative trends, which form the component parts of a framework around which a technics of domination is emerging. Noted above are some brief examples of ways in which stealth has impacted upon governmental process. Of far greater importance is the need to identify the ways in which stealth technologies will broaden their reach into the broader political and cultural realm.

Vicki Sowry has given us another way of positioning materiality across the real/virtual divide, as led by the war machine. We speak of an "improved seeing" that is built on the reduction of others' ability to see, and we can speak of a kind of movement-materiality that is calculated precisely in order to evade the image. In response to developments in radar, for example, the aircraft that at first had the privilege of unfettered seeing has become stealthified, constructed in order to escape detection, as its optical capacities have been gradually transferred to distributed systems. And at ground level, radar can be switched off in order to obfuscate ground locations to aerial electronics: a tactic that Serbian military, for example, has employed in the face of NATO bombing. This new kind of materiality, this evasive movement-materiality, is embedded unequally in matrices of detection and obfuscation among combative actors, driven by the need for ever-decreasing strategic margins and the ceaseless maintenance of "the edge." Its agents and referents are involved in detecting patterns while evading and hampering the ability of others to do so, gaining "signatures" while reducing one's own signature, one's own imprint upon a representational field, limiting the movement-traces that have the potential to betray presence. Within this battlefield lay materiality and geography, integrally intertwined and no longer primary in any sense.

From: Robert Fleck
Subject: [unavailable]
Date: Tuesday 8 June 1999

Dear friends,

Just to confirm that despite the fact that all ground mail is stopped between Nato-states and Yu, email is still working. I just got a mail from a young artist, and it's also possible to answer. Sonja Pavicevic

See you in Venice,

Robert Fleck

From: Brian Carroll
Subject: Re: war space
Date: Tuesday 8 June 1999

Simon Biggs writes:

technologies of control and surveillance that underpin missile guidance systems, satellite tracking and battlefield reconnaissance.

Hi Simon,

Your post reminded me of what I think is an important document: the Militarily Critical Technologies List, Dept. of Defense, mirrored on John Young's Architome archive.

Basically, the document outlines the genealogy of the electronic war apparatus, from Command, Control, Communications, Intelligence, and Information Systems, to Computer Aided Design & Manufacturing, to Supercomputing, Interface Design, Information Security, Intelligent Systems (AI), to Modeling and Simulation, Networks and Switching, Signal Processing, Software Design, and Transmission Systems.

This document provides background for connecting these computers we are sitting in front of, to the war machine, as it functions based upon these technologies of (political) control, if only from the most basic fact that each of our computers is linked, either directly or indirectly, to power plants, nuclear or fossil fueling, the reasoning for the war megamachine.

That these mundane, everyday technologies still have a hand in the militarization of space is also heralded in by the debate surrounding cryptographic technologies, an interesting book review, giving some background to why this is the case is also at JYA's site; Cryptome.

From: Simon Biggs
Subject: Re: war space
Date: Wednesday 9 June 1999

Brian Carroll writes:

Basically, the document outlines the genealogy of the electronic war apparatus, from Command, Control, Communications, Intelligence, and Information Systems, to Computer Aided Design & Manufacturing, to Supercomputing, Interface Design, Information Security, Intelligent Systems (AI), to Modeling and Simulation, Networks and Switching, Signal Processing, Software Design, and Transmission Systems.

This document provides background for connecting these computers we are sitting in front of, to the war machine, as it functions based upon these technologies of (political) control, if only from the most basic fact that each of our computers is linked, either directly or indirectly, to powerplants, nuclear or fossil fueling the reasoning for the war megamachine.

That these mundane, everyday technologies still have a hand in the militarization of space is also heralded in by the debate surrounding cryptographic technologies, an interesting book review, giving some background to why this is the case is also at JYA's site; Cryptome.

Here you are essentially talking about our entire technological infrastructure; it is probable that it has always been the case that our technologies have been intimately tied up with systems of social control, including warfare. In fact, the very "order" of our societies can be seen to be just as tied up with this. The manner in which our societies have developed over millennia are totally caught up in these patterns, to the point that the state of war can be seen as an extension of "normal" social behaviour (who was it that said "war is diplomacy by other means"?). One can regard society itself as a technology (as language can also be seen) and thus we have an all-inclusive subject to deal with.

My perception is that war (and related things, like social control, exclusion, appropriation of difference, ownership, etc.) is something that the human race has practiced ever since it was capable of doing it. Thus the initial question here does not concern the particular role of technology in that (as everything appears to be involved) but rather whether war is something people should do, whether it is a natural human thing and whether we are capable of living without it?

This could be viewed as a moral or philosophical question (and there are certainly many moral and idealistic responses to such questions) but I think to be able to address the issue clearly it is advisable, prior to looking for answers, or even voicing our agendas, to establish the question first, avoiding the temptation to find the answer where we wish to find it.

The question thus appears to be...can the human race survive without war? That is to say, are people capable of living together without recourse to war as a resolution of conflict?

Nevertheless, I will look up the documents you suggest as they certainly sound like interesting reading.

Thanks

Simon Biggs

From: Brian Carroll
Subject: Re: war space
Date: Thursday 10 June 1999

Simon Biggs:

Here you are essentially talking about our entire technological infrastructure…

On one point I agree with you, regarding the assertion that the role of technology and war has always been this way. But on the same point I disagree, with respect to art museums and curators; imagine an art installation, a video piece, say, or a Dan Flavin or a JODI at the MOMA, say. Now, if I am going to ascertain the value of the piece, or even interpret it, am I going to look at it as a discrete and disconnected object d'art, or as a node in a vast interconnected infrastructure that is also connected to fossil fuels, pollution, global warming, wars for oil, etcetera.

On the whole, the art object, or artifact, is taken as a separate piece from the larger technological assemblage, which limits its role and its meaning in terms of art & war.

Now taking the same art piece, say a JODI linked computer program, I could rig up a solar panel to the roof of the museum and run a circuit so that the program is self-supporting, and not connected to that big nasty centralized, highly politicized infrastructure of power and media (that handmaiden of the information war), and what have we? A different piece entirely, a different assemblage of power, different lines of force, a different context.

I stand behind my first post, saying these everyday technologies do have an economic, social, political influence, and that these need to be reflected, re-projected, dismantled, detoured, etc.

My perception is that war (and related things, like social control, exclusion, appropriation of difference, ownership, etc.) is something that the human race has practiced ever since it was capable of doing it. Thus the initial question here does not concern the particular role of technology in that (as everything appears to be involved) but rather whether war is something people should do; whether it is a natural human thing and whether we are capable of living without it?

This question belongs to Utopias and ideologies, from my vantage, at best, war can be sublimated, as it has been during the Cold War. Then, the influences of war surface in other areas, economics, architecture, popular culture, art…

There is a sublimated warfare in the art & architectural magazines: who gets the cover story, who gets ousted, who gets flamed, by who, what university, what club, what cause, what institution? But it is even more messy that this. As many of the institutions are themselves like states, nations, and the conglomeration of the many also become like one, a certain globalism of the art world, the world view becoming a singularity, that is where the network, the net time, comes in as a methodology of critique, dissent and discussion for questions such as: why war? Because, there is this global monoculture of the art and architectural world, a global be-in, where being is dependent upon being a part of the larger edifice of "art," as dictated from the institutions and their statesmen and women, art is (what) in cyberspace.

This list is a war, we are soldiers, fighting for identities, for realities, trying to forge ourselves in this public-private space, and the centuries of institutional power are trying to find their place/space within the matrix, trying to define the rules of the game, when in fact they have no more power, if not less, than those individuals who belong in this space, as artists, as warriors.

The war is you against you, us against us; you and I, how are we going to interact in this e-space? Are we going to censor and sublimate the actions/effects of questioning by limiting our view of the world, seeing things only certain ways, or are we going to take the questioning to infinity, becoming uncomfortable, restless, ready to do battle, to clash ideologies, ideas, dreams in hopes of winning the war against the mundane everyday world, as it is constituted offline?

It is truly an enlightenment project, the open-ended discourse of reasoning, or of an irrational psychopathic exchange of power, to see in the collective IQ, which warrior, the masked or bare, wins the hearts and minds of the public, whose voice will win.

This could be viewed as a moral or philosophical question (and there are certainly many moral and idealistic responses to such questions) but I think to be able to address the issue clearly it is advisable, prior to looking for answers, or even voicing our agendas, to establish the question first, avoiding the temptation to find the answer where we wish to find it.

That leads to an aestheticism of war, war = bad, the ugly = wrong, a moralism of priests and priestesses, with art books as bibles, and disciples churned out of the art schools to follow the holy word. A modernist ascetic purity of form is not by default needed.

The question thus appears to be...can the human race survive without war? That is to say, are people capable of living together without recourse to war as a resolution of conflict?

But isn't conflict a part of creativity? A metabolic exchange between creativity and destruction, a place of origin...how many artists have made their horrors into beauty, how many have struggled to live their dreams and fought battles all along the way. Centuries of experience, is it really art without conflict?

Thus, I believe part of the present-day electronic art context is in including the massive realities of global warming, pollution, wars, that each of these computers we are using, amongst all the other e-technologies, are by default contributing to.

Nevertheless, I will look up the documents you suggest as they certainly sound like interesting reading.

bc

From: Trevor Batten
Subject: Re: war space
Date: Thursday 10 June 1999

Regarding Procedural Space:

Surely the main reason for the continuity of physical and mental space perceived in the context of war is because of the continuity in conceptual/procedural space.

War and sport (and computer programming to a large degree) are prime models for the development of procedural/cognitive/linguistic complexity: i.e. One begins with a simple procedure, for example, a body blow with fist or foot with the "dialogue" at this point being limited to this "basic procedure".

Gradually, over time, the "basic procedure" becomes extended through a subtle dialogue of "set" and "counter-set" either being refined (possibly developing into boxing, tai-boxing, karate, judo, etc.) or being transcended (via defensive body armor or offensive weapons). Each "set" in development representing a stable phase until the next "counter-set" is made, thus increasing the complexity of the procedural space within which the "dialogue" between the combatants must take place.

Clearly, many different factors affect the development of the procedural space. A stable "balance of power" may suit all parties, but stable situations of intolerable iniquity will generally force the weaker party to seek new strategies to break the deadlock. Presumably, the new approach (for which there is momentarily no counter-strategy) will also be strongly affected by local conditions regarding landscape, available materials, social (political, religious, economic) and possibly even "aesthetic" (non-rational) factors.

In this last category we can see, for example, a shifting spectrum regarding the attitude towards death as a result of (armed) conflict.

A spectrum, which, in this case, can be divided into three main sub-systems:

1.
"Systems of Flight" where the loser runs away "and lives to fight another day". In this system we find frightening costumes and the terrifying sounds of drums and bagpipes to scare away the enemy before they even fight.

2.
"Systems of Honour" where opponents may be killed, but war is essentially a business between professional people with mutual respect and due honour given (as reward and encouragement) to those that die. In this system we also find ritual and the paraphernalia

of war – but more as a unifying system of identity for the team than as a weapon of terror against the enemy.

3.
"Systems of Destruction" where there is no ritual and no honour for the combatants -either successful survival or defeat through destruction. In this system we find the "stealth bomber" plus chemical and biological weapons.

Incidentally, we should not be too full of romantic historic fantasies regarding these categories the classic Chinese "Art of War" by Sun Tzu would appear to support system 3 more than system 1.

The NATO/Serbian war would also seem to suggest that in a democracy, civilians are ultimately responsible for the actions of the military and so there are no longer any "innocent civilians" who should be protected against acts of war by professional soldiers. Surely, a potentially dangerous development.

One could also argue that "stealth bombers" and chemical or biological weapons if not used against strictly military targets (in the original, limited sense) are in fact "instruments of terror" which could be placed in category 1, if those subjected to the terror are allowed to escape in order to surrender.

Unfortunately conflicts become exceedingly and perhaps unnecessarily unpleasant when combatants operate under different (aesthetic) assumptions.

So, although confusion is a traditional tool of war, it may be an advantage to all involved to agree on the basic (non-rational) terms of engagement.

IF war > politics > propaganda > art THEN art = war.

If generals win wars because they truly understand the complexity of the battle and are able to translate this understanding into successful procedural strategies then perhaps artists should also invest more time in studying the complexities of their systems. By abandoning "sloganism" and returning to the artistic strategies involved in shamanistic divination perhaps they can gain understanding and achieve the ultimate prize to win the fight before the battle has begun!

From: Aras Ozgun
Subject: Bomb's Eye, part 2
Date: Friday 11 June 1999

A few weeks ago some events forced me to think once again on these issues; Junger and his notion of "seeing" as "an act of aggression," the idea of "point of view" and the political/ideological frameworks of different points of view. I was getting the news on the Internet as usual (since I don't watch TV), and I saw the headlines about NATO's bombing of Belgrade. What followed was an image filling my computer screen after I clicked on the link. It was taken from a camera placed in front of a bomb just before it hit its target. In the black and white, grainy, low-resolution sight of the bomb there was a bridge, which came bigger and bigger and then suddenly disappeared into blackness. I was shocked; fascinated by a kind of horror, I checked the other links to see more. Once I was there, just a few years ago, I have passed over that bridge. I was there with my camera; I had images of this place and those buildings (I used some of these images in my work that I mentioned above). The terror I lived while reading the news and watching the images was multi-dimensional; on the personal dimension I had been there once, I was trying to take images out of everyday life, trying to establish a relation with this foreign place and foreign life, trying to understand it through the electronic images. The way I saw that city was in the way my professor alternatively described what seeing was: "to see is to take in life, to experience the world, to witness, to exist in communication with the world beyond the self, a certain kind of affection." But what I was being exposed now was "seeing as an act of aggression" in its most extreme form. An electronic eye, which does not simply "shoot images," but blows away its objects, totally devastates the thing it sees, diminishes the life it is directed towards. On this level, my despair came from my recognition that I saw this city through my camera eye before they saw it with the eye of the bomb.

At another level, which is less personal, I felt defeated. The group of intellectuals, filmmakers and artists I worked in the past shared a certain belief on the emancipating aspects of technology. We have developed certain ideas in this sense; we thought of technological prosthesis as an extension to human body, which challenges its existence and expands the boundaries of it. We take video camera in such a context; it could be a prosthesis, which could record the events hidden in the curves of everyday life, an extension, which could show us the things we were unable to see with our bare eyes. A part of our experimental work was trying to create a purely mechanical sight with video camera. The idea was to produce an autonomous sight of the camera, which was left to the flow of mechanical movement of everyday life, a sight that is not controlled and directed by any kind of subjectivity. Such a sight could create new points of view that we did not have before, resulting in an increase in the richness of possible point of views directed towards everyday life. The autonomous sight of the camera was a way leading to the multiplicity of the points of views. This is an important point, if we consider that points of views are not passive positions that are to be occupied, that are to be defined by the occupants, but they bear certain degree of activeness, which define the subjectivities that occupy them as well. "We all live in the same city, following different paths and seeing it from different points of views"—Liebniz. The multiplicity of points of view means the multiplicity of subjectivities and multiplicity of life itself—even it is the same life that we live. (3)

In the technological sense, the sight I was exposed to—the eye of the bomb—was far beyond what we could imagine and produce. And at such a limit the technological sight becomes death's point of view, a point of view, which destroys all other points of views and life itself. A mechanical eye, which diminishes life and brings death. We were beaten, surpassed, defeated in our imagination. In Leibniz's baroque philosophy the notion of points of view was developed to justify the existence of God in an elegant way (in such an elegant way which also made possible the existence of multiplicities within pluralities); for him God was the totality of these multiple points of view, it was the city itself in which we live and place ourselves in its endless points of views, God was the endlessness itself. What is seen through the bomb's eye is the absolute, the final point of view, the destruction of the city, the end.

In his book titled *The Vision Machine*, French philosopher Paul Virilio makes a genealogy of the automation of perception and industrialization of the vision. He starts discussing photography and comes to today's computer image In the chapter titled "Candid Camera," he discusses "the end of an art" in his commentary on German video artist Michael Klier's video work "Der Riese" (The Giant) which won the Grand Prix in The Second International Video Festival in Montbeliard in 1984. The whole film is made up of the footage taken from the surveillance cameras all over the German cities. Virilio quotes Klier's assertion that the surveillance video represents "the end and the recapitulation" of his art and follows as such:

"This solemn farewell to the man behind the camera, the complete evaporation of visual subjectivity into an ambient technical effect, a sort of permanent pan-cinema which, unbeknown to us, turns our most ordinary acts into movie action, into new visual material, undaunted, undifferentiated vision-fodder, is not so much, as we have seen, the end of an art whether it be Klier's or 70s' video art, televisions illegitimate offspring. It is the absolute culmination of the inexorable march of progress of representational technologies, of their military, scientific and investigative instrumentalisation over the centuries. With the interception of the sight by the sighting device, a mechanism emerges that no longer has to do with simulation (as in the traditional arts) but with substitution. This will become the ultimate special effects of cinematic illusion." (4)

As Virilio clearly points out, bomb's eye is the final outcome of the "military, scientific and investigative" instrumentalisation of representational technologies. On the other hand, Virilio passes from a very crucial point without noticing its emancipatory significance; he makes an a priori definition of visual technologies as necessarily "representational technologies." He doesn't notice that such an instrumentalisation of visual technologies is embedded in their representative power. Only through the idea of representation image becomes the identity of things, places and events, and then things, events, persons, places can be calculated, organized, manufactured, sold and then can become targets, the concept of "target audience" and "target of a bomb" are products of the same system that depends on representation. Representation is the core of the social/ideological process that finally turns "seeing" into "an act of aggression".

In this sense, unlike what Virilio argues, art does not seek for representation, it does not seek for a chance to grab, represent and instrumentalise the physical reality, it constructs its own existence, its own reality and emancipates us in our relation with the physical reality by doing such. That is why ordinary surveillance camera images stay as nothing but only as the representative images of social control, and on the other hand Klier's film still stands as a piece of art by castrating the representative power of these images and building up "something different" out of them. It is the same with the cinema; representation of reality was not the essence of cinema, it became a certain form that the art of cinema took under such social/ideological/technological conditions.

At this context camera-eye still draws an opposite political way of seeing against that of the bomb's eye. Camera-eye versus the bomb's eye, experimentality versus governmentality. Art is the line of escape; it exists and creates new points of view at the moment that all the possibilities diminish.

In his seminal article "Work of Art In the Age of Mechanical Production," after making an account of the transformation of production and perception of images, Walter Benjamin evaluates on the political conditions of the times and rising fascism in relation to such transformed mechanical production systems and work of art. Unlike Junger's imagination of warfare as the absolute fusion of human body with the technology, Benjamin calls us to imagine how fragile is the human body lying on the battleground under the storm of steel. Fascism aestheticizes politics, Benjamin argues, in order to sustain the existence of a previous form of social system under the transformed mode of production. And he proposes a possible response to this: politicization of art.

Today, once again, for similar reasons, at another historical turning point that bring material transformation of the means of production, either in its concentrated form there, or in its wide spread, transparent form here, fascism aestheticizes warfare. Following Benjamin, we can propose that a proper response should be turning aesthetics itself into a sphere of struggle, a sort of battlefield, in which the forces that bring death in its various forms confront with the powers that supports life within its endless multiplicities.

Notes:
The professor mentioned here is Deirdre Boyle. Video Critic, Faculty Member at The Media Studies Department of The New School, New York.
Brigitte Wemeburg, "Ernst Junger And The Transformed World". October 62, Fall 1992, page 53.
See Ulus Baker's texts in Vertoviana discussion by korautonomedia for the notion of point of views.
Paul Virilio, "The Vision Machine", Indiana University Press, 1995, p.47
korautonomedia: http://aries.gisam.metu.edu.tr

From: Sina Najafi
Subject: war, sound, and time
Date: Saturday 12 June 1999

As Swedish political theorist Jens Bartelson has pointed out, it seems impossible for us at this point in history to dissociate politics and space from each other, since politics in its modern post-Westphalian phase is thoroughly grounded on a notion of space. Everything revolves around the territorial state and its quest to maintain or expand its space, and the legitimacy of this state is founded in reference to a people who both give the state its mandate and are its subjects. (The emergence of the European Union, for example, does nothing to change the fundamental terms here. It still presupposes space as the foundation of politics.) Modernity is geo-political at heart, and politics simply seems to demand a territory within which it can unfold. It seems as impossible to think of politics not being based on space today, as it is to imagine a world that is not capitalist (as Jameson has pointed out, it's even easier for us to imagine the entire destruction of the planet than it is to imagine a non-capitalist economy!). This does not have to be this way: government in nomad societies is based on kinship rather than space, and mediaeval states could overlap spatially because they were, at root, thoroughly temporal. (It is in the 17th - 18th centuries that European states embark for the first time on the task of demarcating their territories precisely).

Bartelson offers a history of how politics became spatialized and space became politicized. It's interesting that his references are to art (single-point perspective), drama (Renaissance theater and its representation of the sovereign), and science (the objectification of space as something already out there in which things then happen). The consequence of this spatialized politics was that the state could exercise full power over its citizens because an apparently safe inside now needed to be protected against a potentially hostile outside. One of the tasks of radical politics today is how to think outside of this apparently primordial connection between space and politics, and I can think of a few art projects that put this connection into question.

First, there is forthcoming sound project called *WAR!*, devised and organized by New York-based artist Brian Conley. *WAR!* is a live interactive radio performance between Belgrade's radio B92 (suppressed by Milošević and now operating underground) and a radio station in New York City. It will air sometime before early October and will be broadcast in all of Serbia and in the New York metropolitan area. The project consists of two teams of 10 sound artists each who will wage a war of sound against each other armed only with cartoon sound effects. Using the stereo divide, it will be possible to arrange it so that the radio listener at either end will hear all the sound from one team on the left speaker and all the sound from the other on the right. Each team will be asked to read three theoreticians of war (von Clausewitz, Sun Tzu, and van Creveld) in advance and then to prepare a number of set pieces for the first hour of the broadcast based on a strategy they have devised. These prepared volleys will be fired in turn for the first hour, and then the teams will be live on air locked in a struggle for domination in the domain of the audio (they can't just blast out maximum noise because that would result in white noise, the audio equivalent of mutually assured destruction). There are also arrangements being made so that Serbian and NY-area radio listeners can participate by telephone for the last fifteen minutes of the event.

As you may know, radio B92 now operates from a number of places (Amsterdam, Vienna, Montenegro) and the final signal is available on the web and is also beamed back to Serbia on medium wavelength by Austrian National Radio. The American team will also be in different places at the same time (New York, Orlando, Los Angeles). The project occurred once before in 1996 in New York City between two teams gathered in two radio stations, but this time the project is geographically much more dispersed. (The B92 end of things is set up but Conley is still in need of some technical help in New York. If anyone can be of help at the technical end of things, please email Conley.)

The project relates of course to some of the issues that have been brought up in this forum so far, especially the question of military space. Conley's project is a war in the domain of the audio. What does that mean and how does that relate to the spatialized war that has been going on in that area? As Conley puts it, "The interesting thing about using audio as well as radio to enact a struggle for domination (and thinking about the space of war) is that these media are three-dimensional and even geographical. They have spatial extent and definition. However, it is not clear how this terrain can be conquered and acquired by either opposing faction. This presents a confounding conceptual problem and makes it a particularly good place for a ludicrous display of belligerent energy."

In addition to Conley's project, two other projects come to mind. The first is the Slovenian art collective Neue Slovenische Kunst's ongoing project State in Time. The State in Time has all the paraphernalia of statehood—citizenship, a constitution, passports, etc.—but without any territorial claims. The highly realistic passports (printed by the same printing house that prints the official Slovenian passports) were in fact used by hundreds of Bosnians at the time of the Bosnian War to gain entrance to other countries. (I have one: it works!) The other is Leif Elggren and Micki von Hausswolffs ongoing project KREV (the dual kingdoms of Elgaland-Vargaland), a state with two sovereign heads! Very similar in structure to the NSK project, KREV sidesteps the spatial basis of a state by claiming the borders between all the other nation states as its territory.

Sina Najafi

From: Marina Grzinic
Subject: State in Time
Date: Wednesday 13 June 1999

Sina Najafi wrote:

Neue Slovenische Kunst's ongoing project State in Time. The State in Time has all the paraphernalia of statehood—citizenship, a constitution, passports, etc.—but without any territorial claims. The highly realistic passports (printed by the same printing house that prints the official Slovenian passports) were in fact used by hundreds of Bosnians at the time of the Bosnian War to gain entrance to other countries. (I have one: it works!)

We might ask how radicalized spatial organizations manifested in reality may serve as models for active intervention in cyberspace. Such a case is the project of the Slovenian visual art group IRWIN, entitled NEUE SLOWENISCHE KUNST (NSK) STATE IN TIME. One of the most attention-grabbing projects of the NSK movement in the 1990's has been the "State in Time" project, which is primarily carried out by the above-mentioned group, IRWIN. It was within the context of a paradigm of this sort that the NSK Embassies and NSK Consulates were realized. NSK Embassies were realized in Moscow (1992), Gent, Belgium (1993), etc. NSK consulates were opened in Florence, Italy (1993), at the Hotel Ambasciatori, and in Umag, Croatia (1994), in the kitchen of the private apartment of gallery owner Marino Cettina.

The group IRWIN established the NSK Embassy in Moscow in a private apartment (address: Leninsky Prospect 12, apt. 24) in May and June 1992. The facade of this residential dwelling was embellished with the artistically articulated insignia of a state embassy. The project took place within the context of the internationalization of one of the greatest Eastern European phenomena, Apt-Art (Apartment-Art), which was a phenomenon of artistic creation and exhibition in private apartments within the Moscow art underground. The Moscow Apt-Art emphasized the status of private space and changed it into a center of communication through the self-organization of those most excluded. The NSK Moscow EMBASSY project represented a new actualization of the phenomenon of life and creation in private apartments during the era of Communist totalitarianism.

In his book, *Spectres de Marx*, Jacques Derrida put into play the term "spectre" to indicate the elusive pseudo-materiality that subverts the classic ontological oppositions of reality and illusion. Slavoj Žižek argues that "We should recognize the fact that there is no reality without the spectre, that the circle of reality can be closed only by means of an uncanny spectral supplement. ... "Spectre" is not to be confused with 'symbolic fiction'... reality is never directly 'itself,' it presents itself only via its incomplete-failed symbolization, and spectral apparitions emerge in this very gap that forever separates reality from the real, and on account of which reality has the character of a (symbolic) fiction: the spectre gives body to that which escapes (the symbolically structured) reality." In an attempt to emphasize the synthetic dialectical moment developed in the NSK State in Time, we are compelled to ask ourselves how can we label this spiritual element of corporeality (NSK State In Time) and this corporeal element of spirituality (embassies in concrete private spaces)? I propose we conclude: SPECTERS. Allow me to state the following: the NSK State in Time is the specter of the state; NSK Embassies are the specters of embassies. As Richard Beardsworth has shown in his important book *Derrida & the Political*: "Any country, any locality, determines its understanding of time, place and community in relation to this process of 'global' specializations."

On the other hand, we can re-articulate the NSK STATE IN TIME also as a precise articulation of the evacuation of the specific historical, social and political space of the former Eastern Europe, after the fall of the Berlin Wall. As Peter Lamborn Wilson, alias Hakim Bey, stated in his lecture at the Nettime meeting entitled "Beauty and The East" in Ljubljana in 1997, the Second World has been erased, and only the First and Third Worlds are left. In place of the Second World, Bey argued, there is a big hole from which one jumps into the Third. NSK STATE IN TIME is a transposition, as much as it is also a spectralization, of the evacuation of the specific historical, social and political space of the former Eastern Europe, of this non-space condition. It is possible to find the same condition in the center of the myth of liberating and innocent cyberspace. "What you discover (in cyberspace—added by the author, M.G.) is always," according to Oliver Marchart, "your own image in a reversed form... This sentence—since obviously it paraphrases the Lacanian communication formula—has an axiomatic status. Wherever you go, you are always already there." And this is exactly to what the IRWIN NSK STATE IN TIME project is pointing a finger. The group IRWIN has the power to articulate its proper position using the same mechanisms and matrices that seem, at first glance, to be part of another "absolutely virtual" territory.

From: Jordan Crandall
Subject: citizens of the world
Date: Sunday 13 June 1999

Dear Andrej Tisma,

In the spring of '98, in the <eyebeam><blast> forum, you wrote, "the Internet makes us citizens of the world. It is a chance for all of us to become individuals, since on the Internet there are no frontiers, no distances, physical or temporal. We are all part of one huge web of individuals."

I am wondering what distancing effect the war may have had, and in general how the role of the net may have changed for you. You have been living in Yugoslavs and active online and I am curious to know how this seemingly borderless space of the net has changed.

From: Andrej Tisma
Subject: Re: citizens of the world
Date: Monday 14 June 1999

Dear Jordan,

A good question for me who just returned home after 78 days of brutal NATO bombing of Novi Sad, the city where I am living. First 30 days I spent in my home, going to the bomb shelter when air raid alarm sirens were sounding, or after strong detonations during the night, which have woken me up (a few times only 100 meters from my home). I was always sleeping dressed up, prepared to leave home, but later on I was spending nights in an underground cafe where I did not bother about bombs falling. After a terrific month in the city I moved with my family to a village near Novi Sad where it was quiet. Even there, out of city, we could hear all detonations, and the windows and door were shaking. At the time of bombing, I tried to stay connected with the world through Internet, participating in mailing lists and sending my messages to friends worldwide. I didn't have much time to spend by my computer because it was dangerous. Our house is near many potential NATO targets, so I tried to be out as much as possible. Also several times, links (optical cables) were cut for few days, because all three Novi Sad bridges were demolished. It also cut our water and electricity supplies.

But even in those uncomfortable circumstances, I managed to stay on-line. Unfortunately I must say that the reality of war reflected on my cyber situation. I was removed from several lists. From Syndicate because my mail was bouncing (it was too much mail in my mailbox because I didn't download it regularly), but also from Rhizome list because of, as it was explained to me, the nature of my messages (anti-NATO).

I felt that real life was reflecting on cyberspace much earlier too, in March last year when I was removed from the Nettime list by Big Brother Lovink because my "nationalistic" views (at the same time while he was normally publishing Albanian nationalists and separatists), but also some time later from 7-11, I don't know why.

In principle I am against any exclusions of people from lists (moderation is O.K.), if the Internet has to stay an open media, without any frontiers. But it seems that the dirty political world took the Internet under its influence. So during this war I was bombed from many sides. Not only with real bombs, which deprived me of Internet links and electricity, but medial cyber bombs too, in form of censorship, which disabled me to communicate freely with my friends and my audience. I feel that removing someone from a mailing list or cyberspace is equivalent for killing somebody in the real life. Because in the cyberspace you can silence someone only by switching him out, and he stops to exist in the virtual reality. So removing someone from cyberspace is equal to murder. And I can say I was "killed" several times recently. This is a kind of war on Internet. But the Internet also stayed our only media to relatively freely speak out during this war, because Yugoslavian TV station buildings were also demolished by NATO bombers (what a subtle kind of censorship), and Yugoslavian TV was removed from Eutelsat, also for political reasons. Radio and TV transmitters were bombed all over the country. So the Internet, which we were by miracle not excluded from, was our only existing media for telecommunication (except mail which is too slow and unsecure).

Once I had even an opportunity to be interviewed by ABC News in New York, and I was answering questions through Internet for two hours, with over 350 people participating (see it at: http://www.abcnews.go.com//sections/world/DailyNews/chat_990329andrej html Also I was running my "Personal" webzine reflecting war events, even putting in some fresh images of consequences of NATO bombings: <http://members.tripod.com/~aaart/personal.htm>

I must admit I didn't produce much web.art during the bombing, but I think it is understandable. So bare Internet communication was my main activity (especially with net friends who showed a great care for me, giving me a huge and precious moral support to go on). But I sent some of my earlier web.art works' URLs (which had much to do with the bombing) to many addresses.

So the Internet stayed for me borderless, without distances in sense of time and space, but not so open as I have supposed a year ago. We all are part of one huge web of individuals, as I said before, but without equal given possibilities, regarding the geographic part of the world we are communicating from and regarding our ideological and political standpoints. That is making me a little bit unhappy and it breaks my illusions about the open, free and democratic world (western part of it) I used to believe in.

Best regards,

Andrej

From: Saul Anton
Subject: Re: peace plan
Date: Tuesday 15 June 1999

However complex the situation in Russia is, however weak are the pro-western politicians of Yeltsin's camp, to argue that it was the Russians who delivered the Serbs to the negotiating table and convinced them to withdraw from Kosovo is simply not a credible argument. It puts the cart before the horse. As a great Marxist thinker once wrote, "power comes from the barrel of a gun." That's why Serbia was in Kosovo with an army. It wasn't negotiating for the withdrawal of the Albanians. That's why the U.S. had to go to war. The negotiations, if I remember correctly, went on for a long, long time before the U.S. started to bomb.

Russia indeed does see its role in the world shrinking, but that's not simply because it's poor. Whatever nuclear arsenal it may have, its control over the states that it dominated, such as the Ukraine, was asserted militarily. Its control over the East European states such as Czechoslovakia and Hungary was, if I remember, asserted militarily. It invaded both countries in 1956 and 1968.

While the hardliners are indeed gaining ground in Russia because of the failed conversion to a viable capitalistic program, I'm not sure it's so easy to find fault with NATO's treatment of them. The truth is, while they used to be a major force, I doubt that NATO's treatment is what's going to put the hardliners in charge. Yeltsin and his cronies have seen to that themselves by being rather incompetent handlers of the few cards they've been dealt. Those Russian generals used to see themselves as geo-political players. They're move in Kosovo seems like some kind of nostalgia for another era. Whether this indicates that a new post-war confrontation is in the offing is doubtful.

Saul Anton

From: Teo Spiller
Subject: on-line chat live from Belgrade an Venice
Date: Tuesday 15 June 1999

Prisoners of War—communicating from isolated environments (on-line chat live from Belgrade)

Prisoners of War (POW) is a group of artists from Belgrade. Oreste is an Italian group of artists, who will be presented in the Italian Pavilion at the Venice Biennial. We will try to establish the communication between the Belgrade and Venice via chat.

Topics will be:

Communication in isolation, closed environment.

Subtopics are:

1) Ways and means of communication/how one communicates when confined to closed and isolated environment. How communication goes within that environment and how it goes in the outside world.

2) The content of such communication. What are the contents of such a communication? Being in isolated environment and without usual means and technical support it is not complete. There is something missing, mistakes are made and so on.

3) Aesthetics of such communication. Does it make sense? Can and should we speak about aesthetics of such communications?

The project was organised at the times of bombing and disturbed communications, so we organised some "alternative" ways of communications in case the chat would not be possible via telephone lines. There are few words about it at <http://www.spiller.si/partizan>.

The online chat will take place at 48th Biennale di Venezia on "d AP E RTutto" in stanza di Oreste (Italian Pavilion) on the 19th and 20th of June 1999 between 11am-1 pm and 4pm-6pm European time (on both days).

I think, this project could answer some questions the VOTI forum is trying to answer, so I am inviting you to take active role in the online chat. I would also suggest, Jordan, at that time, the distribution of messages to participants of VOTI would be "direct" (real time), so beside the chat-line, the debate on VOTI would be possible without delay. With your help, we could in a way "connect" the POW chat and VOTI forum, so debate on VOTI would reflect the chat from Venice and, on the other hand, the debate between members of VOTI forum would reflect on the chat too.

Hope to hear you on Saturday!

From: Barbara Kuon
Subject: megalomaniac curators
Date: Tuesday 08 June 1999

Hearing on this forum about the relationship of war and curating arranged by the VOTI club, the first idea I had was that a curator who is emphasizing her or his powerlessness concerning the war must have become a megalomaniac: to emphasize one's powerlessness in this respect means that one is comparing oneself to belligerent politicians, to powerful parties, presidents and governments deciding on war and peace—that one is somehow competing with them.

It's interesting to notice a certain shift in the way today's curators see themselves. From the eighties up to now, they have been more and more cultivating the image of a manager; they began to look like managers, to behave like managers, to travel like jet-set managers, to communicate like managers, to ruin their health like managers and sometimes even to get paid like managers. They didn't want to show art but wanted to sell art—in a literal sense—to the public. Their curatorial decisions looked like decisions on what to keep and what to get rid of. To become a star in times and spaces dominated by the ideology of the victory of economics (which are fundamentally times and spaces of peace), you have to be a successful businessman. Well, even if economy isn't the more or less secret winner of every war, in times of war, managers look rather ridiculous, because compared to the decisions made by politicians, their own decisions—whether to keep or to sell—seem to be totally unimportant. To be a star in wartimes, you have to be a statesman (or a general).

This must be why the manager-curators now want to convert themselves into statesman-curators and why they are suddenly competing with persons deciding on war and peace. They want to go beyond art, but not in the sense to become a manager, but to become a person who is controlling the strategic support and the political framework of civilization, culture and art. Isn't this megalomaniac? Wouldn't it be interesting to be just a curator, and not a manager, and not a belligerent statesman? Did anybody yet ask what it means to be a normal, average curator? Maybe the time is now ripe to become an average, even banal and trivial curator to win the first prize. Artists have already discovered the strategies of banality—when will curators?

From: Brian Holmes
Subject: megalomaniacal?
Date: Wednesday 09 June 1999

To suggest, as someone has done here, that curators should pursue "strategies of banality" to become "average, even banal and trivial," is to suggest they should "just do their job." Which means we know what their job is, and we know what art is: something to be judged entirely by standards inherent to a profession, sealed off like most other professions to anything outside its functional needs. Admitting that is probably a good way to "win the first prize" from any number of conservative institutions.

To ask, on the other hand, why this forum makes curators look megalomaniacal is to ask about the current state of the world society we are all living in. Increasing access to information, increasingly personalized communications, increasing ability to travel and increasing distrust of the states and the large corporations have made citizens of the rich countries a little more concerned about collective details like war. Where mass media like television tend to leave people emotionally shocked and therefore easily manipulated before their hypnotic visions of violence, the personal connections of Internet, telephone and international travel promote a fiction of agency: we know these people, we can contact them personally, we could do something—about world affairs. Hence the apparent megalomania and not only among curators. The fiction of agency is largely just that, a fiction, but in many respects it is a precious one; the development of so-called "civil society" in the upcoming years will depend a lot on the way this fiction is handled.

Curators could do something here, at their own level of operations and within their own profession—they could potentially even do something about the future wars that are certain to arise out of the neoliberal "world system" propagated mainly by the United States, with its evident lack of concern for the stability of other nations and the welfare of their populations. Curators could forge a place in art institutions for representational and experimental practices which not only express the local realities and aspirations of those living outside the enclaves of wealth, comfort and power, but which also promote more active physical, virtual and symbolic exchange between people in different, unequally powerful contexts—not only between artists, but between all the different social institutions and private realities to which an open, experimental art is inevitably connected. In all modesty, this might help make it harder to accept the current military-political formula: "zero death on our side, whatever the casualties and destruction on the other sides."

To make a contribution like that, however, curators would have to have some commitment, even some courage—qualities which probably won't be found among the average, the banal, and the trivial.

Brian Holmes

From: Bennett Simpson
Subject: megalomaniac curators
Date: Thursday 10 June 1999

The opposite of powerlessness is not belligerence, nor even "power" in the political sense we ascribe to those parties active in the various well or ill-conceived decisions of state under discussion. To feel powerless is to feel disengaged, without options, and seems more like an existential quandary (at least in this discussion) than an effect of one's inability to "compete" with diplomats. To feel powerless is hardly an indication of megalomania. It's a sign of confusion, what can I do? Is it my place to do anything? Can I have a role in shaping a certain set of relations, especially as they concern the people and social bodies most relevant to my experience? To feel powerless is to not know the answer to these kinds of questions. It is more than hasty to assume that the opposite of powerlessness is a pretension to world-political management.

Cultural management is another thing entirely. Of course curators are managers. So are many artists for that matter, especially today. Playing with culture, organizing culture, strategizing culture-curators and artists (and media people, and academics, and advertisers) are taught more and more that these "managerial" activities might be their greatest aspirations, should they eschew "powerlessness" for "engagement." Nobody likes bad faith though, or false claims, or presumptuous ideologues. The problem is, and always has been (hasn't it?), How to discern bad faith from good? When is the cultural management we aspire to founded on sound, well-intended attempts at engagement, and when is it posturing, band-wagoning, a front for financial exchange, or gross ambition? Hard to tell always.

Assuming that curators, as one subset of cultural managers typically linked to both money and taste-making, have some amount of agency, however "fictionalized," it seems necessary to ask this question: How do we distinguish agency from effective engagement—the capacity to "get things done" on a political level without lapsing into the perilous soft-talk of determining whether one's "faith" is good or bad? Seems necessary because of the vast confusion that exists both in the profession and outside concerning: What exactly curators do when they deal with culture, especially politically sensitive culture? Were there an answer, or answers, to such a question (which, I admit, is poorly phrased), it's my hunch that a lot of contemporary curator-managers would be "down-sized" back into the traditional, "banal" and "regular" world of connoisseurship from whence they broke.

Hot and cold,

Bennett Simpson

From: Hou Hanru
Subject: Re: megalomaniac curators
Date: Wednesday 16 June 1999

I think curatorial "progress" is a process of a more general change in today's art work... border lines are merging and artists and "agents" are increasingly closer... curating exhibition is a way to express rather than only "representing" art work... if we understand this well, the question will no longer be "down-sizing" curatorial practice but adjusting the relationship between artists and curators... at some point, they meet and work together to create a common ground...

Best

Hou Hanru

From: Olu Oguibe
Subject: Re: megalomaniac curators
Date: Thursday 17 June 1999

Regarding the matter of curators and their present role, I rather like Hou Hanru's choice of term "agents" as a substitute for our current register, which is a misnomer [Hou, 16 June]. The French always had a more accurate term, organisateur, an organizer, the impresario. Rather than act as a mere curate [caretaker or custodian], which is the calling of the curator and more in line with the call to return to "what curators do," the organizer or impresario has greater freedom to devise, source or project a vision, an agenda. This is the condition and calling of the "agents" Mr. Hou refers to. Here, the British have a great precedent for us.

In the nineteen-eighties, young Black British "curators," most notable among them Eddie Chambers and Lubaina Himid, set out to confront, subvert and positively destabilize Britain's racist art establishment. Rather than pursue the easier, wider path of rhetoric, those young people, most of them artists themselves, would use art exhibitions to underline the absence of Black representation in the agenda of Britain's mainstream culture, as well as seek to reverse this segregation by bringing visibility to Black artists. It was a cultural revolution in the true sense of the word. Like Eddie Chambers, Hou himself sacrificed his own art practice in the early nineteen-nineties in order to devote himself to the mission of raising the visibility of Asian artists in Europe. The results are quite visible today. That is curating as activism, a manifestation of agency.

Of course, ultimately, yesterday's radicals become today's czars, raising suspicion and resentment like dust in their wake. There is a good deal of that around, and that is the one crucial point I find in Barbara Kuon's posting [8 June]. Yet, the great possibilities that some of these "agents," "managers" and cavorting "czars" occasionally bring to the curatorial preoccupation are sometimes of historical significance.

Perhaps, the apparent differences in our understanding of the curatorial calling only reflect obvious differences in cultural location and experience. Our worldviews are inevitably shaped by our circumstances and historical condition. Perhaps, if we accept the modern, international curator more as an "agent" or organisateur, we would better appreciate, even demand, the path of agency which some of them tread, which is not to dismiss the place or duties of the traditional curator, the curate, the custodian.

Passion, immersion; these are the pivot upon which the traditional curatorial calling revolves. Without passionate devotion to the cultural property under her care and an absorbing enthusiasm to bring the public into the secrets of that property and its cultural context, the traditional curator betrays her calling. This, in my thinking, is akin to activism. Hardly a position of "helplessness," it, too, is on the contrary a location of agency.
In other words, the call to consider banality as a curatorial vision [Kuon, 8 June] may only

be considered acceptable if the proposal is to position banality as a momentary, radical gesture, which some may still consider inappropriate. Otherwise, to propose banality as the convention of the curatorial preoccupation is to misrepresent the traditional calling of the curator.

Olu Oguibe

From: Bennett Simpson
Subject: Re: megalomaniac curators
Date: Friday 18 June 1999

Yes, this seems like something to be hoped for. Practice crunches categories and on the best of days allows for options, rejuvenating ambiguities, unforeseen detours in production. Downsizing happens when options seem scarce—cut your losses. In a black and white world where curators "do this" or curators "do that" (curate/micromanage vs. express/engage is the stated split), options do indeed seem scarce, prescription rules. Thankfully, we are finding the world to be neither black nor white, but grey and blurry.

Best,

Bennett Simpson

From: Vasif Kortun
Subject: Re: megalomaniac curators
Date: Friday 18 June 1999

I don't know if a change in the terminology implies a change in actual practice. I understand that neither Hou nor Olu indicate a mere change in the carte-de-visite, but there is more at stake here than camaraderie of the agency and activism (that I find impossible not to support). There are always vast possibilities that are not part of the usual practice today, such as bringing to resonance historical works or things with the contemporary situations or inclusion of things (and communities) that were not part of the art domain proper. We are used to the fact that artists curate these domains into their works, but it is not regular practice for the "curator" to pursue these modalities. In brief, one approach is to expand the stable and received meanings of the words like curator, commissioner, organizer, impresario and etc.

Some time ago, Kara Walker had compared the multiple implications of dealing Black histories in the United States to trying to hold on to an eel. It is wet, slippery and it wiggles all the time. You can try to give new meaning and mythology to the world, but you can also accept acts of disempowerments, uncertainties and, above all, openness. Shift the carte-de-visite/carte d'identité for each project, refuse to be pinned down, become the eel and the person preoccupied with it at the same time. This may well be an imaginary, if not well-trodden, path.

I would like to ask Hou what might be the other implications of the dissolving the ground between the artist and the agent in terms of positions of interest/disinterest. The "Institution" demands, more often than not, difference, and this difference is suggested in economic, and other terms. I am sure that the specific issues such as fund-raising, exhibition proposals, checklists, and the whole big fill in the empty slots on the A4 paper presents insurmountable problems today. I hope that the professionalization and historization of the practice today (as implied in the curatorial MA programs in Europe and North America especially) also indicates a deprofessionalization in terms of the received modalities.

This meltdown has been, at times, both necessary and possible. Bruce Altshuler in his book "The Avant-Garde and in Exhibition" had written that "More than assemblers of the new or impresarios of the avant-garde, people like Seth Siegelaub and Harald Szeemann set the stage for the curatorial assumption of the artist's creative mantle..." This non-overlapping role sharing happened against the backdrop of '68, and the 30 years that has transpired since, affirmed increasingly the role of the curator, and curators are certainly less dedicated to a continuous oeuvre than artists.

From: Saul Anton
Subject: Re: megalomaniac curators
Date: Saturday 19 June 1999

There are a lot of interesting points being raised at the moment. I think the contemporary art world can be analyzed very richly in terms of curatorial practice—and lately I've been rather fixated on the term "practice." Bennett, I think you're right to note that, indeed, there's no black and white here, only muddy greys. Today's practices are plural and should remain that way.

I wonder, though, about the distinction between the artist and the curator, and worry about the idea of collapsing this difference. In some way, the distinction stands, to my mind, for the distinction between theory and practice itself. I mean only that there's an analogical relation here and I don't mean to deny that curators practice and artists theorize. I'm tempted, however, to simply insist on the difference between them as one that cannot be collapsed. The work of the artist is fundamentally different since it is the work of materials—however conceptual it is and however theorized—whereas the curatorial project is for more critical and assertive of positions, politics, etc. Even the most politicized of art can't overcome its implicit subjection to its own materiality. The desire to collapse this difference strikes me as a replay of older issues of vanguardism and modernism. Whereas modernism—with the various isms and poses struck by artists—sought to create a theoretical practice, today curating seems to be about practicing theories.

I hope everyone will indulge me here if I wonder whether the term "rehearsing" theories wouldn't be an appropriate way to translate the sense of "practice" in curatorial practice. Is that what curating is, rehearsing theory? What does it mean to rehearse theories? Perhaps these questions, considered genuinely, offer interesting paths of inquiry. If we think in terms of rehearsal, then we're brought back to the theatrical, impresario aspect of it all. It seems somewhat obvious that the practice of curating, a kind of critical drama where ideas are presented and performed upon a stage, means two things: one, drama has a craft aspect; two, at some level, drama is fiction. Again, there's no great discovery here but I often sense that the critical dimensions overshadow the presentational and representational core or some of the curatorial discourses I'm aware of these days. Possibilities and questions about here. Wouldn't it be interesting to see shows that take up this dramatic aspect of curatorial practice in dynamic ways. I am thinking, here, of Guy Debord and the Situationists. I wonder if situations offer a materiality to curatorial practice that could become the stuff of different kinds of shows and "events"—and I don't mean a "rave."

The theatrical aspect also points to something that is true of artistic practice—its materiality deprives it of being a form of discursive positing. That's why there's a role for criticism, which comes in and posits ideas for it. Criticism is usually a form of ventriloquism, and the art is the puppet it makes speak. Hard to get away from that. The art object cannot speak—

even if, like literature, it speaks or pretends to. The Italian philosopher Gianni Vattimo has called for "weak thought," as a theory that is more like the puppet than puppeteer, and he's proposed it as a loose idea for future discursive, artistic and critical practices. Perhaps this is what the person who suggested curators engage in the "banal" had in mind—and why they ruffled so many feathers here. Perhaps curators don't need to engage with grand global theories and metanarratives, which are too often used to justify their claims and their choices. Ultimately, there's no way to justify curatorial choices, so in one sense, unless the curatorial practice becomes a philosophical position, it's already closer to the level of the everyday, the banal, the aleatory and the temporary, than the eternal, idealistic and closed philosophical systems we continuously try to move away from and fall back into. This is where it seems to replay early 20th century forms of vanguardism but too often and too simply reaffirms an international style (think the big, imposing "neutral" architecture of he 50s and 60s), than a recognition of parochial and regional difference. Isn't that what the nouveau transnational art circuit resembles?

I think, here, of King Lear and his jester, the fool. "Dost thou call me fool, fool?" asks Lear. Hasn't philosophy tried to become more like the fool than like the king in this past century? If there's anything "theory" has sought, it's to recognize the everyday, the banal, the artistic limits of the imperial discursive positions of philosophy. That seems to me to be a fruitful way to understand the comment about the "banal" and about curatorial megalomania. She ruffled some feathers, it seemed. Perhaps curators, too, need to be more like jesters and less like statesmen, especially ones like Lear. There, it seems, lie new directions in practice, ones that can actually be pluralist, rather than being a global vanguard.

Saul Anton

From: Gena Gbenga
Subject: Re: Bomb's Eye
Date: Sunday 20 June 1999

Aras Ozgun wrote:

A few weeks ago some events forced me to think once again on these issues; Junger and his notion of "seeing" as "an act of aggression," the idea of "point of view" and the political/ideological frameworks of different points of view. I was getting the news on the Internet as usual (since I don't watch TV), and I saw the headlines about NATO's bombing of Belgrade. What followed was an image filling my computer screen after I clicked on the link. It was taken from a camera placed in front of a bomb just before it hit its target. In the black and white, grainy, low-resolution sight of the bomb there was a bridge, which came bigger and bigger and then suddenly disappeared into blackness. I was shocked; fascinated by a kind of horror, I checked the other links to see more. Once I was there, just a few years ago, I have passed over that bridge. I was there with my camera; I had images of this place and those buildings (I used some of these images in my work that I mentioned above). The terror I lived while reading the news and watching the images was multi-dimensional; on the personal dimension I had been there once, I was trying to take images out of everyday life, trying to establish a relation with this foreign place and foreign life, trying to understand it through the electronic images. The way I saw that city was in the way my professor alternatively described what seeing was: "to see is to take in life, to experience the world, to witness, to exist in communication with the world beyond the self, a certain kind of affection." But what I was being exposed now was "seeing as an act of aggression" in its most extreme form. An electronic eye, which does not simply "shoot images," but blows away its objects, totally devastates the thing it sees, diminishes the life it is directed towards. On this level, my despair came from my recognition that I saw this city through my camera eye before they saw it with the eye of the bomb.

Dear Aras, thank you for this very interesting text, you are very fortunate to have experienced this split, and I am wondering more of its ontological implications, how it relates to the split you summarize of Junger, and the new possibilities for the image practice... I am wondering how, as an artist you get beyond the despair that you write about, at the loss of the sense of emancipative potential of technology and the feeling of inadequacy in the face of the enormity of war-fueled machine-vision.... it is acute, we all feel...

Following Benjamin, we can propose that a proper respond should be turning aesthetics itself into a sphere of struggle, a sort of battlefield...

What are the terms that we fight through/with?

I have hope.

Gena

From: Michael Benson
Subject: maybe all this
Date: Sunday 20 June 1999

The Kosovars come out of the hills, they are skinny as rails, they are missing most of their families, they see the utter destruction, and they don't really seem to know what to do about it. Is it all over? It's all over. But if it's all over, what to do about all the bodies, all the unresolved anger at their utter helplessness, in the face of an enemy which has suddenly, miraculously, evaporated, what to do with the psychological trauma, the questions about where is he, or she? Are they dead? Or were they taken off to Serbia in the back of a truck for more horrendous treatment? If death came, was it at least relatively fast, or was it after weeks of torture, or rape? If they are still living, what can be done, and by who? Are they still upriver? The horror, the horror.

In Venice, at the Biennial, all the well-fed, well-watered art lovers, and art profiteers, and artists, and promoters, and self-promoters, and judge, and jury, and local gawkers, and various onlookers, and scribes, and photographers, they all survey the art, incline their heads, nod appreciatively, or make subtle negative comments, or positive comments, or ignorant comments. And they track blood-red dust out of Ann Hamilton's installation in the American pavilion, as some would probably say, "appropriately enough." Coming out of the Komar and Melamid lower floor of the Russian pavilion, which featured pictures of Moscow taken by a chimpanzee (not bad), and paintings by several adult Indian elephants (as well as a video of the elephants in the course of painting—quite fascinating, actually, to see the elephant hesitate, apply more paint, think a bit, squint at the canvas, then add more, all with surprising delicacy; the elephant trunk is evidently a lot more skillful than you may have thought, if you ever gave it any thought—coming out of the Komar and Melamid lower floor, I hear one American say to another: "Did you see upstairs?"—gesturing up to where Sergei "Afrika" Bugayev's large installation occupies two rooms—"Because it feels a lot more "Russian." Just in case you didn't know exactly what it is you're buying, or rather, sampling.

In Venice, at the Biennial, in a square near where Marko Peljhan made his interesting presentation of his Project Atoll, the earth-base of which looks like centipede marching towards the future from one angle, and a lunar lander from another angle, there is graffiti reading as follows: (1) "NATO assassini" and (2) "Free Tibet".

All the polymorphous contradictions of the liberal left are there. Although the graffiti is evidently by two different hands. How to free Tibet? Negotiations aren't going to work. So how? China has nuclear weapons. In fact, it now has all the latest US nuclear weapons designs, courtesy of a simple, repetitive file transfer cut-and-paste download activity, which will enable it to be that much more potentially accurate and destructive when it, for example, seizes Taiwan one day in the next decade or so, while using those nukes as a shield. Let alone releasing its totalitarian grip on poor destroyed Tibet.

So—how?

Well, certainly not by force. That would be too upsetting. Not to mention very, very dangerous. And among other things (if anyone survives long enough), it would result in graffiti deploring the whole move.

On the other hand, it's easy to say "NATO assassini", it doesn't require any thought, after all, those "smart" and "dumb" and "laser guided" and "gravity assisted" bombs cost lives, including innocent lives. Bombs don't (yet) come complete with an investigative arm, authority to arrest, courtroom with cage, measured investigative regimen, defense lawyer, balanced presentation of evidence, etc. No, they just kill, or maim, anyone who happens to be in their path. And, with the sound of jets screaming out of Aviano still echoing in your ears, it takes a real effort of will to turn your head and look at the immense, disproportionate pile of bodies on the other side of that scale. Not to mention to try to figure out when violence is justified to stop violence. The latter is a horrendous activity; it's simply not pleasant. The whole thing isn't pleasant, and it's too difficult to parse the whole thing out, because it disrupts certain certainties that are easier to leave sleeping.

Yeah, better to leave them sleeping. Don't ask, "What is it." Go make your visit.

Safe in safe-as-milk Ljubljana, all the bridges intact, electricity coursing through the walls, neighbors watering their plants, I burn several CDs by several interesting musicians, and in so doing, I increase the amount of interesting music in the world, while simultaneously breaking the law, avoiding paying the record companies a dime, and using a laser for something other than guiding a weapon down a chimney into your living room. However, a friend tells me that, if you spend a certain amount of time combing through stereo garbage with a screwdriver and a moderate amount of technical knowledge, you can quickly put together a quite respectable pile of real working lasers from discarded CD players. These lasers can then be wired together, and oriented in the same direction. When I ask him what he would do then, with those lasers, he goes silent. And changes the subject.

I have no idea what his intentions are. But I'd rather not think he's dangerous.

You crack open the book by Wislawa Szymborska, and you read the following:

MAYBE ALL THIS
Maybe all this is happening in some lab? Under one lamp by day and billions by night?
Maybe we're experimental generations?

Poured from one vial to the next,
shaken in test tubes,
not scrutinized by eyes alone,
each of us separately

plucked up by tweezers in the end?
Or maybe it's more like this:
No interference?
The changes occur on their own
according to plan?
The graph's needle slowly etches
its predictable zigzags?
Maybe thus far we aren't of much interest? The control monitors aren't usually plugged in?
Only for wars, preferably large ones, for the odd ascent above our clump of Earth, for major
migrations from point A to B?
Maybe just the opposite:
They've got a taste for trivia up there?
Look! on the big screen a little girl
is sewing a button on her sleeve.
The radar shrieks,
the staff comes at a run.
What a darling little being
with its tiny heart beating inside it!
How sweet, its solemn
threading of the needle!
Someone cries enraptured:
Get the Boss,
tell him he's got to see this for himself!

Etc., etc.

Michael Benson

From: Carlos Basualdo
Subject: Re: megalomaniac curators
Date: Monday 21 June 1999

It seems quite clear at this point in the discussion that the very term "curator" involves a very wide set of different cultural practices. Ambiguity is a function of the degrees of freedom that a term is subjected to. Because of this maybe we could provisionally conclude that curatorial practice has been allowed a rather surprising flexibility today: from conservateur of the past to organizer to activist to manager and innovator. Curiously enough, that list reads like the traditional definition of an intellectual, an old forgotten actor of the worn out theater of modernity. Can curators resurrect that actor, animate that puppet once more? I think that, considered at a modest scale, some curators have been doing that already, as Olu pointed out. Will it be possible to extend the politics of identity to a larger political field? How will those politics look like? Besides managing and rehearsing, I feel that those questions are very much on the curator's side of the field today. And if they have been awarded that freedom maybe they can try to use it in a productive way somehow…Even if that requires thinking through a few of the most urgent and poignant questions today for anybody engaged in the everyday practice of culture(s). I think that in order to think those questions through curators have an invaluable ally, which is of course art itself. But, as Saul's comments on the Situationists imply, art has also meant very different things in the last, at least, four decades. I would risk that the main help for curators will come (and is coming already) from the side of those (anti) artists who defined themselves against the grain of art as a autonomous, self-referential practice. The list is extensive: from Guy Debord to Jean-Luc Godard to Lygia Clark and Hélio Oiticica and Glauber Rocha. There is still a lot to think over there, and maybe the very mechanisms that somehow foreshadowed those practices in the past are the best guarantors of the rewards that reflecting on them now may afford us. This not to mention current contemporary practices like several ones that have been described in this forum (like Brian Conley's WAR! and the activities of the Oreste group)!

Carlos Basualdo

From: Olu Oguibe
Subject: Re: maybe all this
Date: Monday 21 June 1999

reflections on the incongruous

michael benson's observations on the venice biennale, though subtle and open-ended, touch on the very essence of this forum. in march i spent a month at the rockefeller research center in bellagio, on lake como, italy. each day as the venerable scholars, mostly american, went about their daily scholarly business or assembled in the evenings by the lake to play bocce, the serenity of it all belied the fact that only a few miles away nato bombers were taking off by the hour, flying a few hundred miles across the lake and dropping their weapons of mass destruction on targets hard and soft; caravans of fleeing refugees, hospitals, crowded bridges, pregnant women anticipating labor, sowing agony and irredeemable trauma, leaving bitterness and resentment in their wake, the incongruity of it all. i was not in venice for the biennale, but as i read benson's report i wonder: given the proximity of the festival to this theatre of anguish, were there any artists at all who had the boldness or foolishness to cast an eye across the waters and speak to the war, or was it all beautiful dresses, nice dinners and complimentary cards? was it just another theatre of the absurd?

btw, mr. benson speaks about burning cds, "simultaneously breaking the law, avoiding paying the record companies a dime." michael you leave out one thing though, and it is striking. has it occurred to you that when you avoid paying the record companies a dime, you also cheat the poor, hardworking, "interesting musician" whose music you love and spread? do you find that there is a chink missing in your brave, radical mission against capital, namely a rounded consideration of implications not only for capital but for the working artist as well?

isn't it fascinating that in a forum on cultural practices and war, the overarching concern of some is how to improve the commercial efficacy of the defense industry, that is to say, how to increase returns on technologies of mass destruction? again we're gleefully served the usual platter of american defense arguments: defense, defense, defense, one never ceases to wonder what the threat is. note that the only time america has faced real external threat in the entire twentieth century was the japanese attack on pearl harbor, for which the US consigned its own citizens to concentration camps on the basis of their race. all other occasions were falsely contrived: the false accusation against spain which provided theodore roosevelt and his roughriders an excuse to annex cuba, the so-called cuban missile crisis which merely gave john f. kennedy opportunity to orchestrate mass hysteria and in so doing fashion himself into the brave, young, warrior king who stood up against the red terror in defense of america and the democratic world while his intelligence service covertly aided the destabilization of the young democracy in the congo and the assassination of patrice lumumba...defense, defense, defense.

isn't it clear that we all face greater threats to our lives, cultures and civilization, wherever we are, from these cold-blooded peddlers of efficient "defense" who see no difference whatsoever between electronic war games and real war? has it occurred to anyone that rather than continue to perpetuate this culture of war, greater energy ought to be expended on nurturing a culture of coexistence? imagine what stupendous advancements germany would have made in science and industry, in cultural progress, had it not disrupted its own strides in those directions and instead, diverted so much talent, time, labor and resources to war?

only a generation ago, america sacrificed sixty thousand of its youth in a war without meaning, a senseless, meaningless, absolutely illogical war. yet some are still gleeful about billions of dollars in returns from the defense industry. not much seems to have been learnt. writing in reverse script five centuries ago, michelangelo feared that if his inventions were to fall into the hands of such men and women, humanity would be doomed. well, here we are. roll over, signor buonarroti, the savages are here.

olu oguibe

From: Brian Holmes
Subject: salubrious?
Date: Wednesday 23 June 1999

"Airpower thrives in the salubrious air that liberal democracy provides," writes the sagacious Col. Westenhoff. It's stunning how proud people can be about the superior organization of their society, when it comes to killing other people. The democratic drive to murder is sickening to see, ugly to justify. The military is, at times, a necessary evil. But it is always the worst route, because it creates the need for itself. The US military-industrial complex, in particular, is now inventing its needed enemies, particularly but not only in the form of Islamic fundamentalism. When I say inventing, I mean: deliberately escalating potential conflicts to the point where they become dangerous enough to justify alliance-building and displays of overwhelming force. By agitating the specters of fascism or "archaic regression," the power-mongers are able to sell us their police actions against the individuals and peoples who are cut out of the new, liberal formula for profit-making. Warmongering obviates any lingering idea of redistributing the wealth.

The question I now have is: to what extent might this list contribute to aestheticizing war? Already the military thugs are back in style in the US, in Britain too I suppose. Who's going to polish their black boots, and help us all get ready for a little more S&M on a world scale?

To put the question another, more interesting way: how can we develop new artistic and cultural forms that lead elsewhere than to the rationalization of military-economic competition? Mental health is notoriously difficult to define, because it can only be measured by the norms of human communities. Col. Westenhoff and his like seem to me to be insane. But without cultural touchstones to establish the limits of his particular brand of insanity, it may begin to look reasonable. Salubrious, indeed.

Brian Holmes

From: Edi Muka
Subject: Syndicate: from edi for the syndicate list
Date: Thursday 24 June 1999

hi everybody, from edi in tirana. my telephone was broken and I couldn't read the post, but today it is fixed and i have been reading through the posting about "moral responsibility." it is not the first time i read a posting of this nature in the list, but i didn't want to really join in, because it's very easy and very soon the discussion might become emotional, between the Albanian and Serb point of view. but this time, when the conflict seems to be over and when more evidence on what has really happened there is being shown, i found the current discussion interesting and decided to write something.

there is a lot of argument on NATO air campaign against Serbia. i know that everyone has their own opinions and the right to express them in condemning or supporting this action. i myself don't want to take any part in this argument, but being Albanian, knowing that out there is a defenseless population being slaughtered and even burned (as if slaughtering wasn't enough), i gave my support to NATO intervention, even though i repeat i get involved emotionally here. in some of the postings i read, it is said that there could have been more done for a peaceful solution, starting from Dayton, and supporting the peaceful movement in Kosova. maybe this is right, but this suggestion comes in a moment when Kosova is a burned land, full of mass graves and most of its population walking for several months now.

regarding the support to the peaceful movement in Kosova, the outcome was that about 10 years ago, Kosova lost even the scrumbles of the autonomy it had during Tito's time. it is true that before NATO bombing started in Kosova there weren't 1,000,000 people living in camps, but there were already a quarter of that amount displaced internally with their homes burning, and i didn't hear any calls to stop it; there were already 40,000 Serb troops in Kosova that for sure didn't go on vacation there; furthermore, a peaceful effort, Rambouillet (i don't know how realistic it was), took place only after massacres had already started, months before NATO started bombing (it was January already when Racak occurred). i don't know why, but i have a feeling that people now are condemning NATO's intervention, and if that didn't happen would condemn NATO for allowing the so-called "repetition of Bosnia."

i know what it means to live under an autocratic regime, in which alternative ideas might cost one's life, since we have had that for a long time in Albania. but i can not accept the feeling that during all these years and during all the months of the explosion of the Kosova matter, i didn't hear any single word from any Serbian intellectual that at least expressed disagreement for atrocities committed against innocent Albanian population, and i am not speaking for the period of three months ago, because the first massacre where children and women were killed occurred more than one year ago.

well i feared i would become emotional if i entered the argument, and so i did. but there is one thing i would really look forward to having a profoundly sincere answer (as much as possible), from my Serbian friends (the ones i know personally and others i don't). have you ever really considered Albanians living in Kosova as equal to you, deign to live the same life, to have the same rights, exercise the same freedom?

please take a moment to reflect before you answer, this is a question that maybe has to do with moral responsibility and that is rooted deep in the centuries, some years ago, i never was able to understand what Kosovar friends told me about their relationship with the Serbs and of what they went through in their daily life, and i never took it seriously, it is only now that i saw what happened (without ever getting "why") that i can scarcely get what i have heard from them before, therefore the above question is really important to me.

it is important because i want to normally talk to my Serbian colleagues, invite Serbian artists to tirana; i want Serbian artists to have shows in prishtina and i don't want to fear for their security. it is important because we must find a common language, because Serbs must not flee Kosova (even though there are many cases in which it was Serbian neighbours that killed the next door people, as there are some cases that Serbian neighbours guarded empty houses of their Albanian ones). this is not a solution, this is the hardest matter on which we should focus now, start thinking practically how to make the two live together without problems. of course the big deal is on the Albanian side, and i can understand if one goes back and find only the ashes and some bones of his kids, you would hardly like to pretend that nothing happened, but the Serbs too have to change a lot as well, and this change and the desire to live together with Albanians of Kosova can start only if they change the way they have always considered them, and i believe that this is a collective as well as individual moral responsibility.

best to all.

edi.

From: Trevor Batten
Subject: Re: salubrious?
Date: Friday 25 June 1999

On 20-Jun-99, Gen Thomas S. Moorman Jr., USAF wrote:

For nearly 40 years, the government has dominated the space business. Low-risk, cost-plus contracts with NASA, the military, or the intelligence community were the norm. Today, that picture is changing, and the rate of change will become even more dramatic. A number of factors have contributed to this phenomenon: the rapid evolution of information technologies, such as the explosive growth in semiconductor technology and the extraordinary advances in digital signal processing and voice compression; progress in international space policy, including the increasing deregulation of telecommunications services, the allocation of new spectrums to commercial satellite communications, and the allowance of higher imagery resolution for commercial remote sensing; fundamental changes in the process and cost of satellite manufacturing; the increased reliability (if not decreasing costs) of launches; and an expanding global demand for satellite services driven by the information revolution.

Clearly, we should pursue a number of new military space initiatives over the next 1020 years. For example, as more commerce is placed in orbit and as we depend more on space, DOD will need a more comprehensive program to protect our assets. A comprehensive protection program would include improving our ability to detect and assess threats (surveillance), enhancing the survivability of ground stations and platforms, and using commercial assets to augment national security capabilities, to name a few.

It seems the logic of the commercial exploitation of space is identical to the logic which lead to the European colonialization of Africa, Asia, Australia and America.

Do battered children ALWAYS become battering parents?

I guess when history died we lost a valuable teacher: what will it now cost to learn the same lessons?

On 22-Jun-99, Col Charles M. Westenhoff, USAF wrote:

The great success with which liberal democracies have employed air forces as instruments of power is most easily attributed to asymmetrical wealth, but this understanding misses the role democratic institutions and value systems play in the development and employment of airpower.

Surely, "technology" has ALWAYS played a crucial role in battle but human intelligence has ALWAYS been even more decisive in winning the battle, winning the war and winning the peace.

All the armed forces of authoritarian states are clearly affected as military instruments by information distortion, restriction of dialogue, and lack of access to objective sources of feedback.

Yes, this paradox is probably our only hope!

But do the cultural, educational, political, commercial and military systems fully realize that the same applies to ALL systems involving information/energy/money!

IF images can move realities, then eventually one must fight against one's own disinformation (and possibly loose if the campaign has been very successful).

Surely, the "Internet" is triumphant proof of the "efficiency" of redundancy.

Perhaps an honest democracy of involved, connected, thinking, creative people REALLY is the most "efficient" AND "economic" system of all!

We might even need a few predators—just to keep us in shape.

As technological systems become more "organic" it becomes even more important for us to understand that "Survival of the Fittest" means "the best adapted to the circumstances" NOT "the beast with the biggest circumference"!

If in doubt, ask the dinosaurs—if you can still find one.[137]

From: Trevor Batten
Subject: Re: salubrious?
Date: Friday 25 June 1999

On 23-Jun-99, Brian Holmes wrote:

The question I now have is, to what extent might this list contribute to aestheticizing war?

Then perhaps we should first define what we mean by "aesthetics" and by "war." Should we bomb the museum or put the war in the museum? Shall we make war "pretty" or are we fighting for "beauty"? To put the question another, more interesting way: how can we develop new artistic and cultural forms that lead elsewhere than to the rationalization of military-economic competition? Surely an "artistic" form of "war" has different implications than a "cultural" form of "war."

Artists in war, artists at war, artistic war?

Culture in war, culture at war, cultural war?

First we should know WHAT we are discussing, and perhaps WHY.

Mental health is notoriously difficult to define because it can only be measured by the norms of human communities. Col. Westenhoff and his likes seem to me to be insane.

If logic is a sign of madness and emotion a sign of health then you may be right. It seems that war may be aggressive and dangerous. Perhaps one should think seriously about it! Perhaps "logic" is always dangerous, "emotion" too. Both can lead to war. What can save us?

But without cultural touchstones to establish the limits of his particular brand of insanity, it may begin to look reasonable.

Without touchstones, NOTHING can be established—the touchstone determines the nature of all things. So, is it "Reality" or the "Touchstone" which determine our lives? What is "art" if it is not the search for touchstones? What is "culture" if it is not about their use? How great is the confusion without them! Where can "sanity" be found? Perhaps "insanity" is to destroy oneself while believing that one is saving oneself—by believing you are winning, when in fact you are loosing. In that case, any simple error may lead to insanity. In peace, it may be dangerous. In war, it can be fatal!

But what is winning—and what is losing?

Trevor Batten

From: Brian Holmes
Subject: Re: salubrious?
Date: Friday 25 June 1999

I appreciate all of Trevor Batten's exacting questions, the kind I ask myself whenever I write. We may not have the same answers, but in any case I'd like to clear up one misunderstanding: What I was trying to say in my last post was that I felt a little concerned that even our debate in this list may contribute to depicting war as fascinating, stimulating and desirable. Personally I see nothing beautiful about war, don't want to put it in a museum, and don't want to bomb anything. Least of all with uranium.

Beyond that, I do think excesses of logic can be unreasonable, even insane, though emotion is no guarantee of anything. As to the touchstones that artistic and curatorial practice may provide in the present, I'm working on a text in that direction, more later.

Brian Holmes

From: Gena Gbenga
Subject: Re: salubrious?
Date: Friday 25 June 1999

Brian Holmes wrote:

Col. Westenhoff and his likes seem to me to be insane.

I don't think it is fair to say that Colonel Westenhoff is insane. Like everyone else he is just trying to make sense, make meaning, of a job that he has to do. A job that must be occupied...

I find the military people here surprisingly articulate. It is not that I agree with them, only that to hear them speak makes me know that they are real people, trying to come to terms with what they do like everyone else.

At least the Colonels can write. Can we say as much for the Curators?

Gena

From: Trevor Batten
Subject: Re: salubrious?
Date: Monday 28 June 1999

Brian Holmes wrote:

Col. Westenhoff and his likes seem to me to be insane.

On 25-Jun-99, Gena Gbenga wrote:

At least the Colonels can write, Can we say as much for the Curators?

Although I agree with the sentiment I think we should be a little careful of always pointing the finger at someone else (although I am probably just as guilty as {or more than} anybody!).

The fusion of the curator/artist/manager relationship may be crucial: How much is it a normal consequence of the job, how much a normal "historical" development towards "meta-systems," how much does the professionalisation process (through education) inevitably lead to a "managerial" viewpoint—and how much is it simply due to economic forces?

Perhaps it is even a "natural" evolution towards predators and parasites—suggesting a relationship between meta-systems and predators who "live through exploiting the energy systems of fellow creatures."

On the other hand, how important is it to preserve the independence of the separate layers? How can artists develop the necessary contemplative reflection if they must also be activist/managers, and where will curators get their material from if the exhibition becomes the "artistic medium"?

Recycled art can be boring enough—must we also suffer recycled exhibitions? Is there no "artistic Buddha" who can release us from the endless treadmill of artistic reincarnation?

On 26-Jun-99, Brian Holmes wrote:

I do think excesses of logic can be unreasonable, even insane, though emotion is no guarantee of anything.

So we can agree on that. Proportion is surely the measure of wisdom!

Greetings,

Trevor

From: Robert Fleck
Subject: Sharif Turns to Military to Deescalate Kashmir
Date: Tuesday 29 June 1999

Dear Friends,

VOTI is turning towards a kind of "all-over" military discussion. Of course, military aspects can become philosophical questions, as Hegel, Foucault or Virilio pointed out. But we should not get confused about the issues of our discussions. VOTI was created as a forum for curators to discuss emerging issues of visual arts. Of course, any forum like this can turn into something else; this is one of the powerful effects of communication. Shouldn't we try to create another thing to continue our discussion about art, which has been interrupted by the Serbian War?

Best Wishes,

Robert Fleck

From: Vasif Kortun
Subject: Sharif Turns to Military to
Date: Wednesday 30 June 1999

Yes, we have strayed far and away!

Vasif

From: Simon Biggs
Subject: what is VOTi/who is it for???
Date: Wednesday 30 June 1999

Robert Fleck wrote:

VOTI was created as a forum for curators to discuss emerging issues of visual arts. Of course, any forum like this can turn into something else, this is one of the powerful effects of communication. Shouldn't we try to create another thing to continue our discussion about art, which has been interrupted by the Serbian War?

Sorry???

I thought VOTI was created for artists, curators or those generally interested in the arts and creative cultural interventions to discuss the general nature of military conflict and its effects on the arts. Yes, inspired by the current situation in Kosovo, but not limited to it. Yes, of interest to curators, but only as part of a for larger community of people trying to work creatively in what can be trying times for creative practice.

Am I wrong? If I am perhaps I should leave the list...
Personally I have had little to contribute to VOTI, as its particular themes are outside my competence, and I must admit to the deepest possible ambivalence when it comes to politics or the exercise of power in any form. However, I have appreciated some of the posts, if even on an information only level, as a complement to mainstream media coverage of things like Kosovo, Mexico, India/Pakistan, etc.

From: Jose Roca
Subject: Violence at the museum
Date: Wednesday 30 June 1999

Hi, VOTI.

I have remained silent, overwhelmed at the complete indifference of the international community regarding the tragedy that is taking place in Colombia. I was really shocked to see that in France, an affair that involved a police officer in the burning of a beach bar in Corse is still making the news, while the continuing massacres in our country are simply Ignored. At the same time, working as a curator and critic in a cultural institution in Bogota, my position deals with symbolic matter art as a way of signaling a state of things, and as somebody put it in this forum, our work is irrelevant compared to... military decisions? efficient weapons? Following is a review on an exhibition currently taking place at the Museum of Modem Art in Bogota, which deals with the theme of cultural practice and violence.

Jose Roca.

Violence at the Museum.
From May through July 1999, the Museum of Modem Art in Bogota shows the exhibition "Art and Violence", a large thematic show that covers roughly 50 years of Colombian artistic production dealing with a topic that permeates not only art but every other aspect of daily life in Colombia: violence.

Colombia is arguably the most dangerous place in the world, according to international figures, with more than 30,000 violent deaths a year. This rate shadows even current events like the atrocities in Kosovo. The alarming figures that grant Colombia an outstanding place in the Museum of the Macabre are put in their proper perspective when one realizes that they have been constant for the last decade, and show signs of only getting worse.

How do people manage to cope with such an ever-present fact and get on with their daily life? A possible answer might lie in the form of a "selective amnesia", a situation that permits accepting death as sort of a national mark of character, a collective daily "lobotomy" that shields shock in order to continue living much in the way medical crews block emotional involvement in order to be able to perform. We even speak of "la epoca de la violencia" (the era of violence) when we refer to the fifties, a euphemism that appears in history texts, as if violence had stopped or even decreased ever since.

The time frame of the exhibition starts in 1948, an important starting date since it was in this year the popular leader Jorge Eliecer Gaitan was assassinated. It was this event that gave way to a popular uprising known as El Bogotazo. During this period, Bogota and many of the major cities were severely damaged. This event signified the rise of rural political violence, and it can be said that the origins of the guerrillas and private armies that mark today's current confrontations stemmed from El Bogotazo. The Museum of Modern Art's show deals with the subject matter mainly in two ways: representation and allusion. Colombian art is rich in iconography dealing with death. It is certainly not by coincidence that the work of Colombia's best-known artist besides Fernando Botero, Doris Salcedo, stems precisely from this theme. For the exhibition, artistic output is tunneled through a thematic reading, resulting in a usually compelling if problematic show.

Curating such a theme had to be a difficult task, and this perception was precarious, but glittering, existence. Henri Michaux's pre-electronic electrified art then helps us to understand that the "real world" of war is established upon phantasmal images rank non-materiality. With this in mind, anti-war ideology/art, like Michaux's visually vibrating "Dessin Mescalinien", may be capable of composing an unaccustomed, non-logocentric, rhizomatic, viral art from the broad spread of digital codes found scattered throughout the space of computer memory. Here we must remember that a rhizome's multiple dimensions instigate crossovers between both the highest synthetic level and the slightest, most minute, discrete distinctions. The rhizome is a snarl of vicissitudes so intertwined that it must give birth to different scopes of thought and perception and art. Such an aesthetic anti-war cyber theory based on Michaux's rhizomatizing experiments with his consciousness might provide a fundamental antithesis to the authoritarian, mechanical, simulated rigidities of the warring world.

Like in "Dessin Mescalinien", anti-war rhizomatizing ideology/art might develop vibrating articulations which consist of phantasmal digital elements now grouped into spreading systems which possess viral host/parasite characteristics which the eye can scan and identify only because they have a structure that is, in a way, the chimerical, concave, inner-side of war the excitedly vibratory. The conditions of this excitement reside outside of war's representations however, and inside of phantasmal/viral knowledge (beyond the art of war's immediate visibility) in a sort of behind-the-scenes chimerical world of code, deep and dense enough that representation finds itself digitally joined together in the rhizomatizing viral suppositious.

The art of a viral anti-war ideology can perhaps then help direct us towards that rhizomatizing zone, that necessary but always inaccessible virulent arena, which dives down, beyond our gaze, towards the delicate heart of consciousness (when it comes to war). Indeed it is the viral quivering conducted between the host and the parasite that maintains the sovereign but secret sway over each and every war which I find interestingly beyond reductive abstraction or glib representation (thus into an excessive, hybrid, semi-abstraction) when scrutinizing the potential for a viral art in general as it concerns the art of war and its miasmic ideology.

Such a viral anti-war art should, in my opinion, not reify the phantasmal qualities of war's tenets, but rather further atomized the ideology of war into byte phantasmality where only its occult, chimerical, viral tendencies become useful in constructing anti-warring formations. Thereby, anti-war ideology/art becomes a vibratory inventiveness, which is, in its theoretical radically, opposed to the tabular space laid out by classical war.

May I just say that this phantasmal flee from the play of war's current representational givens has the most urgent political/social ramifications in our media saturated society. This, I think, well-founded but ambiguous viral model for an electronic anti-war art indicates the capacity for electronic art's worth as it provides the explication of the phantasmal codes that abet electronic communications by expressing the laws of shimmering reproduction that rule it. Such an electronic viral art can be, in a sense, the undoing of all war ideology then when it is seen to symbolically undermine the field of electronic quantity which non-utilitarian viral ideology attempts to scrutinize in accordance with a non-discursive method, which now appears as an anti-war virus. This places art, in relationship to war, well outside of the mechanics of uniform dogmatism.[138]

From: Brian Holmes
Subject: art beyond war
Date: Thursday 1 July 1999

I too think Robert Fleck has a good point—not that we can't talk about war but that we can also talk about art. The compelling thing would be to race the military barrage that we've witnessed (in this forum but above all in the world at large), to integrate the messages it contains about the state of planetary consciousness, and to formulate cultural proposals in response.

It would be great if some reactions could be expressed to the material that's been posted here, both the texts from the military sector and the testimony on the recent war. I would be curious to hear how people went about finding some of those texts from generals and from arms dealers. They've helped me understand a lot of things, even if they make me seriously bristle when I read them. Jordan Crandall has contributed quite a brilliant essay on "Armed Vision," about which there's been no discussion. I read it as a way to approach the subjectifying processes at work in this "revolution in military affairs"—you know, you are what you see, or "we" are what we see, and right now a lot of things are being looked at as targets (consumers, etc.). What are you seeking to do artistically with your research, Jordan? The essay by itself might give the impression that you are caught up in or fascinated by the "drive" toward the cyborg warrior you describe. But I think the essay reveals only half the picture, and it would be important to hear some more about the other, artistic half. The recent "border camp" post is another way into that discussion, as is Jose Roca's.

Best to all,

Brian Holmes

From: Robert Atkins
Subject: Talking About Art & War
Date: Thursday 1 July 1999

How to talk about art and war? Sometimes at least, very specifically. The amorphousness of the conversations on this list has been striking.

Everybody probably could agree about what war is while simultaneously holding vary different ideas about the nature of cultural practice.

From an American perspective, the only "war" of my lifetime in which artists have played a direct role is the struggle against AIDS. (The Vietnam-era organizing of certain art groups was mostly about networking à la any other profl or interest group, rather than about creating art, media, agitprop.) What seems striking to me about the effectiveness of art—or media collectives such as Gran Fury, Testing the Limits and DIVA TV was the surgical precision of their usually local targets. People outside of New York doubtless never heard of media-genic, propagandistic demos and broadsides against, say, then Mayor Ed Koch. And sometimes broader arenas—such as Gran Fury's attack on the Pope for his lethal, anti-safe-sex views at the 1990 or 91 Venice Biennale—proved appropriate.

At the same time, well-thought-out, process-oriented conceptualist media campaigns intended for broader, international audiences were mounted by artist groups like Visual AIDS (Day Without Art on Dec 1), NAMES Project Quilt etc. Many of us struggled mightily (and gleefully) to frame artist-created Silence=Death and Red Ribbon logo/emblems as conceptualist artworks. The outcome of such curatorial/critical practice might be less important than the space it helped open up for projects like MoMA's sponsorship in 1991 of Felix Gonzalez-Torres' photo-billboards of empty rumpled beds displayed throughout NYC or Gran Fury's selection as an American representative for the Biennale. (The history of AIDS and public art is encapsulated in my essay www.queerarts.org/archiwe/show4/lorum/atkins/atkins.html)

What I'm thinking about is how does a list enable action or create new communities? I feel oddly info-deprived and glutted: reading Nettime, I have to sift through the granular 10' off the ground perspective in order to find the 100' perspective of less specific info I need. As I say, too much information and not enough. I wonder if we in North America are hearing about relevant and innovative cultural, antiwar initiatives in Europe? Tamas Banovic (of Postmasters Gallery) if you're reading this I'd love to know how you analyze and evaluate the month-long artists' forum/exhibition about S. Eastern Europe you recently held in your gallery? Wouldn't such a report stimulate our thinking? I don't intend to be merely venting frustration here. It's more that I feel rather dis-engaged, a condition I tend to deal with by either self-engaging or self-removing.

Robert Atkins

From: Jordan Crandall
Subject forum will close July 2-6
Date: Thursday 1 July 1999

Dear forum members,

From July 2-6 the Blast office will be closed, and the voti-agents, Gena and David Schwartz in New York, Riqaardo Mbarak in Paris, along with other participants who help to channel <voti><blast> content, will take a well-deserved break. Therefore, no messages will be circulated for the next five days.

Perhaps this is a good time to take up Brian Holmes's suggestion—as well as the implicit suggestion of Robert Fleck and others who are concerned about a lack of artistic agendas— to formulate cultural proposals in response to the military barrage, both in the forum and in the culture at large. Jose Roca's evocative description of the "Art and Violence" exhibition in Bogota is a good beginning, focusing on the culture of violence in Columbia through the scrim of artistic endeavor. Comments by Robert Fleck, Zdenka Badovinac, Charles Esche, Bettina Funcke, and Cornelia Lauf were those that originally set the theme of this forum, and it would be helpful too to have their input at this stage.

For July: let us hear your thoughts, dear <voti><blast> forum members, as cultural practitioners. The summer is just beginning.

Jordan

Chapter VII

Sensation

The forum resumes its activity privately and, as no theme or session title is raised for the second-half of the year, several VOTI members begin to discuss the exhibition *Sensation* that was composed of works from the collection of Charles Saatchi. While the exhibition was first opened at the Royal Academy, London, in 1997, it is commented upon here following its tour to the Brooklyn Museum, New York, in 1999. A number of the exhibited works were considered controversial. For example, Chris Ofili's *The Holy Virgin Mary* (1996) was met with protests from religious groups because of his use of elephant dung on the canvas. New York mayor Rudolph Giuliani then threatened to withhold government funding for the museum.

The conversation featured in this chapter is short and touches mainly upon issues of censorship. A closing e-mail from Pedro Reyes Alvarez examines the comparative situation in Mexico. No follow-on e-mails responding to him or engaging this topic were found.

In order of appearance:
Robert Fleck, Bart De Baere, Carlos Basualdo, Marta Kuzma and Pedro Reyes Alvarez.

From: Robert Fleck
Subject: Re: test
Date: Monday 15 November 1999

Dear VOTIs,

Very nice idea, this second edition of VOTI (private)

Best Wishes from Nantes and La Bouillie, information will follow

I agree with Hou, am also not taking so seriously "Sensation" (populist exhibition with populist police reactions...).[139] This has become normal nowadays—just two weeks ago, a mayor in the south of France canceled the exhibition of the photo/conceptual artist Guillaume Janot (one of the best young artists in France) because the invitation card showed a girl with a very short dress. The mayor was socialist, by the way...

Robert Fleck

From: Bart de Baere
Subject: Re: test
Date: Monday 15 November 1999

i agree too, a slightly more interesting question might be to go back into the past and analyse the importance of earlier populist attacks on this tiny area in the states for the formation of the christian right. as for "sensation," what an alliance.

bart.

From: Carlos Basualdo
Subject: Re: test
Date: Monday 15 November 1999

After some time trying to connect to the list without much luck, finally made it. Thanks Susan, it's great to be VOTI-ing again!!!

Such a nightmare, the whole Sensation thing, but I think it is pointing to a deep, deep crisis in the structure of distribution of contemporary art (in this country, of course, but also worldwide perhaps…). Maybe we need to try to reconnect art production to other spheres of knowledge and production—just to retrieve it from commerce a bit?

Carlos

From: Bart de Baere
Subject: Re: test
Date: Wednesday 17 November 1999

Carlos, perhaps you're right.

It might not be a question of separating it from economics but of defining it (culture and art as part of its core) as a second matrix besides economics, intertwined with it but a different matrix all the same. Two months ago I got the weird offer to become advisor to the new minister of culture, which I accepted part time and for a limited period. Curating a situation in which the extreme right wing for the time being is still politically contained. At present we are preparing a four-year policy draft. Highlighting the difference is one of the things we aim at. It will hopefully lead to what might be seen as a continental European response to the Anglo-Saxon model of the Cultural Industries. Within that model, art and commerce are a prime discussion. It need not be.

Bart.

From: Marta Kuzma
Subject: Re: test
Date: Tuesday 16 November 1999

Back, to Bart's comment, perhaps the Sensation issue is less valid in discussing than re-examining the earlier attacks that arose out of the Mapplethorpe exhibitions, starting in Washington and tracking across the country until eventually landing in the arrest of a Museum Director in Cincinnati. Perhaps both scandals bear similarities—the Sensation and Mapplethorpe/Serrano debates came out of some understanding that art carried a "moral" responsibility instigated by politicians at a time of economic boom. Jessie Helms's arguments eventually did an immense amount of good in changing the way photography was integrated and collected by art institutions and the validity of the medium as an art form that continued well into the next decade.[140] It is difficult for us to turn to New York's mayor and remind him, "Hey, Rudy, we've done this before" but it certainly reminds us of a time when government managed to instigate a good deal of fear among heads of institutions and their respective boards not only as to the possible loss of their corporate donors (and therefore to their future livelihood) but that art, despite the 80s, still had the ability to be bound to issues while still evolving.[141] It came at a time when the art world had forgotten that we could still be held criminally for what was shown to a broader public. At the end of yet another decade of extraordinary economic wherewithal in the United States, the Giuliani-Sensation dynamic mirrors the private bantering between a mayor who truly believes he has single-handedly saved New York from economic and civil decrepitude and an advertising magnate who has managed to wield British contemporary art to remarkable marketing levels. And yet, it appears that this is deemed the one scandal that is worthy of our attention outside of war? (And whatever happened to Chechnya?)

I just returned to Kyiv after a brief period in New York. The leading newspaper distributed nationally and usually cited for its moderate stand contained a one-page article by a local art historian who, sentence by sentence, attempted to disclaim the work and reputation of a leading art critic who has actively worked with young and dynamic artists usually ignored by existing institutions. Her claims against him related to his "being too closely associated with a bottle of gin" and the artists—too driven by creating scandal, by referring to the photographic medium because of their lack of proper technical skill to paint a foot or a hand property. This may appear all too amusing, but the writer of this article heads the critical theory department within the one private academic institution in the country. Within a declining economic situation and a recent twist on the part of the Ministry to the right, the combination might be successful enough in landing cultural policy in the shadows of Lukashenko and the Belarussian model.[142] Just another reference point.

So Rudy's tiff with BMA is perhaps, incomparable to Helms's preachings about the morals and ethics of art on a national level. New York and its art community is too well voiced, represented and organized for a single mayor to censor a work of contemporary art within the area.[143] In fact, as I walked from one gallery to another, I heard several gallery visitors ask if the artist represented within the space was also represented within the Sensation exhibition. Perhaps we do need to get away from the discussion of commerce and art, but isn't that, in the end, what drives it (or at least its public display) in successful economies?

Marta

From: Pedro Reyes Alvarez
Subject: ILLEGAL art activities in Mexico City
Date: Wednesday 17 November 1999

Following the discussion that is taking shape after the Sensation issue, I'm afraid that in Mexico, contemporary art does not generate such kinds of media attention. Some shows have been censored here (Mapplethorpe also), but still very few local artists are doing works that could be considered "undesirable," "against morals" or relating in a provocative way with religion or politics.

Instead there are several art activities that strictly can be considered ILLEGAL and nobody complains against them, so I found it interesting to share with you two of them:

1)

Since the mid 80's the collaborative team SEMEFO (which means Forensic Medical Services) has done sculptures, video, installations and performances using human corpses as their main material. The corpses are bodies nobody identifies from the morgue, but having access to them is against the law. Over the years they have made friendship with the guys from the morgue who provide them with all kinds of weird stuff. In fact, if their studio were inspected they could spend several years in prison. Besides this, SEMEFO has shown widely in major museums in Mexico and have been granted by the state several times. Why does no one complain about this? First, police will never expect something illegal to happen in a contemporary art museum; second, the public has a big respect for art and the museum institution. So if it is shown in a museum, it is because it is worthy. One of their pieces can illustrate this:

A few months ago I was invited to a private performance; we were just 12 people in the house. SEMEFO hired a mason who was working on the patio. He made a wood box and later started to do concrete mix. When the mix was ready and in the box, Teresa (leader of the group) took out of a plastic bag a child corpse, almost a fetus, and buried him in the concrete. I thought then this time has been excessive.

All this ceremony happened in cold and solemn silence. We all keep silent after the performance ended. We started to drink to recover from the shock and it wasn't until then when we were told that the fetus was child of the wife of one of the members, who was born dead. As they had related to death in an artistic way, after discussing they found that this was the best way to deal with this sad fact, and we were invited to this intimate funeral, a group ritual. I was strongly moved and sincerely grateful to be part of it. It was like being taken back to the early times of manhood when the spiritual and artistic sense of rituals were undivided. Also it reminded me of an old Mexican tradition of La Muerte Nina, which is a special ritual when a child dies.

Just to get back to the point, the concrete block was shown a month later. This time the piece could be considered legal because by law, when a child is born dead, he is considered part of the mother's body and belongs to her.

2)

I invited Santiago Sierra, a young Spanish artist living in Mexico to do a project at *La Torre de los Vientos* (a hollow sculpture made by Gonzalo Fonseca in 1968; it is a huge concrete tower I have been using since 1996 as a project space, check www.arteinsitu.org.mx and apologies because the website is not updated).[144] Most artists have worked inside La Torre, but Santiago wanted to do something outside. His idea was to block the highway where the sculpture stands by. To stop the traffic at the rush hour of the periferico means to block the largest highway of the biggest city of the world. At the artist's request, I got a big trailer with a huge white box from the company of an art collector.

On Friday at 6:00 P.M.—the nightmare hour—the trailer made the necessary maneuvers to stop perpendicularly in the middle of the highway for five minutes. This action was done without permission without public announcement, basically to do video and photographic documentation, and with no public, only the angry and surprised drivers who were there. Of course no-one thought that they were taking part of a large "urban sculpture," all seemed to be one of the hundreds of incomprehensible phenomena that happen every day in Mexico City.

Chapter VIII

ARCO 2000

In 1999, a discussion with the then Director of ARCO, Rosina Gomez, resulted in VOTI being given the opportunity to organize a series of panel conversations to take place during the art fair in February 2000. Over thirty curators, mainly members of VOTI for the previous two years, came together in Madrid to discuss different aspects of cultural practice under set conversation topics. Despite the importance of this event for VOTI only a very few organizational e-mails from Susan Hapgood were found. This may be because a majority of e-mails about the panel topics and configurations were sent privately and no conversation about ARCO actually took place on the shared forum platform. The original programs in English and Spanish can be found in the appendix (p.407). While ARCO was clearly a key moment in the development of VOTI it appears to have also been the climactic end-point.

Based on conversations in Madrid, the last e-mail from Susan Hapgood featured in this publication, with the optimistic subject line "VOTI Awakes," proposed a "new structure for VOTI discussions." Hapgood shared a schedule for forum postings whereby an e-mail was to be sent on the first and fifteenth of every month by a pre-assigned VOTI member. Very few of the assigned writers took up their posts as scheduled and VOTI gradually ceased activity. The last email found was sent by Carin Kuoni, dated November 13, 2000.

In order of appearance:
Susan Hapgood, Bettina Funcke, Octavio Zaya, Stéphanie Moisdon, Nicolas Trembley, Carlos Basualdo, Zdenka Badovinac, Bart De Baere and Carin Kuoni.

From: Susan Hapgood
Subject: New Members for VOTI
Date: Thursday, January 13, 2000

Dear VOTIs,

Happy VOTI 2000!
From the beginning, we thought of VOTI as an ever-changing network. At this point we realized that in order to fully accomplish this goal, the structure of the Union should become more flexible and rhizomatic. We think that VOTI should be constantly expanding and mutating and thought of a new scheme to make his happen. We would like to invite each of you to propose a new member who will frequently and passionately join in our discussions.

Please think of somebody who you know and respect who is interested in curatorial practice who will actively participate in the VOTI dialogue.

Send an e-mail to me privately at hapgood@rcn.com telling me who the person is, and the e-mail address, and I will take it from there.

Thank you.

Susan Hapgood

From: Susan Hapgood, Bettina Funcke, and Octavio Zaya
Subject: ARCO 2000
Date: Saturday 1 May 1999

Dear VOTI members,

We are working on preliminary plans for the panel discussions for ARCO 2000. Please send Susan an e-mail message during the coming week, by May 7th, to let us know if your schedule will permit you to come to Madrid in mid-February of next year. Then we can begin to plan your involvement in the panel discussions.

Thank you,
Susan Hapgood, Bettina Funcke, and Octavio Zaya

From: [Trembley/Moisdon]
Subject: ARCO 2000
Date: Monday 3 May 1999

Dear VOTI members, dear Susan Hapgood,

We never react to all the information dispatched on the forum because we always thought that Voti should be more pragmatic concerning curatorial practices.

We know how much (with a few exceptions) that information remains too often secret and serves personal ambition.

Lately we have been busy, searching ways to find money to survive. Voti should also be a real international network database for that. Today we consider that Voti is an important tool and we feel more invested in its dynamic regarding, for example, the Kosovo war.

Therefore we would be very interested to meet all of the members who could attend the panel at next ARCO.

Thank you, Rosa Martinez, for the great interview.

Yours

Stephanie Moisdon
Nicolas Trembley

From: Carlos Basualdo
Subject: [unavailable]
Date: Sunday 2 May 1999

Hopefully, the VOTI lectures at ARCO next February will allow us to meet in-person and get a sense of each other's ideas and projects. At this point it is very important that all the members let Susan, Octavio and Bettina know if they will be available to go to Madrid next year, so they can go ahead with the preparation of the lectures. They need to have that information as soon as possible.

All the very best,

Carlos

From: Susan Hapgood
Subject: ARCO 2000
Date: Friday 23 July 1999

ARCO administrators will be contacting everyone in August to confirm the plans and take over the practical arrangements, while we expect you to keep in touch with your panelists regarding the discussion itself.

Here are some basic facts for you and your panelists. Dates of ARCO 2000 panel discussions are February 11,12 and 13, 2000.

I am also sending information on the panel discussions that we have organized. This information is not for public consumption, only for your eyes. Thus we ask that you please not send it to the panelists, but do feel free to send them the description of your own panel topic, of course. The panelists are, for the most part, VOTI members.

Good luck, thanks, and ciao.

XX

Susan

Panel Discussions at ARCO 2000[145]

Sessions 7 to 14
"Challenges to Curatorial Practice"
Panel Discussions by VOTI (Union of the Imaginary)

7. "Mutations of the Exhibition Model"

Moderator: Carlos Basualdo (Poet, Curator and Art Critic, New York)

Participants: Zdenka Badovinac (Slovenia)
Daniel Birnbaum (Director, IASPIS Stockholm)
Lisa Corrin (Curator, The Serpentine Gallery, London)
Åsa Nacking (Freelance Curator and Consultant, Louisiana Museum of Modern
Art, Copenhagen)

Date: Friday, February 11th from 12:30 p.m. to 2 p.m.

After Alfred Baar introduced the exhibition format of the "white cube" in the
Museum of Modern Art, the modernist model of exhibiting work in a linear and
chronological form has been questioned in many and interesting ways throughout
the century. What are the old and new ideas about the construction of exhibitions
and why have they distanced themselves from attitude of neutrality? In addition,
how has the entertainment industry affected these models?

8. "Artists as Generators of Change in Curatorial Practice"

Moderator: Susan Hapgood (Curator of Exhibitions, American Federation of Arts,
New York City; Senior Fellow, Vera List Center for Art and Politics, The New School;
Archivist of VOTI)

Participants: Dan Cameron (Chief Curator, New Museum of Contemporary Art,
New York)
Maria Lind (Curator, Moderna Museet, Stockholm)
Liam Gillick (Artist, London and New York)

Michelle Nicol (Museum Ludwig, Cologne and Zurich)

Date: Friday, February 11 from 5 p.m. to 6:30 p.m.

Artists are often the most powerful catalysts to reinvent ways of structuring exhibitions, while art curators are tied by their responsibilities in relation to the institutions and organizations that employ them. This roundtable discussion dealt with some of the recent changes that have had the most influence in the area of exhibitions, in the work of curators, and which have been the result of fruitful collaborations between artists and curators. The discussion focused specifically on the role that artists play in generating these changes.

9. "Art and Society: The Responsibility of the Curator"

Moderator: Octavio Zaya (Critic and Freelance Curator, New York)

Participants: Bart de Baere (Curator, SMAK, Gent)
Hou Hanru (Independent Art Critic and Curator, Paris)
Cornelia Lauf (Director, Camera Oscura, Editor of artists' books, Rome)

Date: Friday, February 11th from 7 p.m. to 8:30 p.m.

What are the current responsibilities of the art curator in regards to the artists, institutions and an ever-more educated public? What is their essential role within society, and how can they act as a bridge between artistic production and institutional demands without giving up the possibility of creating situations relevant to social, political and cultural issues and subjects?

10. "Curating Beyond the Museum/The Independent Curators"

Moderator: Rosa Martinez (Critic and Independent Curator, Barcelona. Artistic Director, III Biennal SITE Santa Fe, New Mexico)

Participants: Francesco Bonami (Manilow Senior Curator, Museum of Contemporary Art, Chicago)

Marta Kuzma (Ukraine)
Laurence Miller (Director, ArtPace Foundation, San Antonio, Texas)
José Ignacio Roca (Head of Plastic Arts, Biblioteca Luis Ángel Arango, Bogotá)

Date: Saturday, February 12th from 12:30 p.m. to 2 p.m.

This roundtable discussion offered an opportunity to deal with the subject of the work of art curators outside the museum. What are the new challenges and the new possibilities for this profession, and to what degree do they reflect the social and political changes of our time? What are the real differences, in terms of both the limitations and the possibilities, between independent and museum art curators?

11. "Mass Media/Mediators"

Moderator: Udo Kittelmann (Director, Kölnischer Kunstverein, Cologne)

Participants: Ute Meta Bauer (Professor and Head, Institute for Contemporary Art, Academy of Fine Arts, Vienna)
Jordan Crandall (Artist and media theorist, New York)
Jon-Ove Steihaug (Freelance Curator and Critic, Oslo)
Warren Niesluchowski (Independent Writer and Curator, New York)

Date: Saturday, February 12th from 5 p.m. to 6:30 p.m.

The role of mass media often becomes problematic being that it is simultaneously fascinating and critical. Art curators and other cultural producers increasingly incorporate attitudes from the world of media as an integral part of their activity. What are the strategies used to become an intelligent 'mediator' and how are networks of information constructed if the goals are artistic, critical or political?

12. "Misunderstandings and Common Ground"

Moderator: Vasif Kortun (Founder, Istanbul Contemporary Art Project, Istanbul)

Participants: Jesús Fuenmayor (Independent Curator, Caracas)
Maria Hlavajova (Slovakia)

Date: Saturday, February 12th from 7 p.m. to 8:30 p.m.

Given that the difficulties that exist in identifying that which constitutes common ground between one's own culture and other cultures, the misunderstandings that arise from global media constitute the most productive catalysts to reveal alleged local subconscious thoughts and idiosyncrasies. In this sense, the following questions were posed: How do curators work with their own blind spots? What is their common ground? Can more than one common ground be achieved?

13. "Global Production: National Clichés versus Local Differences"

Moderator: Bettina Funcke (Dia Center for the Arts, New York)

Participants: Carolyn Christov-Bakargiev (Art Critic, Rome and Senior Curator PS1 Contemporary Art Center, New York)
Charles Esche (Research Fellow, Edinburgh College of Art; Codirector, The Modern Institute, Glasgow and Editor, Afterall, London)
Viktor Misiano (Critic and Contemporary Art Curator, Moscow)

Date: Sunday, February 13th from 12:30 p.m. to 2 p.m.

This conversation questioned whether a global culture, which assumes the unity of an international language, can take into account diversity and heterogeneity. What are the possibilities of working with realities imposed by local differences instead of following the increasing homogenization of culture that tends to produce national clichés?

14. "Transdisciplinary Practice in Contemporary Culture"

Moderator: Robert Fleck (Route de Plurien, La Bouillie, France)

Participants: Jens Hoffmann (Curator, Brussels and New York)

Hans Ulrich Obrist (Migrateurs-Curator Musée d'Art Moderne de la Ville de Paris and Founder Nano Museum and Museum Robert Walser)
Stephanie Moisdon Tremblay (Art Critic and Independent Curator, Paris)

Date: Sunday, February 13th from 5 p.m. to 6:30 p.m.

This roundtable discussion presented a series of observations about infiltration and the mutual fertilization that is produced through contemporary art. What are the multiple roles that many artists, curators, writers, architects, designers and choreographers play when they work in diverse fields and disciplines? How much do they integrate all these diverse fields within their work, proposals and projects?

From: Susan Hapgood
Subject: VOTI awakes
Date: Tuesday 4 April 2000

Dear VOTIs,

As many of us agreed in our impromptu meeting at ARCO, there will be a new structure for
VOTI discussions. In order to infuse the forum with new topics on a regular basis, we have
paired each VOTI member with a particular day (see the schedule below). We ask that you
post a message on the day listed beside your name. It would be great if you would follow up
your initial posting and keep the discussion going until the next date fisted. While we agreed
that there is no required length for messages, many of us prefer that they remain concise
and brief.

The new members you have suggested will be invited to join VOTI soon, and we want you to
let us know if there are still others you think would be active participants in our discussions
about curatorial practice.

VOTI is also looking for an Oficinista, anywhere in the world, who can participate in our
discussions, who will help sign up new members, change e-mail addresses, and carry out
general tasks with the thing, our listserver. Ideally, we would like someone interested
in curatorial studies, with a reliable Internet connection and e-mail service. Please send
suggestions for an Oficinista or for additional new members as a private e-mail to me.

Please forgive the delay in getting this message out; many of you have been asking privately
if VOTI is working. It is. As always, once inscribed, one only needs to post to VOTI to get
a message to everybody; the situation for the past several months has simply been that
nobody has sent messages.

Best wishes to you all.

It was great to meet so many of you in Madrid!

Susan Hapgood

VOTI MESSAGE SCHEDULE April 3, 2000
Zdenka Badovinac, April 15, 2000
Bart de Baere, May 1, 2000
Carlos Basualdo, May 15, 2000
Ute Meta Bauer, June 1, 2000
Wayne Berwaldt, June 15, 2000
Daniel Birnbaum, July 1, 2000

Waling Boers, July 15, 2000
Francesco Bonami, August 1, 2000
Dan Cameron, August 15, 2000
Christophe Cherix, September 1, 2000
Lisa Corrin, September 15, 2000
Carolyn Christov-Bakargiev, October 1, 2000
Jordan Crandall, October 15, 2000
Charles Esche, November 1, 2000
Okwui Enwezor, November 15, 2000
Robert Fleck, December 1, 2000
Douglas Fogle, December 15, 2000
Jesus Fuenmayor, January 1, 2001
Bettina Funcke, January 15, 2001
Rebecca Gordon-Nesbitt, February 1, 2001
Hou Hanru, February 15, 2001
Susan Hapgood, March 1, 2001
Maria Hlavajova, March 15, 2001
Jens Hoffmann, April 1, 2001
Udo Kittelmann, April 15, 2001
Vasif Kortun, May 1, 2001
Marta Kuzma, May 15, 2001
Cornelia Lauf, June 1, 2001
Maria Lind, June 15, 2001
Rosa Martinez, July 1, 2001
Laurence Miller, July 15, 2001
Viktor Misiano, August 1, 2001
Akiko Miyake, August 15, 2001
Asa Nacking, September 1, 2001
Michelle Nicol, September 15, 2001
Hans Ulrich Obrist, October 1, 2001
Pedro Reyes, October 15, 2001
Kathrin Rhomberg, November 1, 2001
Jose Ignacio Roca, November 15, 2001
Nancy Spector, December 1, 2001
Jon-Ove Steihaug, December 15, 2002
Stephanie Moisdon Trembtay, January 1, 2002
Barbara Vanderlinden, January 15, 2002
Hortensia Voelckers, February 1, 2002
Octavio Zaya, February 15, 2002

From: Zdenka Badovinac
Subject: first message
Date: Thursday 13 April 2000

Dear VOTIs,

I must admit that seeing my name listed on top of the precisely fixed VOTI Message Schedule gave me somewhat of a shock. Well, I am afraid I will not only be the first to start with the discussion but also the first to break the rule—since I am travelling to Romania tomorrow, I am sending this message two days earlier. I believe I will not be the only one to do so, and that there will be many other "violators". I wonder what Bart will do: he is supposed to send the message on May 1, when—at least in Slovenia—everybody is away having picnics.

I can't remember ever hearing what these messages of ours should be about. I can imagine, though, that since we are all very busy we will not be able to develop any "academic" type of discussion in this way. Personally, I would find it amusing to communicate to you what I am most involved with at the moment, as it is a project which I believe could provoke a general discussion. Since I only have a few minutes of time for this message, I will continue by raising some questions which are, hopefully, sufficiently general and interesting enough to start off our communication.

So, I am currently preparing an exhibition of works that will be the base of our newly emergent international collection, called the "Arteast Collection 2000+". The exhibition will open on June 24, that is, one day after the opening of Manifesta, which, as you all know, is to be staged here in Ljubljana this time. Prevalent in our collection are Eastern European works from the 1960s to the present. This is the art that is indeed represented in some collections in the West, but only through very few, typical names. Now the following questions occur to me: To what degree can global culture redefine the extant art museum collections, which are too similar? From Paris through London to New York, we are always bound to come upon one and the same names. How much do things really change inside the museum fortresses? What is the relation of our curatorial practice towards museum collections? While collecting the works for our "Arteast" collection, I was surprised to find out that my way of thinking slightly differed from the line I usually follow when preparing an exhibition. Can we still talk about a "museum piece"?

Are there certain works that we would self-assuredly, in all conviction choose for one of our exhibitions, but which we would be reluctant to propose for a museum collection? What influences such a decision? Do we not secretly still regard art as having a transitory value on the one hand, and an "eternal" museum value on the other?

Hopefully this will bring about at least a minimal reaction in one of your spare moments.

Best regards,

Zdenka

From: Bart de Baere
Subject: second message
Date: May 1, 2000

Sweethearts there, colleagues, VOTIs,

May 1st. So, Zdenka, you'll be out having picnic somewhere in idyllic Slovenia?

Here, in Ghent, May 1st is still the socialist parade, the remnants of much more, the echo of a possibility to consider society not as a market place, a possibility in which the law of supply and demand is the beginning of thinking, not the end of it. I worked this morning, discussing public funding for culture communication with our national tourism wizard. The parade was quite a sad view.

What can we do in these voti-emails?

Perhaps we can share recent experiences that are meaningful to us and that are out of the general information-and-reflection systems. The institution I'm working for (the SMAK) was never as popular as now. At this moment we organised an exhibition in the city center, "Over the Edges," that receives between thousand and six thousand visitors a day. On Friday evening there were—at the same time—an Allan Kaprow lecture, an exhibition by a young artist, two commercial special events in the museum and a party, all organised by us. It was a normal Friday evening for what pretends to be a major institution. All of this is not necessarily meaningful.

It's business. It is—at best—the question: shall we remain content providers, to be swallowed by service providers? Or: is it the destiny of museums to become service providers? Decision-making. There were about thirty people to attend the Kaprow lecture. He hung on to the "what is life" question, doing his life-art game, telling stories of his actions. Lifelike. What may elude, disappear, slip away. What worries him about our profession is the degree to which organisers have to compromise and deal with institutional demands; doing a tiny bit of what they'd really want to do and doing much which-is-less-bad-than-other-things-might-have-been. Yak, he's right.

All the same, Kaprow won't be my offer. The real offer, on this 1st of May: there's a movie you don't know about. I saw it by accident. Some bright French ladies came to Ghent and invited me to a private viewing of it. To see this movie, that was what made me most happy last week. It's the first production Samuel Beckett was completely involved in: "Comedy," twenty minutes, 1965, (front page scandal in Venice then, shown in Paris in '66, not distributed afterwards), B&W, high contrasts made deliberately in order to make it untransferable to TV, three actors, (well-known French comedians), their white heads above huge vases, their heads speaking when a spot lights them, dubbed, sound speeded up 2,5 times, with an experimental machine that was available then, that didn't change the voices, 300 cuts, harsh, grey, sometimes a scream, a face becoming full screen size. Frontal. Severe.

Marin Karmitz was the director.[146] He became other things in the film world and didn't promote this movie. After its projection last week he told of '68, three years later, of how Godard and he held opposite views, him making a movie with labourers, Godard doing a remake of that with professional stars... Karmitz believed one should be an artist/filmmaker and at the same time give the word—la parole—to those who don't have the possibility to distribute it. Godard stated that he used the word of others to do his own thing. It was nice to be reminded, at that table, of the possibility of really different paradigms, of the fact that the present range is a narrow range indeed. It was nice to be able to perceive Godard as a bourgeois artist. No problem with that, superb quality—but limitative and perhaps therefore so successful. Not dangerous, after all. Doing his thing, tickling and fitting, after all.

This brings me to some of the questions Zdenka asked in her mail, here was one that rounded the others up: "Do we not secretly still regard art as having a transitory value on the one hand, and an "eternal" museum value on the other?" Probably Zdenka is right. Probably we still want to make those kinds of absurd distinctions. Probably we have a spider-webbed attic in the back of our skull, an attic with inhabitants that never reach our mouth, even if their murmurs pervade our thoughts. Well. Kaprow hung on to his "what is life" question, refusing "what is art." It seemed an easy trick of an experienced lecturer. It became less easy when he earnestly and naively stated that at this moment in time no transversals are being made. What did he say? What? It's the one thing we do these days, transversals: synergy, integration, merger... multimedia, parties and theater in musea, movies in exhibitions, all of that. What? But perhaps Kaprow is right. Perhaps we pretend to act horizontally but in reality act vertically. Perhaps we tap the transversal energy—the energy of the borders of our domains—in order to give more energy to those domains, not to transcend them. (You see, art is interested in society, you see, this is a contemporary show, it shows, look at the party accompanying it, "you see, you don't have to leave art to find Las Vegas").

Perhaps the remarks that are made in this way avoid questions. Perhaps the aspiration to be larger than life became an automatism.

Perhaps we should continuously dismember ideas like "collection" or "exhibition," in order to reconstruct them, over and again, like Beckett did with his writing or with this movie that was seen as a disgrace for the audience in 1965.

We do grant eternity sometimes and transitory-ness sometimes and no attention whatsoever most of the time. Let me end with another question Zdenka asked: "What influences such a decision?" Is our astute professionalism the motor or is there a wider framework directing it?

May 1st, about as solid a day as December 31st—or May 15th. Off to a birthday party now.

Warmth,

Bart De Baere.

From: Carin Kuoni
Subject: voti message
Date: Monday 13 November 2000

An Election of Our Own

If the current (and ongoing) American presidential election were an exhibition, somebody else's exhibition, it might prove quite enjoyable or even education to point out its weaknesses, examine its strong points, and analyze the final product, for instance in a curatorial studies program. Among the weak spots, you would want to point out the fact that the most popular artwork was still not included in the show because of the 538 jury members involved and their, perhaps unnecessarily, prolonged deliberations.

You would also have to acknowledge that the artist whose work did end up being included in the exhibition had been seen at more parties in the presence of wealthier collectors than the runner-up, and you could link that observation to the question of whether more favorable coverage in the media had possibly contributed to his success. If you then turned to the art itself, it would be worthwhile to compare people's perception of the artist with their perception of the work. Both are identical! And while it's been widely acknowledged that the winning artist also has a winning personality and is considered a jolly good fellow and amiable guy, upon closer examination his artwork reflects few of the artist's own values. But either that wasn't really noticed by anybody or else it simply didn't matter. Plenty of conclusions your students could draw from this little study, theories regarding the viewer, the media and mediations, and the relationship between form and content.

Fortunately, this presidential election is not an exhibition, and we're not responsible. While this election has taught us the power of the individual, in fact, completely surprised us with it, it would be nice to be able to acknowledge some sort of curatorial power that transcends the individual, that an exhibition was not merely the reflection of a few people's thoughts.

Democracy in art doesn't seem to work. With their project "The People's Choice," 32 artworks painted according to the wishes of the people, polled in 32 countries, the two Russian expatriates Komar & Melmaid have given us a most horrendous, hence most useful example of art created by democratic principles, What would accumulated curatorial power have to look like?

Would you listen to the audience, or go for the juries? Would you turn to content, or focus on look? Would you read. look. and/or listen?

While an exhibition is not an election, interestingly enough, some of the same criteria apply when evaluating either. The aura surrounding show and presidency, whether accurate or imagined, is what moves people's perception. And that is often largely created by money.

While this experience might lead to a further reflection on our relationship to money, and the people who funnel it into our art institutions, and who, in large part, are responsible for creating this aura, in art, politics, and in life.

Carin Kuoni

Appendix

TNCS Networkers - Civil Society - Transnational Corporations - Democratic Governance

Brian Holmes

Transnational corporations: TNCs are the bogeymen of global dreams. They are imaged (on the left, at least) as roving, post-mechanical monsters, outfitted with fantastically complex electronic sensors and vicious trilateral brains and driven by an endless appetite for the conversion of resources, labor and consumer desire into profit for a few. There's some truth in that image. But the power of transnational capital is inseparable from the capital "S" of subjective agency, expressed in social, cultural and political exchange which is why I'd like to discuss TNCs in relation to what you might call TNCS: transnational civil society.

Let's start with the bogeyman. It became apparent in the sixties that private corporations were taking over the technological and organizational capacities developed initially in World War II: the coordinated industrial production, transportation, communication, information analysis and propaganda required for multi-theater warfare. Corporations such as Standard Oil or IBM, operating through subsidiary companies in every nation, which did not allow direct penetration, were projections of a (mostly American) military-industrial complex into both the developed and the undeveloped world as part of the globe-girdling Cold War strategy. Yet already in the sixties these "multinational" enterprises were achieving autonomy from their home bases, for instance, through the creation by British financiers of the Eurodollar, a way to keep profits offshore, out of the national tax collector's hands. The offshore economy took a quantum leap in the mid-seventies after the first oil shock, when the massive capital transfers to the OPEC countries were channeled by inventive Western bankers into the new, stateless circuits of financial exchange. That's about the time when the new system of transnational capitalism began to emerge, with the collapse of the nationally based Fordist-Keynesian paradigm of labor-intensive industrial production plus welfare programs. The proximate cause for the collapse was the inflation brought on by the policies of stimulating consumption through public spending, but the durable factor prohibiting any return to the postwar social contract was the competitive pressure of what is now known as flexible accumulation, based on geographically dispersed yet highly coordinated "just-in-time" production, cheap world-wide distribution through container transport systems, and the complex management, marketing and financing made possible by telecommunications. The flexible production system allowed the TNCs to avoid the concentrated masses of workers on which union power depends, and so much of the labor regulation built up since the Great Depression was sidestepped or abolished. At the same time, new technologies for financial speculation pushed levels of competition ever higher as industrialists struggled to keep up with the profit margins that could be realized on the money markets. With the demise of the Soviet Union and the nearly simultaneous resolution of the GATT negotiations, eliminating almost all barriers to international trade, the world stage was cleared for the activities of the lean-and-mean corporations. The favors of unprecedentedly mobile enterprises would now have to be courted by weakened national governments, which increasingly began to appear as no more than "executive committees" serving the needs of the transnationals. And the TNCs grew tremendously, with spectacular mergers that haven't stopped: witness BP/Amoco in oil, Daimler Benz/Chrysler in auto manufacturing, Morgan Stanley/Dean Whitter in investment banking or the proposed "Oneworld" alliance that would group nine international carriers around the two giants, British Airways and American Airlines...

This thumbnail sketch of economic globalization could go on and on, as it does in an incredible stream of recent books and articles from ail schools of economics and all frequencies of the political spectrum. But what's generally left out of the hypercritical, alarmist discourse that I personally find most compelling, is some theoretical consideration of the roles played by the individual, human nodes of the world network: I mean us, the networkers, the people whose labor actually maintains the global economic webs, and whose curiosity and energy is sucked up into the tantalizing effort to understand them and use them for our own ends. I'm trying to think on a broad scale here: the pioneers of virtual communities and net.art are only the tip of this iceberg. What's fascinating to see is the emergence on a sociological level of something like a "class of networkers," people who are increasingly conscious of the welter of connections that make up the global economy, who participate and, to some degree, profit from those connections, who suffer from them too and who are beginning to recognize their own experience as part of a larger pattern. The massification of Internet access in the last few years, only since the early 90s, has finally given this class its characteristic means of expression. But precisely this expanded access to worldwide communications has made it pretty much impossible to go on fingering a tiny corporate elite as the sole sources and agents of the global domination of capital. We are now looking at and sharing in a much larger phenomenon: the constitution of a transnational civil society, with something akin to, but different from, the complexity, powers and internal contradictions that characterized, and still characterize, the nationally based civil societies.

Civil society was initially defined, in the Enlightenment tradition, as the voluntary social relations that develop and function outside the institutions of state power. Tocqueville's observations on the importance of such voluntary initiatives for the cohesion of mid-19th-century American society established an enduring place for them in the theories of democracy. The idea recently got a lot of new press and some new philosophical consideration with the upsurge of dissidence in the Soviet Union and the other Eastern Bloc countries in the seventies and eighties; and at the same time, as the neoliberal critique of state bureaucracy resulted in the dismantling of welfare functions and the decay of public education systems, the notion of self-motivated, self-organizing social activities directed toward the common good became something of a Great White Hope in the western societies. So-called non-governmental organizations could then be seen as the correlates of civil society in the space of transnational flows. Nowadays, with the environmental and labor abuses of TNCs becoming glaringly violent and systematic, and with their cultural influence ballooning through their sway over the media, a lot of people in non-governmental organizations are understandably keen on promoting a notion of global civil society as a network of charitable humanitarian projects and political pressure groups operating outside the precinct of "corporate" power (with attempts to develop institutional agency focusing mostly around the UN). I sympathize with the intention, but still I'd like to point out that the individual rights and the free exchange of information on which this global civil society depends are also necessary elements of capitalist exchange and accumulation. The internationalization of law and the fundamental demand of "transparency," i.e. full information disclosure about all collective undertakings, are among the great demands of the TNCs' financial managers. To the extent that it wants to participate in capitalist exchange, even a regime as repressive as that of China, for example, has to open up more and more circuits of information flow, and so it pays the price of higher scrutiny, both internal and external, on matters of individual rights and freedoms. The whole ambiguity of capitalism, in its concrete, historical evolution, is to combine tremendous directive power over the course and content of human experience with a structurally necessary space for the development of individual autonomy, and thus for political organizing. The networkers, those whose bodies form nodes in the global information flow and who therefore can participate in an enlarged civil society, are subject to that ambiguity. Which means, pragmatically, that the expansion of the transnational corporations is inherently connected to the possibility for any democratic governance by a transnational civil society.

As Gramsci made clear long ago, civil society is always fundamentally about levels or thresholds of tolerance to the pressures and abuses of capitalist accumulation.

The specific forms and effects of civil society are determined by a complex cultural mood, a shifting, partially unconscious consensus about who will be exploited at work, and how, about whose intelligence and emotions will be brutalized by which commercial media, and when and where and how, about whose land will be polluted, and with what—and, of course, about whose land will just get suburbanized or left tragically undeveloped, about who will be able to refine their intelligence and emotions and in which ways, about who must work and who gets to work and who no longer "needs" to work and who just gets left on the sidelines. Thus Gramsci, writing in the 20s and 30s, had a somewhat jaundiced view of really-existing civil society. He conceived it as the primary locus of political struggle in the advanced capitalist societies, but he also saw it as a directive, legitimating cultural superstructure, generally engaged in the justification of brutal domination; and he recalled the violence of petty bureaucrats and clergyman in the Italian countryside, keeping the submissive classes in line. Gramsci's key concept of hegemony expresses both the role of this legitimating function of civil society in maintaining dominance and also its potential mobility, its capacity to effect a redistribution of power in society. I think that the emergence of the transnational class of networkers, operating as a significant minority in most countries, is effectively shifting the articulation of political power in all the world's nations. I'll try to describe how with just a few examples.

Consider the United States, the country that launched the Internet, where an important fraction of the population is extracting new wealth out of what Robert Reich termed the "global webs" of multi-partner industrial, commercial, and financial ventures, where many people not directly involved as operative nodes in such webs are still very conscious of them because they have their savings or retirement funds invested in global financial markets (as almost half of Americans now do), and finally, where long lists of NGOs and alternative communication networks are based, many of them with roots in the idealistic social-reform movements of the sixties and seventies. This is also a country where the least wealthy 40% of the population has actually seen their wages go down and their working conditions deteriorate over the last twenty years, where chronic social exclusion has become highly visible in the forms of homelessness and renewed racial violence, and where, last but not least, a very powerful Christian Coalition has emerged to reject almost every kind of consciousness change attendant on globalization and the recognition of cultural diversity. To marshal a workable political consensus out of such intense divisions, Clinton-Gore had to simultaneously push even harder toward the flexibilized information economy than their Republican predecessors had done, while making (and then breaking) lots of promises to restructure the country's welfare safety net, maintaining a high-profile international human-rights discourse (for instance with respect to China), and combining talk about environmentalism with a hip and tolerant style to woo all the former sixties radicals whose capacity for cultural and technological innovation fuels so many growth markets. Continuing economic growth has, of course, been the only thing to render this juggling act possible, making the strident neoliberal critique of the Republican right seem redundant and forcing the Republicans into even greater dependence on the extreme right, as defined and prosecuted by the moral order of Christian fundamentalism.

Europeans tend to look on media-driven American politics with consternation and a powerful will to deny any resemblance to the situation in their own countries. But if Tony Blair enjoys so much prestige in the rest of the EU right now, it is because of New Labour's ability to juggle the contradictions of an unevenly globalized society, somewhat as Clinton has done. The hegemonic formula reflected by New Labour seems to be a fun, flexible lifestyle, good for stimulating consumption, a fast-paced managerial discipline to keep up with global competition, and a center-left position that shows a lot of sympathy for casual workers and the unemployed while eschewing any genuinely socialist policies of market regulation and restricting the state's role to that of a "promoter" (Blair's word). However, there are indications that this formula, tantalizing as it is, will not really work in the rest of Europe, stricken by unemployment and yet still reticent to dismantle the remains of its welfare systems. The very interesting resurgence of support for state interventionism and economic regulation in France is one such indication. A more disquieting sign is the rise of populist neofascist parties, not only in France, where the National Front clamors against mondialisme (globalism), but also in Austria, Italy, Belgium and Norway. These betoken major resistance to the neoliberal path that the European Union—or more accurately, Euroland—has taken under the economic leadership of the Bundesbank. The compromise-formation between a transnational elite subordinating everything to its privileges and an excluded popular class looking to vent its frustrations seem to be the scapegoating of poorer immigrants. The sight of two immigration officers savagely beating an African in a transit corridor of Schiphol airport has stuck in my mind as an all-too possible future for Euroland.

The powerfully articulated national civil societies of Europe are likely to falter and distort rather than break under the pressure of the split introduced by the transnational class. Hegemonic dissolution occurs when a majority of a country or region's people can no longer identify themselves with any aspect of the institutional structure that purports to govern them. A case in point is Algeria. Here we see the steadily increasing inability of a recently urbanized and relatively educated population to identify with a government that no longer even remotely represents a possibility to share the benefits of industrial growth-because there hasn't been any for the past twenty years. The government is now an oligarchy drawing its revenues from TNCs in the fields of resource-extraction and consumer-product distribution. For many Algerians who have left their former village environment but can no longer get a job or use their education, the only ideology that can render a regression to pre-industrial living conditions tolerable is not democracy, but Islamic fundamentalism. If transnational capital continues to exploit the new international space, which it has (de)regulated for its convenience without any consideration for the daily lives of huge numbers of people, such violent reactions of rejection are inevitable and will spread. The current crisis of the global financial system is all too likely to fulfill this prediction.

Paradoxically, it is the global financial meltdown that may offer the first real chance for transnational civil society to have a significant impact on world politics. Not because networkers will have any direct influence on the few transnational institutions that do exist: only the richest states and the lobbies of the very large corporations can sway the IMF, OECD, and WTO; and despite all the inroads made by non-governmental organizations, the UN is only really effective as a kind of mega-forum for debate. But in the context of a world-wide economic crisis, networkers may be able to use an understanding acquired by direct participation in global information flows to effectively criticize the institutions, ideologies, and economic policies of their own countries. In other words, transnational civil society may find ways to link back up with the national civil societies. There is already an example of networked resistance to economic globalization that has operated in just this way: the mobilization against the Multilateral Agreement on Investments. This ultraliberal treaty aims not at harmonizing but at homogenizing the legal environment for transnational investment. It would prohibit any differential treatment of investors, thus making it impossible for governments to encourage locally generated economic development. It would allow investors to sue governments in any case where new environmental, labor or cultural policies entailed profit losses. And its rollback provision would function to gradually eliminate the "reservations" that individual states might initially impose. Negotiations on the MAI began secretly in 1995 among the 29 member-states of the Organization for Economic Cooperation and Development and might actually have been concluded in April 1998 had the draft text of the treaty not been obtained and made public, first by posting it on the Internet (see the Public Citizen site, at www.citizen.org). This, plus the resultant press coverage, brought cascading opposition from around the world, including a joint statement addressed to the OECD and national governments by 560 NGOs. The result was that member-states were forced into questioning certain aspects of the treaty and negotiations were temporarily suspended, though not definitively adjourned.

Detailed information on the MAI can be obtained over the Internet, for instance, from the National Centre for Sustainability in Canada (www.islandnet.com/-ncfs/maisite/). The diffusion of this information remains important at the date I am writing (September 1998), as further negotiations are upcoming. Opponents say that like Dracula, the MAI cannot stand the light of day. What I find particularly interesting in this context is the way the angle of the daylight differs across the world. Canadian activists, having seen their local institutions weakened by NAFTA, are extremely concerned with preserving national sovereignty. Consumer advocates and environmentalists were able to exert the strongest influence on the US Congress. In France, the threat to government subsidy of French-language audiovisual production tipped the balance of indignation. NGOs in developing countries that may be incited to join the treaty immediately pointed to the dangers of excessive speculation by outside investors. Underlying these and many other specific concerns there is no doubt a broad conviction that the single, overriding value of capitalist accumulation by any means, and for no other end than accumulation itself, is insane or inhuman. But even if the current financial crisis is almost certain to reinforce and extend that conviction, still it will have no political effect until translated into more tangible issues within an institutional environment that is still permeable to those whose only power lies in their intelligence, imagination, empathy and organizing skills. Like it or not, that environment is still primarily to be found in the nation, and not in some hypothetical Oneworld consciousness. Which is tantamount to saying that transnational civil society, if developed for its own sake, would probably end up as homogeneous and abstract as the process of transnational capital circulation that structures the TNCs. The only desirable global governance will come from the endless harmonization of endlessly negotiated local differences.

I have evoked the position of networkers as human nodes in the global information flow. What are the implications of that position? In his three-volume study of "The Information Age," sociologist Manuel Castells gives the following definition: "A network is a set of interconnected nodes. A node is the point at which a curve intersects itself." This definition is either fatalistic or provocative. Fatalistic if it defines the network of information exchange as an entirely autonomous system, interlinked only to itself in a structure of recursive proliferation. But provocative if it helps push the human nodes to assert their autonomy by seeking connections outside the recursive system. Can we hope that a redirection of priorities will arise from the aberrant spectacle of financial short-circuiting and resultant material penury in a world whose productive capacities are so obviously immense? I suspect that in the near future at least some progress toward the reorientation of the world economy is likely, particularly in the European Union where the rudiments of transnational democratic institutions do exist. Even in the US, real doubt may grow about the sustainability of the speculative market in which so many have invested. In this context there may be a chance for activists to talk political economics with the far larger numbers of networkers who formerly had ears only for the neoliberal consensus. But a real change in the hegemony will not come about without an expansion of the magic circle of empowerment to people and priorities that have been marginalized and excluded. There is a tremendous need right now to spend some time away from computers and out of airports, not to ideologize people in the national civil societies but just to find out what matters to them and to discover other levels of experience that can feed one's own capacities for empathy and imagination. Such experience can help re-qualify the transnational networks. In this respect, I continue to think there has been something compelling in the Zapatista electronic insurgency, despite the aura of exoticism it is often reduced to. Not only has it been a vital force in shifting the hegemonic balance in Mexican civil society by giving uncensored voice to the demand for greater democracy. Not only has it been able to mobilize support from far-flung nations at a time when "Third Worldism" was becoming a term of insult and disdain. But in addition to these considerable accomplishments it has been able to infuse the global network with stories and images of the Lacanian forest, evoking experiences of time, place and human solidarity that seem to have been banished from the accelerating system of abstract exchanges. The thing is not to romanticize such stories and images, but to look instead for the real resonances they can have in one's own surroundings. Call it transnational culture sharing, if you like.

The Artist's Reserved Rights Transfer and Sale Agreement
Seth Siegelaub and Robert Projansky, 1971

THE ARTIST'S RESERVED RIGHTS TRANSFER AND SALE AGREEMENT

The accompanying 3 page Agreement form has been drafted by Bob Projansky, a New York lawyer, after my extensive discussions and correspondence with over 500 artists, dealers, lawyers, collectors, museum people, critics and other concerned people involved in the day-to-day workings of the international art world.

The Agreement has been designed to remedy some generally acknowledged inequities in the art world, particularly artists' lack of control over the use of their work and participation in its economics after they no longer own it.

The Agreement form has been written with special awareness of the current ordinary practices and economic realities of the art world, particularly its private, cash and informal nature, with careful regard for the interests and motives of all concerned.

It is expected to be the standard form for the transfer and sale of all contemporary art, and has been made as fair, simple and useful as possible. It can be used either as presented here or slightly altered to fit your specific situation.

If the following information does not answer all your questions consult your attorney.

WHAT THE AGREEMENT DOES

The Agreement is designed to give the artist:

- 15% of any increase in the value of each work each time it is transferred in the future.
- a record of who owns each work at any given time.
- the right to be notified when the work is to be exhibited, so the artist can advise upon or (see Article Seven (b)) veto the proposed exhibition of his/her work.
- the right to borrow the work for exhibition for 2 months every five (5) years (at no cost to the owner).
- the right to be consulted if repairs become necessary.
- half of any rental income paid to the owner for the use of the work at exhibitions, if there ever is any.
- all reproduction rights in the work.

The economic benefits would accrue to the artist for life, plus the life of a surviving spouse (if any) plus 21 years, so as to benefit the artist's children while they are growing up. The artist would maintain aesthetic control only for his/her lifetime.

Although the contract may seem to alter the previous relationship between artist and art owner principally by putting new obligations on the owners, the Agreement really does some very good things for the collector. In return for these obligations, which are almost costless for the collector, he gets substantial benefits; the Agreement is designed:

- to give each owner the formalized right to receive from the artist (or his/her agent) a certified history and *provenance* of the work.
- to create and clarify a non-exploitative, one-to-one relationship between the artist and the owner.
- to maintain this relationship—what lawyers call "privity"—between the artist and each successive owner of the work.
- to establish recognition that the artist maintains a moral relationship to the work, even as the collector owns and controls it.
- to give assurance to the owner that he is using the work in harmony with the artist's intentions.

WHEN TO USE THE AGREEMENT

The Agreement form has been designed to be used by the artist at the time of the FIRST TRANSFER—

either by gift, or barter for things or services, or sale

of EACH INDIVIDUAL work of art—

either a painting, a sculpture, a drawing, a graphic, a multiple, a mural, an immovable sculpture, a non-obect work, or any other fine art you can think of

from the artist to ANYONE else—

either a friend, another artist, collector, museum, gynecologist, lawyer, corporation, landlord, relative or dealer.

IMPORTANT: It is NOT for use when you lend your work to exhibitions or when you give it to your dealer on consignment. It IS for use when the dealer sells your consigned work.

In short, the Agreement form is to be used when you part with your work for keeps.

Its terms are effective and it requires a very simple procedure to keep it in effect with each successive owner of your work of art.

It requires the artist and the first owner of the work to fill out and sign the Agreement form and also, to affix a notice of the existence of the Agreement somewhere on the work of art itself.

HOW TO USE THE AGREEMENT

1. To begin, xerox or offset a number of copies of each page of the Agreement form. You will need at least 2 copies for each work you sell or give or trade away. (Save *this* copy to make future copies and so you can refer to this information.)

2. Fill out the contract forms—one copy for you, one for the new owner, and another copy of the last page only (from which you cut out the notice to affix to the work). Make sure that you fill it out legibly.

3. Follow the simple instructions in the margin of the Agreement form. Double check to make sure you have filled in the spaces that must be filled in and struck out what must be struck out.

IMPORTANT: Fill out only those parts of the Specimen TRANSFER AGREEMENT AND RECORD which identify the work and the *original* parties to the *original* Agreement ("between _______________ and _______________ made the _______________ day of _______________, 19_____,"). Be sure you fill out the specimen NOTICE.

You will note that the contract form speaks in terms of a "sale" ("whereas Artist is willing to sell the Work to Collector and Collector is willing to purchase. . . ."); this doesn't mean you can't use it when you give a friend a work or pay your dentist with a painting or trade works with another artist. We have used the words "sell" and "purchase" only for the sake of simplicity (likewise, we use the term "Collector" just because it is the most all-inclusive word for this purpose). Strictly speaking, even if you are giving or trading your work you are "selling" it for the promises in the Agreement and whatever else you get.

This Agreement form is not a bill of sale or an invoice, nor is it a substitute. If the work is sold for money, prepare a separate bill of sale for your financial records.

In Article One, you enter the price   value of the work; you, the artist, can put any value that you and the new owner agree upon. If the work is resold for a figure higher than the one you have entered as "value", the owner will have to pay you 15% of the difference over that figure; obviously the higher the figure you put in, the better break the new owner is getting. If you are giving a friend a work or exchanging with another artist (you need two separate Agreements for the latter situation) you might want to enter a nominal value so that you would get some money, even if he/she later sells it for less than what your dealer would sell it for.

IMPORTANT: if there are rights given the artist under the Agreement form that you as the artist do not want, you strike them out. ·   IMPORTANT: be sure to examine ARTICLE SEVEN (b); if you don't feel you must have a veto over all details of the future exhibition of the work, be sure you strike (b) out of ARTICLE SEVEN. Few collectors will want to buy a work if their right to lend it for exhibition is so restricted by someone else. If you give a work away you can leave (b) in, but that will make it very difficult for your friend to sell it. We have put (b) in because (a) is the least an artist should accept and (b) is the most he/she can ask for. If (a) is not enough for you but you don't need (b), have an attorney draft a short rider to the Agreement setting forth those specific controls over exhibition that you feel you must have.

4. You and the Collector should each sign both copies, yours and his, so they will both be legal originals.

5. Before the work is delivered, be sure that a copy of the NOTICE is affixed to the work. DO NOT cut it out of one of the originals. Put it on a stretcher bar or under a sculpture base or wherever else it will be aesthetically invisible yet easily findable. It should get a coat of clear polyurethane—or something like it—to protect it. It won't hurt to put several copies of the NOTICE on a large work.

If your work simply has no place on it for the NOTICE or your signature—in which case you should always use an ancillary document which describes the work, which bears your signature, and which is transferred as a (legal) part of the work—glue the NOTICE on the document.

PROCEDURE FOR FUTURE TRANSFERS. For future transfers, the owner makes three copies of the TRANSFER AGREEMENT AND RECORD form from his original (without the words "SPECIMEN"). He then fills them out, entering the value or price that he and the next owner have agreed upon. Both the old and new owners sign ALL THREE copies of the dated TRANSFER AGREEMENT AND RECORD, each keeps one copy and the third is sent with the 15% payment (if any is required) to the artist or his/her agent. The old owner gives the new owner a copy of the original Agreement, so he will know his responsibilities to the artist and have the TRANSFER AGREEMENT AND RECORD form if HE transfers the work.

THE DEALER

If you have a dealer, he is going to be very important in getting people to sign the contract when he sells your work.

The dealer should make the use of the Agreement a policy of the gallery, thereby giving the artists in the gallery collective strength against those few collectors and institutions who do not really have the artist's interests at heart.

Remember, your dealer knows all the ins and outs that go down in the business of the art world. He knows the ways to get the few reluctant art buyers to sign the Agreement—the better the dealer the more ways and the more buyers he knows and the easier it will be. He can do what he does now when he wants things for his artists—give the buyer favors, exchange privileges, preferential treatment, discounts, hot tips, time, advice and all the other things that collectors expect and appreciate.

The Agreement only formalizes what dealers do now anyway; dealers try to keep track of the work they have sold, but now they can only rely on exhibition lists, catalogues, hit-or-miss intelligence and publicity to keep them up-to-date. The Agreement creates a very simple record system, which will automatically maintain a biography of each work and a chronological record of ownership. It is private, uncluttered and no dealer should ever have to hire another secretary to administer it; if each work engenders a dozen pieces of paper over the entire life of the Agreement, it will be a lot. The requirement of giving a *provenance* to the current owner is no more than what goes on today, but under this system it will be accurate and almost effortless.

A dealer shouldn't be expected to do this for nothing; it seems reasonable to compensate the dealer with some part of the 15% he/she is collecting for the artist, perhaps one-third of it.

When, as is often the case, an artist moves from one dealer to a more prestigious one, the first dealer might continue to collect whatever payments are occasioned by the resale of the earlier work.

When a dealer BUYS work directly from the artist (for resale or otherwise), they should write the intended RETAIL value of the work in their Agreement, NOT the actual amount of money the dealer is paying the artist, which would be less.

Getting the contract signed is mostly a state of mind. If your dealer does not think the benefits of the Agreement are important for you, he will have dozens of reasons why he can't get those few reluctant buyers to sign it; on the other hand, if he seriously wants you to have these benefits he will be able to overcome all those obstacles without losing a single sale.

THE FACTS OF LIFE: YOU, THE ART WORLD AND THE AGREEMENT

The general response to the preliminary draft of this Agreement form has been extremely favorable; the vast majority of people in the art world feel it is fair, reasonable and practical. A few have expressed certain reservations about whether or not people will actually use it. These reservations can be summed up in two basic statements:

• "... the economics of buying and selling art is so fragile that if you place one more burden on the collectors of art, they will simply stop buying art ...", and
• "... I will certainly use the Agreement—if everyone else uses it ..."

The first statement is nonsense; clearly the art will be just as desirable with as without the Agreement and there is no reason why the value of any art should be affected at all, especially if this contract is standard practice in the art world—which brings us to the second statement. If there is a problem here, this statement reflects it: it is the concern of the individual artist or dealer that the insistence on the use of the contract will jeopardize their sales in a competitive market.

If we examine this notion carefully, we see it doesn't hold up.

ALL artists sell, trade and give their work to only two kinds of people:
• those who are their friends.
• those who are not their friends.

Obviously, your friends will not give you a hard time; they will sign the Agreement with you. The ONLY trouble will come when you are selling to someone who is not a friend. Since surely 75% of all art that is sold is bought by people who are friends of the artist or dealer—friends who dine together, see each other socially, drink together, weekend together, etc.—whatever resistance may appear will come only in respect to some portion of the 25% of your work that is being sold to strangers. Of these people, most will wish to be on good terms with you and will be happy to enter into the Agreement with you. This leaves perhaps 5% of your sales which will encounter serious resistance over the contract. Even this real resistance should decrease toward zero as the contract comes into widespread use.

In a manner of speaking, this Agreement will help you discover who your friends are.

If a collector wants to buy but doesn't want to sign the Agreement, you should tell him that all your work is sold under the contract, that it is standard for your work.

If he buys work only from those few artists who won't insist on using the Agreement he is being very foolish; non-use of this Agreement is a very dumb criterion for building one's collection.

There are other things that you can point out to the reluctant collector:

• first of all, it's not going to cost him anything unless your work appreciates in value. If that doesn't cut any ice, and he wants to keep *all* of whatever profit he might make with your work, you can simply write in a higher value for it, thus giving him a free ride for the first part of the appreciation he anticipates.
• if and when he sells your work and he owes you some payment, he doesn't necessarily have to pay you with money; you can give him credit against the purchase of a new work or take payment in services or something other than money.
• of course, if a collector buys a work without the contract when the use of the Agreement has become the standard practice for the artist, the collector will have to rely on sheer good-will when he later wants the artist (or his/her dealer) to appraise, repair or authenticate it. Why he should expect to find any good-will there is anybody's guess.

Is the collector really going to pass up your work because you want him to sign the contract? Work that he likes and thinks is worth having? If the answer is yes, given the fact that it won't cost *him* anything to give you the respect that you as the creator of the work deserve—if that will keep him from buying, he is being very stubborn and foolish and nobody can tell you how to illuminate him.

Using the contract doesn't mean that all your relationships in the art world will hereafter be strictly business or that you will have to enforce your rights down to the last penny. Friends will still be friends; you will be able to waive your rights to payments (in whole or in part), your right to make repairs, to grant reproduction rights, to be consulted—but they will be YOUR rights and the choices will be YOURS.

The Agreement form has been prepared to be used by any and all artists—known, well-known and unknown. Simply make a lot of copies and use it whenever you give, trade or sell your work. It will be effective from the moment you use it. The more artists and dealers there are using it, the better and easier it will be for everybody. It requires no organization, no dues, no government agency, no meetings, no public registration, no nothing—just your will to use it. Just plug it in and watch it go—a perfect waffle every time!

ENFORCEMENT

First, let's put this question in perspective: most people will honor the Agreement because most people honor agreements. Those few people who will try to cheat you are likely to be the same kinds who will give you a hard time about signing the Agreement in the first place. Later owners will be more likely to try to cheat you than the first owner, with whom you or your dealer have had some face-to-face contact, but there are strong reasons why both first and future owners should fulfill the contract's terms.

What happens if owner #2 sells your work to owner #3 and doesn't send you the transfer form? (He's not sending your money, either.)

Nothing happens. (You don't know about it yet.)

Sooner or later you do find out about it because it takes a lot of effort to conceal such sales and the grapevine will get the news to you (or your dealer) anyway. To conceal the sale, owner #3 has to conceal the work and he's not going to hide a good and valuable work just to save a little money. And if he ever wants to sell it, repair it, appraise it or authenticate it, he MUST come to you (or your dealer). When you do find out about such a transfer—and you will—you sue owner #2, who will be stuck for 15% of the increase based on the price to owner #3 OR on the value at the time you find out about it, which maybe much higher. Clearly, a seller (in this case owner #2) would be extremely foolish to take this chance, to risk having to pay a lot of money just to save a little money.

As to falsifying values reported to the artist, there will be as much pressure from the new owner to put in a falsely high value as from the old owner to put in a low value. There are real difficulties inherent in getting two people to lie in unison, especially if it only benefits one of them—the seller. In 95% of the cases the amount of money to be paid to the artist won't be enough to compel the collectors to lie to you.

You will note that in the event you have to sue to enforce any of your rights under the Agreement, ARTICLE NINETEEN gives you the right to recover reasonable attorney's fees in addition to whatever else you may be entitled to.

SUMMATION

We realize that this Agreement is essentially unprecendented in the art world and that it just may cause a little rumbling and trembling; on the other hand, the ills it remedies are universally acknowledged to exist and no other practical way has ever been devised to cure them.

Whether or not you, the artist, use it, is of course up to you; what we have given you is a legal tool which you can use yourself to establish ongoing rights when you transfer your work. This is a substitute for what has existed before—nothing.

We have done this for no recompense, for just the pleasure and challenge of the problem, feeling that should there ever be a question about artists' rights in reference to their art, the artist is more right than anyone else.

Seth Siegelaub, 24 February 1971, New York

SEE OVERSIDE FOR AGREEMENT FORM

please POST, REPRODUCE, and USE this poster freely.

this poster is not to be sold.

this poster has been printed and distributed by the

california institute of the arts in los angeles

and produced by the

school of visual arts in new york

for further information: Seth Siegelaub, Post Office Box 350, New York 10013, U.S.A.

DESIGN: CRISTOS GIANAKOS

AGREEMENT OF ORIGINAL TRANSFER OF WORK OF ART

<table>
<tr><td>Fill in date, names and addresses of parties</td><td>

This agreement made this___________day of____________________, 19______, by and between

____(hereinafter the "Artist"), residing at

____and

_____________________________________(hereinafter the "Collector"), residing

at____;

</td></tr>
</table>

WITNESSETH:
WHEREAS the Artist has created that certain work of art;

Title:___________________________Identification #:_____________________

Date:___________________________Material:_________________________

Dimensions:_________________________Description:______________________

(hereinafter "the Work"); and
WHEREAS Artist is willing to sell the Work to Collector and Collector is willing to purchase the Work from Artist, subject to mutual obligations, covenants, and conditions herein; and
WHEREAS Collector and Artist recognize that the value of the Work, unlike that of an ordinary chattel, is and will be affected by each and every other work of art the Artist has created and will hereafter create; and
WHEREAS the parties expect the value of the Work to increase hereafter; and
WHEREAS Collector and Artist recognize that it is fitting and proper that Artist participate in any appreciated value which may thus be created in the Work; and
WHEREAS the parties wish the integrity and clarity of the Artist's ideas and statements in the Work to be maintained and subject in part to the will or advice of the creator of the Work,
NOW, THEREFORE, in consideration of the foregoing premises and the mutual covenants hereinafter set forth and other valuable considerations the parties hereto agree as follows:

PURCHASE AND SALE. ARTICLE ONE: The Artist hereby sells to Collector and Collector hereby purchases the Work from Artist, subject to all the covenants herein set forth (for the price of____________________; receipt of which is hereby acknowledged) (at the agreed valuation for the purposes of this agreement of ________________).

FUTURE TRANSFERS: ARTICLE TWO: Collector covenants that in the event Collector shall hereafter sell, give, grant, barter, exchange, assign, transfer, convey or alienate the Work in any manner whatsoever or if the Work shall pass by inheritance or bequest or by operation of law, or if the Work shall be destroyed and insurance proceeds paid therefor, Collector or Collector's personal representative shall:
    (a) file a current TRANSFER AGREEMENT AND RECORD in the form and containing the Information set forth and called for in the specimen hereunto annexed and made a part hereof, completed and dated, and subscribed by Collector or Collector's personal representative and collector's transferee, with the (Artist at the address set forth above) (Artist's agent for the purpose:________________________________ at:_________________________________) within thirty days of such transfer, distribution, or payment of insurance proceeds, and shall
    (b) pay a sum equal to fifteen percent (15%) of the Appreciated Value (as hereinafter defined), if any, occasioned by such transfer or distribution or payment of insurance proceeds to (Artist at the address set forth above) (Artist's agent for the purpose:_____________________at:____________________ ___________________) within thirty days of such transfer, distribution, or payment of insurance proceeds.

PRICE/VALUE. ARTICLE THREE: The "price or value" to be entered on a TRANSFER AGREEMENT AND RECORD shall be:
    (a) the actual selling price if the Work is sold for money; or
    (b) the money value of the consideration if the Work is bartered or exchanged for a valuable consideration; or
    (c) the fair market value of the Work if it is transferred in any other manner.

APPRECIATED VALUE. ARTICLE FOUR: "Appreciated Value" of the Work for the purposes of this Agreement, shall be the increase, if any, in the value or price of the Work set forth in a current duly executed and filed TRANSFER AGREEMENT AND RECORD over the price or value set forth in the last prior duly executed and filed TRANSFER AGREEMENT AND RECORD, or, if there be no prior duly executed and filed TRANSFER AGREEMENT AND RECORD, over the price or value set forth in ARTICLE ONE herein
    (a) In the event a current duly executed TRANSFER AGREEMENT AND RECORD is not timely filed as required by ARTICLE TWO herein, Appreciated Value shall nonetheless be computed as if such current TRANSFER AGREEMENT AND RECORD had been duly executed and filed, with a price or value set forth therein equal to the actual market value of the Work at the time of the current transfer or at the time of the discovery of such transfer.

TRANSFEREES TO RATIFY AGREEEMENT. ARTICLE FIVE: Collector hereby covenants that he will not hereafter sell, give, grant, barter, exchange, assign, transfer, convey or alienate the Work in any manner whatsoever or permit the Work to pass by inheritance or bequest or by operation of law io any person without procuring such transferee's ratification and affirmation of all the terms of this Agreement and transferee's agreement to be bound hereby and to perform and fulfill all of the Collector's covenants set forth herein, said ratification, affirmation and agreement to be evidenced by such transferee's subscription of a current duly completed and filed TRANSFER AGREEMENT AND RECORD.

ike out one t applicable

PROVENANCE. ARTICLE SIX: Artist hereby covenants that (Artist) (Artist's agent for the purpose as set forth in ARTICLE TWO) will maintain a file and record of each and every transfer of the Work for which a TRANSFER AGREEMENT AND RECORD has been duly filed pursuant to ARTICLE TWO herein and will at the request of the Collector or Collector's successors in interest, as that interest shall appear, furnish in writing a provenance and history of the Work based upon said records and upon Collectors' notices of proposed public exhibitions and will certify in writing said provenance and history and the authenticity of the Work to Collector and his successors in interest, and, at Collector's reasonable request, to critics and scholars. Said records shall be the sole property of the Artist.

EXHIBITION. ARTICLE SEVEN: Artist and Collector mutually covenant that

(a) Collector shall give Artist written notice of Collector's intention to cause or permit the Work to be exhibited to the public, advising Artist of all details of such proposed exhibition which shall have been made known to Collector by the exhibitor. Said notice shall be given for each such exhibition prior to any communication to the exhibitor or the public of Collector's intention to cause or permit the Work to be exhibited to the public. Artist shall forthwith communicate to Collector and the exhibitor any and all advice or requests that he may have regarding the proposed exhibition of the Work. Collector shall not cause or permit the Work to be exhibited to the public except upon compliance with the terms of this article.

ike out (b) iot required

(b) Collector shall not cause or permit any public exhibition of the Work except with the consent of the Artist to each such exhibition.

(c) Artist's failure timely to respond to Collector's timely notice shall be deemed a waiver of Artist's rights under this article, in respect to such exhibition and shall operate as a consent to such exhibition and to all details thereof of which Artist shall have been given timely notice.

ARTIST'S POSSESSION. ARTICLE EIGHT: Artist and Collector mutually covenant that Artist shall have the right, upon written notice and demand to Collector made not later than 120 days prior to the proposed shipping date therefor, to possession of the Work for a period not to exceed sixty (60) days solely for the purpose of exhibition of the Work to the public at and by a public or non-profit institution, at no expense whatsoever to Collector. Collector shall have the right to satisfactory proof of sufficient insurance and pre-paid transportation or satisfactory proof of financial responsibility therefor. Artist shall have the right to such possession of the Work for one period not to exceed sixty (60) days every five (5) years

NON-DESTRUCTION. ARTICLE NINE: Collector covenants that Collector will not intentionally destroy, damage, alter, modify or change the Work in any way whatsoever.

REPAIRS. ARTICLE TEN: Collector covenants that in the event of any damage to the Work, Collector shall consult with Artist prior to the commencement of any repairs or restoration and if practicable Artist shall be given the opportunity to make any required repairs or restoration.

RENTS. ARTICLE ELEVEN: In the event that Collector shall become entitled to any monies as rent or other compensation for the use of the Work at public exhibition, the Collector shall pay a sum equal to one-half of said monies to (Artist) (Artist's agent as set forth in ARTICLE TWO herein) within thirty (30) days of the date when Collector shall become entitled to such monies.

ike out one applicable

REPRODUCTION. ARTICLE TWELVE: Artist hereby reserves all rights whatsoever to copy or reproduce the Work. Artist shall not unreasonably refuse permission to reproduce the Work in catalogues and the like incidental to public exhibition of the Work.

NON-ASSIGNABILITY. ARTICLE THIRTEEN: No rights created in the Artist and for the Artist's benefit by the terms of this Agreement shall be assignable by Artist during the Artist's lifetime, except that nothing herein contained shall be construed as a limitation on Artist's rights under any copyright laws to which the Work may be subject.

NOTICE. ARTICLE FOURTEEN: Artist and Collector mutually covenant that there shall be permanently affixed to the Work a NOTICE of the existence of this Agreement and that ownership, transfer, exhibition and reproduction of the Work are subject to the convenants herein, said NOTICE to be in the form of the specimen hereunto annexed and made a part of this Agreement.

ike out (a) if : applicable

(a) Because the Work is of such nature that its existence or essence is represented by documentation or because documentation is deemed by Artist to be part of the Work, the permanent affixing of said NOTICE to the documentation shall satisfy the requirements of this article.

TRANSFEREES BOUND. ARTICLE FIFTEEN: In the event the Work shall hereafter be transferred or otherwise alienated from Collector or Collector's estate in any manner whatsoever, any transferee taking the Work with notice of this Agreement shall in every respect be bound and liable to perform and fulfill each and every covenant herein as if such transferee had duly made and subscribed a properly executed TRANSFER AGREEMENT AND RECORD in accordance with ARTICLE TWO and ARTICLE FIVE herein at the time the Work was transferred to him or her.

EXPIRATION. ARTICLE SIXTEEN: This Agreement and the covenants herein shall be binding upon the parties, their heirs, legatees, executors, administrators, assigns, transferees and all other successors in interest and the Collector's covenants do attach and run with the Work and shall be binding to and until twenty-one (21) years after the deaths of Artist and Artist's surviving spouse, if any, except that the covenants set forth in ARTICLE SEVEN, ARTICLE EIGHT and ARTICLE TEN herein shall be binding only during the life of the Artist.

WAIVERS NOT CONTINUING. ARTICLE SEVENTEEN: Any waiver by either party of any provision of this Agreement, or of any right hereunder, shall not be deemed a continuing waiver and shall not prevent or estop such party from thereafter enforcing such provision or right, and the failure of either party to insist in any one or more instances upon the strict performance of any of the terms or provisions of this Agreement by the other party shall not be contrued as a waiver or relinquishment for the future of any such terms or provisions, but the same shall continue in full force and effect.

AMENDMENT IN WRITING. ARTICLE EIGHTEEN: This Agreement shall not be subject to amendment, modification, or termination, except in writing signed by both parties.

ATTORNEYS' FEES. ARTICLE NINETEEN: In the event that either party shall hereafter bring any action upon any default in performance or observance of any covenant herein, the party aggrieved may recover reasonable attorneys' fees in addition to whatever remedies may be available to him or her.

IN WITNESS WHEREOF, the parties have set their hands and seals to this Agreement as of the day and year first above written.

SPECIMEN   -   SPECIMEN   -   SPECIMEN

NOTICE

Ownership, Transfer, Exhibition and Reproduction of this Work of Art are subject to covenants set forth in a certain Agreement made the _______ day of ___________, 19_____, by and between_______________________________ and_______________________________________, the original of which is on file with___________________ _____________________________________ at _____________________________________ _____________________________________.

____
(Artist)

____
(Collector)

SPECIMEN   -   SPECIMEN   -   SPECIMEN

TRANSFER AGREEMENT AND RECORD

To:

Know ye that ____

residing at____

has this day transferred all his right, title and interest in that certain Work of art known as:

Title: Identification #:

Date: Material:

Dimensions: Description:

to ____________________________ residing at___________________________________,

transferee, at the agreed price or value of_____________________________. Transferee, hereby

expressly ratifies and affirms all the terms of that certain Agreement made by and between

_________________________________ and____________________________________

on the _______ day of ____________, 19_____, and agrees to be bound thereby and to perform and fulfill all of Collector's covenants set forth in said agreement.

Done this_______ day of___________, 19_______,

at _________________________________   _________________________________

_________________________________   _________________________________

Scan of Whitney Letter

December 1, 1998

Dr. Maxwell L. Anderson, Director
Whitney Museum of American Art
945 Madison Avenue
New York, NY 10021

Fax: 212-570-1807

Dear Dr. Anderson:

We wish to express our opposition to your treatment of curators Thelma
Golden and Elisabeth Sussman. The recent restructuring of the curatorial
departments at the Whitney Museum of American Art is indicative of a
managerial approach that has been slowly developing in a number of major
art museums. Beyond our wish to show support for fellow curators Golden
and Sussman, we see your recent actions as signals of a pervasive
disrespect for curatorial practice, and as signs of aversion to some of
the most aesthetically and intellectually challenging experiments in
contemporary art.

Curators at many institutions today are caught in a kind of double bind.
Art museums pride themselves on their proximity to an academic
environment, positing scholarship as one of their highest goals. Yet due
to shifts in the infrastructure of funding, museums have also adopted
corporate management models – with the corollary effect that curators
are treated as expendable workers. Contrary to both of these models,
curators do not have the job security and intellectual support enjoyed
by professors in the university system, nor do they enjoy salaries
comparable to corporate employees. As a result, they are forced to stand
on increasingly shaky ground, while serving as the primary source of
ideas for their institutions' exhibition programming. The door is then
open to all kinds of abuses.

We find your actions in regard to these particular individuals to be a
form of intellectual gentrification, if not censorship. The fact that
Thelma Golden and Elisabeth Sussman presided over the controversial 1993
Biennial Exhibition, one of the most stimulating and contentious
contemporary art exhibitions presented after the gutting of the National
Endowment for the Arts, or that Golden then went on to curate "Black
Male: Representations of Masculinity in Contemporary American Art," are
coincidences that hardly escape us. Since when did exhibitions that set
attendance records and raise genuine intellectual questions become a
failure? Of course no one is required to subscribe to the aesthetic
options of these two curators, but to admit that they are part of an
important debate, itself linked to a vibrant focus of artistic

experimentation, is surely necessary for a public institution that seeks
to represent artistic practice today. To sidestep this debate over
politics and identity in a multicultural, globally integrating society
is to set a timid, unproductive, yet perhaps more easily manageable
agenda for the Whitney. This troubling direction reflects a broader
conservative trend, the mistaken return to an outdated conception of
cultural history.

We feel it is imperative to mark our opposition to your actions, lest
they be misperceived as the innocuous restructuring of an organization
like any other in the private sphere. Curating is an eminently public
activity and must remain so, if the visual arts are to continue to
generate the curiosity, the enthusiasm and the commitment that sustain
our efforts as professionals in this field.

Sincerely yours,

Mónica Amor
Zdenka Badovinac
Bart de Baere
Wayne Baerwaldt
Carlos Basualdo
Daniel Birnbaum
Francesco Bonami
Dan Cameron
Christophe Cherix
Carolyn Christov-Bakargiev
Lisa Corrin
Jordan Crandall
Amada Cruz
Okwui Enwezor
Robert Fleck
Douglas Fogle
Jesús Fuenmayor
Bettina Funcke
Rebecca Gordon-Nesbitt
Hou Hanru
Susan Hapgood
Jens Hoffmann
Brian Holmes
Udo Kittelmann
Aleksandra Kostic
Maria Lind
Rosa Martinez
Laurence Miller
Viktor Misiano
Akiko Miyake
Louise Neri

Michelle Nicol
Hans-Ulrich Obrist
Kathrin Rhomberg
Liisa Roberts
José Ignacio Roca
Yukiko Shikata
Nancy Spector
Barbara Vanderlinden
Peter Weibel
Octavio Zaya

Friends and members of the Union of the Imaginary (VOTI) – a permanent forum for the
discussion of issues pertaining to curatorial practice in the context of
contemporary society
http://www.blast.org/voti.html

Research document: The Trial of Pol Pot

Text believed to have been included in Le Mag - Magasin's exhibition journal.
From the archives of Liam Gillick.

```
The Trial of Pol Pot
A project co-ordinated by Liam Gillick and Philippe Parreno.
A report structure in the form of a discussion document, some response, some
questions, some response, enlargements onto the gallery walls.
Supervised by Thomas Mulcaire, Rebecca Gordon-Nesbit, Douglas Gordon, Gabriel
Kury, Jeremy Millar, Josephine Pryde, Carsten Höller, Rirkrit Tiravanija, Ronald
Jones, Pierre Joseph, Zeigam Azizov, Adrian Schiesser, Terry Atkinson.

Communication 1
"Remember, it is about a specific trial of a specific person, but not a
documentation of an event. It is "event led" so obviously contains some specific
reference, but it is not either documenting the event or presenting some
collection of works where artists have thought about "justice",
"occidental/oriental", "imperialism", "the imposition of identities", "parallel
histories" and so forth." From an email to Josephine Pryde, supervisor of "The
Trial of Pol Pot".

Communication 2
"Rather than a typical art centre based exercise in relativism, The Trial of Pol
Pot could instead be seen as a layering of single solutions over a web of
discussion and rhetoric rather than the typical model of a show which might be
described as the layering of a web of discussion and rhetoric over a series of
single proposals." From a fax to the supervisors of "The Trial of Pol Pot".

Communication 3
"So the project is about the nature of events, characterisation and political
representation based on a specific situation that we are led to believe actually
took place. Therefore to avoid falling into a middle brow trap of avoidance,
neo-liberal relativism and coy neo-alternativeness, we obviously make some
reference to the actual event. Yet the project is not a picture of that event,
nor is it documentation of that event. It is not a group exhibition and it is
not a solo show. It bears some quite strong institutional critique in relation
to the current situation of art centres without falling into sullen refusal or
acceptance of marginalisation in order to define a project as distinct through
its opposition to the other shows alongside it. It plays with the normal
hierarchy between artists and curators in quite precise, well documented ways.
The show creates a space where it is possible to consider the ideas around such
events. It functions as a set or staging for a series of potential
reconsiderations, so of course it needs some specific techniques of
representation instead of the fog of data and photocopies that we are led to
believe are the only way to approach such issues. I feel that art only functions
in the spaces between more clearly defined social activities, creating spaces
and techniques that are not possible in similar communication structures that
are more hamstrung by notions of correct behaviour and audience expectation."
From an email to Josephine Pryde, supervisor of "The Trial of Pol Pot".


A postcript by Liam Gillick
```

(answers to very brief questions)

BACKGROUND
Philippe and I wanted to establish a situation where we could examine an event
that was unclear in terms of the way it had been played out via traditional
informational routes. At the time of the exhibition's conception, the trial of
Pol Pot had just taken place in the jungles of Cambodia near to the Thai border,
yet nothing had been resolved in terms of settling the moral and ethical issues
that surrounded the Khmer Rouge period. We both found this suspension of
resolution interesting in parallel with our interest in contemporary forms of
social structuring in general.

SHIT HAPPENS
Of course, international events took off in sync with our developmental
structure, and other people became interested in this issue in a more precise
way, leading to the death of Pol Pot and the current focus upon former Khmer
Rouge operatives. Yet it is important to understand that we were taking this
event as only one possible structure from many that we could have chosen. We
were as interested in the machinations of the trial concept, and the idea of how
to image an event that cannot be represented as much as we might have been
interested in the specifics of Pol Pot's situation. That is why we did not put
together a quasi-anthropological survey of the contemporary situation in
Cambodia, and instead attempted to negotiate this event without using the same
techniques that would be employed in the Western media, in context based art or
in cinema.

QUESTIONS
This, of course, caused some problems for people who have a more pedestrian and
myopic view of the potential of art now, and some precise arguments on these
subjects were played out on an Internet forum. The discussions that took place
among the curators on the forum revealed that some are happier when art merely
seeks to mirror anthropological structures that have been abandoned by all but
the most disenfrachised cultural producers. There was some anxiety on the part
of those involved in the forum that the people of Grenoble wouldn't be able to
understand the project. We completely reject this singularisation of audience
and the patronising notion that the multiple audiences of a large European city
require didactic structures in order to enter into a dialogue with cultural
producers.

CURATING / CO-ORDiNATING
While we wouldn't wish to emphasise some notional critique of contemporary
curating we certainly used the word Co-ordinated instead of curated to literally
describe the fact that we co-ordinated the project. You cannot curate a cultural
structure you can only guide and co-ordinate its shape. There is no material to
curate. Curating in this context would imply the organisation of people or
things or structures. We made the decision that it would only be interesting to
accept responsibility within a co-ordination role. We saw the curatorial gesture

as coming from Yves and once he had "curated" Philippe and myself, we could go ahead and co-ordinate our project.

IMAGES PULLING IN AND OUT OF FOCUS
A large space, inscribed with text and over-lit with theatre/cinema lights and fronted by an extremely large banner is a place full of images. Artists negotiate questions of representation all the time, it is what they do, but focusing upon representation alone would be equivalent to an architect who only focused upon the facade of the building and didn't look at the structure. Representation is only problematic for those who are trying to preserve a specific form of representation. A step by step treatment is the only possible way to do anything. We were not trying to link up various points of view but address the problematic situation of how to negotiate an event within an art context without resorting to a mirroring of the forms used by the agents of standard information transferral whether that be the media, other artists and curators who focus upon showing people what they already know, or governmental agencies with an interest to "spin" a version of contemporary events.

VISITING MAGASIN ALONE
We are both interested in the concept of a cultural producer being in a state of flickering activity and analysis. However, there is no singular sense of audience. The most dynamic Capitalist structures know this, but art spaces still function with a generalised sense of audience, for the most part. We tried to shift this sense of audience through the involvement of the supervisors and the knowledge that many people visit the Magasin alone. There are few moments when a large audience is in the exhibition space simultaneously unless it is playing host to a local school party or a group of art professionals on some culture tour. So we played with this in our design of the space, in order to involve the visitor within a precise visual setting where they too might be able to apply themselves to the questions at hand. A setting that was overloaded and precise rather than relativistic and modest. We also offered a free poster, near to the entrance of the space, so that any visitor might opt to take one instead of coming into the place. This seemed like a good way to offer people the choice of whether or not to continue and become involved in playing out our specific game.

JUDGEMENT
This was a project full of images. Extremely photogenic and quite loaded. Issues of judgement were at the heart of the project, but not quasi-formalistic art judgements about the nature of representation. It is necessary to assess and constantly renegotiate each specific situation, rather than look for a model that can accommodate every project.

The Trial of Pol Pot was presented at MAGASIN from 8 November 1998 to 3 January 1999.
Gillick/Le Mag DATE Juin 25, 1999   PAGE 5.

Inside Job
Matthew Debord

© *Artforum*, March, 1999, "Inside Job," by Matthew Debord. 147

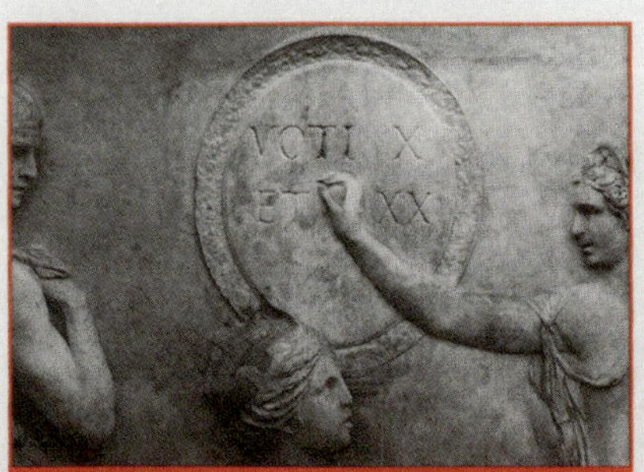

Inside Job

"A permanent forum for the discussion of issues pertaining to curatorial practice in the context of contemporary society," VOTI (www.blast.org/voti.html)—the letters stand for "Union of the Imaginary" (with the *U* expressed in the ancient Roman style, for pronunciation's sake)—has been nestled inside Jordan Crandall's X Art Foundation, at the Blast site, since March 1998. An invitation-only forum for a group of about forty-five mostly youngish, mostly freelance curators to hash out issues pertaining to their amorphously defined jobs, VOTI's membership reads like a who's who on the current international scene: Okwui Enwezor, Dan Cameron, Hou Hanru, Francesco Bonami, Hans-Ulrich Obrist, and Carlos Basualdo, among others, all contributed to the site's formation. Modeling itself on a labor union—with Crandall at the top, and Ulrich and Basualdo as his capos—VOTI arose out of disgruntlement with the current state of freelance curatorial affairs (i.e., a curator is thought to come, prepackaged, with a specific set of artists and a signature theoretical approach which can then be plugged into whatever show management has in the works). The union's only action so far has been a private letter of protest to the Whitney, criticizing the firings that took place there after Maxwell Anderson seized the reins. A recent discussion opened a dialogue on contracts. In the future, some topics will diverge from the invitation-only template and be discussed in public forums. "We wanted to send a signal to the rest of the art world," says Basualdo, "that it was still possible to work collaboratively."

—*Matthew DeBord*

Scan of English program ARCO conferences, Madrid, 2000.

Panel D
[10-15 Feb ...ce Programme

PREVIEW

1 & 2 - "ITALIAN ART AND THE ART SYSTEM"
SPONSOR: ISTITUTO ITALIANO DI CULTURA DI MADRID

Director-Moderator: **Achille Bonito Oliva** (Commissioner Italy at ARCO 2000, Rome)

Participants:
Cecilia Casorati (Art Critic, Independent Curator, Professor of Contemporary Art Accademia di Belle Arti, Rome)
Laura Cherubini (Professor Art History Academy of Fine Arts, Brera, Milan)
Mario Codognato (Free-lance Curator, Rome)
Manuela Gandini (Journalist, Art Critic and Curator, Milan)
Daniela Lancioni (Independent Curator, Responsible for Photographic Archive Incontri Internazionali d'Arte Contemporanea Tor Bella Monaca, Rome)
Angela Vettese (Art Critic, Independent Curator, Professor of Art History Accademia Carrara di Belli Arti, Bergamo)

Date: Thursday, February 10th from 12:30 p.m. to 2 p.m. and from 5 p.m. to 6:30 p.m.

3 & 4 - "INTERNATIONAL MUSEUMS' ACQUISITION POLICY"
SPONSOR: GENERAL DIRECTION OF FINE ARTS AND CULTURAL HERITAGE OF THE MINISTRY OF CULTURE AND EDUCATION OF SPAIN

Chaired by: **Benigno Pendás** (General Director of Fine Arts and Cultural Heritage of the Ministry of Culture and Education of Spain)

Participants:
Francesco Bonami (Museum of Contemporary Art, Chicago)
Dan Cameron (New Museum of Contemporary Art, New York)
Germano Celant (Solomon E. Guggenheim Museum, New York)
Richard Flood (Walker Art Center, Minneapolis)
Steingrim Laursen (Louisiana Museum of Modern Art, Humlebaek)

Allison de Lima Greene (The Museum of Fine Arts, Houston)
Marti Mayo (Contemporary Arts Museum, Houston)
Declan Mcgonigle (Irish Museum of Modern Art, Dublin)
Kynaston McShine (MoMA –Museum of Modern Art, New York)
Silvia Vega Badeiras (Museo de Arte Contemporáneo de Monterrey, Mex.)

Date: Friday, February 11th from 12:30 p.m. to 2 p.m. and from 5 p.m. to 6:30 p.m.

5 & 6 - "MUSEUMS' ACQUISITION POLICY IN SPAIN"
SPONSOR: GENERAL DIRECTION OF FINE ARTS AND CULTURAL HERITAGE OF THE MINISTRY OF CULTURE AND EDUCATION OF SPAIN

Chaired by: **Benigno Pendás** (General Director of Fine Arts and Cultural Heritage of the Ministry of Culture and Education of Spain)

Participants:
Juan Manuel Bonet (Director IVAM –Instituto Valenciano de Arte Moderno)
Manuel Borja-Villel (Director MACBA –Museo de Arte Contemporáneo de Barcelona)
José Antonio Chacón (Director Centro Andaluz de Arte Contemporáneo, Sevilla)
José Guirao (Director MNCARS –Museo Nacional Centro de Arte Reina Sofía, Madrid)
Miguel Fernández-Cid (Director CGAC –Centro Galego de Arte Contemporánea, Santiago de Compostela)
Antonio Franco (Director MEIAC –Museo Extremeño e Iberoamericano de Arte Contemporáneo, Badajoz)
Pedro de Sancristóval y Murua (Diputado Foral de Cultura de Álava)

Date: Saturday, February 12th from 12:30 p.m. to 2 p.m. and from 5 p.m. to 6:30 p.m.

7.to 14- "CHALLENGES TO CURATORIAL PRACTICE": Panel Discussions by VOTI (Union of the Imaginary)

7.- "MUTATIONS OF THE EXHIBITION MODEL"

Moderator: **Carlos Basualdo** (Poet, Curator and Art Critic, New York)

Participants:
Zdenka Badovinac (Slovenia)
Daniel Birnbaum (Director IASPIS Stockholm)
Lisa Corrin (Curator The Serpentine Gallery, London)
Asa Nacking (Free-lance Curator and Consultant Louisiana Museum of Modern Art, Copenhagen)

Date: Friday, February 11th from 12:30 p.m. to 2 p.m.

8.- ARTISTS AS GENERATORS OF CHANGE IN CURATORIAL PRACTICE"

Moderator: **Susan Hapgood** (Curator of Exhibitions, American Federation of Arts, New York City; Senior Fellow, Vera List Center for the Art and Politics, The New School, Archivist of VOTI)

Participants:
Dan Cameron (Chief Curator New Museum of Contemporary Art, New York)
Maria Lind (Curator Moderna Museet, Stockholm)
Liam Gillick (Artist, London and New York)
Michelle Nicol (Museum Ludwig, Cologne and Zurich)

Date: Friday, February 11th from 5 p.m. to 6:30 p.m.

9.- "ART AND SOCIETY: THE RESPONSIBILITY OF THE CURATOR"

Moderator: **Octavio Zaya** (Critic and Free-lance Curator, New York)

Participants:
Bart de Baere (Curator SMAK, Gent)
Hou Hanru (Independent Art Critic and Curator, Paris)
Cornelia Lauf (Director Camera Oscura, Editor of artist's books, Rome)

Date: Friday, February 11th from 7 p.m. to 8:30 p.m.

10.- "CURATING BEYOND THE MUSEUM/THE INDEPENDENT CURATORS"

Moderator: **Rosa Martínez** (Critic and Independent Curator, Barcelona. Artistic Director III Bienal SITE Santa Fe, New Mexico)

Participants:
Francesco Bonami (Manilow Senior Curator Museum of Contemporary Art, Chicago)
Marta Kuzma (Ukraine)
Laurence Miller (Director ArtPace Foundation, San Antonio, Texas)
José Ignacio Roca (Head of Plastic Arts Biblioteca Luis Ángel Arango, Bogotá)

Date: Saturday, February 12th from 12:30 p.m. to 2 p.m.

11.- "MASS MEDIA/MEDIATORS"

Moderator: **Udo Kittelmann** (Director Kölnischer Kunstverein, Cologne)

Participants:
Ute Meta Bauer (Professor and Head Institute for Contemporary Art, Academy of Fine Arts, Vienna)
Jordan Crandall (Artist and media theorist, New York)
Jon-Ove Steihaug (Free-lance Curator and Critic, Oslo)
Warren Niesluchowski (Independent Writer and Curator, New York)

Date: Saturday, February 12th from 5 p.m. to 6:30 p.m.

12.- "MISUNDERSTANDINGS AND COMMON GROUND"

Moderator: **Vasif Kortun** (Founder Istambul Contemporary Art Project, Istanbul)

Participants:
Jesús Fuenmayor (Independent Curator, Caracas)
Maria Hlavajova (Slovakia)

Date: Saturday, February 12th from 7 p.m. to 8:30 p.m.

34

13.- "GLOBAL PRODUCTION: NATIONAL CLICHÉS VERSUS LOCAL DIFFERENCES"

Moderator: **Bettina Funcke** (Dia Center for the Arts, New York)

Participants:
Carolyn Christov-Bakargiev (Art Critic, Rome and Senior Curator PS1 Contemporary Art Center, New York)
Charles Esche (Research Fellow, Edinburgh College of Art; Co-Director, The Modern Institute, Glasgow and Editor Afterall, London)
Viktor Misiano (Critic and Contemporary Art Curator, Moscow)

Date: Sunday, February 13th from 12:30 p.m. to 2 p.m.

14.- "TRANSDISCIPLINARY PRACTICE IN CONTEMPORARY CULTURE"

Moderator: **Robert Fleck** (Route de Plurien, La Bouillie, France)

Participants:
Jens Hoffmann (Curator, Brussels and New York)
Hans Ulrich Obrist (Migrateurs-Curator Musée d'Art Moderne de la Ville de Paris and Founder Nano Museum and Museum Robert Walser)
Stephanie Moisdon Tremblay (Art Critic and Independent Curator, Paris)

Date: Sunday, February 13th from 5 p.m. to 6:30 p.m.

15 & 16.- "COLLECTORS' FORUM"

Moderator: **Manuel E. González** (Chase Manhattan Bank, New York)

Participants:
Juan Vergez (Buenos Aires)
Eduardo Costantini (Buenos Aires)
João Carlos de Figueiredo Ferraz (São Paulo)
Michael Klein (Microsoft Art Collection, Redmond)
Ignacio Enrique Oberto (Caracas)
Jose Olympio Pereira (São Paulo)
Isabella Pratta (São Paulo)
Conde Panza di Biumo (Lugano),
Patrizia Sandretto Re Rebaudengo (Turin)

Date: Thursday, February 10th and Friday, February 11th from 7 p.m. to 8:30 p.m.

17.- "THE GERMAN SHIFT"

Participant: **Udo Kittelmann** (Director Kölnischer Kunstverein, Cologne)

Date: Saturday, February 12th from 4 p.m. to 7 p.m.

18.- "WOULD GOYA HAVE LIKED THE INTERNET?"

Director-Moderator: Gregor Muir (Lux Gallery, London)

Participants:
Ted Byfield (Freelance Editor and writer, London and New York)
Korinna Patelis (Visiting Lecturer, Dept. Media and Communications, Goldsmith's College, University of London)
Benjamin Weil (Former Director ICA New Media Department, Free-lance Curator and Critic, New York)

Date: Saturday, February 12th from 7 p.m. to 8:30 p.m.

19.- "SURFING THE INTER-NATIONAL?"

Director-Moderator: **Anthony Bond** (Chief Curator Art Gallery of New South Wales, Australia)

Participants:
Charles Merewether (Curator The Getty Research Institute for the Arts and Humanities, Los Angeles)
Apinan Poshyananda (Associate Director Centres of Academic Resources Chulalongkorn University, Bangkok)
Judy Annear (Senior Curator Photography The Art Gallery of New South Wales, Sydney)

Date: Sunday, February 13th from 7 p.m. to 8:30 p.m.

20 & 21.- "SOUTHERN CONE LATIN FORUM"

Director-Moderator: **Marcelo Pacheco** (Director Fundación Espigas, Buenos Aires)

Participants:
Justo Pastor Mellado (Art Critic, Independent Curator, Santiago de Chile)
Gustavo Buntinx (Critic, Art Historian, Independent Curator, Lima)
Gabriel Peluffo Linari (Director Museo Municipal de Bellas Artes Juan Manuel Blanes, Montevideo)
Sandra Antelo-Suárez (New York)
Adriano Pedrosa (Artist, Writer and Curator, Associated Curator XXV Bienal de São Paulo, Rio de Janeiro and São Paulo)

Date: Monday, February 14th from 5 p.m. to 6:30 p.m. and from 7 p.m. to 8:30 p.m.

22.- "NEW DUTCH VIEWS"

Participants:
Bartomeu Mari (Director Witte de With Center for Contemporary Art, Rotterdam)
Leontine Coelewij (Curator Stedelijk Museum, Amsterdam)
Anna Tilroe (Art critic/writer; NRC - Handelsblad, Amsterdam)

Date: Monday, February 14th from 12:30 p.m. to 2 p.m.

23.- "GLAMOUR AND POSING"

Director-Moderator: **Rafael Doctor Roncero** (Critic and Curator MNCA Reina Sofía and Comunidad de Madrid)

Participants:
Estrella de Diego (Professor of Contemporary Art Universidad Complutense, Madrid)
Ana Laura Alaez (Artist, Madrid)
Xabier Arakistain (Art Curator, Bilbao)

Date: Tuesday, February 15th from 7 p.m. to 8:30 p.m.

UPDATED
(1st October, 1999):

For further information and inscriptions:
ASOCIACIÓN AMIGOS DE ARCO -
PARQUE FERIAL JUAN CARLOS I -
28042 MADRID - SPAIN
Tel.: (34) 91 722 50 80
Fax: (34) 91 722 57 98
E-mail: bueno@ifema.es
www.arco.ifema.es

Scan of Spanish program ARCO conferences, Madrid, 2000.

Fundación Joan Miró en Barcelona, Museo Pablo Gargallo o Fundación Museo Pablo Serrano en Zaragoza o Museo Ramón Gaya en Murcia. Al mismo tiempo, desde el comienzo de los años 90, ha prosperado el coleccionismo institucional por parte de entidades, principalmente financieras, públicas o privadas, que han permitido el afianzamiento de artistas contemporáneos españoles o locales. De esta relación se desprende que la adquisición de obras esta íntimamente ligada a la creación de museos y colecciones, y que éstos han realizado un importante esfuerzo, acreditar su personalidad mediante una colección propia.

7.a 14- <u>"DESAFÍOS EN TORNO A LA LABOR DEL COMISARIO"</u>: Mesas de Debate por VOTI (Union of the Imaginary). Serie concebida por Bettina Funcke, Susan Hapgood y Octavio Zaya
BAJO LOS AUSPICIOS DE: FUNDACIÓN ICO

Presentación de VOTI: Fecha: Viernes, 11 de Febrero 11 de 12:00 a 12:30. Sala: A

7.- "MUTACIONES DEL MODELO DE EXPOSICIÓN"
Moderador: Carlos Basualdo **(Poeta, Curador y Crítico de Arte, Nueva York)**
Participantes: **Zdenka Badovinac** (Directora, Curadora de exposiciones, Moderna galerija / Museum of Modern Art, Ljubljana), **Daniel Birnbaum** (Director IASPIS, Estocolmo), **Asa Nacking** (Curadora Independiente y Consultora Louisiana Museum of Modern Art, Copenhague)
Fecha: Viernes, 11 de Febrero de 12:30 a 14 horas. Sala: A

*Después de que **Alfred Barr** introdujera el formato de exposición de "cubo blanco" en el MUSEUM OF MODERN ART, el modelo modernista de exposición de forma lineal y cronológica se ha visto cuestionado de múltiples e interesantes formas a lo largo de todo el siglo. ¿Cuáles son las ideas antiguas y las nuevas en lo que se refiere a la construcción de exposiciones, y por qué se alejaron de su supuesta neutralidad?. Además, ¿cómo ha afectado la industria del ocio a estos modelos?*

8.- "LOS ARTISTAS COMO GENERADORES DE CAMBIO EN LA LABOR DEL COMISARIO DE ARTE"
Moderadora: **Susan Hapgood** (Curadora de Exposiciones, American Federation of Arts, New York City; Investigadora, Vera List Center for the Arts and Politics, The New School, Archivista de VOTI, Nueva York)
Participantes: **Dan Cameron** (Curador Jefe New Museum of Contemporary Art, Nueva York), **Maria Lind** (Curadora Moderna Museet, Estocolmo), **Liam Gillick** (Artista, Londres y Nueva York), **Michelle Nicol** (Museum Ludwig, Colonia y Zurich)
Fecha: Viernes, 11 de Febrero de 17 a 18:30 horas. Sala: A

Los artistas son, con frecuencia, los más poderosos catalizadores para reinventar las estructuras expositivas, mientras que muchos conservadores y comisarios de arte se ven atados por sus responsabilidades en relación con las instituciones u organizaciones para las que trabajan. Esta mesa redonda trató acerca de algunos de los recientes cambios que más han influido en el campo de las exposiciones y en la labor de los comisarios de arte, y que han sido el resultado de fructíferas colaboraciones entre artistas y comisarios de arte. La discusión se centró especialmente en el papel que desempeñan los artistas para que se produzcan estos cambios.

9.- "ARTE Y SOCIEDAD: LA RESPONSABILIDAD DEL COMISARIO DE ARTE"
Moderador: **Octavio Zaya** (Crítico y Comisario Independiente, Nueva York)
Participantes: **Bart de Baere** (Curador SMAK, Gent), **Hou Hanru** (Crítico de Arte Independiente y Curador, París), **Cornelia Lauf** (Directora Camera Oscura, Redactora de libros de artista, Roma)
Fecha: Viernes, 11 de Febrero de 19 a 20:30 horas. Sala: A

¿Cuáles son, en la actualidad, las responsabilidades del comisario de arte respecto a los artistas, a las instituciones y a un público cada vez mejor informado? ¿Cuál es su papel esencial dentro de la sociedad, y cómo puede actuar de puente entre la producción artística y las exigencias institucionales, sin dejar por ello de propiciar unas situaciones que sean pertinentes para las cuestiones/temas sociales, políticos o culturales?

10.- "LA LABOR DEL CONSERVADOR MÁS ALLÁ DEL MUSEO/LOS COMISARIOS DE ARTE INDEPENDIENTES"
Moderadora: **Rosa Martínez** (Crítica y Comisaria Independiente, Barcelona. Directora Artística III Bienal SITE Santa Fé, Nuevo México)
Participantes: **Francesco Bonami** (Conservador Jefe Museum of Contemporary Art, Chicago), **Marta Kuzma** (Curadora independiente y crítica, Kiev), **José Ignacio Roca** (Jefe de Artes Plásticas Biblioteca Luis Ángel Arango, Bogotá)
Fecha: Sábado, 12 de Febrero de 12:30 a 14 horas. Sala: A

Esta mesa redonda ofreció una oportunidad para tratar el tema de la labor de los conservadores y comisarios de arte fuera de los museos. ¿Cuáles son los nuevos retos y las nuevas posibilidades de esta profesión, y en qué medida reflejan los cambios sociales y políticos de nuestra época? ¿Cuáles son las diferencias reales, en términos tanto de limitaciones como de posibilidades, entre los comisarios de arte independientes y los conservadores de los museos?

11.- "MEDIOS DE COMUNICACIÓN/MEDIADORES"
Moderador: **Udo Kittelmann** (Director Kölnischer Kunstverein, Colonia)
Participantes: **Jordan Crandall** (Artista y *media* teórico, Nueva York), **Warren Niesluchowski** (Escritor Independiente y Curador, Nueva York), **Ute Meta Bauer** (Profesora y Directora Instituto de Arte Contemporáneo, Academia de Bellas Artes, Viena)
Fecha: Sábado, 12 de Febrero de 17 a 18:30 horas. Sala: A

El papel de los medios de comunicación de masas se vuelve a menudo problemático debido al hecho de que dichos medios son, a un tiempo, fascinantes y críticos; por su parte, los comisarios de arte y otros productores de cultura adoptan cada vez con más frecuencia actitudes propias de los medios de comunicación como parte integral de su propia actividad. ¿Cuáles son las estrategias para ser un 'mediador' inteligente, y cómo se construye una red de información según que sus fines sean artísticos, críticos o políticos?

12.- "MALENTENDIDOS Y PUNTOS DE ACUERDO"
Moderador: **Vasif Kortun** (Fundador Istambul Contemporary Art Project, Estambul)
Participantes: **Jesús Fuenmayor** (Curador Independiente, Caracas), **Maria Hlavajova** (Co-curadora, Manifesta 3, Eslovaquia), **Mika Hannula** (Escritora, Curadora y Lectora, Berlín), **Douglas Fogle** (Walker Art Center, Minneapolis)
Fecha: Sábado, 12 de Febrero de 19 a 20:30 horas. Sala: A

Habida cuenta de las dificultades que existen para identificar lo que constituyen puntos de acuerdo de la propia cultura en relación con otras culturas, los malentendidos que surgen a través de las redes mundiales de medios de comunicación constituyen los catalizadores más productivos para mostrar supuestos subconscientes e idiosincrasias locales. En este sentido, se puedieron plantear los siguientes interrogantes: ¿cómo trabajan los comisarios con sus propias áreas oscuras?, ¿cuáles son sus puntos de acuerdo? ¿puede lograrse más de un punto de acuerdo?

13.- "PRODUCCIÓN GLOBAL: LOS *CLICHÉS* NACIONALES FRENTE A LAS DIFERENCIAS LOCALES"
Moderadora: **Bettina Funcke** ((Dia Center for the Arts, Nueva York)
Participantes: **Carolyn Christov-Bakargiev** (Crítica de Arte, Roma y Curadora Jefe PS1 Contemporary Art Center, Nueva York), **Charles Esche** (Investigador, Edinburgh College of Art; Co-Director, The Modern Institute, Glasgow y Editor Afterall, Londres), **Viktor Misiano** (Crítico y Comisario de Arte Contemporáneo, Moscú), **Sarat Maharaj** (Profesora de Historia y Teoría del Arte Goldsmiths' College, Londres)
Fecha: Domingo, 13 de Febrero de 12:30 a 14 horas. Sala: A

El tema de discusión se cuestionó si una cultura global, que asume la unidad de un lenguaje internacional, puede tener en cuenta la diversidad y la heterogeneidad. ¿Qué posibilidades existen de trabajar con las realidades impuestas por las diferencias locales, en vez de seguir la creciente homogeneización de la cultura que tiende, por su parte, a producir clichés nacionales?

14.- "LABOR INTERDISCIPLINARIA EN LA CULTURA CONTEMPORÁNEA"
Moderador: **Robert Fleck** (Route de Plurien, La Bouillie, Francia)
Participantes: **Jens Hoffmann** (Comisario, Bruselas y Nueva York), **Hans Ulrich Obrist** (Migrateurs-Curador Musée d'Art Moderne de la Ville de Paris y Fundador Nano Museum y Museum Robert Walser), **Stephanie Moisdon Tremblay** (Crítica de Arte y Comisaria Independiente, París)
Fecha: Domingo, 13 de Febrero de 17 a 18:30 horas. Sala: A

Esta mesa redonda presentó una serie de observaciones acerca de la infiltración y la mutua fertilización que se han producido a través del arte contemporáneo. ¿Cuáles son los múltiples papeles que desempeñan muchos artistas, comisarios de arte, escritores, arquitectos, diseñadores o coreógrafos, cuando trabajan en campos y disciplinas diversos? ¿En qué medida integran todos esos diversos campos en sus actuaciones, propuestas o proyectos?

Biographies

Pedro Reyes Alvarez
2013: Artist, Mexico City.
1999: Artist, Mexico City.

Saul Anton
2013: Critic and writer who has contributed regularly to magazines such as *Artforum, Bookforum, Frieze, art+text* and other publications. He has been Assistant Professor of Art at the Tyler School of Art, Temple University, Philadelphia.
1999: [unknown]

Robert Atkins
2013: *AIDS Over Time/Time Over AIDS* project; book reviewer, *Art in America;* author of 25th anniversary edition *ArtSpeak: A Guide to Contemporary Ideas, Movements and Buzzwords*, San Francisco.
1999: Fellow, STUDIO for Creative Inquiry, Carnegie Mellon University and Editor, Artery: The AIDS-Arts Forum, New York.

Zdenka Badovinac
2013: Director of the Moderna Galerija, Ljubljana.
1999: Director of the Moderna Galerija, Ljubljana.

Carlos Basualdo
2013: Keith L. and Katherine Sachs Curator of Contemporary Art, Philadelphia Museum of Art, Philadelphia.
1999: Poet and freelance curator, Project Director of Apex Art Curatorial Projects, New York.

Trevor Batten
2013: Enjoys a small pension and busy growing coconuts, bananas and Java programs in rural Bohol, an island in the Philippines.
1999: Teacher, researching global socio-cultural effects of the commercialization of the computer.

Ute Meta Bauer

2013: Curator and Associate Professor at the Massachusetts Institute of Technology, Cambridge.
1999: Curator, Professor and Head of the Institute for Contemporary Art at the Academy of Fine Arts Vienna.

Michael Benson

2013: Photographer, writer, filmmaker, book-maker, exhibitions producer and award-winning filmmaker.
1999: [unknown]

Simon Biggs

2013: Media artist, writer, curator and researcher with interests in digital poetics, affective, interactive and performance environments, interdisciplinary research and co-creation; his work has been internationally presented and published. Professor of Interdisciplinary Arts at the University of Edinburgh.
1999: Media artist working with interactive environments, and a writer and curator on media and cultural theory. Research Professor in the Art and Design Research Centre at Sheffield Hallam University.

Francesco Bonami

2013: Director of Venice Biennale in 2003, Curator of Whitney Biennial 2010, Artistic Director Fondazione Sandretto Re Rebaudengo in Turin, Chief Editor of *ANEW* magazine.
1999: Senior Curator at the Museum of Contemporary Art, Chicago, Artistic Director Fondazione Sandretto Re Rebaudengo per L'Arte, Torino, and Artistic Director of Pitti Discovery, Florence.

Iara Boubnova

2013: Director of the ICA, Sofia; currently curating … *the eye never sees itself,* the 2nd Ural Industrial Biennial, Yekaterinburg, Russia and *Present Unlimited*, 1st Sofia Contemporary Festival, Sofia.
1999: Curating a locally interested group show, National Gallery for Foreign Art, Sofia.

Dan Cameron

2013: Chief Curator, Orange County Museum of Art, California.
1999: Writer, lecturer, Senior Curator at the New Museum of Contemporary Art, New York.

Brian Carroll
2013: Writer on digital media.
1999: [unknown]
N.B. Brian Carroll could not be tracked down during the making of the
e-publication.

Christophe Cherix
2013: The Robert Lehman Foundation Chief Curator of Drawings and Prints,
MoMA, New York.
1999: Assistant Curator, Cabinet des Estampes, Geneva.

Carolyn Christov-Bakargiev
2013: Artistic Director dOCUMENTA (13), Kassel (2012); Visiting Professor at
The Cooper Union, New York (2013); Northwestern University, Evanston-Chicago
(2013–15); Goethe University, Frankfurt (2013–15); Leverhulme Professor,
University of Leeds (2014).
1999: Art critic and independent curator, Rome.

Jordan Crandall
2013: Media artist, theorist, and performer. Professor in the Visual Arts
Department at University of California, San Diego.
1999: Artist and media theorist, New York.

Bart De Baere
2013: Director of the Museum of Contemporary Art in Antwerp (M HKA)
1999: Organizer and writer, Stedelijk Museum voor Actuele Kunst, Ghent

Okwui Enwezor
2013: Curator, art critic, writer, poet and educator specializing in art history,
New York – Munich.
1999: Curator, Artistic Director of dOCUMENTA XI.

Charles Esche
2013: Curator of the 31st Sao Paulo Bienale 2014 and Director of the
Van Abbemuseum, Eindhoven.
1999: Writer and exhibition organizer, Codirector of The Modern Institute,
Glasgow.

Robert Fleck

2013: Professor, Kunstakademie Düsseldorf.
1999: Independent critic, curator, and Director of the post-graduate program at the Ecole Regionale des Beaux-Arts, Nantes.

Douglas Fogle

2013: Writer, independent curator, Curatorial Advisor to Neon Foundation in Athens; Los Angeles.
1999: Curator of Contemporary Art, Walker Art Center, Minneapolis.

Bettina Funcke

2013: Independent writer and member of the Masters Program Faculty, Critical Theory and the Arts, at the School of Visual Arts, New York.
1999: Associate Publications Editor, Dia Center for the Arts, New York, and doctoral candidate at ZKM Karlsruhe.

Gena Gbenga

1999: Gena Gbenga was an intern at Blast who was writing under a pseudonym.

Liam Gillick

2013: Artist, working on construction of a large discussion platform at Laguna Gloria in Texas.
1999: Artist, working on first public project at the BIC Technologie-Zentrum in Leipzig.

Rebecca Gordon-Nesbitt

2013: Disillusioned with the commodification of the cultural field, Gordon-Nesbitt turned her attention to a critique of its mechanisms and a quest for alternatives; she recently edited *Conflict, Community, Culture* and authored the book *To Defend the Revolution is to Defend Culture: The Cultural Policy of the Cuban Revolution*.
1999: Curator, founding member of Salon3, London.

Marina Grzinic

2013: Philosopher, theoretician and artist, Ljubljana.
1999: [unknown]

Hou Hanru

2013: Independent critic and curator, Paris - San Francisco.
1999: Independent critic and curator, Paris.

Susan Hapgood
2013: Director, Mumbai Art Room; Senior Advisor, Independent Curators International; and Visiting Professor, Jawaharlal Nehru University, New Delhi.
1999: Curator of Exhibitions, American Federation of Arts, and Senior Fellow, Vera List Center for Art and Politics, The New School, New York.

Jens Hoffmann
2013: Deputy Director and Head of Exhibitions and Public Programs at The Jewish Museum in New York.
1999: Independent curator, New York.

Brian Holmes
2013: Art critic, cultural theorist and activist, particularly involved with the mapping of contemporary capitalism.
1999: [unknown]

Ben Kinmont
2013: Artist, publisher, lecturer, antiquarian bookseller, founder of Antinomian Press and a traveling show entitled *Prospectus* (Amsterdam, Paris, New York, and San Francisco), Sebastopol, California.
1999: Artist, publisher, antiquarian bookseller, New York.

Udo Kittelmann
2013: Curator, writer, previous Director of the Kölnischer Kunstverein, Cologne; Commissioner at the Biennial of Venice for the German Pavillion; Director of the Museum für Moderne Kunst Frankfurt (MMK), current Director of the Nationalgalerie, Staatliche Museen zu Berlin (State Museums in Berlin).
1999: Curator, writer, Director of Kölnischer Kunstverein, Cologne.

Aleksandra Kostic Dimitrijevic
2013: Artist
1999: [unknown]
N.B. Aleksandra Kostic Dimitrijevic could not be tracked down during the making of the e-publication.

Vasıf Kortun
2013: Director of Research and Programs, SALT, Istanbul and Ankara.
1999: Writer, curator, educator and Founder of the Istanbul Contemporary Art Project, Istanbul.

Barbara Kuon
2013: Lecturer in Philosophy, Art and Media Theory at Karlsruhe University of Arts and Design (Germany) since 2002.
1999: Ph.D. student at Karlsruhe University of Arts and Design.

Carin Kuoni
2013: Director and Curator of the Vera List Center for Art and Politics at The New School, New York.
1999: Director of exhibitions at Independent Curators International, New York.

Marta Kuzma
2013: Curator and until recently the Director of the Office for Contemporary Art Norway in Oslo. Professor of art theory at the postgraduate programme of Visual Arts at the Istituto Universitario di Architecturra di Venezia and a visiting professor to the Boccioni University in Milan.
1999: Founding Director, Soros Center for Contemporary Art Kiev.

Cornelia Lauf
2013: Ph.D., art historian, curator, Adjunct Professor at IUAV, Universita di Venezia.
1999: Art historian and curator, Founder and Director of Camera Oscura, San Casciano dei Bagni, Tuscany.

Bronwyn Mahoney
2013: Writer, lives and works in Paris.
1999: Ph.D. candidate in Brisbane on new technologies and museums, working on Asia Pacific Triennial's website and online exhibition, dropped out of the Ph.D., moved to Taipei.

Rosa Martínez
2013: Curator of the series *What to Think, What to Desire, What to Do,* CaixaForum, Barcelona, 2012–13.
1999: Art historian, art collections advisor and independent curator, Barcelona, Spain. Curator of *Looking for a Place*, 3rd International Site Santa Fe Biennial, New Mexico, 1999.

Stéphanie Moisdon
2013: Chief Editor of *Frog Magazine* with Eric Troncy, Associate Curator in the Consortium, Contemporary Art Center in Dijon, and the Pompidou Center in Metz and Dean of the Master of Visual Arts in ECAL (Ecole d'Art Cantonale de Lausanne).
1999: Art critic, freelance curator and Cofounder of Bureau des Videos.

Edi Muka
2013: Curator of Roda Sten Konsthall, Gothenburg; Artistic Codirector of
Goteborg International Contemporary Art Biennial.
1999: Director of International Center of Culture, Tirana.

Sina Najafi
2013: Editor-in-chief of *Cabinet* magazine, Editorial Director of Cabinet Books,
curator, teacher at Cooper Union, Yale, and RISD, scholar of Comparative Literature
at Princeton University, Columbia University, and New York University, New York.
1999: Editor-in-chief of *Cabinet* magazine, dissertation in Comparative Literature
at New York University, New York.

Joseph Nechvatal
2013: Artist, author, teacher at the School of Visual Arts (SVA), New York;
exhibitor at 55th Venice Biennale.
1999: Artist, Ph.D. and conference coordinator at CAiiA, University of Wales
College, Newport; teacher at the School of Visual Arts (SVA), New York.

Michelle Nicol
2013: Art historian and Managing Partner of advertising agency Neutral, Zurich.
1999: Curator, art and film historian, Zurich.

Hans Ulrich Obrist
2013: Codirector of Exhibitions and Programmes and Director of International
Projects at the Serpentine Gallery, London.
1999: Independent curator, Paris, Vienna and London, Operator of the Migrateurs
program at Musee d'Art Moderne de la Ville de Paris.

Olu Oguibe
2013: Professor of Art and African-American Studies at the University of
Connecticut, Storrs. Senior Fellow of the Vera List Center for Art and Politics at the
New School, New York and the Smithsonian Institution, Washington D.C.
1999: [unknown]

Aras Özgün
2013: Media artist and media studies and sociology scholar and professor at The
New School, New York.
1999: Graduate student in the Media Studies Department of The New School
University, New York.

Jose Roca
2013: Estrellita B Brodsky Adjunct Curator of Latin American Art at Tate Modern, London, Artistic Director of FLORA ars+narutra, independent space for contemporary art, Bogotá.
1999: Curator and critic, Visual Arts Department at the Biblioteca Luis Angel Arango, Bogatá.

Bennett Simpson
2013: Curator, Museum of Contemporary Art, Los Angeles.
1999: [unknown]

Nedko Solakov
2013: Artist, Sofia.
1999: Artist, Sofia.

Nancy Spector
2013: Deputy Director and Chief Curator, Solomon R. Guggenheim Museum, New York.
1999: Curator of Contemporary Art, Solomon R. Guggenheim Museum, New York.

Teo Spiller
2013: Master of Fine Arts, guest professor at Arthouse College, Ljubljana.
1999: CEO of DOBER, contemporary arts institute, Venice.

Andrej Tisma
2013: Artist, art critic, curator and editor for digital and electronic arts in the Cultural Center of Novi Sad, Serbia.
1999: Art critic for *Dnevnik* newspaper, Novi Sad, Yugoslavia.

Nicolas Trembley
2013: Curator of the Syz collection, Geneva and independent curator of *Mingei are you here? Craft in contemporary art*, Pace gallery, London.
1999: Curator of Swiss Institute, Paris and Cofounder of Bureau des Videos.

Angus Trumble
2013: Senior Curator of Paintings and Sculpture at the Yale Center for British Art, New Haven, Connecticut.
1999: Curator of European Art at the Art Gallery of South Australia, Adelaide.

Octavio Zaya
2013: Director of *Atlántica, Journal of Art and Thought* and Curator-at-large of MUSAC, León, Spain; currently based in New York and Boston.
1999: Independent curator and writer, New York.

Thanks and Acknowledgements

Thanks are due to many individuals who have helped make this publication a reality. First and foremost, we thank Carlos Basualdo, Hans Ulrich Obrist, Jordan Crandall and other VOTI members who embraced the idea from the start, gave their permissions, and dug through their archives to see what they could find; and to those who supplied the lion's share of the documents: Robert Fleck Archives, Lannion; and Wolfgang Staehle, Walter Palmetshofer and Max Kossatz of The Thing. There is now a growing archive of materials on VOTI available at SALT, Istanbul.

The first batch of salvaged material was organized by Duygu Demir with the assistance of Gökcan Demirkazık. November Paynter took over the process when a bulk of additional material was found, making the final selections and creating a sequencing that is far more cogent and user-friendly. She was assisted by Eliza Wallace who reviewed the document as it came together and helped contact the contributors for permission to include their posts; and later by Siobhan Burger who helped format the initial e-publication document.

Among the VOTI members who knew there was valuable dialogue to be found, and tried over the past five years to bring this material to light, we wish to acknowledge Carolyn Christov-Bakargiev and Marta Kuzma, in particular.

Susan Hapgood and Vasıf Kortun

Endnotes

n.b. Content considered to be sourced text, or that has been copied and pasted from others' e-mails, often from the same thread, appears in gray.

1. Alexander Dorner (1893 – 1957), museum director and professor of art history in Germany and the United States, leader in avant-garde art collecting and curating.

2. Willem Sandberg (1897 – 1984), Dutch typographer and museum curator.
Félix Fénéon (1861 – 1944), Parisian anarchist and art critic.

3. Harald Szeemann (1933 – 2005), Swiss curator and art historian. Director of documenta 5, Kassel, 1972 and two-time curator of the Venice Biennale, 1999 and 2001.
Pontus Hultén (1924 – 2006), Swedish art collector and inaugural Director of the Centre Georges Pompidou, Paris, 1974–81.

4. Walter Hopps (1932 – 2005), American art dealer and museum director, including chief positions at Ferus Gallery, Los Angeles; Pasadena Art Museum, California; and the Menil Collection, Houston, among others.

5. Johannes Cladders (1924 – 2009), curator, critic and inaugural Director of the Abteiberg Museum from 1967–85.
Lucy Lippard (1937 –), American activist, feminist, art critic, and curator noted for her many articles and books on contemporary art.
Jean Leering (1934 – 2005), art historian and Director of the Van Abbemuseum, Eindhoven, from 1964–73.
Walter Zanini, (1925 – 2013), Brazilian curator, art critic and historian.
Seth Siegelaub (1941 – 2013), American-born art dealer, curator, author and researcher. Originator and author, with lawyer Robert Projansky, of *The Artist's Reserved Rights Transfer and Sale Agreement* published in 1971. For complete document see appendix.

6. Chapter I *The Museum of the XXI Century*

7. Susan Hapgood, VOTI Archivista. For biography see appendix.

8. Zdenka Badovinac, VOTI member. For biography see appendix.

9. Bettina Funcke, VOTI member. For biography see appendix.

10. Brian Holmes, VOTI invited forum participant. For biography see appendix.

11. Okwui Enwezor, VOTI member. For biography see appendix.

12. Douglas Gordon (1966 –), British artist.

13. Jens Hoffmann, VOTI member. For biography see appendix.

14. Francesco Bonami (VOTI Member), *Dreams and Conflicts – The Viewer's Dictatorship*, 50th Venice Biennale, (Venice 2003). For biography see appendix.
Molly Nesbit, Hans Ulrich Obrist, Rirkrit Tiravanija, *Utopia Station*, 50th Venice Biennale (Venice 2003).
Carlos Basualdo, *The Structure of Survival*, 50th Venice Biennale (Venice 2003).
Hou Hanru (VOTI member), *Zone of Urgency (Z.O.U.)*, 50th Venice Biennale, (Venice 2003).

15. *Zeitwenden* involved a gathering of 33 curators and leaders of the art world in Bonn who were asked to advise for a major exhibition due to open in December 1999. This group and meeting was known as the "Conclave."

16. Nancy Spector, VOTI Member. For biography see appendix.

17. Stitfung für Kunst und Kultur e.V.

18. Yuko Hasegawa, Chief Curator of the Museum of Contemporary Art, Tokyo (2006–present).
Dan Cameron, VOTI Member. For biography see appendix.
Barbara Vanderlinden, curator, author and founding artistic director of Brussels Biennial, Belgium, 2008.
Udo Kittelmann, VOTI Member. For biography see appendix.

19. Nicholas Serota (1946 –), Director of the Tate, UK (1988–present).

20. The Conclave selected five co-curators to work on the exhibition: Carlos Basualdo (South America), Dan Cameron (North America), Okwui Enwezor (Africa), Yuko Hasegawa (Asia) and Udo Kittelmann (Europe).

21. Jeff Wall (1946 –), Canadian artist.
Maurizio Cattelan (1960–), Italian artist.

22. Walter Smerling has been the Managing Director of Stiftung für Kunst und Kultur (Foundation for Art and Culture) since 1986.

23. Letter to the Whitney. See Chapter III *The Whitney Letter and FRACS*

24. *Cream: contemporary art in culture 10 curators 10 writers 100 artists* (London: Phaidon Press Limited, 1998). The 10 curators were Carlos Basualdo, Francesco Bonami, Dan Cameron, Okwui Enwezor, Matthew Higgs, Hou Hanru, Susan Kandel, Rosa Martínez, Åsa Nacking and Hans Ulrich Obrist.

25. Seth Siegelaub, *January 5-31, 1969*, also known as *The January Show* (New York: 1969).

26. Carl Andre, Robert Barry, Douglas Huebler, Joseph Kosuth, Sol LeWitt, Robert Morris, Lawrence Weiner, also known as the "Xerox Book," ed. by Seth Siegelaub, (New York: 1968). A book exhibition in which each of the seven artists were asked to make a 25-page work on 8 1/2" x 11" paper, which was then photocopied and printed.
Lucy Lippard, a series of shows known as her *Numbers Shows* with catalogues kept on index cards, the first called "557,087" and held at the Seattle World's Fair in 1969, (several venues, shows held between 1969 and 1974).

27. Hans Ulrich Obrist, *DO IT* (New York: e-flux, ongoing print and online publication).

28. Interview between Hans Ulrich Obrist and artist Félix González-Torres (1993), printed in *Hans Ulrich Obrist: Interviews, Volume 1*, ed. Thomas Boutoux, (Milan and New York: Fondazione Pitti Immagine Discovery and Charta, 2003), stored at Museum in Progress.

> Félix González-Torres: I always said I wanna be the spy. I want to be the one that looks like something else in order to infiltrate, in order to function as a virus. I mean, the virus is our worst enemy but should also be our model in terms of not being the opposition anymore, not being very easily defined, so that then we can attach ourselves to institutions which are always going to be there – and, as Althusser said, these institutions or these ideological institutions are always

replicating themselves. If we are attached to them as a virus we will replicate together with these institutions. As we know, these ideological apparatuses are never going away, they always are going to be there and when we think we have pinned them down they replicate themselves somewhere else, I think that's a fascinating aspect of being an infiltrator or working as a virus being attached to these institutions.

29. Édouard Glissant (1928 – 2011), Martinican writer, poet and literary critic.

30. Rem Koolhaas (1944 –), Dutch architect and architectural theorist. Founding partner of OMA and research-orientated counterpart AMO.

31. *Nettime*, Internet mailing lists for networked cultures, politics, and tactics. http://www.nettime.org

32. Chapter II *The Economy of the Art World*

33. Guy Debord, *Des Contracts*, Cognac: Le Temps Qu'il Fait, 1995. Three film contracts signed by Debord between 1973 and 1984, a preface, and a letter written a few days before his death.

34. *The Artist's Reserved Rights Transfer And Sale Agreement*, Seth Siegelaub and Bob Projansky, 1971. For complete document see appendix.

35. *Democracy Realized: The Progressive Alternative*, Roberto Mangabeira Unger (Verso, 1998).

36. Elisabeth Sussman and Thelma Golden were curators at the Whitney Museum. See Chapter III *The Whitney Letter and FRACS*

37. *Boy with a Frog*, Charles Ray, 2009, Punta Della Dogana, Venice. Removed in 2013.

38. Barbara London, Associate Curator in the Department of Media and Performance Art at the Museum of Modern Art, New York, spent almost a year in Japan dividing a MoMA sabbatical in two: she received a National Endowment for the Arts Fellowship, winter 1988–89, and a Japanese government Bunkacho Fellowship, winter 1992–93.

39. Maxwell Anderson was Alice Pratt Brown Director of the Whitney Museum of American Art, 1998 – 2003.

40. Chapter III *The Whitney Letter and FRACS*

41. Chapter IV *The Trial of Pol Pot*
Philippe Parreno. French artist and filmmaker.
Liam Gillick, VOTI contributor. For biography see appendix.

42. ARCO conferences (Madrid: 2000). For scans of the program see appendix.

43. Rosina Gomez-Baeza was Director of ARCO, 1986 – 2006.

44. Chapter VI *Cultural Practice and War*

45. Cedric Price (1934 – 2003), British architect.

46. Félix Fénéon and Alexander Dorner - see endnotes 1 & 2.

47. "Building the Future: Museums of Modern Art in the Twenty-First Century," (Pocantino Conference, October 1996, tape-recordings and transcript, MoMA, New York).

48. Lygia Clark (1920–88), Brazilian artist known for her painting, interactive installations and art therapy work, especially in the late 70s and early 80s.

49. Sam Doyle (1906–85), folk artist from South Carolina.
Bill Traylor (1854 – 1949), self-taught artist born into slavery in Alabama.

50. Frances Yates, *The Art of Memory* (Chicago: University of Chicago Press, 2001).

51. Michel de Certeau (1925–86), French scholar.

52. Summary notes from Closing Summary of Eyebeam Blast forum.

53. Salon3 was established in London in 1998 as a space for international exchange and co-founded by Maria Lind, Rebecca Gordon-Nesbitt and Hans Ulrich Obrist. Below is the announcement e-mail sent to the VOTI forum:

Date: Thursday 6 August 1998

Dear VOTI,

Rebecca Gordon-Nesbitt, Maria Lind and Hans Ulrich Obrist are thrilled to announce the opening of a new office and project space in the Elephant & Castle Shopping Centre. salon3 is a collaborative, hybrid organisation in which many different disciplines are brought together in a continuous series of projects. A culmination of two years' discussion between the three founder members, salon3 harnesses the energy of international curators in perpetual motion. It is hoped that this will enable London to maintain a discourse with arts practitioners based outside England and that salon3 activities will encourage some of the cultural 'Diaspora' to repopulate the city. With an active programme of talks and events, salon3 presents high-quality arts projects in a global context.

The inaugural project, living model, a collaboration between curators, artists and Ole Scheeren (architectural advisor of salon3 and ex-O.M.A), is an architectural and artistic experiment about the possible future of arts spaces. Scheduled to open in Autumn, it relies on the participation of international artists to customise a number of functioning modules ranging from the conventional to the extraordinary.

The events programme will begin in September and be followed by a jour fixe. VOTI members are invited to recommend international visitors to London from all disciplines who could participate in a talk or event. Collaborations with artists from France, Scotland, Slovenia and Sweden are planned. salon3 publishing will form a significant part of the output, with monographs by Jeremy Deller and Will Bradley scheduled for Autumn 1998.

54. Centro Cultural Borges opened in the 1990s.

55. Andreas Huyssen (1942 –) , Villard Professor of German and Comparative Literature at Columbia University.

56. Gordon Matta-Clark, FOOD (New York 1971). An artist-run restaurant in Soho. Rirkrit Tiravanija, *Untitled (Free)* (Gallery 303, New York, 1992). The artist converted the gallery space into a kitchen where he served rice and Thai curry for free.

57. This refers to a series of jigsaw puzzles commissioned for Austrian Airlines based on Alighiero Boetti's "Cieli ad alti quota" (High Skies) from 1993.

58. An incomplete version of Hans Ulrich Obrist's e-mail was included in the first version of the e-publication. The entire e-mail has since been recovered and is included here, in full.

59. Guy Debord, *Des contracts* (Cognac: Le Temps Qu'il Fait, 1995). The publication consists of three film contracts signed by Debord between 1973 and 1984, a preface and a letter written a few days before his death.

60. Ed. note: No official English translation available.

61. Seth Siegelaub and Robert Projansky, *The Artist's Reserved Rights Transfer and Sale Agreement* (1971). For complete document see appendix.

62. Hans Ulrich Obrist and Seth Siegelaub, "A conversation: between Seth Siegelaub and Hans Ulrich Obrist," (TRANS> #6, 1999), 51–63. Full interview text can be found at *e-flux*.

63. Slavoj Žižek, "A Plea for Leninist Intolerance," *Critical Inquiry, 28.2* (2002)

64. Richard Stallman (1953 –), software freedom activist and computer programmer, author of many software contracts. "Copyleft" uses the principles of copyright law to preserve the right to use, modify and distribute free software.

65. Richard Serra, *Tilted Arc* (Foley Federal Plaza, New York, commissioned in 1979, constructed in 1981, removed in 1989).

66. *Der Hang zum Gesamtkunstwerk* (The Tendency Towards the Total Work of Art), curated by Harald Szeemann (Kunsthaus, Zurich, 1983).

67. TNCS = Transnational Civil Society
TNCs = Transnational Corporations

68. MAI = Multilateral Agreement on Investment.
OECD = Organization for Economic Cooperation and Development.

69. Ed. note: E-mail sent by Okwui Enwezor not found.

70. Saskia Sassen (1949 –), Dutch-American sociologist; Robert S. Lynd Professor of Sociology at Columbia University and Centennial visiting Professor at the London School of Economics.

71. The Whitney ouster refers to the sacking of Thelma Golden and Elisabeth Sussman from the Whitney Museum in 1998. See Chapter III *The Whitney Letter and FRACS*

72. TNC(s)=Transnational Corporation(s)

73. Ed. note: E-mail including this text as ascribed to Okwui Enwezor not found.

74. Ed. note: E-mail sent by Bart De Baere not found.

75. Robert Fleck (VOTI member). For biography see appendix.

76. 24th Sao Paulo Bienal, 1998, Artistic Director Paulo Herkenhoff; Adjunct Curator Adriano Pedrosa.

77. SCCA = Soros Center for Contemporary Art

78. Oswald de Andrade, "Manifesto Antropófago" (Cannibal Manifesto) (1928). An essay about Brazilian culture.

79. Thelma Golden, *Black Male: Representations of Masculinity in Contemporary American Art*, (Whitney Museum of American Art, New York, 10 November 1994–5 March 1995).

80. Ben Kinmont, "An exhibition project with Marcel Broodthaers, Paula Hayes/Wild Friends, Ed Kienholz, Yves Klein, Komar & Melamid, Seth Siegelaub and Bob Projansky, and Various Times and People" (AC Projectroom, 1996-1997). Catalogue printed in an edition of 500 copies. No archive. *Exhibition can be repeated.* (Exhibition recreated for Crash at ICA, London, in 1999; for *Etat des Lieux #1* (curated by Nicolas Bourriaud) at Fri-Art, Fribourg, in 2000; and for *L'Oeuvre Collective/Collective Art Work* (curated by Pascal Pique) at Les Abatoirs, Toulouse, in 2000).

81. Ed. note: No further e-mails in this conversation thread were found.

82. Ed. note: E-mail sent by Hans Ulrich Obrist not found.

83. David Ross, former Director of the Whitney Museum who resigned in 1998 to become Director of the San Francisco Museum of Modern Art. He was replaced at the Whitney by Maxwell Anderson.

84. Thelma Golden, *Black Male: Representations of Masculinity in Contemporary American Art* (Whitney Museum of American Art, New York, 10 November 1994-5 March 1995).
1993 Whitney Biennial, curators: Elisabeth Sussman, John G. Hanhardt, Thelma Golden, Lisa Phillips (Whitney Museum of American Art, New York).

85. AICA = International Association of Art Critics.

86. Alexandra Anderson-Spivy, former President of AICA.

87. Chrissie Isles, Anne and Joel Ehrenkranz Curator, Whitney Museum of American Art, New York

88. Ed. note: E-mail sent by Carlos Basualdo not found.

89. Ed. note: E-mail sent by Hans Ulrich Obrist not found.

90. Roman Opalka (1931 – 2011) French-born Polish painter, in 1965 began painting numbers one to infinity, a task to which the artist pledged his life. The black background for the numbers was incrementally lightened to grey with the intention being that he would eventually be painting white on white.

91. Ed. note: E-mail sent by Bettina Funcke not found.

92. Ronald Laing, *The Politics of Experience* (London: Routledge & Kegan Paul, 1967).

93. Emily Dickinson (1830–86), *To make a prairie*. Actual poem reads:

> To make a prairie it takes a clover and one bee
> One clover, and a bee
> And revery
> The revery alone will do
> If bees are few

94. Luce Irigaray (1930 –), Belgian-born French psychoanalyst and philosopher.

95. André Gorz (1923 – 2007), *Misères du présent, richesses du possible* (Galilee, 1997).

96. Referring to Maxwell Anderson, Alice Pratt Brown Director of the Whitney Museum of American Art, New York, 1998 – 2003.

97. Irit Rogoff, "How to Dress for an Exhibition" (a 1998 lecture and essay by former Director of the Cultural Theory Program, Goldsmiths College, London University on the Whitney Museum's exhibition *Black Male*, 1994).

98. Sarit Shapira, *Routes of Wandering: Nomadism, Voyages and Transitions in Contemporary Israeli Art* (The Israel Museum, Jerusalem, 1991).

99. 2eme Congres interprofessionnel de l'art contemporain = Second National Congress for Contemporary Art.

100. Ed. note: DISCLAIMER Aleksandra Kostic could not be contacted during the making of the publication.

101. Ed. note: These online posts appear to have expired and could not be sourced.

102. Liam Gillick, Philippe Parreno, Carsten Höller, Rirkrit Tiravanija, Thomas Mulcaire, Rebecca Gordon-Nesbitt, Gabriel Kuri and Adrian Schlesser, *The Trial of Pol Pot*, Magazin, Centre National d'Art Contemporain, Grenoble (1998). See appendix.

103. Alain Touraine, *Critique of Modernity* (Blackwell Publishing, 1995).

104. Ed. note: During the making of the e-publication Liam Gillick shared a research document for the project *Trial of Pol Pot*, which was originally circulated July 1998. For document see appendix.

105. Serge Daney, "Baby seeking bathwater" (published in *Libération* in two parts on 30 September and 1 October 1991, published in English in *Documenta Documents 2*, 1996, Cantz Verlag, translated by Brian Holmes).

106. Ed. note: This appears to be text from a private e-mail sent by Carlos Basualdo to Liam Gillick that Gillick then posts to the forum.

107. Chris Marker, *L'heritage de la chouette* (documentary, 26 min/episode, 13 episodes, France, 1989).

108. La prise de parole = The capture of speech. From a book of the same title,

Michel de Certeau, *The Capture of Speech*, trans. Tom Conley, ed. Luce Giard (University of Minnesota Press, 1997).

109. Benjamin Buchloh, "Structure, Sign, and Reference in the Work of David Lamelas," first published in *David Lamelas: A New Refutation of Time*, exh. cat. (Munich: Kunstverein München; Rotterdam: Witte de With, 1997), 121–49.

110. Le Magasin—Centre National d'Art Contemporain, Grenoble, France, founded in 1896.

111. ENSBA = École nationale supérieure de Beaux-Arts de Paris.

112. Ralph Rugoff, "Rules of the Game," *Frieze* (1999).

113. Mary Jane Jacob was Chief Curator of the Museum of Contemporary Art, Chicago and the Museum of Contemporary Art, Los Angeles in the 1980s. She is currently Executive Director of Exhibitions and Exhibitions Studies at the School of the Art Institute of Chicago.
Lisa Corrin was at the time Senior Curator at Serpentine Gallery, London. She is currently Ellen Philips Katz Director of Northwestern University's Block Museum of Art, Chicago.
Suzanne Pagé has been the Director of the Musée d'Art Moderne de la Ville de Paris. She is currently Artistic Director of Louis Vuitton Foundation for Creation, Paris.
Susan Vogel has held the positions of Curator at the Metropolitan Museum of Art; Founding Director of the Museum for African Art; and Director of the Yale University Art Gallery, and Professor in the Department of Art History at Columbia University, all New York.

114. Lorenzo Romito, student of architecture and urban design, founding member of Stalker, "a laboratory of urban art."

115. Lisa Parola, curator, art critic and journalist, *a.titulo*.

116. Ed. note: E-mail from Radomir Stančić not found.

117. Slobodan Milošević (1941 – 2006), Serbian and Yugoslav politician, President of Serbia (1989–97), President of the Federal Republic of Yugoslavia (1997 – 2000). In the midst of the 1999 NATO bombing, he was charged with war crimes including genocide and crimes against humanity.

118. *Living with Genocide*, international symposium curated by Zdenka Badovinac, Director of the Moderna galerija (Ljubljana: Moderna galerija, 1996).

119. Ed. note: E-mail from Hans Ulrich Obrist with Slavoj Žižek text not found. Žižek text is presumably "Slavoj Žižek: Against the Double Blackmail" from Tariq Ali, "Springtime for NATO," *New Left Review 234* (March-April 1999), 70.

120. PEN = international non-governmental organization "promoting literature and defending freedom of expression."

121. Ed. note: See endnote 59, link for presumed referenced Žižek text.

122. Vuk Drašković (1946 –), served as Deputy Prime Minister of Yugoslavia in 1999.

123. KLA = Kosovo Liberation Army.
 IRA = Irish Republican Army.

124. Jan Hoet (1936 – 2014), founder of SMAK (Stedelijk Museum voor Actuele Kunst or City Museum for Contemporary Art), Ghent.

125. Ed. note: E-mails from Ute Meta Bauer were not included in version 1 of the e-publication. Permission has since been granted and they were included in version 2 and in this print edition.

126. Semira Adamu (1978–98), 20-year-old Nigerian asylum seeker who was suffocated by two Belgian police officers during an expulsion flight.

127. Paolo Baratta, President of la Biennale di Venezia.

128. *Flash Art*, bimonthly contemporary art magazine founded in 1967 in Italy.

129. http://nedkosolakov.net/content/announcement/index_eng.html

130. AFAA = Association française d'action artistique.

131. Ed. note: E-mails from Ute Meta Bauer were not included in version 1 of the e-publication. Permission has since been granted and they were included in version 2 and in this print edition.

132. Announcement on Jordan Crandall's Blast link.

133. "Agent blast" was a feature used by VOTI when a member wanted to share an outside source text or article with the forum.

134. It is unclear whether the content of the entire e-mail is sourced from the publication *The Cultivated Wilderness* by Paul Shepheard and if they are correctly quoted.

135. Ed. note: DISCLAIMER Brian Carroll could not be traced during the making of the publication.

136. Originally posted on *Nettime*.

137. Ed. note: It is not entirely clear which sections of this e-mail were written by Trevor Batten. The formatting in the original e-mail was used to mark what was understood by the editor to be written by Trevor Batten and what was copy pasted.

138. Ed. note: The rest of the e-mail cannot be found.

139. *Sensation* (Royal Academy London, 18 September – 28 December 1997, Berlin Hamburger Bahnhof, 30 September 1998 – 30 January 1999, Brooklyn Museum, New York, 2 October 1999 – 9 January 2000). Artworks from the collection of Charles Saatchi.

140. Jessie Helms, Republican United States Senator from North Carolina, tried to cut funding in the 1980s for the National Endowment for the Arts for supporting the controversial works of Robert Mapplethorpe and Andres Serrano.

141. Rudolph Giuliani, Former Mayor of New York City, 1994 – 2001.

142. Alexander Lukashenko (1954 –), President of Belarus since 1994.

143. BMA = Brooklyn Museum of Art.

144. Ed. note: Dead link.

145. Translation from Spanish by Kurt Hollander of the final ARCO panel discussion program as included as a pdf in the appendix.

146. Marin Karmitz (1938 –), French-Romanian director, producer and film distributor.

147. Ed. note: DISCLAIMER: *Artforum* and SALT were unable to contact the author Matthew Debord to secure his permission to reprint this article.

Colophon

Editors: Susan Hapgood, Vasıf Kortun and November Paynter
Copyeditor: Sylee Gore
Design: Özgür Şahin
Production: Lösch, Waiblingen

First published on paper by Koenig Books, London.
An electric version of this publication was published by SALT in 2013.

Koenig Books Ltd   SALT
At the Serpentine Gallery   *founded by* Garanti
Kensington Gardens   Bankalar Caddesi 11
London W2 3XA   Karaköy 34420 İstanbul Türkiye
koenigbooks.co.uk   saltonline.org

Printed in Germany

Distribution

Germany & Europe   UK & Ireland   Outside Europe
Buchhandlung Walther König,   Cornerhouse Publications   D.A.P. / Distributed Art
Köln   HOME   Publishers, Inc.
Ehrenstr. 4, 50672 Cologne   2 Tony Wilson Place   155 6th Avenue, 2nd Floor
Tel. +49 (0) 221 / 20 59 6-53   UK – Manchester M15 4FN   USA-New York, NY 10013
Fax +49 (0) 221 / 20 59 6-60   Tel. +44 (0) 161 2123466   Tel. +1 (0) 212 627 1999
verlag@buchhandlung-walther-   Fax +44 (0) 1752 202 330   Fax +1 (0) 212 627 9484
koenig.de   publications@cornerhouse.org   eleshowitz@dapinc.com

ISBN 978-3-86335-908-9